VIRGIL was born near Mantua in
through the death-struggles of the Roman Republic and the
establishment of Augustus as Emperor. He wrote the *Eclogues*, a
collection of short pastoral poems *c.*42–38 BC and became associated
with Maecenas, the millionaire aesthete and powerful associate of
Augustus, who was a great patron of poets. He composed a substan-
tial poem on country life, the *Georgics*, from about 37 to 29 BC. The
next ten years he spent working on his epic poem, the *Aeneid*, which
dramatizes and glorifies the story of the founding of Rome. Virgil
died at Brindisi in 19 BC on his way home from a trip to Athens,
leaving his epic not fully revised. It was immediately recognized as
the greatest masterpiece of Roman literature, a position which it has
never lost.

JASPER GRIFFIN is a Fellow and Tutor at Balliol College, Oxford.
His other publications include *Homer on Life and Death* (1980),
Homer (Past Master, 1980), *The Oxford Book of Snobs* (1982), *Latin
Poets and Roman Life* (1985), *The Mirror of Myth* (1986), and *Virgil*
(Past Master, 1986). He is an editor of the *Oxford History of the
Classical World* (1986).

OXFORD WORLD'S CLASSICS

For over 100 years Oxford World's Classics have brought readers closer to the world's great literature. Now with over 700 titles—from the 4,000-year-old myths of Mesopotamia to the twentieth century's greatest novels—the series makes available lesser-known as well as celebrated writing.

The pocket-sized hardbacks of the early years contained introductions by Virginia Woolf, T. S. Eliot, Graham Greene, and other literary figures which enriched the experience of reading. Today the series is recognized for its fine scholarship and reliability in texts that span world literature, drama and poetry, religion, philosophy and politics. Each edition includes perceptive commentary and essential background information to meet the changing needs of readers.

OXFORD WORLD'S CLASSICS

VIRGIL

The Aeneid

Translated by
C. DAY LEWIS

With an Introduction and Notes by
JASPER GRIFFIN

OXFORD
UNIVERSITY PRESS

OXFORD

UNIVERSITY PRESS

Great Clarendon Street, Oxford OX2 6DP

Oxford University Press is a department of the University of Oxford.
It furthers the University's objective of excellence in research, scholarship,
and education by publishing worldwide in

Oxford New York

Athens Auckland Bangkok Bogotá Buenos Aires Calcutta
Cape Town Chennai Dar es Salaam Delhi Florence Hong Kong Istanbul
Karachi Kuala Lumpur Madrid Melbourne Mexico City Mumbai
Nairobi Paris São Paulo Singapore Taipei Tokyo Toronto Warsaw

with associated companies in Berlin Ibadan

Oxford is a registered trade mark of Oxford University Press
in the UK and in certain other countries

Published in the United States
by Oxford University Press Inc., New York

First published as a World's Classics paperback 1986
Reissued as an Oxford World's Classics paperback 1998
Reissued 2008

British Library Cataloguing in Publication Data

Data available

ISBN 978–0–19–953748–8

2

Printed in Great Britain by
Clays Ltd, St Ives plc

CONTENTS

Foreword   vi

Introduction   ix

Select Bibliography   xxv

A Chronology of Virgil   xxvi

THE AENEID

Book I   *page* 3   Book VII   *page* 188

Book II   31   Book VIII   220

Book III   63   Book IX   248

Book IV   90   Book X   283

Book V   118   Book XI   322

Book VI   154   Book XII   361

Explanatory Notes   401

FOREWORD

To the 1966 Oxford Paperbacks Edition of the *Eclogues*,
Georgics and *Aeneid*

MY translation of the *Georgics* was first published (by
Jonathan Cape) in 1940; that of the *Aeneid*, which had been
commissioned for broadcasting by the Third Programme of
the B.B.C., in 1952 (by the Hogarth Press); the *Eclogues* in
1963 (by Jonathan Cape). I am most grateful to these firms
for allowing the several books to be brought together in the
present edition. I have left untouched the original transla-
tions of the *Eclogues* and *Georgics*; but I have weeded out
from the *Aeneid* some of the modernisms and colloquialisms
which, though they may have served a purpose for broad-
casting, now seem to me unacceptable in print.

Reading through these translations again after a space of
years, I find it easier than I did at the time to distinguish
the points where Virgil is most approachable by the con-
temporary translator—or at any rate by me—and those
where we can make little or nothing of him. It is primarily
a matter of language. However complex his pattern of
images, however elliptic his thought, the English poet has
tended over the last twenty-five years towards a simplicity of
language, a habit of putting down words in an order approxi-
mating to that of prose. It is a use of words more suited to the
down-to-earth matter and manner of the *Georgics* than to
the ornate, formally intricate style of the *Aeneid*—a style for
which, I fancy, Tennyson was the last English poet who
could have found an adequate poetic equivalent.

It would be perfectly possible for a writer to use the
Aeneid as a diagram for a very free rendering: there is good
precedent for such renderings in the Elizabethan translators,
in Dryden, Pope, and Cowper; and younger poets have
approached Homer recently in the same way. My own
inclination, however, was to use Virgil as a text rather than

a springboard: grappling close with an original can exercise unaccustomed muscles in one's own language. Each of my versions is line-for-line and aims at a precise explication of the original, though I have taken more liberties when trying to rise to some heightened passage of Virgil, and have used rhythms of English and Irish folk-song for translating the singing matches in the *Eclogues*.

I have said elsewhere that, while there is seldom any insuperable difficulty about discovering what Virgil meant, it is all but impossible to convey how he said it. Most especially is this true of the *Aeneid*. But the translator's problems are not only linguistic. There are many passages in this epic which cannot appeal to the modern reader as they must have done to the Roman. The antiquarian aspect of the *Aeneid*—the frequent place-names and family names, some of the customs and legends even, which Virgil introduced to glorify the Roman people and its history—can be of interest only to scholars nowadays: I found it almost impossible to reproduce such passages without causing the narrative to lose grip.

On the other hand, the scenes of action remain superb, none the less so although the modern reader may well detect in Virgil a conflict between the excitement of war and the pity of it, most clearly exemplified in the death of Turnus. Virgil, as the *tot bella per orbem* lines of his *Georgics* had already shown, was sick of civil war and hoped for a long period of peace under Augustus. The compassion he brought to his epic, the pathos with which he invested certain scenes, though in a sense they weakened the poem, enlarged the epic form. This note of compassion had been struck in the *Eclogues*, when Virgil described the plight of smallholders dispossessed by war veterans. Akin to it is the wonderful tenderness with which, in the *Georgics*, he wrote about animals, birds, bees, weather signs, the coming of spring: a countryman born and bred, he brought to such subjects a countryman's practical understanding together with a poet's playfulness and imaginative sympathy. Many of the similes

of the *Aeneid* are drawn from nature, too: if they are some-
times more vivid than the actions for which they offer
similitudes, this shows again how powerfully the poet's mind
was drawn to nature.

For me, the most rewarding passages to translate were
those in which, writing of country scenes and pursuits, Vir-
gil raised his language to a lyric utterance, and those where
he charged the classical epic with a current of romantic feel-
ing. Every translator must have or hope for certain moments
when he is in close touch with the mind of his great original—
when the spirit of that original enters into him, a little of it
for a little time. He will also, if he is himself a poet, wish to
make a poem of his own out of the foreign material which
confronts him. This paradox conveys the mystique of
translating. The poet-translator must use the language and
rhythms of his own day, I believe, or else he will fall into the
wrong kind of artificiality; but he must also submit himself
with humility to the thought of his original. He can do no
more than provide a working model of it—a model which,
for his own generation, works.

C. DAY LEWIS

INTRODUCTION

PUBLIUS VERGILIUS MARO, in English usually called Virgil, was born in a small town near Mantua (the modern Mantova) in the year 70 BC. His family seems to have been respectable but not at all grand. He received a good education, but only in Italy: the equivalent of a period at a modern University, a stay in Athens studying philosophy, was apparently beyond his reach. In 19 BC he did make a journey to Athens, but he fell ill and died on the way home.

Virgil was born in a traumatic time of transition for Rome. The aristocratic republican system which had conquered the world was visibly failing to cope with the situation created by its own success. Polybius, an intelligent Greek of the second century, had ascribed the Roman triumph to the public spirit and republican virtues of her people; but ever since 133 BC there had been an accelerating series of violent conflicts. In the nineties great parts of Italy tried to overthrow Rome in a war which lasted four years. In 84, for the first time, a Roman general marched on Rome: that was Sulla, and he followed his victory with a blood-bath of his political opponents. In the year in which Virgil was born Pompey and Crassus, two powerful dynasts, forced their own election as consuls. In 63 Catiline, an aristocratic revolutionary, fell fighting against Roman legions. The fifties were a disastrous decade: the Senate was impotent to counter the informal alliance of Pompey, Crassus, and Julius Caesar (the 'First Triumvirate'); gang warfare became a commonplace in Rome, and on occasion it was not even possible to hold elections. Finally, after Crassus was killed in a great Roman defeat by the Parthians in 53, Pompey and Caesar fell out: Caesar crossed the Rubicon in 49 and marched on Rome, and a civil war followed which took three years to end with Caesar's victory. Two years later, in 44, he was assassinated.

A fresh round of civil war followed, between the assassins and the Caesarian party led by Mark Antony and Caesar's grand-nephew and adopted son Octavian, later known as Augustus. Brutus and Cassius were defeated; the Second Triumvirate—Antony, Octavian, and the aristocratic general Lepidus—ordered a fearful proscription and massacre, in which Cicero was murdered. Property was looted, and to settle the veteran soldiers of the victorious legions large areas of Italy suffered confiscation of land. It appears that Virgil, Horace, Tibullus, and Propertius all lost some or all of their estate at this time, a fact which gives some idea of the extent of the expropriations. The thirties were dominated by minor civil wars (Pompey's son Sextus challenged the triumvirs and was finally defeated) and the fear of a major one. It came in 31: Antony and Cleopatra were defeated at Actium, and Octavian was the sole ruler of the world. The question of his intentions obsessed every mind: what would he do when he came back from the East? Would there be another round of massacres and proscriptions? In fact he chose to be benevolent and moderate. There were no reprisals, and Octavian took the unheard-of name 'Augustus'—something between 'venerable' and 'super-human'—and settled down to reorganize the State and revitalize the national morale.

That brief sketch of political events gives the setting in which Virgil lived and wrote. It was a time in which people despaired of Rome. Some of the earliest publications of Virgil's friend, the poet Horace, express that despair with violence and bitterness (*Epodes* VII and XVI). It had begun to seem that all was over: that the Empire against which the barbarians were powerless would destroy itself, opening the way for savage horsemen, in the words of Horace, to ride over the ashes of the Imperial City. All the poems of Virgil have that fearful prospect, and the moral faults which were causing it, somewhere in view; and the alternation of hope and despair is one of the vital threads running through his work.

There was also, however, another crisis confronting the

poet, and that was a literary one. Roman literature had so far had a curious history. It came into existence as a response to the challenge of the ancient and overwhelming literature of Greece. Rome's Eastern conquests had brought her inescapably face to face with the phenomenon of Greek cultural superiority. A hard-headed, tight-fisted race of farmers and soldiers confronted a culture which in all the arts, visual and literary, had produced works of a daunting formal perfection. That is indeed the single most striking thing about Greek culture: the overriding concern with form. That is as true of the subtle mathematical calculations which are embodied in the Parthenon and in the representation of the human body in sculpture, as it is of the complex and exact metres of Greek poetry and the measured cadences and supple variations of Plato's Greek prose. This is what above all explains the terrific impact of Greek art on the other peoples with whom they came into contact. It had the effect of making their own productions seem, in comparison, intolerably uncouth and provincial; and so the Etruscans and the Lycians and all the rest fell under the spell of Greek style and did their best to emulate it. That is one reason for the disappearance of their languages—they wrote in Greek forms and in Greek.

Rome took a different path. In the late third century there were Roman grandees who were writing histories of Rome in Greek, and it might have seemed likely that such productions would be all that Rome would produce: while Greece became on the political level a province of Rome, Rome on the cultural level would be no more than another province of Greece. This was averted by the efforts of men of non-Roman origin and of far humbler social position than the senators who were happily writing in Greek, men like the Greek slave Livius Andronicus, Ennius from southern Italy, Plautus from Umbria, Terence from north Africa. These men embarked on the laborious task of raising the Latin language to equality with Greek, and of creating in it a literature which could stand beside the splendid literature of Greece. That meant taking over the Greek literary forms—tragedy, comedy, oratory, philosophy, history, epic—and recreating them in Latin. It also meant extending, enriching, and refining the Latin language itself.

The poets of the generation before Virgil, that of Catullus, having been brought up on the great works produced in the second century BC, felt blasé about their achievements and superior to their technique. There was a vogue for short poems of exquisite polish, ostentatiously imitating those of late and sophisticated Greek poets: about four hundred lines seems to have been the maximum length for serious narrative verse. Catullus' *Peleus and Thetis* (poem LXIV) is a surviving example, but we know of a number of others. Catullus told of Ariadne deserted by Theseus and lamenting on Naxos; his friend Cinna wrote a *Zmyrna*, about a mythological princess who fell in love with her own father: it took nine years to write and was soon provided with a commentary to explain its obscurities. Calvus wrote about Io, a mythological princess who was turned into a cow. And so on. These poems were highly polished, mellifluous, erudite, cool, remote from life. Life, indeed, pullulated in short squibs: poems of six or twelve or twenty lines, expressing love, hate, contempt, affection, amusement, polemic. As for politics, Catullus composed obscene epigrams on Julius Caesar and in another poem informed him that he had no wish to please him, and no curiosity to find out whether he was black or white. Only the isolated figure of Lucretius, as far as we know, was at work on a long poem with a serious purpose—passionate propaganda for the tranquil philosophy of Epicurus.

It will be seen that the explicit aims of Catullus and his friends are of a rather decadent sort. The long poem in the grand style is a bore and, for the serious artist, an impossibility. Refinement of technique and exotic and perverse subjects: we see a vista opening at the end of which stands Oscar Wilde's preposterous *Salome*. Yet Latin literature had not yet had its classical period, and this decadence, so self-consciously chosen, is particularly artificial. The natural shape of the literature is being deformed. For the next generation of poets the position was a difficult one. Virgil felt and expressed, even in his earliest work, the desire to write, one day, a serious epic; but it was not possible simply to disregard the technical advances and the elitist notions of his immediate predecessors. Somehow all that would have to be included, if the projected epic was to live up to the highest standards of artistic conscience; and above all a way must be found to unite the two sides, to express in the high style and in substantial works the emotion and vigour that marked the short lyrics of Catullus.

Virgil's first published work, the *Eclogues*, can be treated only very briefly here.[1] He chose as his Greek model a highly sophisticated poet of the third century BC, Theocritus of Syracuse. Theocritus wrote short poems in dramatic or quasi-dramatic form, some as monologues, others for several speakers. The part of his varied output which interested and attracted Virgil was the pastoral poems: elegant scenes presenting shepherds, goatherds, and oxherds, who (in verse whose artfulness consisted partly in the calculated affectation of simplicity) spoke and sang of their flocks, their singing contests, and their loves. Virgil found here a form which combined polished technique, artificiality, and a sort of realism. In his *Eclogues* he emulated that technical refinement, producing Latin verse which for suppleness and melody excelled anything that had yet been written in the language. He emphasized the unreality of the form by setting his shepherds not, like Theocritus, in Sicily, but in a place not to be found on a map. This place was Arcadia, which is not simply an area in the middle of the Peloponnese, but an unreal locality, where at times the scene evokes Sicily, and at others it appears to be set near Mantua—a Mantua close to the sea-shore and surrounded by hills which cast their evening shadows at the end of so many of the *Eclogues*. Idle to go to Mantua and remonstrate

---

[1] On the *Eclogues* and *Georgics* see the Introduction by my colleague R. O. A. M. Lyne to Day Lewis's translation of the *Eclogues* and *Georgics* (Oxford 1983: also in the World's Classics series), and my own *Virgil* (Oxford 1986: in the Past Master series), chapters 2 and 3.

that the sea is far away and the countryside absolutely flat. Virgil has discovered the Arcadia of Claude Lorrain and of Watteau, a temperament and an ideal rather than a place.

He also extended the form in the opposite direction, allowing into his pastoral world the jarring intrusion of Roman politics. The first *Eclogue* tells how Meliboeus is expelled from his land, ousted by a godless soldier, while Tityrus was miraculously saved by a 'divine young man' in Rome. He has made it impossible for the reader to work out exactly what happened, or what relation, if any, Tityrus is supposed to have to the poet himself: but no reader could miss the context. The evictions of 42 and 41 BC, when Italians were turned out to make room for the troops of the victorious party, are unmistakable, although disguised by being projected into a world of musical shepherds with Greek names. And it is worth observing that while the first half of the poem belongs to Tityrus and his joy at his deliverance, the second half is dominated by Meliboeus with his bitter lamentations at the injustice of his fate. Virgil has already found a way of expressing strong emotion yet creating in his poem an exquisite balance between acceptance and rejection of events, between optimism and despair.

His next work, the *Georgics*, marked a great increase in scale. A poem of some two thousand lines is far longer than anything ever envisaged by Horace, Tibullus, or Propertius. Again the form is Greek: this time the model is the archaic and distant figure of the peasant-poet Hesiod of Ascra, who versified ethical and practical instructions for peasant farmers about 700 BC. Virgil actually calls the *Georgics* 'an Ascraean song', but the reader was to be in no doubt that what he actually produced was something extremely unlike Hesiod. Hesiod's rugged technique—hobnailed lines and awkward transitions—is as impossible for Virgil as his frugality, misogyny, and superstition. The thinnest possible Hesiodic veneer sufficed, consisting of the occasional quotation and a few more substantial echoes significantly accumulated in the first book of the *Georgics*.

Virgil's poem was about Italy, to which he devotes rhapsodic passages of praise, and while the practical instructions which he conveys are so selective and so elliptic as to be of no practical help, the poem is intensely serious in conveying a moral and religious picture of the world and of human life. Hard work as a moral virtue, coupled with the delightful ease that the bounteous earth will bestow in just return for effort; the virtuous figure of the rustic contrasted with the criminal madness of war, yet also the insistence that is through the virtues of rustic Italy that Rome conquered the world: the *Georgics* hold in delicate equilibrium conflicting and contradictory values. This is especially so of their attitude to Augustus and the idea of Rome. He is the hope of a world turned upside-down, the offspring of gods and bound himself for apotheosis and Olympus; Virgil hopes to live long enough to build a stately temple of verse in his honour.[2] Yet the poem loves peace, the undisturbed and uncorrupted countryside, and a philosophical perspective in which the mind can view with indifference all transient things, even 'Roman history and the kingdoms which pass away'.[3]

So much by way of build-up to the great epic which, in the end, Virgil wrote. The *Georgics* were published in 29 BC, and the poet turned to his heroic poem. He was to die before completing it, which accounts for the metrically incomplete lines in the poem, and doubtless also for a few loose ends and traces of change of plan, which he would have tidied up had he lived. It is worth observing that the survival of a visibly unfinished poem in antiquity is a very rare thing: ancient taste was not attracted by the romantic appeal of the fragmentary and suggestive but looked for perfection and completeness. None of the many imitators of Virgil included unfinished lines in their Virgilian pastiches. That the *Aeneid* was none the less accepted shows the high position which Virgil had at the time of his death, the expectation which the poem had aroused, and the

---

[2] *Georgics*, I. 500; I. 24–42; III. 10–48.
[3] Ibid., II. 498.

immediate impression which it made on its first readers. I take
the opportunity to say also that we can be confident that Virgil
did not intend to go with his story beyond the end of the twelfth
book as we have it. He gave the poem twelve books as a gesture
of courteous modesty to the epics of Homer, each of which was
divided into twenty-four books: he would not have written an
epic in thirteen, and Book XII is already the longest in the
Aeneid. The end, bold and unexpected as it is, follows the poet's
plan.

At the beginning of the third book of the *Georgics* Virgil
appeared to promise that what he would write was an epic poem
recording and glorifying the warlike deeds of Augustus: 'I shall
build a great temple . . . Augustus shall be in the centre . . . on
the portals I shall depict his conquest of Egypt and Asia and his
subjection of the whole world. There also shall be statues of his
Trojan ancestors . . .'⁴ That is to say, an epic on Augustus with
glimpses back to the mythical origins of his family in Troy.
What he actually produced was a poem about Augustus'
Trojan ancestor, with glimpses forward to himself. It was
natural that Augustus should expect an epic about his own
career: much less eminent Romans had received such poems in
the past. But as Virgil contemplated writing it, he came to see
that it would not do. The ancients regarded epic and tragedy as
the highest forms of poetry, epic perhaps the highest of all:
those who succeeded in such a high genre were the greatest
poets. Conscious of great powers, ambitious for achievement
both for himself and for Rome, which at last could now receive
an epic poem worthy to stand beside the *Iliad* and *Odyssey* of
Homer, Virgil had put himself through a testing apprenticeship
in his progression from *Eclogues* to *Georgics.* He was now ready
to challenge Homer himself. That meant the full panoply of the
heroic scale, personal interventions by gods, great battles
fought out hand to hand, stories of magic and the supernatural:
and how could such a poem be written about a man still alive,
and about recent history? No amount of tact and skill could

⁴ *Georgics*, III. 16ff.

prevent it from collapsing into bathos and absurdity, if Augustus was to be shown conversing with deities and mowing down warriors in battle. And, no less importantly, such a poem would be inescapably committed to a simple and straight-forward interpretation of events: Augustus must always be right, his enemies must be villains and monsters. There could be no sympathy for Antony, or for Cleopatra.

Such considerations doubtless weighed with Virgil. A poem written in that way would be hack-work. He turned instead to the mythical world in which epic was traditionally at home. By a fortunate chance (or so it may seem: but it was Virgil's insight in seeing and seizing the opportunity which made it seem so) the family of the Julii, to which Caesar and Augustus belonged, was a clan of high antiquity claiming to descend through many centuries from the nobility of Alba Longa, a city older than Rome, founded by Iulus, the son of Aeneas: there they derived from Aeneas and from his mother, the goddess Aphrodite, whom the Romans called Venus. Caesar had made consider-able play with this claim, which was one of a number made, in the late Republic, by aristocratic Roman families.

Now, Aeneas was an eminently suitable hero for an epic, far removed in time from the prosaic light of the contemporary world; he was in fact a character who appears quite prominently in the *Iliad.* At that distance, encounters with gods were quite a different thing from inventing them for contemporaries; and a hero who fought at Troy was naturally a champion in the old swashbuckling way, so incongruous for Augustus, whose victories were won by subordinates and who had been, so his friends said, unwell at the Battle of Philippi (his enemies put it more harshly). The *Aeneid* is an eminently Homeric poem, and its plot can be seen to combine both the great Homeric epics. In the first half of the poem Aeneas wanders the Mediterranean, making his way from Troy to the Tiber; that recalls the *Odyssey.* In the second half he fights great battles in Italy, and that recalls the *Iliad.* It is natural to think that Virgil consciously aimed to create a poem which should supply Rome with a challenger to both the supreme poems of Greece.

But Aeneas was more than one suitable hero among others for a Roman epic. Himself a personage who linked the poem with Homer, he was in addition the only one of the heroes who linked the mythology of Greece with the one great myth produced and valued by Romans: the myth of Rome herself. For a Roman it was Rome which served as a focus for the reverence and the interest which Greeks gave to their various myths and the relations which they revealed of humanity and the gods. And Virgil was also able to discern a way of dealing with Augustus which would be incomparably better and more poetic than the narration of his exploits. The important thing about Augustus was not what he did at the Battle of Actium or what he did at any moment in the thirties, it was that he offered a real chance to arrest and reverse a catastrophic slide of Rome into the abyss. This extraordinary man might yet succeed in establishing an order for Rome which would endure, and even in reviving the virtues which in the past had enabled one city, not to all appearances uniquely fortunate in position or endowment, to conquer the world. A hundred years of decline and disorder was redressed at last: that might count as a second foundation of the city, and present Augustus as another Aeneas, another god-sent deliverer. Such a conception was much better presented in the form of prophetic utterances and visions of the future than in narrative about a central actor in the story, and that is how, in the *Aeneid*, Augustus is represented.

There was, however, a difficulty. Greek scholars said that Troy fell in the twelfth century BC; Roman chronology went back to the foundation of the city in the year 753 BC, a foundation associated with the name of another mythical figure, Romulus. Between the two there yawned a gap of time, and Aeneas after all his adventures and sufferings could not found Rome. Virgil saw how to turn that into an advantage. Among the benefits which came from the decision to write not

about Augustus but about Aeneas one—and not the least—was
that it now became possible to present the hero's destiny in a
light which was not entirely or unambiguously optimistic. Virgil
had meditated deeply on the nature and significance of Roman
history, and the *Aeneid* insists that the destiny of the imperialist
is anything but easy or enjoyable. Aeneas is forced by the gods
to leave his city of Troy, forced to leave Dido and cause her
death, forced to wage fearful wars with the Italians who are to
be his allies and to play a vital part in the making of Rome,
forced to kill attractive people whom he would have preferred
to spare. In all this he is offered only the cool comfort of the
imperial achievement of his descendants, which he will not live
to see, and which he must take on trust. The fact that he cannot
even found Rome adds to the poignancy of that destiny. It is
underlined when in Book VIII the poet actually sends him to
the future site of Rome, unrecognizable in trees and brambles;
and when at the end of that book he is given a marvellous
shield, the work of a god, which presents the pageant of Roman
history—a vista of wars and battles, with the gods of conflict
and discord in the centre, and Bellona the war-goddess
brandishing a blood-stained whip—and the long-suffering
hero gazes at the depiction of a history which he does not know,
before shouldering the weight of the glory and destiny of his
descendants.[5] That is a symbolic scene: the archetypal
imperialist, forced to feel the weight of a brilliant and terrible
history which has not yet happened and which he cannot
understand.

This point is central to the understanding of the *Aeneid*, and
it is important not to over-simplify it. Virgil did not write a
poem which was straightforwardly anti-imperialist. The calling
of Rome to conquer and to rule the world is presented and
endorsed in the grandest style and with the greatest emphasis.
In the first book, in a scene on Olympus which casts its shadow
over the whole poem, Jupiter says 'Empire without limit I have
given them'. The prophetic god Apollo declares that 'The

[5] *Aeneid*, VIII. 337 ff; 729–31.

house of Aeneas shall rule the whole world: and their sons' sons and those who shall be born of them'. The destiny of Rome is to place the whole world under its laws, says Jupiter. On the shield of Aeneas we see an image of Augustus receiving the homage and tribute of a conquered world: 'In they come, the vanquished peoples in long procession . . .'[6] Rome will bring to the world the gifts of peace, justice, order, and law; but they can be brought only by force. In the Underworld Aeneas is shown his mighty descendants, the heroes of republican history, and they are a line of conquerors; Aeneas himself is given a foretaste of the nature of Roman history in the second half of the poem, when he carries the shield, emblazoned with scenes of battle and violence, into a murderous war with the Italians. Without bloodshed and destruction, Empire is impossible. The role of Juno in fermenting war and forcing it on the reluctant hero is, among other things, shorthand for that fact: there is something in heaven which exacts the price of blood. Virgil's plaintive protest 'Can a divine being so persevere in anger?'[7] is left unanswered. The poet is grieved by his own tale.

The episode of Dido, the most popular part of the poem ever since antiquity, makes a similar point. Aeneas lost his wife (no fault of his) at the sack of Troy. On he goes, lonely and unhappy, as he bitterly tells his goddess mother when she allows him an encounter with her, one which she deliberately makes unsatisfying.[8] In Carthage he meets Dido, a widow, beautiful, humane, and capable. That they should fall in love seems humanly inevitable, even without the malicious interference of the meddling goddesses Venus and Juno. But Aeneas is driven on and obliged to desert her for his Italian destiny. We are meant to feel that he is right to leave her: but the poet has so arranged his story that it is Dido who has our sympathy in her despair and suicide, and the hasty departure of the hero presents him in an unhandsome light. Virgil's own talent for

---

[6] *Aeneid*, I. 279; III. 97; IV. 231; VIII. 722.
[7] *Ibid.*, I. 11; cf. XII. 503.   [8] *Ibid.*, I. 372–410.

the emotional description of unhappy love, which found
expression in the *Eclogues* and also in the story of Orpheus and
Eurydice in the fourth book of the *Georgics*, might have seemed
unpromising equipment for a poet of patriotic epic. With
consummate skill he turns it to the service of the central ideas
of the *Aeneid*—the Dido episode is by no means an inorganic
addition—in showing the founder of Roman greatness forced
to deny his own happiness and to destroy what he loved. The
Italian wars will make the same point. Aeneas cannot protect
the young prince Pallas who is entrusted to him, cannot avoid
killing the attractive young prince Lausus, ravages Italy, and
kills Turnus when he might have preferred to let him live.[9] The
princess Lavinia, whose hand he wins, is a young girl: she is
not, as Dido would have been, the appropriate wife for the
battered hero, the Penelope to his Ulysses. Heaven makes it
very clear that the happiness of Aeneas is not its concern.

The *Aeneid* is an epic, a piece of heroic poetry. It exploits all
the traditional features of epic as it was derived from the *Iliad*
and *Odyssey* of Homer—the divine interventions, the long
similes, the journeys and battles and speeches. For those who
have read the Homeric poems the comparison is a fascinating
exercise, and one which has been practised ever since Virgil's
own time. Above all Virgil draws from that tradition the high
style in which he writes, and the justified confidence that his
plot is more than simply a story, that it illuminates the
fundamentals of the relationship of gods and men. But the
Aeneid is something very different from a rewriting of Homer in
Latin. Virgil was a highly cultivated man, a student of literature
and of philosophy. All his reading and his learning has entered
into his great poem, and of course much of it was unthinkable
in the distant archaic world of Homer. Attic tragedy; late Greek
poetry; the works of his Latin predecessors, especially the old
epic of Ennius: the poetry of Lucretius and Catullus; Platonic
philosophy and theology; the divine providence of the Stoic
dogma and the divine indifference of the Epicurean; Greek

---

[9] *Ibid.*, X. 479ff.; X. 802–32; XII. 919ff.

myth and Roman history; the special contribution made to Rome by Italy—all of this, and more, is vital to the poem. Finally, Virgil wanted to create an epic which would be original not only in the complexity of the contents but also in its style and atmosphere. The objective manner of the Homeric epic was to be variegated and transfigured with the strongly subjective and emotional manner of Virgil's own earlier work. That must have been the hardest part of the creation of the *Aeneid*, and his success here made his epic unique in ancient literature.

Aeneas is a hero, and as such he must be brave and dashing. That produces difficulties, when in Book II he must himself narrate the story of his leaving Troy and setting off with a considerable force of men, leaving the city to its fate. That is in a way unheroic, and the poet can be seen emphasizing two things: first, that the ruin of Troy was the work of gods, not of men, already fixed, quite beyond human power to avert, and second, that Aeneas, although explicitly ordered by the gods to leave and serve their long-range purposes, disobeys and rushes off to fight and be killed. Only after repeated divine instructions and signs does he overcome his natural impulse and obey. He is not less heroic than Achilles, Virgil wants us to conclude, but more: to the spontaneous courage and *élan* of the old-style hero is added the painful and onerous obligation to subject his will—even his heroism—to the will of the gods. That is hard to learn and hard to bear: hardest of all, perhaps, when the same heavenly prodding drives him on from Dido. The words *pius* and *pietas*, central to the poem and hard to translate into English, fit in here. *Pietas* was a quality highly valued by Romans: it meant something like 'sense of obligation', especially towards parents, gods, Rome. A sense of obligation, or of duty, is not a quality which has much emotional resonance to us, however much we may admit that it is admirable, but for Romans it had a warmer and more positive feel.

The English word from *pietas* is pity, and that feeling, too, is pervasive in the poem. It is Dido's capacity for pity which first attracts Aeneas to her,[10] and the quality is one of the most pervasive in the poem. The hero Aeneas must fight and kill, both as the successor to the warriors of the Homeric epic and also as the archetype of Roman history, but he takes little pleasure in his victories. What he witnesses of battle at Troy is the sack of the city and the murder of its aged king; the war which he must fight with the Italians has some of the horror of a civil war, and Aeneas repeatedly tries to evade it and to make peace. In Book X the young Etruscan prince Lausus, rescuing his father, persists in forcing Aeneas, who has warned him to stand clear, to kill him. The hero's spear is driven home through the tunic which the boy's mother has embroidered with gold thread: Aeneas groans aloud at the sight of his pale face and the thought that he, too, showed *pietas*. It is a profound image of his whole career when we see him stand with the body in his arms, its neatly ordered hair befouled with blood, calling on Lausus' comrades to take it for burial.

It is perhaps a more powerful image, at the very end of the poem, when he kills his opponent Turnus. Virgil might have made this easy, a fatal wound given in single combat, as when Achilles slays Hector in the *Iliad*. Instead he has created a disquieting and ambiguous scene. Turnus is wounded: on the ground he admits defeat, renounces his claim to Lavinia's hand, and begs for his life. His appeal is taking effect on Aeneas, when suddenly he sees on Turnus the sword-belt which he stripped from the corpse of his victim Pallas. In a transport of justified rage he kills him, and the poem ends with the departure of Turnus' lamenting spirit. The reader is meant to recall that in the *Iliad* the killing of Hector is followed by two whole books, in which Achilles comes to terms first with the other Greeks and then, unexpectedly, with his enemy Priam too. None of that in the *Aeneid*, which ends with an unresolved discord. Why did Virgil do it? Romans were well aware that warfare should not be pursued with passionate hatred, and in

[10] *Aeneid*, I. 46f; I. 630.

the Underworld Aeneas was instructed to spare the
conquered.[11] Virgil perhaps shows a deeper insight into the
nature and consequences of war. Turnus is himself a killer, and
he has caused enormous slaughter by his obstinacy and pride;
but in any case fighting cannot be simply pursued in a cool and
rational spirit. His death, which is from some points of view
clearly justified, is none the less a dreadful thing, the death of
an Italian prince with some fine and attractive qualities. Aeneas
is forced into it by the logic of his god-given destiny of
imperialism; and he finds that he cannot do it without the
passionate destructiveness which it seemed that he was singled
out to avoid. The *Aeneid* begins with Aeneas, the fortunate
survivor, wishing that he had died at Troy,[12] and it ends with
him forced into a blind act of justified revenge. Between those
two points the destiny of Rome is set out and justified. Virgil
does not take either the easy option of denouncing imperialism
or the easier option of endorsing it. The exquisite balance of
his account shows how well he had learned, in the *Eclogues* and
Georgics, to combine plainness with evasion; it made his epic
the truest memorial to the imperial people of Rome; and it
explains why, even after it has become clear that the Roman
Empire was not, after all, history's last word, his poem remains
a profound and moving meditation on the nature and nemesis
of power.

[11] *Aeneid*, VI. 853.   [12] *Ibid.*, I. 94.

SELECT BIBLIOGRAPHY

THERE is a Latin text in the Loeb Classical Library, with facing English translation by H. R. Fairclough. The most interesting of the older translations is that of John Dryden: marvellous in rhetoric and panache, the product of an age saturated in the Latin classics, and well worth reading. It must be said that it is sometimes very far from the literal sense of the original, and that his rhyming couplets inevitably impose a different movement from that of Virgil's long periods.

The historical political background is brilliantly described in R. Syme's classic *The Roman Revolution* (Oxford, 1939: paperback). The early life of Virgil is well treated in the second chapter of L. P. Wilkinson, *The Georgics of Virgil* (Cambridge, 1969: paperback), which is the best book on the *Georgics*. On the *Eclogues* there is a helpful Introduction to Robert Coleman's edition (Cambridge, 1977).

W. A. Camps, *An Introduction to Virgil's 'Aeneid'* (Oxford, 1969) is an admirably compact short book on the *Aeneid*. Brooks Otis, *Virgil: A Study in Civilized Poetry* (Oxford, 1963) is more subjective: exciting, sometimes vulnerable. The sinister and daemonic side of the *Aeneid* is brought out by W. R. Johnson, *Darkness Visible* (California, 1976: paperback). There is a good collection of papers: *Virgil, a Collection of Critical Essays*, edited by S. Commager (Englewood Cliffs, NJ, 1966: paperback). Gordon Williams's *Tradition and Originality in Roman Poetry* (Oxford, 1968) illuminates many passages in Virgil, and in other authors. Domenico Comparetti, *Vergil in the Middle Ages* (English translation, 1895: reprinted, 1966), contains much curious information. Two recent books on Virgil's influence: R. D. Williams and T. S. Pattie, *Virgil: His Poetry through the Ages* (London, 1982), well illustrated; and Charles Martindale (editor), *Virgil and His Influence* (Bristol, 1984), on the debt to him of later poets and artists. Both are available in paperback. My own views on the poet are set out at greater length in Jasper Griffin: *Virgil* (Oxford, Past Master series, October 1986).

A CHRONOLOGY OF VIRGIL

70 BC   Virgil born near Mantua.

63   Consulate of Cicero and attempted coup by Catiline.

59   Consulate of Julius Caesar. The 'First Triumvirate' of Caesar, Pompey, and Crassus dominates Roman politics from 60 BC.

58–49   Caesar conquers Gaul.

53   Crassus is defeated and killed by the Parthians.

49   Caesar crosses the Rubicon and marches on Rome. Civil war begins between Caesar and Pompey.

45   Final defeat of the Pompeian armies.

44   Caesar assassinated. Octavian, his grand-nephew, is adopted in his will.

44–3   Struggle between Caesar's assassins, led by Brutus and Cassius, and the Caesarian party, led by Octavian and Mark Antony. Brutus and Cassius are defeated at Philippi.

43–39   Proscriptions and evictions.

42-38   (approximately) Virgil at work on the *Eclogues*.

42–31   Octavian supreme at Rome and in the West, Mark Antony in the East.

40   Disputes between Octavian and Antony are patched up at Brundisium. Antony marries Octavia, sister of Octavian.

39 or 38   Virgil joins the circle of Maecenas. He introduces his friend, the poet Horace.

38–1   Crescendo of conflict between Octavian and Mark Antony, who deserts Octavia for Cleopatra, queen of Egypt. Antony and Cleopatra are defeated at Actium, 31 BC, and kill themselves.

37–29   (approximately) Virgil at work on the *Georgics*.

29   Octavian returns to Rome from the East and holds a triple
          triumph.

29–19   Virgil at work on the *Aeneid*.

27   Octavian takes the name Augustus. It becomes clear that the
          Republic is at an end.

19   Death of Virgil, on a journey to Athens; the unfinished *Aeneid*
          is published by his literary executors.

THE AENEID

BOOK I

I tell about war and the hero who first from Troy's frontier,
Displaced by destiny, came to the Lavinian*shores,
To Italy—a man much travailed on sea and land
By the powers above, because of the brooding anger of Juno,
Suffering much in war until he could found a city
And march his gods into Latium, whence rose the Latin race,
The royal line of Alba*and the high walls of Rome.
Where lay the cause of it all? How was her godhead injured?
What grievance made the queen of heaven so harry a man
Renowned for piety, through such toils, such a cycle of
    calamity?
Can a divine being so persevere in anger?
There was a town of old—men from Tyre colonized it—
Over against Italy and Tiber mouth, but afar off,
Carthage, rich in resources, fiercely efficient in warfare.
This town, they say, was Juno's favourite dwelling, preferred
To all lands, even Samos: here were her arms, her chariot:
And even from the long-ago time she cherished the aim that
    this
Should be, if fate allowed, the metropolis of all nations.
Nevertheless, she had heard a future race was forming
Of Trojan blood, which one day would topple that Tyrian
    stronghold—
A people arrogant in war, born to be everywhere rulers
And root up her Libyan empire—so the Destiny-Spinners
    planned.
Juno, afraid of this, and remembering well the old war
Wherein she had championed the Greeks whom she loved
    against the Trojans—
Besides, she has other reasons for rage, bitter affronts
Unblotted as yet from her heart: deep in her mind rankle

The judgement of Paris,* the insult of having her beauty
    scorned,
Her hate for Troy's origin, Ganymede* taken and made a
    favourite—
Furious at these things too, she tossed all over the sea
The Trojans, the few that the Greeks and relentless Achilles
    had left,
And rode them off from their goal, Latium. Many years
They were wandering round the seven seas, moved on by
    destiny.
So massive a task it was to found the Roman race.

They were only just out of sight of Sicily, towards deep water
Joyfully crowding on sail and driving the foam-flocks before
    them,
When Juno, who under her heart nursed that inveterate
    wound,
Soliloquized thus:—
                    Shall I give up? own myself beaten?
Impotent now to foil the Trojan lord from Italy?
Fate forbids me, indeed! Did not Athene burn
The Argive fleet and drown the crews, because one man
Had given offence? because of the criminal madness of
    Ajax?*
Why, she herself flung down Jove's firebolt from the clouds,
Blasted that navy and capsized the sea with a storm;
And Ajax, gasping flame out of his cloven breast,
She whisked up in the whirlwind, impaled him on a crag.
But I, who walk in majesty, queen of heaven, Jove's
Sister and consort, I must feud with a single nation
For all these years. Does anyone worship my divinity
After this, or pay my altar a suppliant's homage?

  Such were the thoughts milling round in her angry heart
    as the goddess
Came to the storm-cloud country, the womb-land of brawl-
    ing siroccos,
Aeolia. Here in a huge cavern King Aeolus

Keeps curbed and stalled, chained up in durance to his own
     will,
The heaving winds and far-reverberating tempests.
Behind the bars they bellow, mightily fretting: the mountain is
One immense murmur. Aeolus, aloft on his throne of power,
Sceptre in hand, gentles and disciplines their fierce spirits.
Otherwise, they'd be bolting off with the earth and the
     ocean
And the deep sky—yes, brushing them all away into space.
But to guard against this the Father of heaven put the winds
In a dark cavern and laid a heap of mountains upon them,
And gave them an overlord who was bound by a firm contract
To rein them in or give them their head, as he was ordered.
Him Juno now petitioned. Here are the words she used:—
     Aeolus, the king of gods and men has granted
You the rule of the winds, to lull the waves or lift them.
A breed I have no love for now sails the Tyrrhene sea,*
Transporting Troy's defeated gods to Italy.
Lash fury into your winds! Whelm those ships and sink
     them!
Flail the crews apart! Litter the sea with their fragments!
Fourteen nymphs I have—their charms are quite out of the
     common—
Of whom the fairest in form, Deiopea, I'll join
To you in lasting marriage and seal her yours for ever,
A reward for this great favour I ask, to live out all
The years with you, and make you the father of handsome
     children.
     Aeolus answered thus:—
                              O queen, it is for you to
Be fully aware what you ask: my duty is to obey.
Through you I hold this kingdom, for what it's worth, as
     Jove's
Viceroy; you grant the right to sit at the gods' table;
You are the one who makes me grand master of cloud and
     storm.

Thus he spoke, and pointing his spear at the hollow mountain,
Pushed at its flank: and the winds, as it were in a solid mass,
Hurl themselves through the gates and sweep the land with tornadoes.
They have fallen upon the sea, they are heaving it up from its deepest
Abysses, the whole sea—East wind, South, Sou'-wester
Thick with squalls—and bowling great billows at the shore.
There follows a shouting of men, a shrilling of stays and halyards.
All of a sudden the storm-clouds are snatching the heavens, the daylight
From the eyes of the Trojans; night, black night is fallen on the sea.
The welkin explodes, the firmament flickers with thick-and-fast lightning,
And everything is threatening the instant death of men.
At once a mortal chill went through Aeneas and sapped him;
He groaned, and stretching out his two hands toward the stars,
Uttered these words:—

                 Oh, thrice and four times blessèd you
Whose luck it was to fall before your fathers' eyes
Under Troy's battlements! O Diomed, the bravest
Of the Greek kind, why could not I have fallen to death
On Ilium's plains and shed my soul upon your sword?
Fallen where Hector lies, whom Achilles slew, and tall
Sarpedon fell, and Simois our river rolls so many
Helmets and shields and heroes together down its stream?

Even as he cried out thus, a howling gust from the North
Hit the front of the sail, and a wave climbed the sky.
Oars snapped; then the ship yawed, wallowing broadside on
To the seas: and then, piled up there, a precipice of sea hung.
One vessel was poised on a wave crest; for another the waters, collapsing,

Showed sea-bottom in the trough: the tide-race boiled with
  sand.
Three times did the South wind*spin them towards an
  ambush of rocks
(Those sea-girt rocks which Italians call by the name of 'The
  Altars'),
Rocks like a giant spine on the sea: three times did the East
  wind
Drive them in to the Syrtes shoal,* a piteous spectacle—
Hammering them on the shallows and hemming them round
  with sandbanks.
One ship, which carried in her the Lycians and faithful
  Orontes,
Before Aeneas' eyes is caught by an avalanche wave
And pooped: her helmsman is flicked from off the deck and
  headlong
Sent flying; but three times the vessel is twirled around
By the wave ere the waters open and greedily gulp her down.
A man or two can be seen swimming the huge maelstrom,
With weapons and planks and Trojan treasure spilt on the
  sea.
Now Ilioneus' strong ship, now the ship of valiant Achates,
And the ships that carry Abas and aged Aletes go
Down to the gale; the ships have all sprung leaks and are
  letting
The enemy pour in through the loosened joints of their
  hulls.
  Meanwhile Neptune has felt how greatly the sea is in
    turmoil,
Felt the unbridled storm disturbing the water even
Down to the sea-bed, and sorely troubled has broken surface;
He gazes forth on the deep with a pacific mien.
He sees the fleet of Aeneas all over the main, dismembered,
The Trojans crushed by waves and the sky in ribbons about
  them:
Juno's vindictive stratagems do not escape her brother.

He summons the East and the West winds, and then pro-
    ceeds to say:—
   Does family pride tempt you to such impertinence?
Do you really dare, you Winds, without my divine assent
To confound earth and sky, and raise this riot of water?
You, whom I——! Well, you have made the storm, I must
    lay it.
Next time, I shall not let you so lightly redeem your sins.
Now leave, and quickly leave, and tell your overlord this—
Not to him but to me was allotted the stern trident,
Dominion over the seas. His domain is the mountain of
    rock,
Your domicile, O East wind. Let Aeolus be king of
That castle and let him keep the winds locked up in its
    dungeon.
   He spoke; and before he had finished, the insurgent sea
    was calmed,
The mob of cloud dispersed and the sun restored to power.
Nereid and Triton*heaving together pushed the ships off
From the sharp rock, while Neptune levered them up with
    his trident,
And channelled a way through the sandbanks, and made the
    sea lie down—
Then lightly charioted off over the face of the waters.
Just as so often it happens, when a crowd collects, and
    violence
Brews up, and the mass mind boils nastily over, and next
    thing
Firebrands and brickbats are flying (hysteria soon finds a
    missile)—
That then, if they see some man whose goodness of heart and
    conduct
Have won their respect, they fall silent and stand still, ready
    to hear him;
And he can change their temper and calm their thoughts with
    a speech:

So now the crash of the seas died down, when Neptune gazed
    forth
Over their face, and the sky cleared, and the Father of ocean,
Turning his horses, wheeled away on an easy course.
    Aeneas' men, worn out, with a last effort make for
The nearest landing place; somewhere on the coast of Libya.
A spot there is in a deep inlet, a natural harbour
Formed by an island's flanks upon which the swell from the
    deepsea
Breaks and dividing runs into the land's recesses.
At either end of the lofty cliffs a peak towers up
Formidably to heaven, and under these twin summits
The bay lies still and sheltered: a curtain of overhanging
Woods with their shifting light and shadow forms the back-
    drop;
At the seaward foot of the cliffs there's a cave of stalactites,
Fresh water within, and seats which nature has hewn from
    the stone—
A home of the nymphs. Here, then, tired ships could lie, and
    need
No cable nor the hooking teeth of an anchor to hold them.
Here, with seven ships mustered, all that was left of his
    convoy,
Aeneas now put in: and the Trojans, aching for dry land,
Tumbled out of their ships onto the sands they craved so,
And laid their limbs, crusted with brine, upon the shore.
Then first of all Achates*struck a spark from flint,
Nursed the spark to a flame on tinder, gave it to feed on
Dry fuel packed around it and made the flame blaze up there.
Sick of mischance, the men got ready the gifts and gear of
Ceres,* setting themselves to roast on the fire and grind,
Though tainted it was with the salt water, what grain they
    had salvaged.
    While this was going forward, Aeneas scaled a crag
To get an extensive view of the sea, hoping to sight
Some Trojan ship—Antheus perhaps, safe from the storm,

Or Capys, or the tall ship displaying the shield of Caicus.
Ship there was none in view; but on the shore three stags
Caught his eye as they wandered with a whole herd behind
    them,
A straggling drove of deer which browsed along the valley.
Aeneas, where he stood, snatched up the bow and arrows—
The weapons he had borrowed just now from faithful
    Achates—
And aiming first at the leaders of the herd, which carried
    their heads high
With branching antlers, he laid them low; then shot at the
    herd,
And his arrows sent it dodging all over the leafy woods.
Nor would he stop shooting until triumphantly
He had brought down seven beasts, one for each of his ships.
Then he returned to the harbour and shared them among his
    comrades.
And then he shared out the wine which good Acestes* had
    casked
In Sicily and given them—a generous parting present,
And spoke these words of comfort to his sad-hearted
    friends:—
   Comrades, we're well acquainted with evils, then and now.
Worse than this you have suffered. God will end all this
    too.
You, who have risked the mad bitch, Scylla,* risked the cliffs
So cavernously resounding, and the stony land of the
    Cyclops,*
Take heart again, oh, put your dismal fears away!
One day—who knows?—even these will be grand things to
    look back on.
Through chance and change, through hosts of dangers, our
    road still
Leads on to Latium: there, destiny offers a home
And peace; there duty tells us to build the second Troy.
Hold on, and find salvation in the hope of better things!

Thus spoke Aeneas; and though his heart was sick with
  anxiety,
He wore a confident look and kept his troubles to himself.
The Trojans set to work, preparing the game for a banquet;
Hacked the chines apart from the ribs, and exposed the guts:
Some sliced the meat into steaks which they spitted with
  trembling fingers,
Some set down cooking pots on the beach, and fed the fires.
Then they restored their strength with the food, sprawling
  at ease
On the grass they took their fill of the wine and the rich
  venison.
Afterwards, hunger appeased and the meal cleared away, for
  a long time
They talked of their missing friends, longing to have them
  back,
Half-way between hope and fear, not knowing whether to
  deem them
Alive or utterly perished and far beyond human call.
True-hearted Aeneas grieved especially for the fate of
Ardent Orontes, and Amycus, and the cruel fate of Lycus,
Grieved for Gyas the brave and for the brave Cloanthus.
  At last they made an end. Jupiter from high heaven
Looked down at the flights of sails on the sea, and the earth
  beneath him,
Its shores and its far-flung peoples: so, at the top of the morn-
  ing
He stood, and presently focused his gaze on the Libyan
  realm.
Now, as he deeply pondered the troubles there, came Venus,
Sadder than is her wont, her eyes shining with tears,
And spoke to him:—
                    Sir, you govern the affairs of gods and men
By law unto eternity, you are terrible in the lightning:
Tell me, what wrong could my Aeneas or his Trojans
Have done you, so unforgivable that, after all these deaths,

To stop them reaching Italy they are locked out from the
    whole world?
Verily you had promised that hence, as the years rolled on,
Troy's renaissance would come, would spring the Roman
    people
And rule as sovereigns absolute over earth and sea.
You promised it. Oh, my father, why have you changed your
    mind?
That knowledge once consoled me for the sad fall of Troy:
I could balance fate against fate, past ills with luck to come.
But still the same ill fortune dogs my disaster-ridden
Heroes. Oh when, great king, will you let their ordeal end?
Antenor, slipping away through the Greek army, could safely
Sail right up the Illyrian gulf, pass by the remote
Liburnians, and pass the source of river Timavus
Where tidal water, roaring aloud below rock, spouts up
Through nine mouths, and the fields are hemmed with a
    sound of the sea.
He was allowed to found Padua, make a home for
Trojans there—could give his people a name, and nail up
His arms, could settle down to enjoy peace and quiet.
But we, your seed, for whom you sanction a place in heaven—
Our ships damnably sunk—because of one being's anger
We are cheated, and fenced afar from Italy.
Is this the reward for being true? Is it thus you restore a king?
    The begetter of gods and men inclined towards her the
      smiling
Countenance which calms the sky and makes fair weather,
Gently kissed his daughter's mouth, and began to speak:—
    Fear no more, Cytherea. Take comfort, for your people's
Destiny is unaltered; you shall behold the promised
City walls of Lavinium, and exalt great-hearted Aeneas
Even to the starry skies. I have not changed my mind.
I say it now—for I know these cares constantly gnaw you—
And show you further into the secret book of fate:
Aeneas, mightily warring in Italy, shall crush

Proud tribes, to establish city walls and a way of life,
Till a third summer has seen him reigning in Latium
And winter thrice passed over his camp in the conquered
    land.
His son Ascanius, whose surname is now Iulus—
Ilus it was, before the realm of Ilium fell—
Ascanius for his reign shall have full thirty years
With all their wheeling months; shall move the kingdom
    from
Lavinium and make Long Alba his sure stronghold.
Here for three hundred years*shall rule the dynasty
Of Hector, until a priestess and queen of Trojan blood,*
With child by Mars, shall presently give birth to twin sons.
Romulus, then, gay in the coat of the tawny she-wolf
Which suckled him, shall succeed to power and found the
    city
Of Mars and with his own name endow the Roman nation.
To these I set no bounds, either in space or time;
Unlimited power I give them. Even the spiteful Juno,
Who in her fear now troubles the earth, the sea and the sky,
Shall think better of this and join me in fostering
The cause of the Romans, the lords of creation, the togaed
    people.
Thus it is written. An age shall come, as the years glide by,
When the children of Troy shall enslave the children of
    Agamemnon,
Of Diomed and Achilles, and rule in conquered Argos.
From the fair seed of Troy there shall be born a Caesar—*
Julius, his name derived from great Iulus—whose empire
Shall reach to the ocean's limits, whose fame shall end in the
    stars.
He shall hold the East in fee; one day, cares ended, you shall
Receive him into heaven; him also will mortals pray to.
Then shall the age of violence be mellowing into peace:
Venerable Faith, and the Home, with Romulus and Remus,
Shall make the laws; the grim, steel-welded gates of War*

Be locked; and within, on a heap of armaments, a hundred
Knots of bronze tying his hands behind him, shall sit
Growling and bloody-mouthed the godless spirit of Discord.

So Jupiter spoke, and sent Mercury down from on high
To see that the land and the new-built towers of Carthage
    offered
Asylum to the Trojans, for otherwise might queen Dido,
Blind to destiny, turn them away. He aerially wafted,
Feathering his wings, and post-haste came down on Libyan
    soil.
Now he performs his mission; at the god's will that people
Puts by its haughty temper, the queen at once responds to
An intimation of peace and goodwill towards the Trojans.
True-hearted Aeneas, after a night spent on a treadmill
Of cares, when kindly dawn came, determined to reconnoitre
The strange terrain, find out to what land the storm had
    brought them
And who lived there—was it men or only beasts—for it
    looked like
A wilderness, and bring back a full report to his friends.
He saw that the ships were concealed in a woody creek, be-
    neath
The overhang of the cliff, with trees and shifting shadows
About them; and then set forth, accompanied by Achates
Only, swinging a couple of broad-tipped spears in his hand.
There, from the heart of the woodland, his mother came to
    meet him
Guised as a maiden in face and dress, with a girl's weapons—
A Spartan girl, as it might be, or Thracian Harpalyce,*
Outpacer of horses, swift outrunner of running rivers.
In huntress wise she had handily slung her bow from her
    shoulder,
And her hair was free to blow in the wind, and she went bare-
    kneed
With the flowing folds of her dress kilted up and securely
    knotted.

She spoke first:—

Hullo there, young men! If you have seen
One of my sisters roving hereabouts or in full cry
After a foaming boar—she carries a slung quiver
And wears a spotted lynx-skin—please tell me where she
    went.
   Thus Venus spoke; and the son of Venus began to reply
        thus:—
   No sight or sound have I had of any of your sisters,
O—but what shall I call you, maiden? for your face is
Unmortal, and your speech rings not of humankind.
Goddess surely you are. A nymph? The sister of Phoebus?*
Give luck, whoever you be! Lighten, I pray, our ordeal!
Tell me in what clime, upon what shores of the world
We are cast up: for, driven here by wind and wave,
We have no clue to the peoples or places of our wandering.
Tell this, and we will offer sacrifice at your altar.
   Then Venus said:—

Believe me, such titles are not my due:
It is the fashion for Tyrian girls to carry a quiver
And wear like this the high-laced, crimson hunting boot.
The kingdom you see is Carthage, the Tyrians, the town of
        Agenor;*
But the country around is Libya, no folk to meet in war.
Dido, who left the city of Tyre to escape her brother,
Rules here—a long and labyrinthine tale of wrong
Is hers, but I will touch on its salient points in order.
Her husband was Sychaeus, a man of great estates
Among the Phoenicians and greatly loved by the ill-starred
        Dido
Whose father had given her in marriage to Sychaeus,
A virgin bride. Now the throne of Tyre was held by her
        brother,
Pygmalion, a monster who had no rival in wickedness.
Maniac evil stepped in. Pygmalion, blinded by love for
Gold, godlessly murdered the unsuspecting Sychaeus

In secret before the altar—no pang of compunction for her
    love;
And kept the deed dark for a long time, vilely inventive of
    fictions
To cheat with hollow hope her pining, loving heart.
But there came, one night as she slept, the phantom of her
    unburied
Husband, weirdly floating its clay-white face up to her,
Exposed the atrocious altar, the breast spitted with steel,
And took the cover off that crime hidden in the house.
Then the phantom urged her swiftly to fly the country,
And told her where she could find in the earth an old treasure,
    a secret
Hoard of gold and silver to help her on her way.
Dido, in great disquiet, organized her friends for escape.
They met together, all those who harshly hated the tyrant
Or keenly feared him: they seized some ships which chanced
    to be ready
And loaded them with the gold: so was that treasure sailed
Out of Pygmalion's grasp: a woman led the exploit.
They came to this spot, where today you can behold the
    mighty
Battlements and the rising citadel of New Carthage,
And purchased a site, which was named 'Bull's Hide'*after
    the bargain
By which they should get as much land as they could enclose
    with a bull's hide.
But now, tell me who you are, what land you have come from,
    and whither
Your journey leads.
                    So Venus questioned him; and Aeneas,
Sighing, drew up his voice as it were from the heart's
    depth:—
    Goddess, if I were to tell our tale right through from the
        start
And leisure there was to hear the chronicles of our labours,

Evening would close the sky and the day be asleep ere I
    finished.
We from old Troy (if ever the name of Troy has come to
Your ears) were voyaging, when the weather's caprice
    drove us
Off our course and piled us onto the Libyan shore.
I am true-hearted Aeneas; my fame has been heard of in
    heaven:
I carry my gods of Home which I rescued from the enemy.
I go to my own land, Italy, where Jove began our line.
With twenty ships I embarked on the Phrygian sea, my
    mother,
A goddess, showing the way, I following destiny's bidding:
But seven ships now are left us, battered by wind and wave.
I, a stranger and needy, now roam the Libyan desert,
Driven from Europe and Asia.
                         Venus could bear no longer
To hear him grieve, and so she broke in on his anguish, say-
    ing:—
    Whoever you are, you cannot breathe and live, I am sure,
Hateful to heaven, for soon you'll have reached the Tyrian
    city.
Do but fare on, press on from here to the queen's palace.
Unless what my parents taught me of signs and omens is
    meaningless,
I can declare your friends rallied to you, your missing
Ships brought back to haven here by a shift of the wind.
Look at those twelve swans flying in jubilant formation:
Just now an eagle, swooping from heaven, was scattering
    them
All over the sky: but see how, in a long line, they look down
Where to land or where their fellows already have landed.
Rallied they are, and romping aloft with their wings whoop-
    ing,
And wheeling about the sky in company, and calling.
Even so it is with your ships and your young warriors—either

They're havened already or running free to the harbour
    mouth.
Do but fare on, and firmly step where the road leads you.
    She spoke. She turned away; and as she turned, her neck
Glowed to a rose-flush, her crown of ambrosial hair breathed
    out
A heavenly fragrance, her robe flowed down, down to her
    feet,
And in gait she was all a goddess. Aeneas recognized
His mother, and as she passed from him, sent these words in
    her wake:—
    Must you too be cruel? Must you make game of your son
With shapes of sheer illusion? Oh, why may we not join
Hand to hand, or ever converse straightforwardly?
    Thus he reproached her, and turned his steps toward the
    battlements.
But Venus folded them as they went in an opaque mist,
Magically poured round them an ample cloak of cloud,
Lest any should spy or encounter Aeneas and Achates,
Attempt to delay them or demand to know their business.
Then she herself was gone through the air to Paphos,* joyfully
Homing again where her temple is, and a hundred altars
Glow with Sabaean* incense and blow with fresh-breathed
    flowers.
    Meanwhile the two pressed on apace, where the track
    pointed.
And now they were climbing a hill whose massive bulk looms
    over
The city and commands a prospect of soaring towers.
Aeneas marvels at great buildings, where once were shanties,
Marvels at city gates and the din of the paved streets.
The Tyrians are busy at work there, some extending the walls,
Manhandling blocks of stone and building the citadel,
Others choosing a site for a house and trenching foundations:
Laws are being made, magistrates and a parliament elected:
Here they dig out a harbour basin; here they are laying

Foundations deep for a theatre, and hewing from stone immense

Columns to grace one day a tall proscenium.

So in the youth of summer throughout the flowering land

The bees pursue their labours under the sun: they lead

A young brood from the hive, or press the flowing honey

And fill the cells to bursting with a delicious nectar;

Relieve incoming bees of their burden, or closing ranks

Shoo the drones, that work-shy gang, away from the bee-folds.

The work goes on like wild-fire, the honey smells of thyme.

Ah, fortunate you are, whose town is already building!

Aeneas said, and gazed up at the city's heights.

Then, in his cloak of darkness he went—a miraculous thing—

Into their midst and joined the crowds, but none perceived him.

There was a grove, most genial its shade, at the city centre,

Just where the Carthaginians, after their rough passage,

First dug and found the sign which royal Juno had promised—

The skull of a spirited horse*; it was a sign that henceforth

Their nation would thrive in wealth and war throughout the ages.

Dido was building here, in Juno's honour, a huge

Temple, made rich by offerings and the indwelling presence of Juno:

Bronze was its threshold, approached by a flight of steps; the door-posts

Were braced with bronze, and the door with its grinding hinges was bronze.

This grove had seen Dido's fear*allayed by a chance of renewal

For the first time; and here Aeneas first dared to hope for

Salvation and believe that at last his luck was turning.

For, while he awaited the queen and his eyes roved over the detail

Of that immense façade, amazed by the town's good fortune,

Admiring the skill of the rival craftsmen, the scope of their
    work,
He noticed a series of frescoes depicting the Trojan war,
Whose fame had already gone round the world; the sons of
    Atreus*
Were there, and Priam, Achilles too, hostile to both.
Aeneas stood; wept:—
                            Oh, Achates, is there anywhere,
Any place left on earth unhaunted by our sorrows?
Look!—Priam. Here too we find virtue somehow rewarded,
Tears in the nature of things, hearts touched by human
    transience.
Then cast off fear; the fame of our deeds will ensure your
    welfare.

  He spoke, and fed his soul on those insubstantial figures,
Heavily sighing, the large tears rivering down his cheeks.
Pictured there, he beheld scenes of the fight round Troy—
Here the Greeks fled with the Trojan warriors hard behind
    them,
Here fled the Trojans before the chariot of plumed Achilles.
He recognized through his tears, not far away, the snow-
    white
Tents of Rhesus*taken by surprise, while all slept deep,
And wrecked with terrible slaughter by Diomed, man of blood,
And Diomed driving away to his camp the fiery horses
Before they could graze the meadows of Troy or drink the
    Xanthus.
Another scene was of Troilus*in flight, his weapons gone
(Unhappy the lad, unequal the fight with Achilles): his
    horses
Are bolting; heels over head he hangs backwards out of the
    chariot,
Yet gripping the reins; his neck and his hair are being dragged
    along
Over the ground, and his trailing spearpoint scribbles in the
    dust.

Meanwhile to the shrine of their goddess, their foe's friend,
    the Trojan women
Are walking to make intercession: their hair is unbound, they
    carry
The goddess' ritual robe, they mourn and beat their breasts:
But the goddess keeps her eyes on the ground and regards
    them not.
Thrice round the walls of Troy Achilles has dragged Hector
And now is demanding a ransom of gold for the lifeless body.*
At this point Aeneas uttered a deep groan
To see the spoils, the chariot, the actual body of
His friend, and Priam's defenceless hands stretched out to
    Achilles.
He noticed himself, too, in the forefront of the battle,
Noticed the Aethiopian brigade and the arms of black
    Memnon;*
Picked out Penthesilea leading the crescent shields of
The Amazons and storming through the rack like a fire,
Her bare breast thrusting out over the golden girdle,
A warrior queen, a girl who braved heroes in combat.
    Now while Aeneas viewed with wonder all these scenes,
And stood at gaze, rooted in a deep trance of attention,
There came in royal state to the temple, a crowd of courtiers
Attending her, queen Dido, most beautiful to see.
As, by the banks of Eurotas or over the Cynthian slopes*
Diana foots the dance, and a thousand Oreads*following
Weave a constellation around that arrowy one,
Who in grace of movement excels all goddesses,
And happiness runs through the still heart of Latona—
So Dido was, even so she went her radiant way
Through the crowds, eager to forward the work and growth
    of her realm.
Now, at the holy doors, under the temple porch,
Hedged by the spears of her guard, she throned herself on
    high;
Gave laws and ordinances, appointed the various tasks

In equitable proportions or else by drawing lots.

Just then, all of a sudden, Aeneas saw approaching
Amid the multitude Antheus, Sergestus, valiant
Cloanthus and other Trojans, whom the black hurricane
Had sundered at sea and driven afar to different beaches.

He and Achates together were thrilled through, were dumb-
founded

With anxious joy: they eagerly yearned to join hands with
their friends,

But the mystery of the whole affair disquieted them.

So they keep dark, and peering out from their womb of cloud,

Speculate what befell these friends, where their ships are
beached,

Why they are here: for spokesmen from each of the ships were
coming

To sue the queen's favour, and shouting aloud as they neared
the temple.

When they had entered and Dido had granted to them an
audience,

The eldest, Ilioneus, began in collected tones:—

O queen, who, under God, have founded a new city

And curbed the arrogance of proud clans with your justice,

We hapless Trojans, wanderers over a world of seas,

Implore you, stop your people from wickedly burning our
ships.

God-fearing men we are. Incline your heart to spare us.

We are not come as pirates to waste your Libyan homes

With the sword, and carry down their plunder to the beaches.

We've no mind for marauding; the conquered lack such
effrontery.

There is a place—the Greeks call it Hesperia—*

An antique land, well warded, possessed of a rich soil:

Oenotrians colonized it; whose heirs, so rumour says now,

Have named it, after their first founder, Italy.

That was our bourne. . . .

But rainy Orion rose, and the sea got up of a sudden:

We drove on chartless shoals, the winds wantonly pitched us
Far apart on the deep amid toppling waves and unchannelled
Reefs. A handful of us have drifted to your shores.
What manner of men are these? What land is this that allows
    them
Such barbarous ways? They bar us even from the sanctuary
Of the sands: they threaten, and forbid us to touch the hem of
    their country.
If humankind and mortal arms mean nothing to you,
Think of the gods—they do not forget good deeds and bad.
Aeneas was our king: never was a man more just,
More duteous of heart, more adept in warlike arts, than he.
If destiny has preserved him, if still he breathes the air
Of day, and is not sleeping in death's unwelcome shade,
We need not fear; and you should have no cause to regret
That you were prompt to aid us. In Sicily, too, we have towns
And resources, and noble Acestes* who comes of Trojan
    stock.
We pray you, let us lay up the vessels the storm shattered,
And shape new oars and timbers for them out of your forests;
So that, if we are meant to get back our friends and our king
And make for Italy, to Italy we may go;
But if that hope is lost—if the Libyan sea has drowned you,
Lord Aeneas, and there's no future for Iulus—
We may at least sail back to our last port of call, to Sicily,
Where homes are ready for us, and make Acestes our king.
    Ilioneus stopped speaking. A shout of assent rose from
The Trojans all. . . .
Then Dido, with her eyes downcast, addressed them
    briefly:—
    Trojans, put fear away from your hearts and forget your
    troubles!
Mine's a hard task, with a young country: that's why I have to
Do such things, to guard my frontiers everywhere.
Who has not heard of Troy and the men of Aeneas—their
    manly

Virtues, and all that famous conflagration of war?
We Carthaginians are not so insensitive of heart,
Nor is our city quite so out of the way or benighted.
Whether your choice is great Hesperia, land of Saturn,*
Or you decide upon Sicily and king Acestes,
I will give you an escort there and what provision you need.
Or would you like to share my kingdom, on equal terms?
This city I am building—it's yours: draw up your ships,
    then;
There shall be no preference, I say, between you and us.
Oh, if only your king, Aeneas himself, could come here,
Fetched by the same storm! Well, I will send couriers abroad
With orders to comb the furthest corners of Libya, in case
He is wandering somewhere, in woods or towns, a castaway.

   Arrested by Dido's words, Aeneas and brave Achates
For some time now had been on fire to slough off their cloak
Of darkness. Achates first spoke urgently to Aeneas:—

   Tell me, goddess-born, what idea forms in your mind now.
All is saved, you can see, our fleet and our friends restored
    to us.
One only is missing, and him we saw drowned in the welter
Before our eyes: all else bears out what your mother told us.

   These words were hardly spoken, when in a flash the cloud-
    cloak
They wore was shredded and purged away into pure air.
Aeneas was standing there in an aura of brilliant light,
Godlike of face and figure: for Venus herself had breathed
Beauty upon his head and the roseate sheen of youth on
His manhood and a gallant light into his eyes;
As an artist's hand adds grace to the ivory he works on,
As silver or marble when they're plated with yellow gold.
So then Aeneas addressed the queen, and startling them all
At once began:—

            I am here, before you, the one you look for,
Trojan Aeneas, saved from out the Libyan sea.
O lady, you alone have pitied the tragic ordeal

Of Troy, and now you offer to share your home and city
With us, the remnant of Troy—men utterly spent by
Every disaster on land and sea, deprived of everything.
Dido, we have not the means to repay your goodness, nor
  have
Any of our kin, wherever they are, scattered over the world.
If spirits there be who look after the good, if indeed just
  dealing
And minds informed with the right mean anything to heaven,
May God reward you as you deserve! What happy age,
What great parentage was it gave life to the like of you?
So long as rivers run to the sea, and shadows wheel round
The hollows of the hills, and star-flocks browse in the sky,
Your name, your fame, your glory shall perish not from the
  land
Wherever I am summoned to go.
                                                He spoke: he stretched out
His right hand to Ilioneus, his friend, and his left to Serestus,
Then to others, brave Gyas and brave Cloanthus.
   Sidonian Dido, amazed first by the man's appearance
Then by the magnitude of his downfall, thus addressed
  him:—
   O goddess-born, what doom is pursuing you through so
  many
Hazards? What violent fate casts you on this harsh coast?
Are *you* the famed Aeneas, whom gentle Venus bore
To Trojan Anchises by the waters of Simois?
Indeed I well recollect Teucer*coming to Sidon,
An exile from his homeland, and seeking a new kingdom
With the help of Belus: at that time Belus, my father, was
  sacking
Rich Cyprus and holding the island down in subjection to
  him.
Now from that time I have known about the fall of Troy,
And known your name, Aeneas, and the kings who led the
  Greeks.

Even their enemy held the Trojans in high esteem
And claimed blood kinship with the ancient line of Troy.
So, gentlemen, do not hesitate to come under my roof.
I too have gone through much; like you, have been roughly
     handled
By fortune; but now at last it has willed me to settle here.
Being acquainted with grief, I am learning to help the un-
     lucky.
   She spoke: she led Aeneas into the royal palace,
And ordered a thanksgiving service to be held in the gods'
     temple.
Besides, she sent to his companions on the shore
Twenty bulls, a hundred head of bristle-backed swine,
A hundred fatted lambs together with their ewes,
And the good cheer of the Wine-god.
Within, the palace was being arrayed in all the glitter
Of regal luxury, and a banquet being made ready:
Richly embroidered the hangings of princely purple; a
     service
Of solid silver on the tables; and golden vessels chased
With the legends of family history—a long lineage of glory
Traced through many heroes right from its earliest source.
   Aeneas, whose love for his son would not allow a moment's
Delay, now sent Achates running down to the ships,
Bade him tell Ascanius the news and return with him,
Aeneas being always thoughtful for his dear son, Ascanius.
They were to bring back also some gifts, which had been
     salvaged
From Troy's ruins—a robe of stiff golden brocade
And a veil with a pattern of yellow acanthus round its border;
Argive Helen had worn them once, had brought them with
     her
Out of Mycenae when she eloped to Troy for that lawless
Marriage*; they were a marvellous gift from her mother, Leda.
In addition to these, a sceptre which Ilione, the eldest
Daughter of Priam, had carried once, a pearl necklace,

And a double coronet of gold and precious stones.
With this commission Achates hurried down to the ships.
   But Venus was meditating a new and artful scheme,
Which was to substitute, for little Ascanius, Cupid
Changed into his likeness, and let Cupid inflame
The queen with those gifts and set a match to her very
      marrow:
For Venus felt uneasy about her hospitality
And Tyrian equivocation; the thought of Juno irked her,
Recurring at nightfall. So she talks to her winged Cupid:—
   My son, my only strength, sole agent of my powers,
My son, who laugh at the bolts of giant-killing Jove,
To you I come for a favour, petitioning your godhead.
Your own brother, Aeneas,* is being tossed about
From shore to shore, a victim of Juno's brutal resentment—
This you know well and often have shared my grief at it.
Now Carthaginian Dido clings to him and delays him
With flattery. I fear the results of kindness inspired by
Juno: she'll not give up, when so much hinges on this.
Her I mean to forestall by rusefully taking the queen's heart
And throwing a cordon of fire round it: no deity
May swerve her if she is mine, possessed by love for Aeneas.
Now listen to my plan, how you can do this thing.
Sent for by his dear father, the royal child, the apple
Of my own eye, makes ready to go to Dido's city,
With gifts for her—things that escaped the sea and the blaze
      of Troy:
Him I shall hide away, drugged with sleep, in one of
My holy places, on high Cythera or on Idalium,*
Lest he gain knowledge of my plot or interfere.
Do you impersonate him, for the space of one night only;
A boy yourself, put on that boy's familiar features,
So that, when Dido takes you joyfully into her lap
There at the banquet table with the wine passing round,
And when she hugs you close and pours sweet kisses upon you,
Then you may secretly fire her heart and inject your magic.

Cupid obeyed the words of his dear mother: he took off
His wings, and walked rejoicing in the gait of young Ascanius.
But Venus showered a dew of peaceful sleep on the limbs of
Ascanius, snuggled him in her breast, and divinely bore
    him
Up to Idalian groves, where the tender marjoram puts him
To bed in a cradle of flowers and shade and entrancing
    fragrance.
And now, as his mother had bade him, Cupid was on his
    way
Carrying the kingly gifts and delighted to walk with Achates.
When he arrived, the queen had taken her place in the midst
And reclined on her golden couch beneath a magnificent
    awning.
Aeneas and his Trojan followers now assembled,
Disposed themselves upon the purple-upholstered couches.
Manservants brought round water to wash their hands, and
    offered
Bread in baskets, and gave out napkins of fine wool.
Within there were fifty maids, whose task it was by rote
To keep up the kitchen fire and a good supply of victuals:
A hundred maids and a hundred manservants, all of the same
    age,
Were there to load the banqueting tables and set the wine
    cups.
Carthaginians too, great numbers of them, were met
In the festive hall, invited to sit at the painted couches.
They admire the gifts of Aeneas, admire the boy Ascanius—
Or rather the radiant looks and plausible speech of Cupid—
Admire the robe and the veil with its pattern of yellow
    acanthus.
But above all poor Dido, fated to be destroyed,
Can't slake her soul with gazing, and in the gazing grows
Ever more ardent, moved alike by the boy and the gifts.
Cupid, when he had put his arms round Aeneas' neck
And been embraced, appeasing the love of his feigned father,

Went to the queen. With her eyes, with all her heart she
    devoured him,
Fondled him oft in her bosom—poor Dido, little she knew
The strength of him who was settling insidiously there. But
    Cupid,
Obeying his mother, began to efface little by little
The memory of Sychaeus from Dido's mind and tempt her
Disused, long-slumbering heart to awake to a living love.

  When first there was a lull in the feast, and a course was
    removed,
Great bowls of wine were brought to the tables and garlanded.
A rumble of talk went up, the wide hall surged with voices:
The chandeliers that hung from the gold-fretted ceiling
Were lit, and cressets of torches subdued the night with their
    flames.
The queen now called for a goblet of gold, jewel-encrusted,
And filled it up with wine, a goblet Belus had used
And all his heirs; then did the company fall silent.

  Jupiter—yours, they say, are the laws of hospitality—
Grant this be a happy day for the Carthaginians and those
Who come from Troy, a day that our children will remem-
    ber!
May Bacchus, giver of joy, be here, and bounteous Juno!
And you, my people bless our feast with friendly hearts!

  With these words, Dido poured a libation of wine on the
    table,
And after the toast was first to touch her lips to the goblet;
Then passed it to Bitias with a challenge, who eagerly drained
The foaming golden cup, left not a drop within it.
Next, other chieftains drank. Then the long-haired Iopas,
A pupil of Atlas, made the hall hum with his golden zither*:
He sang of the travelling moon and the sun's manifold
    labours;
He sang the creation of man and beast, of fire and water;
Arcturus he sang and the rainy Hyades and the twin Bears;
The reason why winter suns race on to dip in the ocean

And what slows down the long nights. Round after round of
    applause
Came from the Carthaginians; the Trojans followed suit.
Yes, and ill-starred Dido talked on into the small hours,
Talked over many things as she drank deep of love,
Asking over and over again about Priam and Hector,
Asking about the armour the son of Aurora*had come in,
The points of Diomed's horses and the stature of great
    Achilles.

  But now, dear guest, tell us, please tell us from the beginning
The story of Greek stratagems, and how your comrades fell,
And your own wanderings; for now is the seventh summer
That over land and sea you have been widely wandering.

BOOK II

All fell silent now, and their faces were all attention
When from his place of honour Aeneas began to speak:—
    O queen, the griefs you bid me reopen are inexpressible—
The tale of Troy, a rich and a most tragic empire
Erased by the Greeks; most piteous events I saw with my
        own eyes
And played no minor part in. What Myrmidon*or Thessalian,
What soldier of fell Ulysses could talk about such events
And keep from tears? Besides, the dewy night drops fast
From heaven, and the declining stars invite to sleep.
But if you want so much to know what happened to us
And hear in brief a recital of Troy's last agony,
Although the memory makes me shudder, and shrink from
        its sadness,
I will attempt it.
                        Broken in war and foiled by fate,
With so many years already slipping away,* the Greek staff
Constructed a horse, employing the craft of the goddess
        Athene—
It was high as a hill, and its ribs were made from planks of
        pinewood—
To pay for their safe return to Greece, they pretended: this
        rumour
Got round. But, choosing warriors by lot, they secretly
Put them in on the blind side of the horse, until its vast
And cavernous belly was crammed with a party of armed
        men.
    In sight of Troy there's an island, a well-known island,
        Tenedos—
Rich and powerful it was, while Priam's empire stood;
Now, little but a bay, a roadstead unsafe for shipping.

Thither the Greeks sailed out, and hid on its desolate coast.
This was evacuation, we thought—they had sailed for Greece.
So all Troy threw off the chains of her long anguish.
We opened the gates, we enjoyed visiting the Greek camp,
Viewing the derelict positions on the abandoned beaches.
Here the Dolopes camped; there, ferocious Achilles:
Here was beached their navy, and here the battle raged.
Some of us gaped at the gift—so deadly—the Greeks had left
  for
Minerva, and its stupendous bulk. Thymoetes first,
Either from treachery or because Troy's fate now was sealed,
Urged that the horse be brought through the walls and placed
  in our citadel.
But Capys and all those of sounder views recommended
Hurling it into the sea or setting fire to it, as some
Booby-trap of the Greeks and not to be trusted—or else
Boring holes in its belly to see what might be inside it.
So the rank and file were violently torn between contraries.
Then out in front of them all, hundreds straggling behind
  him,
In a great temper Laocoon came tearing down from the
  citadel,
Crying from far:—
      Citizens, are you all stark mad?
Do you really believe our foes are gone? Do you imagine
Any Greek gift is guileless? Is that your idea of Ulysses?
This thing of wood conceals Greek soldiers, or else it is
A mechanism designed against our walls—to pry into
Our homes and to bear down on the city; sure, some trick
Is there. No, you must never feel safe with the horse, Trojans.
Whatever it is, I distrust the Greeks, even when they are
  generous.
 He spoke: he put forth his strength, and spun his huge
  great spear
At the flank of the monster, right into its belly's rounded
  frame.

The spear stuck quivering; the hollow womb of the creature
Grunted at the concussion and rumbled hollowly.
If destiny, if our own will had not been so contrary,
Laocoon would have made us rip open that cache of Greek
    troops—
There'd still be a Troy—O topless towers, you'd be standing
    now!
  But listen, just at this moment some Trojan shepherds
    were noisily
Dragging a young man, handcuffed, into our king's presence.
The fellow had quite deliberately put himself in their path;
He was assured in nerve, and prepared one way or the other—
To bring off his underhand scheme (for they did not know
    him) or meet
A certain death: his game was to prise open Troy for the
    Greeks.
Eager to stare at him, the youth of Troy came mobbing
All round the man, and vied in jeering at him for being
    captured.
  Now hear how the Greeks tricked us; learn from one case
    of their wickedness
What every Greek is like.
Well then, he came to a halt—stared at, worried, unarmed—
Stood there, and ran his eyes round the Trojan spectators,
    and spoke:—
  O god! Is there now a single land or sea to accept me?
What awaits me now at the latter end? Oh, it is hopeless!
I have no foothold at all with the Greeks, and now the
    Trojans
Are my vindictive foes and they will have my blood.
  His pitiable tones produced a revulsion of feeling; our
    violence
Was checked: we encouraged him to tell us who he was,
What he could say for himself, and what he relied on in
    letting
Himself be taken. Finally, he laid aside fear, and spoke:—

Sir, I will tell you all, of course, come what come may,
And tell you the whole truth. I will not deny that I am a Greek;
This first: if Fortune has cast Sinon for tragedy,
She shall not wantonly shape me into a liar as well.
Some talk has come to your ears, perhaps, about Palamedes*
Of the family of Belus, and his bright reputation:
Him the Greeks framed on a monstrous charge of being a
      traitor,
And put him down to death, an innocent man, because
He was against the war. Now they are sorry they killed him.
Well, I was poor, so my father sent me to be his squire
At an early age, since he was a relative of ours.
While his authority was unshaken, his influence strong in
Our High Command, I too enjoyed a certain distinction
And honour. But when my kinsman, through the spiteful
      intrigues of Ulysses
(I daresay you know the tale), was driven from the land of the
      living,
I was ruined; I dragged out the days under a cloud, grieving,
Bitter about the downfall of my innocent friend.
I had not the sense to keep quiet: I volunteered that if ever
We won and I got back to Greece, to my home, when a chance
      offered,
I'd take revenge. Those words inspired a vicious hatred.
From then, my fortunes slipped; from then did Ulysses con-
      stantly
Persecute me with new slanders, dripping his subtle poison
Into the popular ear, and conspire to find allies against me.
Nor did he rest until, with Calchas*under his influence—
But what's the point, I ask you, going on with the sorry tale
And delaying you, if you think all Greeks are alike, and
      merely
To be one condemns me? Take your long-due reprisal.
      Ulysses
Would love it: the sons of Atreus would pay you handsomely
      for it.

Then of course we were all the more eager to find out the
    whole of his story—
Greek cunning, evil on such a scale, being as yet beyond
    us.
So he went on, trembling, and spoke with pretended emo-
    tion:—
    Often, sick of the way the war dragged on, the Greeks
Longed to withdraw from Troy, to sail home and be shut of
    fighting.
If only they'd done it! But always a stormy, vicious mood
Of the sea intervened and the South wind frightened them
    off sailing.
Especially when that horse, that fabric of maple, already
Was standing here, did the whole sky reverberate with storm
    clouds.
In this quandary, we sent Eurypylus to inquire
Of Phoebus' oracle; who brought back this message of gloom
    from the shrine:—
With human sacrifice, O Greeks, with a young girl's blood
Did you appease the winds when first you sailed to Troy:*
With human blood, with a Greek life, you must make sacri-
    fice
If you're to get safe home. The words went round: our
    people's
Spirits were paralysed; an icy shuddering coursed through
Their bones—whom would fate fix on? whom does Apollo
    require?
At this stage Ulysses made a great scene, pulling the seer
Calchas into our midst, pestering him to tell us
The god's will. Yes, and already many surmised that I
    was
That heartless schemer's victim, and silently saw what was
    coming.
For ten days Calchas was dumb, stayed in retreat, and would
    not
Name or commit to death anyone by his utterance.

But at long last, as Ulysses got ever more importunate,
According to plan he broke silence and smelt me out for the
    altar.
They all approved: what each had feared for himself, was
    easy
To tolerate when it became the death of this one poor scape-
    goat.
And now the hideous day was here; the last rites made ready
For me—the salted meal, the headband to go round my
    temples.
I dodged away then from death, I confess it; I broke prison,
And lay all night concealed in the mud of a lake, among reeds,
Giving them time to sail, on the chance that indeed they
    would sail.
No more hope have I now of seeing the old country, seeing
My little sons or the father I yearn for: on them the Greeks
Maybe will exact reprisals because of my escape
And make them pay, poor things, with their life for what I
    have done.
Yet by the gods I beg you, by the high powers that are witness
To truth, by Fidelity—if anywhere upon earth
She still can be found inviolate—I beg you to pity so dreadful
An ordeal, pity one who has too much to bear.
    We gave him his life for those tears: they even aroused our
    compassion.
Priam himself at once ordered the handcuffs, the cramping
Chains to be struck off the fellow, and spoke him a friendly
    word:—
    Whoever you are, from now on give up the Greeks, you
    are clear of them:
Be one of us, and answer these questions of mine truthfully.
Why did they build this huge monster of a horse? Who
    advised it?
Is their object religious? or was it to be some engine of war?
    So Priam spoke. Sinon, well up in the Greek art of trickery,
Raised to heaven his hands, free of the fetters, crying:—

You everlasting lights, and your inviolate deity,
I call you to witness—the altar too, and the damnable knife
Which I escaped, and the holy headband I wore to be sacri-
      ficed!
No sin that I should relax the solemn code of the Greeks;
No sin to loathe them, or to disclose their secrets, if any
There are: I can have no guilt at law in my own land.
Only abide by your promise, Trojans, and with your pre-
      server
Keep faith, if my words prove true and give good value for
      sparing me.
   All the hope of the Greeks, their assurance in starting the
      war,
Was sustained by the backing of Pallas Athene. But when the
      godless
Diomed and that master-craftsman of crime, Ulysses,
Set out to steal Troy's luck, Athene's image, away from
Her holy place,* massacred the sentries high on the citadel,
Snatched up the sacred image, and dared to lay their blood-
      stained
Hands on her virginal headband—from that day forth, the
      hopes
Of the Greeks were caught in an undertow and carried away,
      their strength
Was shattered, for the goddess hardened her heart against
      them.
Unmistakable were the signs of anger she gave us.
The image was hardly set up in our camp, when its eyes
      glared
Balefully glittering fire, salt sweat broke out all over it,
And thrice—oh, supernatural!—did the statue, untouched,
      dart forth
From her base, the spear and shield she carried quivering.
Straightaway, Calchas pronounced we must dare the sea and
      be gone,
For Troy would never now be destroyed by Greek weapons

Unless we sailed back home to fetch new luck, and returned
    with
The gods' blessing as when we first sailed here in our fine
    ships.
So at this moment they're running free towards Mycenae
To get fresh force and the gods on their side again: they'll
    be back
Unexpectedly over the sea. So Calchas interprets the omens.
Thus advised, they built this horse to dispel the curse of
Guilt for stealing Athene's image and wounding her god-
    head.
But Calchas bade them build the horse of enormous size
With strong oak planks, a real sky-scraping monster, so that
It could not get through your gates or be towed within the
    walls,
And thus become your guardian, serving the old cult.
For if your hands had outraged this offering to Minerva,*
It would be quite disastrous (may the omen sooner recoil
On its own prophet!) for Priam's rule and for the Trojans:
But if your hands should have got the horse up into the city,
Then would you carry Asia in war right up to the Grecian
Strongholds; such is the fate that is reserved for our children.
    Such was the artful, treacherous perjury Sinon used
To impose on us. We were tricked by cunning and crocodile
    tears—
We whom neither Diomed nor Larissaean*Achilles
Could conquer, not in ten years, not with a thousand war-
    ships.
Just then another event, the most alarming yet,
Befell us wretches, muddling still further our hooded minds.
Laocoon, whom we'd elected by lot as Neptune's priest,
Was sacrificing a great bull at the official altar,
When over the tranquil deep, from Tenedos, we saw—
Telling it makes me shudder—twin snakes with immense
    coils
Thrusting the sea and together streaking towards the shore:

Rampant they were among the waves, their blood-red crests
Reared up over the water; the rest of them slithered along
The surface, coil after coil sinuously trailing behind them.
We heard a hiss of salt spray. Next, they were on dry land,
In the same field—a glare and blaze of bloodshot eyes,
Tongues flickering like flame from their mouths, and the
     mouths hissing.
Our blood drained away at the sight; we broke and ran. The
     serpents
Went straight for Laocoon. First, each snake knotted itself
Round the body of one of Laocoon's small sons, hugging him
     tight
In its coils, and cropped the piteous flesh with its fangs. Next
     thing,
They fastened upon Laocoon, as he hurried, weapon in hand,
To help the boys, and lashed him up in their giant whorls.
With a double grip round his waist and his neck, the scaly
     creatures
Embrace him, their heads and throats powerfully poised
     above him.
All the while his hands are struggling to break their knots,
His priestly headband is spattered with blood and pitchy
     venom;
All the while, his appalling cries go up to heaven—
A bellowing, such as you hear when a wounded bull escapes
     from
The altar, after it's shrugged off an ill-aimed blow at its
     neck.
But now the twin monsters are gliding away and escaping
     towards
The shrine of relentless Minerva, high up on our citadel,
Disappearing behind the round of the goddess' shield, at her
     feet there.
Then, my god! a strange panic crept into our people's flutter-
     ing
Hearts: they argued Laocoon had got what he deserved

For the crime, the sacrilege of throwing his spear at the wooden
Horse and so profaning its holiness with the stroke.
Bring the horse to Minerva's shrine! Pray for her goodwill!
All of our people shouted.
We cut into our walls, laid open the heart of the city.
Everyone set about the task: we inserted rollers
Under its hooves, put hawsers of hemp around its neck,
And strained. The disastrous engine was jockeyed over our walls,
An army in its womb. Boys and unmarried maidens
Escorted it, singing psalms, joyfully gripping the traces.
The menace mounts, comes trundling into the city centre.
O, my country! O Ilium, home of the gods! O Troy town,
Famous through war! Four times the monster stopped, at entrance,
And every time it stopped the accoutrements clanged in its belly.
Yet we persevered, with never a thought—we were madly blind—
Until we had lodged the ominous thing in our holy place.
Then, to cap all, Cassandra* opened her mouth for prophecy—
She whom her god had doomed to be never believed by the Trojans.
But we poor fools, whose very last day it was, festooned
The shrines of the gods with holiday foliage all over the city.
  So now the sky rolled round, and night raced up from the ocean
Voluminously shrouding the earth and heaven's vault
And the villainous scheme of the Greeks. Not a sound from the Trojans, supine
Along the walls, tired out, in the embrace of sleep.
And now the main Greek army was moving from Tenedos
In fleet formation, under the favouring silences
Of a quiet moon, towards the coast they knew so well.

Their leading galley had signalled with flame: Sinon, pro-
    tected
By fate's injustice, stealthily unlocked the wooden horse
And let the Greeks out from its belly. The horse disgorged,
    the men
Burst revelling forth from its hollow flank into the fresh
    air—
Thessander and Sthenelus in the lead, with Ulysses the
    terrible,
Sliding down a rope they had lowered—Acamas, Thoas,
Neoptolemus son of Peleus,* Machaon and Menelaus,
And Epeus—the man who had actually built the clever con-
    traption.
They broke out over a city drowned in drunken sleep;
They killed the sentries and then threw open the gates,
    admitting
Their main body, and joined in the prearranged plan of
    attack.
   It was the hour when worn-out men begin to get
Some rest, and by god's grace genial sleep steals over them.
I dreamt, I seemed to behold our Hector*standing before me,
Most woebegone and shedding great tears, just as he'd looked
    once
In death, after being dragged by the chariot, black with the
    dirt
And blood, his swollen feet pierced where the thongs had
    been threaded.
Ah, god! what a sight he was! how terribly changed from the
    Hector
Who once came back arrayed in the armour of Achilles,*
Who came back from bombarding the Greek navy with fire!
Now his beard is matted, clotted with blood his hair,
He exhibits the many wounds received while defending his
    country
In combat around the walls. I too am weeping. Unasked, I
Address him in my dream, force out these sorrowful words:—

O light of Troy! O surest hope of the Trojans! What has
Been keeping you so long? What shores do you come from,
      Hector?
Long have we looked for you: how happily now we behold
      you—
We whom the death of many friends, the manifold ordeal
Of city and folk have exhausted! But why is your face, serene
      once,
So shamefully disfigured? Why do I see these wounds?
      He gave no heed at all to these futile questions of mine,
But heaving a heavy sigh from the depth of his heart, spoke
      out:—
      Goddess-born, you must go, you must save yourself from
      these flames.
The enemy's within the gates. Troy's tower is falling, falling.
You owe no more to your country or Priam: if strong right
      hands
Could save our town, this hand of mine would have saved it
      long ago.
Her holy things, her home-gods Troy commends to your
      keeping:*
Take these as partners in your fate, for these search out
The walls you are destined to build after long roaming the
      seaways.
      He spoke, he picked up the holy headbands, the puissant
      Vesta*
And her undying fire from out the temple sanctuary.
      Meantime, Troy was shaken through and through by her
      last pangs—
Yes, more and more, although the house of my father,
      Anchises,
Lay far back from the street, detached, and screened by
      trees,
The sounds of death came clearly, the battle alarum swelled.
I shook myself out of sleep, and clambering onto the ridge
Of the roof, I stood up there, straining my ears to listen.

You know how it is when southerly gales are fanning a fire
   through
A cornfield, or when a torrent in spate with mountain water
Smears flat the fields, flattens the crops which the oxen have
   worked for,
Drags forests down in its course—how then a shepherd,
   perched on
A rock, hearing the noise, is bemused and quite at a loss.
Now what I saw in my dream came true, and the Greeks'
   treachery
Was plain to behold. Deiophobus*house flared up and hugely
Collapsed; the house of Ucalegon, next door, was blazing:
You could see the flames reflected all over the Sigean straits.
Everywhere rose the shouting of men, the braying of
   trumpets.
Madly I snatch up my arms, beyond thinking how best to
   employ them;
Only I'm wild to rally some fighters and counter-attack
To relieve the citadel: blind rage and desperation
Drive me; one thought comes—that death in battle is a fine
   thing.
   But look, Panthus arrives, having got through the Greek
   barrage—
Panthus, the son of Othrys, Apollo's priest at the citadel:
Holding the hallows, his conquered divinities,* and leading
His little grandson, he frantically has made his way to my
   doorstep.
Where is the core of the fighting? What is our rallying-point?
I had hardly spoken these words when he, with a sob,
   replied:—
   The very last day has come, the hour inevitable
For Troy. We Trojans, with Ilium*and all its Teucrian glory,
Are things of the past; for cruel Jove has quite gone over
To the Greeks: the city's on fire; the Greeks are masters here.
The towering horse which stands in the heart of the city spilt
   out

Armed men: and flushed with triumph, Sinon is stirring the
    blaze
Everywhere. There are Greeks packing the opened gates—
All who ever came in their thousands from Mycenae:
Wherever the roads are narrow, they're blocked by Greek
    detachments.
A front of steel stands there, the sword-points glitter, the
    swords
Are bared to kill. The sentries guarding our gates could
    hardly
Begin to resist or put up a fight in the blinding darkness.
    So Panthus spoke, revealing the will of heaven. His words
Drove me towards the burning, the fighting. I heard the
    call of
War's sombre Fury—a dull roar, and shouts flung up to
    heaven.
Now Rhipeus and champion Epytus, looming up in the
    moonlight,
Hypanis and Dymas were there to reinforce me
And fell in at my side, together with young Coroebus,
Son of Mygdon. Coroebus, it happened, had come to Troy
But recently, impelled by a crazy love for Cassandra,
Bringing a son-in-law's aid to Priam and the Trojans—
Hard luck that he did not listen to his prophetic Cassandra's
Warnings.
Well, when I saw them in close formation and good shape for
    battle,
I spoke to inspire them further. Men! dear hearts so vainly
Valiant! If you are set on following one who intends
To see the business through to the end, this is the pic-
    ture:—
The gods, by whose grace our kingdom once stood, have
    washed their hands of us,
Abandoning shrine and altar; the city you would relieve
Is ablaze: let us die, let us charge into the battle's heart!
Losers have one salvation—to give up all hope of salvation.

So I fired my men with the fury of desperation. Then, just
    like
Marauding wolves in a black fog, at a time when their rabid
    hunger
Has sent them blindly prowling, and the cubs they have left
    are waiting
At home, their gullets parched, so through the enemy
    barrage
We went as to certain death, we steadily made for the heart of
The city, and were engulfed in the black night's ambient
    shade.
That night!—what words can render its deaths and its
    disaster?
What tears can rise to the level of all that was suffered then?
An ancient city is falling, after long years of power:
So many motionless bodies prostrated everywhere
Along the streets, in the houses, on the gods' holy thresholds.
Not the Trojans alone paid their account in blood:
There were times when courage returned even though we
    knew we were beaten,
And then the conquering Greeks fell. All over the town you
    saw
Heart-rending agony, panic, and every shape of death.
    The first to cross our path was Androgeos, with a fair-sized
Body of Greeks around him: he thought, in his ignorance,
We were friends, and went so far as to hail us with comradely
    words:—
    Get going, men! Whatever has kept you so long? What do
    you
Mean by this slackness? The rest of the Greeks have been
    burning and sacking
Ilium; and here are you only just turned up from the ships.
    He spoke; and at once—for he got no satisfactory answer—
It dawned on him that the men he'd fallen in with were
    hostile.
Startled, he brought up sharp, checked speech, winced away.

Like one who, forcing his way through sharp briars, acci-
    dentally
Has trod on a snake, and in sudden panic shudders away
    from
Its angrily-rearing head, its gunmetal neck puffed out—
Androgeos, unnerved at the sight of us, made to retreat.
We went for him and his party, surrounded them; and since
They had no local knowledge and were paralysed with fear,
Picked them off one by one. So fortune favoured our first
    move.
Flown with success and in high spirits, Coroebus ex-
    claimed:—
    Comrades, let's follow up where fortune has first shown us
A way to survival, and play our luck while it is good!
Change shields with these dead Greeks, put on their badges
    and flashes!
Craft or courage—who cares, when an enemy has to be
    beaten?
The Greeks themselves shall equip us.
                                    So saying, he put on
Androgeos' plumed helmet, his shield with its fine heraldic
Device, and fitted onto his side the Argive sword.
Rhipeus, and Dymas too, and all our warriors gleefully
Followed suit, each arming himself from the spoils just taken.*
Then we went on through the press of the Greeks, under
    false favours
Of alien gods. Many a sharp engagement we fought
In the blindfold night, and many a Greek we despatched to
    Hades.
Some broke and ran for the ships, ran for the sure protection
The beaches gave: one lot, driven by sheer cowardice,
Climbed the horse again and returned to the womb they had
    come from.
    Ah well, there's no trusting the gods for anything, once
        they're against you!—
Over there was Priam's daughter, Cassandra, her hair flying,

Being dragged away from Minerva's house, from its very
      sanctuary,
Her burning eyes uplifted to heaven, but in vain—
Her eyes, for she could not lift her delicate palms, they were
      pinioned.
Coroebus found this sight too much: in a passion of rage
He bores right into the thick of the foe; he wants to be killed.
We followed him, all of us, attacking in close order.
Now, we were first mown down by the fire of our own side,
      shooting
From the high temple roof; a deplorable slaughter began
Through mistaken identity—our Greek equipment and
      crests.
Next, the Greeks rallied, shouting with rage at the attempt to
Rescue Cassandra: they went for us—Ajax most vindictively,
And the two sons of Atreus, with the whole battalion of
      Dolopes:
So, when a hurricane breaks, you may get a clash and a tussle
Of winds—the West, the South, and the East wind rough-
      riding
His orient steeds: then forests whine, and Nereus in wild rage
Churns the sea with his trident and raises it mountains-high.
More Greeks appeared now—the ones whom, in the con-
      fusing darkness
Of night, our ruse had routed and stampeded over the town.
These were the first to recognize our shields, our fraudulent
      weapons;
They noticed, too, the foreign tongue which gave us away.
Well, this was it. We were crushed by weight of numbers.
      Coroebus
Went down to Peneleus' sword at the altar of the war-
      puissant
Goddess; then Rhipeus fell, he who of all the Trojans
Was most fair-minded, the one who was most regardful of
      justice:
God's ways are inscrutable. Now Hypanis fell and Dymas

Shot by their own friends. And Panthus—not all his good-
    ness
Nor the headband he wore as Apollo's priest saved him from
    death.
O ashes of Ilium! O flames that my world died in!
I call you to witness that I, at your setting, was facing the
    Greeks' fire,
Evading no danger in combat: if fate had meant me to die
    then,
I'd have earned that death by the way I fought. But soon
    myself,
Iphitus and Pelias were drawn away—Iphitus
Being old, and Pelias slowed down by a wound Ulysses had
    given him—
Urgently summoned by war-cries we heard from the palace
    of Priam.
Here we beheld so tremendous a struggle as made it seem
    that
Nowhere else in the city could men be fighting and dying—
A bitter battle, the Greeks trying to scale the walls
And ramming a compact wedge of shields at the door they
    assaulted.
They advance ladders to the walls; hard by the very door-
    posts
They climb the rungs, with left hands holding their shields
    above them
To ward off missiles, and grasping the battlements with their
    right hands.
The Trojans for their part are stripping the turrets and roof-
    tops,
Ready, since now the end is in sight, to use the material
For missiles, to put up a stern defence though death is upon
    them:
Yes, they throw down even the gilded beams, the pride of
Their ancestors; while others cluster to guard the doors
Below with a thick-set hedge of naked swords. Our courage

Rekindled now. We would seek to succour the king's palace,
Reinforce the defenders and lend our strength to the con-
    quered.
   There was a door, a secret entrance by which you went
From one block to another, a postern out of the way
Behind the palace: by this, while our empire stood, Andro-
    mache—*
Poor soul—would often come unattended to visit her
    husband's
Parents, bringing her child, Astyanax, to his grandsire.
Using this door, I got out onto the rooftop whence
The luckless Trojans were raining missiles, all to no purpose.
A tower stood over the sheer of the wall, its apex soaring
Skyward: this tower commanded a long-familiar prospect
Across Troyland to the Greek ships and the Achaean lines.
This we attacked with crowbars all round, where the weak
    joints of
Its flooring offered a purchase, prised it off from its deep bed
And pushed hard at it: the tower tottered and fell full length
With a sudden crash, bursting all over the massed attackers.
But still, others came on; still it rained spears and arrows
And stones and every missile unceasingly . . .
   Right on the very threshold of the entrance hall was
    Pyrrhus*
In all his insolent glory, aglitter with bronze accoutrements.
So a snake comes out, full fed on malignant herbs—a snake
Which winter has kept underground sullenly brewing its
    poison,
But now it has sloughed its old skin, is young again and
    glistening;
It coils along on its slithering belly, and lifts to the sunlight
Its vertical throat and flickers a tongue like forked lightning.
With Pyrrhus were giant Periphas, and Achilles' old chario-
    teer
Automedon, now a squire, and all the Scyrian brigade,
Assaulting the palace and tossing firebrands up at its roof.

Pyrrhus himself, in the lead, seized an axe, and battering the
stout door
Smashed through it, and wrenched it away from its hinges,
though it was strengthened
With bronze: now he had hewed out a panel, and made a hole
In the tough wood, opening up a gap the size of a window.
Through this they are able to see the interior, the long gal-
lery;
The private rooms of Priam and Troy's old kings are exposed,
And they see the armed defenders packing the doorway
within.
   Inside the palace, all was confusion, groans, agony.
The echoing halls resounded through and through with the
keening
Of women, whose wails and shrieks beat at the golden stars.
Mothers, distracted with fear, were wandering about the
palace,
Clinging tight to its door-posts and kissing them good-bye.
Pyrrhus attacks, with his father's dash: neither the bolts
Nor the guards have the strength to withstand it: stroke upon
stroke, a ram
Weakens the door, till it's torn away from its hinges and
falls in.
Brute force has made a breach; the Greeks go storming
through,
Massacre those in their way, and the place overflows with
soldiery.
More violent it was than when, banks broken, a foaming
river
Pours through: the dykes have gone down to the thrust of the
water, and now
In a mass it raves forth over the fields, swirling the herds and
Their shippons across the plain. I had to watch Pyrrhus
crazed with
Blood-lust, and the brothers Atrides,* there on the threshold,
Hecuba with her hundred princesses,* and Priam sullying

All over with blood the altar whose fire he had consecrated.
Those fifty bridal rooms, that promised a rich posterity—
Fallen flat were their doors, proudly adorned with eastern
Gold and with spoils. Wherever there was no fire, the Greeks
    were.

   I daresay you are wondering what happened to Priam then.
Once he had seen how the captured city was faring, seen
His doors were hacked away and the enemy deep in the
    palace,
Priam, though tremulous with old age, donned the armour
He had not worn for years—a pathetic gesture—strapped on
His useless sword, and was moving deathwards against the
    foe.
In the central court, beneath the uncovered sweep of the sky,
Stood a massive altar, and near it a very old laurel tree
Leaned over the altar, enfolding the home-gods with its
    shade.
Here Hecuba and her daughters, like a flock of doves dashed
    down
By a black storm, were sitting huddled about the altars
That would not protect them, and clasping the images of the
    gods.
Now, when she saw Priam dressed up in his youthful armour,
She cried:—
    Oh, my poor husband, what fatal intention has made you
Take up arms like this? Where are you running? Our
    present
Predicament is beyond such aid. Weapons won't save us,
Nor would they save us even if my own Hector was here now.
Please come back, over here: this altar shall guard us all,
Or else we will die together.
    This did she say, and taking
The old king to her, made him sit down in sanctuary.
   But picture it, Priam's son, Polites,* had just avoided
A death-blow from Pyrrhus, and wounded was running the
    enemy gauntlet,

Running away down the long colonnades and across the great
    hall
Alone. Pyrrhus hotly pursued him, always about to strike,
Each moment seeming to have him, so close did the spear
    point come.
Just when Polites emerged before his parents' eyes,
He fell, and his life ebbed out in a deep river of blood.
Priam, though death now ringed him round, could not be
    passive,
Could not refrain from uttering his indignation. He cried:—
    Hear me, you criminal! If there is any justice in heaven,
Any eye for such things, may the gods pay you the due re-
    ward
And unstintingly show their gratitude for this most mon-
    strous crime
You have committed—making me witness my son's death,
Fouling a father's eyes like this with the sight of murder!
You are poles apart from Achilles—your father, you lyingly
    claim.
He treated me differently far, though I was his foe; he
    respected
A suppliant's rights, gave up the bloodless remains of Hector
For burial, and gave me safe conduct back to my city.*
    So saying, the old man flung his weapon, but harmlessly—
No strength behind it: a clang when the shield of Pyrrhus
    parried it,
And then the spear was dangling impotently from its centre.
Pyrrhus replied:—
                        All right, you shall go and carry a message
To my father Achilles. Remember to tell him what a milk-
    sop
His son has become, and what shocking deeds he has com-
    mitted.
Now die!
        Even as he spoke, he dragged the old man, trembling,
And sliding in the pool of his son's blood, right to the altar;

Twinèd Priam's hair in his left hand, raised with his right the
    flashing
Sword, and sank it up to the hilt between his ribs.
Such was Priam's end, the close decreed by destiny—
That in his dying hour he should see Troy blazing, falling—
His Troy which boasted once such a wealth of lands and sub-
    jects,
The mistress of Asia once. A great trunk lies on the shore,
A head torn from the shoulders, a body without a name.*

    Then first the full horror of it all was borne in upon me.
    I stood
In a daze: the picture of my dear father came to mind,
As I watched king Priam, a man of the same age, cruelly
    wounded,
Gasping his life away; I pictured my Creusa*
Deserted, my home pillaged, and the fate of my little
    Ascanius.
I glanced round, wishing to see what force of men was left me.
All were gone: utter exhaustion and sickness of heart
Had made them drop from the roof to the ground or into the
    flames.

    Yes, I was now the one man left of my party. But just then,
Hugging close to the threshold of Vesta, speechlessly hiding
    there,
I noticed the daughter of Tyndareus, Helen. The blaze lit up
The whole scene as I wandered, peering this way and that.
Helen, the scourge of Troy and her own land alike,
In dread anticipation of Trojan wrath at Troy's
Downfall, of Greek revenge, of her cuckolded husband's
    anger,—
Helen, that hateful creature, was crouched by the altar, in
    hiding.
A fire broke out in my heart, a passion of rage to avenge
My country's fall and punish her crime by a crime upon her.
Was she going to get away with it? see Sparta again and her
    homeland?

Return as a queen, in triumph? be once more reunited
With husband, home, parents and children? use our Trojan
Ladies for her attendants and Trojan men for slaves?—
All this, with Priam put to the sword, and Troy in ashes,
And Troy's shore time and again bathed in a sweat of blood?
Not so, I said. For although to kill a woman earns one
No fame, and victory over a female wins no decorations,
I shall be praised for stamping out an iniquity, punishing
One who so richly deserves it; and I shall enjoy fulfilling
My soul with a flame of vengeance, appeasing my people's
    ashes.*
Such were my thoughts, the insensate fury that drove me
    onward,
When to my view—and never before had I seen her so clear—
My gentle mother appeared: all glowing with light she came
Through the gloom, a goddess manifest, oh, high and hand-
    some as
The heaven-dwellers know her. She laid a hand on mine,
Restraining me, then shaped these words with her rosy lips:—
    My son, what anguish spurs you to this ungoverned rage?
What madness has driven all thought for love out of your
    heart?
Will you not first find out if your aged father, Anchises,
Is where you left him, and whether your wife, Creusa, be still
Alive, and little Ascanius? A whole Greek army is surging
Round them on every side, and but for my guardian care
The flames would have got them by now, the fell sword
    drained their blood.
It is not the beauty of hated Helen, it is not Paris,
Though you hold him to blame—the gods, the gods, I tell
    you, are hostile,
It's they who have undermined Troy's power and sent it
    tumbling
Look! I shall wipe away the cloud which now occludes
And dulls your mortal vision, even as you gaze, the dank
    mist

Befogging you. Fear not to do whatever your mother
Tells you, and willingly be guided by me. Now, look at
That litter of masonry there, huge blocks, stone torn from
    stone,
And the dust-laden smoke billowing up from the debris—
It's Neptune's work: he gores and tosses with his great
    trident
The walls, the foundations, until the whole city is dis-
    embowelled.
Look over there! At the Scaean gate, panoplied Juno
Heads the shock-troops, and in a vindictive fury calls up
Her allies from the ships.
Look round! See Pallas Athene planted upon the cita-
    del—
The storm-cloud is lurid about her, the Gorgon glares from
    her shield.
Jove supplies fresh courage and a victorious strength
To the Greeks, inciting the gods against the Trojan cause.
Escape then, while you may, my son, and end this ordeal.
I shall be with you, seeing you safe to your father's
    house.
    She had spoken; and now she was vanished into the night's
    thick darkness.
Terrible shapes loom up, set against Troy, the shapes of
Heaven's transcendent will.
    Then indeed I saw that all Ilium was subsiding
Into the flames, and Neptune's Troy quite overthrown.*
Imagine a veteran ash-tree upon some mountain top,
When woodsmen are working to fell it, with blow upon blow
    of their axes
Vigorously hacking: the tree seems always about to fall;
It nods, and the topmost leaves are shivered by each con-
    cussion:
Little by little their blows master it, till at last
With a great groan it snaps off and falls full length on the hill-
    side.

Well, I went down from the roof, and divinely guided
    pressed on
Through flame and foe: the weapons gave way, the flames
    drew back for me.
  But when I reached the door of my father's house, the
    ancestral
Home, my father Anchises, whom first I looked for, wishing
To get him away first to the safety of the hills—Anchises
Flatly refused to prolong his life, now Troy was finished,
Or to endure exile. He said:—
                              O you, whose blood
Is in the prime, who are strong enough to stand on your own
    feet,
Do you try for escape!
But as for me, if the gods had meant me to go on living,
They'd have preserved this place. Enough, more than
    enough
To have seen Troy ruined once and once have survived her
    capture.*
Bid me farewell and leave, O leave this body of mine
Where it is! I shall find death in action. The foe will slay me
For pity, or spoils. And to bury me—that will not cost them
    much.
For years now I have been lingering, obnoxious to heaven and
    useless
To mankind, ever since the ruler of gods and men
Blasted me with the searing breath of his levin-flash.*
  So he went on saying. We could not shift him, although
We implored him with floods of tears—I, and my wife Creusa,
Ascanius and the whole household—not to ruin everything,
Not to add his weight to the doom which was heavy upon us.
He refused: obstinately he clung to his house and his purpose.
Once again I am moved to fight, yearning for death in my
    misery,
Since neither luck nor forethought offered a way out now.
Father, I said, did you really think I could run away

And leave you? Did so shameful a notion escape your lips?
If it's the will of heaven that nothing be left of our city,
And if your mind's made up that you and your family
Shall perish, as well as Troy, a door to that death is wide open:
Pyrrhus is coming, all bathed in Priam's blood; he loves
Butchering sons in front of their fathers, fathers at the altar.
Was it for this, dear mother, you fetched me through fire and
    steel,—
That I should witness the enemy right in our house, witness
Ascanius and my father and my Creusa beside them
Lying slaughtered here in one another's blood?*
To arms, my men! To arms! Their last hour calls the con-
    quered.
Send me back to the Greeks! Let me go back and renew
The fight! It must never be said we died unavenged this day!
    My sword was at my side again; I was fitting my left arm
Through the strap of my shield, and on my way out of the
    house,
When Creusa clung to me at the door, gripping my ankles,
Holding little Ascanius up to his father, and crying:—
    If it's deathwards you go, take us with you! O take us, and
    come what may!
But if your experience tells you that something is to be
    gained by
Fighting, protect this house first! Think what you're leaving
    us to—
Ascanius, your father, and me who loved to be called your
    wife once!
    Loudly she cried these words, and filled the house with her
    crying.
Just then a miracle happened, a wonderful miracle.*
Imagine it!—our hands and our sad eyes were upon
Ascanius, when we beheld a feathery tongue of flame
Luminously alight on his head, licking the soft curls
With fire that harmed them not, and playing about his
    temples.

Anxious, in great alarm, his mother and I hurried to
Beat out, put out with water, that holy blaze on his hair.
But father Anchises, greatly heartened, lifted his eyes up,
Stretched up his hands to heaven, with words of prayer,
    saying:—
    O god omnipotent, if any prayers can sway you,
Give ear to mine. One thing I ask: if by our goodness
We have deserved it, grant your aid,* confirm this omen!
    The old man had hardly spoken when from our left hand
        came
A sudden crash of thunder, and a shooting star*slid down
The sky's dark face, drawing a trail of light behind it.
We watched that star as it glided high over the palace roof,
And blazing a path, buried its brightness deep in the woods of
Ida; when it was gone, it left in its wake a long furrow
Of light, and a sulphurous smoke spread widely over the
    terrain.
That did convince my father. He drew himself upright,
Addressed the gods above, and worshipped the heaven-sent
    star:—
    No more, no more lingering! I follow, I'm there, where
        you guide me!
Gods of our fathers, guard this family, guard my grandson!
This sign is yours, and Troy is still in your heavenly keep-
    ing.*
Yea, I consent. I refuse no longer, my son, to go with you.
    He had spoken; and now more clearly over the town the
        fire's roar
Was heard, and nearer rolled the tide of its conflagration.
Quick, then, dear father, I said, climb onto my back, and I
    will
Carry you on my shoulders—that's a burden will not be
    burdensome.
However things turn out, at least we shall share one danger,
One way of safety, both of us. Let little Ascanius walk
Beside me, and Creusa follow my steps at a distance.*

And you, servants, pay careful attention to what I shall tell
    you.
As you go out of the city, you come to a mound with an
    ancient
Temple of Ceres upon it, secluded; nearby, an old cypress
Stands, which for many years our fathers preserved in
    reverence.
Let this be our rendezvous: we'll get there by different routes.
Do you, my father, carry the sacred relics and home-gods:
Sinful for me to touch them, when I have just withdrawn
From battle, with blood on my hands, until in running water
I am purified.
    With these words, I laid the pelt of a tawny lion
For covering over my broad shoulders and bowed neck;
Then stooped to lift my burden: Ascanius twined his fingers
In mine, hurrying to keep up with his father's longer stride.
My wife came on behind. We fared on, hugging the shadows.
I, who just now had faced the enemy volleys, the Greeks'
Concentrated attack, without turning a hair—I was scared by
Every breeze, alarmed by every sound, so strung up
Was I with anxiety for my burden and my companion.
    And now I was nearing the gates and thinking that we had
    made it,
When on a sudden there came to my ears the sound of many
Footsteps—or so it seemed. Then, peering into the gloom,
My father exclaimed:—
                  Run! They're upon us! Run, Aeneas!
I can see the shine of their shields and the bronze accoutre-
    ments winking.
    Well, I panicked. My wits were fuddled, were snatched away
By some malignant prompting. For even as I darted off
Into by-ways, off my course among streets I knew not—O
    god,
The anguish of it!—my wife Creusa, fate took her—did she
Stop there? or lose her way? Did she sink down in exhaus-
    tion?

We never knew. We never set eyes on her again.
I did not look back for the lost one, I did not give her a
    thought
Until we had reached the mound, the ancient, hallowed place
Of Ceres. Here at last, when all were assembled, one was
Missing, one had denied husband and son her company.
I was out of my mind. What mortal, what god did I not curse?
In all the city's ruin what bitterer thing did I see?
Commending Ascanius, Anchises and the Teucrian home-
    gods
To my friends' care, and hiding them deep in the hollow vale,
I put on my shining armour, I made for the city once more.
To reconstruct those events, to retrace our path through
    Troy
And expose my life to its perils again—that was my purpose.
  For a start, I returned to the shadowed gate in the city wall
By which I had sallied forth, noting my tracks and following
    them
Back through the night, straining my eyes to scan them.
    Everywhere
Dread and the sheer silence reduced my courage to nothing.
Next, I went home, in case—just on the chance that she might
    have
Gone there. The Greeks had broken in, the whole house was
    occupied.
That instant, gluttonous fire was fanned by the draught right
    up to
The roof top; flames burst out there, the blast of the heat
    roared skywards.
I went on, to revisit Priam's house and the citadel.
Here, in the empty colonnades of Juno's sanctuary,
Phoenix and fell Ulysses were engaged on the duty allotted
    them,
Guarding the loot. To this point from all over Troy had
    plunder,
Salvaged from burning shrines, been brought: tables of gods,

Solid gold bowls and looted vestments were being piled up
    here
In heaps. Children and frightened mothers were standing
    about
In a long queue.
I dared (you will hardly believe it) to call out loud through
    the gloom
And fill the streets with shouting: sadly I cried 'Creusa!'—
Called to her over and over again, but it was no good.
As I roamed on that endless, frenzied search through the city
    buildings,
There appeared before my eyes a piteous phantom, yes,
The very ghost of Creusa—a figure larger than life.*
I was appalled: my hair stood on end, and my voice stuck
In my throat. It was she who spoke then, and thus relieved
    my pain:—
    Darling husband, it's madness for you to indulge your
        grief
Like this. These happenings are part of the divine
Purpose. It was not written that you should bring Creusa
Away with you; the great ruler of heaven does not allow it.
For you, long exile is destined, broad tracts of sea to be
    furrowed;
Then you will reach Hesperia, where Lydian*Tiber flows
Gently through a land in good heart, and good men live.
There, your affairs will prosper; a kingdom, a royal bride
Await you. No more tears now for your heart's love, Creusa:
I shall not see the proud halls of the Myrmidons or Dolopes,
Nor work as a slave for Greek women—I, who am Dardan
And daughter-in-law to the goddess Venus.
No, the great Mother of the gods*is going to keep me here.
Good-bye, Aeneas. Cherish our love in the son it gave us.
    With these words, though I wept and had so much to say
To her, she left me, fading out into thin air.
Three times I tried to put my arms round her neck, and three
    times

The phantom slipped my hands, my vain embrace: it was
  like
Grasping a wisp of wind or the wings of a fleeting dream.
So in the end I went back to my friends, the night being over.
I was astonished to find,* when I got there, a great number
Of new arrivals come in, both women and men, a sorry
Concourse of refugees assembled for exile. From all sides
They'd come together, their minds made up, their belongings
  ready,
For me to lead them wherever I wished across the sea.
And now was the dawn star rising over the ridges of Ida,
Bringing another day. The Greeks were holding the gates of
The city in force. Troy was beyond all hope of aid.
I accepted defeat, picked up my father and made for the
  mountains.

BOOK III

After the gods had seen fit to destroy our Asian empire
And Priam's innocent people, after proud Ilium's fall,
When Neptune's Troy was an area of flattened, fuming
   rubble,
We were impelled by signs from heaven to go into exile
In some far-off and virgin land. Hard by Antandros
At the foot of Phrygian Ida we laboured to build a fleet,
Not knowing where*destiny would lead us or let us settle,
And mustered our company. In the first days of summer
Father Anchises*bade us hoist our sails to fate.
I was in tears as I left my country's coast, the harbour,
The plain where Troy had stood. Homeless, I took to the
   deep sea—
I, with my friends, my son, my home-gods and the great
   gods.

   Yonder there lay a land of broad plains, tilled by the
      Thracians,
A land protected by Mars, ruled once by hot-tempered
   Lycurgus,
Allied with Troy from of old through friendly relations and
   marriage,
While fortune smiled on us. Thither I went, and began to
Build a town by its shore (an enterprise which fate
Was biased against), and made up its name from my own,
   Aenea.*
I was sacrificing to Venus, my mother, and to the rest of
The gods, that they should bless our project—was sacrificing
A sleek bull on the shore to the king of the heaven-dwellers.
There was a dune nearby, as it chanced, topped by brush-
   wood
Of cornel and of myrtle sprouted with thick-set shafts.

I approached it, wanting some foliage to festoon over the
    altar,
And tried to root up its dense greenery: as I did so
I saw an uncanny thing, which horrifies me to speak of.
From the first sapling that I tore up, its roots dissevered,
There oozed out, drop by drop, a flow of black blood
Fouling the earth with its stains. My whole frame shook in
    a palsy
Of chilly fear, and my veins were ice-bound. Well, I pro-
    ceeded
To pluck out the whippy shaft of another sapling; I wanted
To investigate the mystery and get at the reason for it.
From the bark of this one too there issued the black blood.
Pondering much, I prayed to the deities of the woodland
And Gradivus*who looks after the Thracian fields, that they
    should
Take the sting out of the omen and turn it to our advantage.
But when, with my knees deep in the sand to get a purchase,
I was putting forth a still greater effort upon a third shaft—
Shall I say it aloud, or be silent?—then, a pathetic moan
Came from the depth of the dune, a voice was saying to
    me:—
    Aeneas, you're tearing me! I am buried here. Don't hurt
        me!
Don't dishonour your guiltless hands. I am a Trojan,
No foreigner. That blood is drawn not from the wood.
Get away from this cruel land, from these hard-fisted shores!
I am Polydorus.* The spears that nailed me down here have
    sprouted
An iron crop above me, a thicket of javelin wood.
    Then an acute conflict appalled my mind. I stood there
Dazed: my hair was on end and my voice stuck in my throat.
This Polydorus had been unluckily sent by Priam
With store of gold, in secret, to lodge with the Thracian king,
At a time when Priam began to have doubts about the resis-
    tance

Of Troy, perceiving how the blockade of the city was
    tightening.
That king, when the Trojan fortunes ebbed and our power
    was crushed,
Went over to Agamemnon, tagged on to the winning side,
Breaking all laws of good faith. He murdered Polydorus
And seized the gold. What lengths is the heart of man
    driven to
By this cursed craving for gold! When I'd got over my panic,
I referred the supernatural affair to our chosen counsellors,
My father foremost, and asked them to give their views
    upon it.
They were unanimous for leaving this guilty land
Where guest-laws had been thus outraged, and setting sail
    again.
So we hold a funeral service for Polydorus: we pile up
Earth on the dune, make an altar for the departed spirit,
Drape it with mourning bands and melancholy cypress;
Our women stand round it, hair unbound as the rites require;
Vessels foaming with fresh milk and bowls of victims' blood
We ceremonially offer: we lay the ghost*in its tomb,
And call aloud on the spirit—a last hail and farewell.
    As soon as we dared launch forth, the winds granting a
    calm sea,
A gently-rustling breeze inviting the voyage, my comrades
Swarmed on the beach and warped our ships down into the
    water.
We glide out of the roadstead: cities and land grow distant.
There is a holy island, sea-girt, in the good graces
Of the Nereids' mother and of Aegean Neptune:
A floating island,*it used to rove the archipelago,
Till Apollo moored it for men's use to Myconus and Gyarus,
Stationary now, no more at the beck and call of the winds.
Hither I came. That peacefullest place—how securely it
    havened
Us weary folk. Disembarking, we worshipped Apollo's city.

King Anius, who held both temporal and spiritual power
    there,
Came to meet us, wearing the sacred laurels and chaplet
Of Phoebus: he recognized Anchises as an old friend:
Host and guests clasped hands; then we went into the temple.
    I worshipped the god's dwelling of antique stone, and
        besought him:—
Grant us a walled home of our own, a place for tired men,
A future, and a continuing city! Ensure for us few,
Left by the Greeks and relentless Achilles, a second Troy!
Who guides us? Where do you bid us go? Where shall we
    settle?
Give us a sign, O Lord, and inspire our minds with your
    wisdom!
    The words were hardly out when a sudden tremor*visibly
Quaked the god's house and his laurel; the mountains shook
    all over,
The doors of the shrine flew open, and the sacred cauldron
    boomed.
We prostrated ourselves on the earth. An utterance came to
    our ears:—
    O long-enduring Trojans, the land which first produced*
The stock from which you come, that same will take you
    back
To her abundant breast. Seek out, then, your first mother.
Here shall your house hold sway over earth, from shore to
    shore—
You and your children's children and the generations after
    them.
    Phoebus had spoken. A great babble of joy broke out:
Everyone was asking, where is that promised land
The god bids us return to out of our wanderings?
Then my father, pondering our people's traditions, said:—
    Give ear, O chieftains, and understand where your hopes
        are centred!
There is a sea-girt island called Crete, Juppiter's birthplace:

Here a Mount Ida*stands, here was our race cradled.
A hundred inhabited cities that prosperous kingdom owns.
Thence, if I recollect the story aright, did Teucer,
Our famous ancestor, migrate once to the Troad,
Choosing a place for a kingdom. This was before Ilium
And Troy's towers had been built: men lived in the valley
    bottoms.
From Crete are derived the Great Mother, the patron of
    Cybele, the cymbals
Of the Corybantes, the grove of Ida, the hush of the faithful
Which belong to Cybele's cult and the lions yoked for her
    chariot.
Come then and let us follow where the gods' guidance leads:
Let us appease the weather and sail for the land of Crete.
It is not far away: if Juppiter favours us,
Our ships should reach the Cretan shore three days from
    now.
    Those were his words. Then he made due sacrifice at the
    altars—
For Neptune a bull, and a bull for you, beauteous Apollo,
A black lamb to the Storm-god, a white to the genial Zephyrs.
    A report went round that king Idomeneus*had been exiled
From his ancestral realm, that the coast of Crete and its
    dwellings
Being emptied of our foe, we'd find homes ready and waiting.
So we left the port of Delos, and skimming the deep we
    coasted
Naxos, the hilly haunt of Bacchantes, and green Donysa,
Olearos, and marble-white Paros, the Cyclades dotted
Over the sea, through straits that blossomed with many an
    island.
The boatswains are calling the stroke, the oarsmen straining
    in rivalry;
Crews shout one to another, Roll on, Crete and our home-
    land!
A following breeze gets up, giving us speedy passage,

Until at last we glide to the ancient shores of Crete.
Eagerly setting to work on the walls of my chosen city,
I name it Pergamea*; I encourage my folk, who delight in
That name, to love it as home and make the town-centre
    imposing.
  Our ships had not been beached long, our men were just
    engaged in
Breaking the soil and taking wives, while I was busy
On laws and housing, when a blight spread over the sky,
A wasting epidemic attacked our bodies, there fell
On trees and crops a hideous plague, a season of death.
Some gave up the ghost, some dragged out life in sickness;
The dog-days seared the fields with a heat-wave till they were
    barren;
Grass died of thirst, the diseased crops denied us nourish-
    ment.
My father now advised we should sail back again
To the oracle of Delos, that the god might graciously tell us
What end was assigned to these crippling mischances, where
    we should look to
For help out of our troubles, and whither should steer our
    course.
  It was night, and sleep enfolded all denizens of earth:
The sacred images of the gods, the Trojan home-gods
Which I had carried with me from out the blazing heart
Of Troy—as I lay asleep now, their presences appeared
Before my eyes, revealed in a fulness of light, where the full
    moon's
Radiance was flooding through the windows of my room.
They spoke to me, and their words relieved my anxious
    heart:—
  That which Apollo would say if you went up to Delos
He utters here. Aye, look! He sends us to you of his own
    grace.
We, when Ilium burned, followed you and your cause,
We went with you on shipboard over the surging sea;

Even so shall we exalt your seed to heaven,
And make their city an empress. Do you seek out a great
    place
For great ones, and never give up, though long and hard your
    exile.
You must change homes. This is not the land which Delian
    Apollo
Oracled for you; it was not in Crete he bade you settle.
There is a place—the Greeks call it Hesperia*—
An antique land, well warded, possessed of a rich soil.
Oenotrians colonized it; whose heirs, so rumour says now,
Have named it, after their first founder, Italy.
There is our real home: there was Dardanus*born,
And old Iasius; there did our line begin.
Rise up then, with a cheerful mind repeat to your father
These sure and certain sayings: let Corythus*be his bourne
And Italy, for Jove forbids you to colonize Crete.

    I was amazed by that vision and voice of the deities—
This was not sleep; I seemed to recognize in the room there,
The aspect, the garlanded hair, the very face of my home-
    gods;
And a cold sweat was trickling over my body then.
I was out of bed in a moment, lifting the palms of my hands
To heaven, putting up a prayer, pouring upon the hearth
A libation of wine unwatered. When the rite was done, I felt
    better
And told Anchises exactly what I had experienced.
He saw that he'd confused two branches of our family
And made a novel mistake in the old topographical lore.
Now he is saying:—

             My son, much wrought by the doom of Ilium,
You must know that Cassandra alone prophesied me such
    happenings.
I recollect now her predicting these things as our people's
    destiny—
Hesperia and Italy were often upon her tongue.

But who could have thought that Trojans would ever come
    to the shores of
Hesperia? Whom could Cassandra's presages influence then?
Let us bow to Apollo's warnings and take the better way.
   He spoke. We agreed with his words. All were enthusiastic.
So this place too we abandoned, leaving a few behind us,
And spreading sail we drove our hulls through the vasty sea.
   When we were well away, in deep water, out of sight now
Of land, with nothing but sea and sky wherever we looked,
An indigo-coloured rain cloud stood overhead, the precursor
Of gloom and storm, and the sea's face darkened with
    shuddering catspaws.
Winds billowed the sea at once, the seas were running high,
And we were hurled in a tossing waste, all contact gone.
Rain-storms muffled the daylight, a streaming night inked
    out
The sky, flash upon flash of lightning shattered the clouds.
Thrown off our course, we blindly groped about on the
    waters,
Palinurus* himself, our steersman, could not tell day from
    night,
Confessed he had lost his way in the wilderness of water.
Three days, three days befogged and unsighted by that dark-
    ness,
We wandered upon the sea, three starless nights we wandered.
At last, on the fourth day, we sighted land in the offing—
A view of faraway mountains and smoke spiralling up.
We struck our sails, we strained at the oars; our mariners
    quickly
Made the foam fly with their hard stroke, sweeping the dark-
    blue sea.
   It was the coast of the Strophades*which rose to welcome
    me
Preserved from the waves—Strophades being the Greek
    name for
Those islands in the broad Ionian Sea where dreadful

Celaeno and her coven of Harpies dwell, now the house of
Phineus*is barred and in fear they have left their pristine
  banquets.
No viler monstrosity than they, no pest more atrocious
Did ever the wrath of god conjure up out of hell's swamp.
Bird-bodied, girl-faced things they are; abominable
Their droppings, their hands are talons, their faces haggard
  with hunger
Insatiable.
When we had made our landfall and entered port, we
  observed
Abundant herds of cattle dotted over the vale
And goat flocks browsing there without any goat-herd by
  them.
We slaughtered some; we invited Jove and the other gods
To take their share of the spoil. Then by the winding shore
Seated on makeshift benches, we are most richly feasting.
But, the next moment, we hear a hoarse vibration of wing-
  beats—
The Harpies are on us, horribly swooping down from the
  mountains.
They tear the banquet to pieces, filthying all with their bestial
Touch. Hideous the sounds, nauseous the stench about us.
We choose a secluded spot under an overhanging
Crag, enclosed by trees and their shifting shadows, to set up
Our tables again and light a fire on a new altar.
Again from their hidden lairs, flying in from different angles,
That noisy coven claws at the feast, hovering around it,
Their mouths tainting the meat. So then I order my friends,
Stand to arms, for we must fight this damnable brood.
They did as they were ordered: they hid their swords in the
  grass
Ready to hand, and put their shields out of sight beside them.
So when the creatures again came screeching round the bay,
Misenus,* from an observation-post above us,
Blew the alarum. My friends went in to an unfamiliar

Combat, trying their steel on sinister birds of the sea.

But blows did not make them turn a feather, their bodies would not

Be wounded—they simply flew off at high speed into the blue,

Leaving a half-devoured feast and their own disgusting traces.

Celaeno alone, perching upon a rock pinnacle, stayed

Behind, and broke into speech, a fortune-teller of evil:—

So you're willing to go to war—to war, sons of Laomedon,*

Over the cattle you slaughtered, over slain bullocks? prepared

To drive us innocent Harpies out of our rightful domain?

Very well: take these words to heart, and never forget them.

What the Father almighty foreshowed to Phoebus Apollo

And he to me, will I, the chief of the Furies, reveal you.

You are making all speed for Italy, and the winds won over,

To Italy you shall go, even enter port you may:

But, before you can wall your promised city, outrageous

Famine shall fasten upon you, in return for trying to kill us,

And force you to chew your tables*—yes, gnaw at them and devour them.

She spoke: she winged away into the sheltering forest.

As for my friends, their blood went cold with the shock of panic

And curdled; their hearts sank: no more fighting, they said—

Through vows and prayers alone we must seek security, whether

Those creatures are of heaven or uncanny birds of ill omen.

Anchises stretched out his hands from the shore in supplication

To the powers above, appointing due sacrifice in their honour.

Ye gods, prevent these threats! Ye gods, avert this calamity!

Incline your hearts to the faithful! Oh, save us!

Then he gave orders

To cast off the moorings, to free the sheets and pay them out.
A South wind filled the sails; we flew before it over
The white-capped waves whither the breeze and our helms-
    man took us.
Presently hove in sight the sea-girt, woody Zacynthos,*
Dulichium and Samé and the sheer cliffs of Néritos.
We ran past the promontories of Ithaca, Laertes'
Kingdom, cursing the land that bred cruel Ulysses.
Later we opened the cloudy peaks of Mount Leucata,
Then the temple of Apollo—a warning land-mark to
    mariners.
Here we put in, exhausted, near to the little town:
Bow anchors were thrown out, the ships were beached by
    the stern.
  So at last, hoping against hope, we'd come to land: we per-
    formed
Purification rites to Jove, we made burnt offerings,
And on the shores of Actium* we held the Trojan Games.
Stripping and oiling their bodies, my comrades practised
    our old
Traditional wrestling bouts. Light-hearted they were to have
    won past
So many Greek cities, made good their escape through the
    enemy.
The sun went rolling on through the circuit of a whole year,
Freezing winter roughened the sea with northerly gales.
A rounded shield of bronze, borne once by the warrior
    Abas,
I nailed to a door, and wrote this line in dedication—
THESE ARMS AENEAS FROM THE VICTORIOUS DANAI.*
Then I gave orders to man the ships and clear from harbour.
Eagerly rowed my comrades, sweeping the sea with long
    strokes.
Soon were the lofty peaks of Corcyra* lost to view;
We coasted along Epirus, and coming to the Chaonian
Harbour, we drew near Buthrotum, that hill city.

Here we heard a rumour of quite extraordinary doings—
That Helenus, son of Priam, was king over Greek cities,
Having acquired Pyrrhus' sceptre and wife, Andromache,*
Who thus had passed again to a man of her own people.
I was astonished: I felt a wonderful strong desire
To talk with Helenus and learn how it all happened.
I set forth from the harbour, leaving our fleet on the shore;
Just then, as it chanced, in a grove near the city, where flowed
     a make-believe
Simois,* was Andromache performing the sad and solemn
Rites of the Dead, with wine for the ashes and invocations
To the spirit, at Hector's cenotaph—an empty mound of
     green turf
And twin altars the widow had consecrated to grief.
When she caught sight of me coming and saw the Trojan
     accoutrements,
She was frightened out of her wits by the marvel of it—her
     body
Went rigid as she gazed, and the warmth ebbed from her
     bones.
She fainted; after a long while she just managed to speak:—
     Are you real—this shape I see? Can you really bring me
     news,
O goddess-born? Are you living? Or, if your day is done,
Tell me, where's Hector?
          With these words, she burst into tears; one could hear
Only her sobs. I can hardly get in a brief answer, she's so
Upset; my own voice is broken and incoherent with feel-
     ing:—
I'm alive, to be sure—living on through every kind of
     adversity;
Doubt not that what you see is real.
But oh, how have you fared since of so great a husband
You were deprived? What fortune, worthy of Hector's
     Andromache,
Has smiled on you? Or are you still united to Pyrrhus?

With eyes downcast, and speaking in a low voice, she
  said:—
Oh, luckiest of us all, that maiden daughter of Priam*
Who was appointed to die on an enemy's tomb beneath
The walls of Troy—the one whom no man drew lots for, the
  one
Who never knew captivity or the bed of a conqueror!
But I, when our home lay in ashes, was carried off overseas,
Endured the contemptuous treatment of Achilles' insolent
  son,
And bore his children in slavery. Afterwards, when he
  wanted
A Greek wife, Leda's Hermione,* he passed me on
To Helenus and made me the slave wife of a slave.
But Orestes then, consumed with violent love for his stolen
Bride, and driven mad by the Furies which punish crime,
Took Pyrrhus off guard and murdered him at his father's
  altar:*
On whose decease, a part of his kingdom was restored
To Helenus, who christened these the Chaonian plains,
Named the whole of the country after Chaon*of Troy and
Rebuilt Troy's very keep upon our foothills here.
But you—what made you come? Was it weather or Provi-
  dence brought you?
Which of the gods impelled you towards this land you knew
  not?
What of your boy, Ascanius? Is he still in the land of the
  living?
He was your son, in the old days, at Troy.
Does he still think about the mother whom he lost?
Does the example of Aeneas and his uncle, Hector,*
Awake in him the old-time virtues, the hero spirit?
  The words poured out. She was weeping—a long-drawn
    fit of fruitless
Weeping, when from the city, with a great retinue round
  him,

Approached the son of Priam, the hero Helenus.
He recognized his kin, and took us back to the palace
Talking to us, interspersing his words with tears of happiness.
As we went, I saw the town was a miniature Troy, a model
Of mighty Pergamum; saw a dry watercourse named for
The Xanthus, and a Scaean gate whose threshold I kissed.
My Trojans enjoyed with me the city's hospitality.
The king was entertaining them in his great hall surrounded
By colonnades; they were drinking from cups of wine, each
    man
Goblet in hand, with a feast on golden plates before them.

One day passed, and another; and now the breezes wooed
Our sails impatiently, and the canvas swelled in a South wind.
So then I approached the seer, making request of him:—
Scion of Troy, and heaven's mouthpiece, you that vibrate to
Apollo's presence, the tripod, the laurels, you the diviner
Of what the stars portend and the songs and flights of birds,
O tell me—since I have had divine sanction for all my
Journey, and all the gods have expressed their will that I
Should make for Italy, should try for that faraway land;
Only the Harpy, Celaeno, prophesies an uncanny
New horror, threatening us with malevolent wrath and a
    gruesome
Famine—tell me what dangers I am first to avoid,
Or in what way I can overcome these numerous troubles.

Helenus sacrificed some bullocks, as is the custom,
Beseeching heavenly grace, unbound the head-dress from
His reverend head, and took me by the hand into Apollo's
Temple (how awed I was by the sense of immanent deity!)
Then was the priestly king inspired to utter these words:—

Goddess-born, it is beyond question true that your voyage
Has higher sanction: the Father of heaven predestines it,
And spinning the wheel of chance, ordains for you such
    fortunes.
Therefore, that you may safelier travel the unfamiliar
Seas, and winning to port, establish yourself in Italy,

A few things out of many will I reveal. The Fates
Deny me further knowledge and Juno forbids me to say
      more.
First, then, the Italy*you imagine so close that you're ready,
Mistakenly, to enter her ports any day now, in fact is
A very long way from here, and the way is far from easy.
You will have to strain at the oars in the Sicilian waters,
Voyage the whole length of the Ausonian sea,
And pass the infernal lakes*and the Tyrrhene island of Circe*
Before you can establish your town in a land safe for you.
These signs will I declare you. Store them up in your
      memory.
When, anxious of heart, you shall come to a lonely river and
      find there
Under the ilex trees lining its bank, a sow*—
A great white sow, with a litter of thirty new-born piglets,
White as she, clustered at the teats of their sprawling
      mother—
There is the site for your city, the terminus of your travails.
And do not let the threat about biting the tables intimidate
      you:
Fate will find out a way, Apollo will come to your call.
What you must shun is that part of Italy yonder, the coast
Nearest to ours and washed by the tides of our own sea,
For ill-disposed Greeks are settled in all the townships there.
In one place the Narycian Locri*have built battlements,
And Lyctian Idomeneus has garrisoned the plains of
The Sallentines: elsewhere, you'd find little Petelia squat on
Its walls, the town of the Meliboean chief, Philoctetes.
Another thing—when your ships have crossed the seas and
      are anchored,
When you perform your vows at the altar set up ashore,
Remember to veil your head*with a purple covering, lest,
As you worship the gods amid the altar fires, some enemy
Visage should meet your gaze and turn the omens awry.
This ceremonial you and your friends must always adhere to:

By this observance your heirs may stand firm in the faith.
Now when you have left that first landfall and sail to Sicily,
At the point where Pelorus*begins to reveal a narrow opening
Steer for the land on your port bow, the seas to port, and
    make
A detour giving a wide berth to shore and breakers a'star-
    board.
Once on a time, they say, these two lands were a single
Country; then there came a convulsion of nature which tore
    them
Hugely asunder—the ages can bring such immense geo-
    logical
Change—and the sea rushed violently in between them,
    dividing
Italy from Sicily, severing their coasts and washing
Cities and fields on either side with a narrow strait.
Scylla guards the right shore, insatiable Charybdis*
The left. Three times a day the latter, down in the depths of
A whirlpool gulps whole tons of wave into her maw,
Then spews them up again, flailing the heavens with spray.
But Scylla lurks unseen in a cavernous lair, from which
She pushes out her lips to drag ships on to the rocks.
Her upper part is human—a girl's beautiful body
Down to the privates; below, she is a weird sea-monster
With dolphin's tail and a belly of wolverine sort. It's advis-
    able
To fetch a long compass, although it protracts the voyage, and
    sail
Right round the Sicilian cape of Pachynum,* a southernmost
    mark,
Rather than to set eyes on that freakish Scylla within
Her cavern vast or the rocks where her sea-blue hounds are
    baying.
Finally, if I have any foresight, if you can trust
My divinings at all, if Apollo inspires my soul to truth,
This one thing, Aeneas, I solemnly tell you—one thing

Which sums up all—and I cannot repeat the warning too
    often:—
It's paramount that Juno should have your prayers and
    homage;*
Be zealous in making your vows to Juno and wooing her
    powerful
Partisanship with a suppliant's gifts. Do this, and at last
You will obtain a fair passage from Sicily to Italy.
Now when you are safely there, close to the city of Cumae*
And the haunted lake Avernus deep in a soughing wood,
You will find an ecstatic, a seeress, who in her antre com-
    municates
Destiny, committing to leaves the mystic messages.
Whatever runes that virgin has written upon the leaves
She files away in her cave, arranged in the right order.
There they remain untouched, just as she put them away:
But suppose that the hinge turns and a light draught blows
    through the door,
Stirs the frail leaves and shuffles them, never thereafter
    cares she
To catch them, as they flutter about the cave, to restore
Their positions or reassemble the runes: so men who have
    come to
Consult the sibyl depart no wiser, hating the place.
Here you must not grudge time spent, although it delays
    you—
However impatient your friends may grow, however fine
The weather for sailing, however strongly the sea calls you—
Time spent in approaching the sibyl, asking an oracle of her,
Praying that she will graciously open her mouth and prophesy.
Then will she tell you of wars to come with the tribes of Italy,
How to evade, or endure, each crisis upon your way;
And if you pay reverence to her, she will give you a favourable
    passage.
Such are the counsels I am permitted to offer you.
Go your way, then, exalting great Troy with famous deeds.

After the prophet had spoken thus, in friendly wise,
He gave instructions for presents to be carried down to the
    ships,
Presents of solid gold, objects inlaid with ivory;
He cargoed us with silver and cauldrons from Dodona,*
A cuirass made of golden chain-mail, triple-meshed,
And a helmet fine with plumes on its tapering crest, which had
    once
Belonged to Pyrrhus. Besides, there were personal gifts for
    my father.
He furnished, as well, horses and guides,
Brought the crews up to strength and fully equipped my
    friends.
Now was Anchises urgent for the sails of our fleet to be
    rigged,
So that a favouring wind should find us not unready.
Whereupon the prophet of Phoebus respectfully addressed
    him :—
    Anchises, once thought worthy of divine marriage by
    Venus,
Close to the heart of the gods, twice saved*from Troy's
    destruction,
Look yonder! There is Italy. Make sail for that land with all
    speed!
Yet is it written that you shall drift past yonder shore.
Far is the region of Italy revealed for you by Apollo.
Fare forth, Anchises, blest in the love of your son! The
    winds
Are rising. No more words from me, no more delaying.
    Andromache too, saddened by this long last farewell,
Brings Ascanius presents—a robe patterned with gold
    thread
And an embroidered cloak: she is not backward in courtesy,
But loads him with the work of her loom, and says to him :—
    Take these things too, dear lad, as keepsakes to remind
    you

Of her who made them, tokens of the abiding love of Andro-
 mache,
Hector's wife. Yes, take these gifts from your kin, these last
 gifts.
You are the image of my son, Astyanax; in eyes
And hands and mien the picture of him, the one picture
 left me:
He would have been your age now, like you growing to man-
 hood.

 Tears came to my eyes as I spoke these parting words:—
Long may you live and lucky,*you who have now accomplished
Your destiny! We are bandied from one vicissitude
To another. For you no ploughing the prairies of sea, no
 endless
Chasing after the ever-receding fields of Italy:
Peace, for you, is born. You behold a Xanthus in replica,
A Troy your hands have built—under better omens, I pray,
Than the old Troy, and further out of the way of the Greeks.
If ever I get to Tiber and the lands adjacent to Tiber,
If ever I set eyes on the place marked out for my people,
One day, from those sister cities, those neighbouring tribes
 in Epirus
And in Hesperia, which share the same ancestor, Dardanus,
And the same tale of disaster, we'll make one single-hearted
Troy. Let that be a charge*we leave to our posterity.

 Forth we went*on the sea, the Ceraunian cliffs being close in
The offing, for that course gave the shortest passage to Italy.
Now the sun went down and the mountains were veiled in
 shadow.
Putting ashore, we shipped the oars, then gratefully sinking
Down on the bosom of earth, we lay scattered about on the
 dry beach
Restoring our strength, while sleep flowed over our spent
 bodies.
Night, driven on by the hours, was not yet in mid-career,
When Palinurus alertly rose from his bed and tested

The weather, pricking his ears for any breath of a breeze;
All the stars he scanned as they slid through the quiet sky,
Arcturus and the rainy Hyades and the Twin Bears;
Orion he observed with its golden sword and sword-belt.
Noting that all was set fair in the calm sky, he blew
A clear trumpet-call from the poop: we left that bivouac,
And spreading the sails' pinions went forth upon our way.
And now, the stars dispersed by the first flush of dawn,
We sighted, far away, dim hills and a low coast-line,
Italy. Achates was the first to hail, 'Italy!'
'Italy!' my comrades echoed in cheerful greeting.
Then did my father, Anchises, garland a mighty bowl
And fill it with wine, and taking his stand high up on the
    stern
Above us, invoked the gods:—
    You deities who control the sea, the earth and the weather,
Grant us fair winds and an easy passage! Breathe kindly
    upon us!
    A freshening breeze answered his prayer: getting nearer,
    we opened
A harbour mouth, and saw on Minerva's Height*a temple.
Furling the sails, my comrades changed course direct for the
    land.
That harbour was hollowed out by the action of heavy seas
In east winds: at its entrance are reefs that smoke in a smother
Of spray, concealing the harbour: turreted cliffs slope down
Two arms to form its walls, and the temple lies back from the
    foreshore.
Here, an initial omen,* I espied four horses freely
Grazing the deep-grassed vale, four horses white as snow.
Then pronounced Anchises:—
                    War is your word, O strange land.
For war are horses needed; and those steeds there mean
    war.
Nevertheless, in time can these same cattle be trained for
The shafts and learn to bear in amity yoke and bridle:

So there are hopes for peace, too.

Then we prayed to the power divine

Of Athene, the clasher of arms, who received our first thanks-
giving,

Veiling our heads at the altar with wraps of embroidered
stuff,

And following the instructions which Helenus had most
emphasized,

Duly offered to Argive Juno*a burnt sacrifice.

At once, as soon as our vows had been properly performed,

Trimming our yards to the wind, under a press of canvas

We left that abode of Greeks, that unreassuring district.

Next we raised*the gulf of Tarentum—Hercules' town,

If the legend is true; and opposite, the temple of the
' Lacinian

Goddess, Caulonia's heights and shipwrecking Scylacéum.

Then we made out Trinacrian Aetna on the horizon,

And from afar we heard a thunder of waves throbbing

On rocks, and inshore noises broke fitfully on our ears;

The race was dancing with fury, the shoal-water boiling with
sand.

Anchises cried:—

That must be the infamous Charybdis!

Those are the reefs, the terrible rocks that Helenus told of!

Row for your lives, my comrades! Pull together! Pull!

Yarely they all obeyed my father's command. Palinurus

Turned away first to port, the bows of his vessel creaking;

Then the whole convoy, with oars and sails, clawed off to
port.

We were tossed up high*on an arching surge, then down we
went

In the trough as the wave fell away, down to the very Pit.

Thrice roared aloud the reefs and the caverns of rock be-
neath us,

Thrice we beheld the sky through a spattering flounce of
spindrift.

Time passed. The wind went down with the sun. Utterly
    spent,
Not knowing where we were, we crept to the shores of the
    Cyclops.
   There lies a haven, sheltered from all four winds; it is calm
And roomy too; but, nearby, Aetna thunderously erupts.
Ever and anon it discharges at heaven a mirky cloud,
A swirl of pitch-black smoke lurid with white-hot cinders,
And volleys huge balls of flame, singeing the very stars.
Ever and anon, as if the mountain's guts were being coughed
    up,
It belches rock, and groaning, vomits out thick streams
Of lava, seething up from its roots. The story goes
That Enceladus,* charred by Jove's lightning, is crushed be-
    neath
This mountain mass—that Aetna was dumped down bodily
    on him,
And like a leaky furnace jets out the fire which consumes
    him;
So, every time he turns over to rest one aching side,
Sicily quakes and rumbles, smoke hangs above like an
    awning.
That night we hid in the woods, enduring these gigantic
Phenomena, and unable to see what caused the din;
For the lights of the stars were out, there was no shine on the
    face of
Heaven from the constellations, only a fog which bandaged
Its eyes, and clouds which muffled the moon at this dead of
    night.
   And now tomorrow was here, with the first star of the
    morning,
And sunrise had uncurtained the dark dew-dropping sky,
When suddenly there stepped out of the woods a strange
    individual,*
A man unknown to us, in rags and a state of extreme
Emaciation, who stretched imploring hands to us

On the shore. We looked round. Appallingly dirty, his beard
    overgrown,
His rags held together with thorns, in all else he was a Greek,
A man who had gone to Troy once in the Greek expeditionary
    force.
He, when from a distance he saw our Trojan dress
And equipment, stood stock still for a little, scared at the
    sight,
Unable to move. But soon he was frantically running
    down to
The beach, sobbing out entreaties:—
                        By the heavens above, Trojans,
By the gods in heaven, by the breath and light of life, I
    beseech you
Rescue me! Get me away! to whatever land, I care not.
That's all I ask. I know I was one of the Greek invaders,
I own that I helped to make war against your Trojan homes.
If you feel what I did was so dreadful a crime, then punish
    me—
Tear me limb from limb and sink my remains in the broad
    sea.
If I must die, at least I'll have died at the hands of humans.
  He spoke: he clasped our knees and clung, writhing about
    them.
So we encouraged him to tell us his name and his family,
Tell us what fate had brought him to this. My father,
    Anchises,
After a brief hesitation offered the man his hand—
A gesture of immediate good-faith to reassure him.
He, at last throwing off his apprehensions, spoke out:—
  I am of Ithaca, a comrade of luckless Ulysses,
Achemenides by name: my father Adamastus
Being poor (would that we'd stayed as we were!), I went to
    Troy.
Here, in the Cyclops' cave, my companions left me behind,
Forgetting me in their panicky haste to quit the ogre's

Demesne. A house of blood and bloody feasts that cave is,
Gloomy within, immense. So tall is its master, he knocks
His head on the stars (ye gods, rid the earth of such cankers!).
He is not easy on the eye, not one you can cosily talk to.
He fancies the flesh and dark blood of wretched human
    victims.
I saw him myself seize two of our company with his huge
    hand,
Then, lolling back in the cave, smash their bodies against
A rock, until the whole place was spattered and swimming
    with gore:
And then I saw him munching my friends' blood-boultered
    bodies,
Saw the still-warm limbs quivering under his teeth.
Ulysses did not let the Cyclops go unpunished:
Dire was the extremity, but Ulysses kept his head.
For when, gorged on the meal and sodden with wine, the
    Cyclops
Bowed his neck, lay down, stretched himself the whole
Length of the cave, and was belching blood and human frag-
    ments
Mingled with bloody wine in his sleep, we then, after praying
The gods for strength and drawing by lot our places, hemmed
The ogre round, bored into his eye with a sharp stake—
That single, gigantic eye deep-set in his savage brow,
That eye as huge as an Argive shield or the sun itself.
So, with fierce joy, we avenged our comrades in the end.
But you must get out of here. Quick! Cut the cables, or else
You'll rue it!
That Polyphemus, folding his woolly flocks in the cave
And milking them—he is not unique. There are a hundred
Other Cyclops, as big and fierce as he, at large
Over these winding shores and these high hills, the monsters.
Three times now have the horns of the moon filled up with
    light
Since I began to lead this life in the woods, among dens

And uninhabited haunts of wild beasts, on crags looking out
     for
The one-eyed giants, trembling at the sound of their voice
     and tread.
A starveling diet of berries and stone-hard cornels was all
The woods supplied, with roots of herbs I plucked to feed on.
Though long and everywhere I gazed, I saw no help
Till your ships hove in sight. To you, however it turned out,
I committed myself: anything to have escaped that brood of
Abomination. At your hands would any death be preferable.
   Scarce had he finished speaking when, moving down from
     the mountain
Towards the well-known shore, mammoth in bulk, his sheep
     flock
Round him, we saw that same shepherd, that Polyphemus—
A monster, grisly, misshapen, titanic, his eye gone.
He carries the trunk of a pine tree to guide and support him
     walking:
The fleecy sheep go with him—they are his only pleasure
And consolation in woe.
When he had come to the sea's edge and touched the surging
     deep,
He washed the socket of his eye, which oozed blood, with
     sea-water,
Gritting his teeth and groaning; then waded into the deep sea,
Yet even there the water did not come up to his waist.
Frightened, we hurried to get far away, taking on board
That Greek who so merited mercy, and stealthily cutting the
     cables:
Frantically we tugged at the oars, we swept the sea's face.
He sensed us, veered his steps towards the noise of our
     passage.
But when he found there was no way of laying his hands
     upon us
And he was falling behind in his race with the waves which
     carried us,

Then he let out a stupendous bellow, shivering the whole
Expanse of the sea, shaking Italy to its core
With fright, and reverberating through Aetna's anfractuous
     caves.
Whereupon the Cyclops people were roused; from hill and
     forest
They ran down towards the roadstead and swarmed upon the
     beach.
There they stood, the fraternity of Aetna, impotent,
With baleful eyes and their sky-scraping heads—we saw
     them—
A terrifying assembly: so on some mountain top
Head-in-air oaks are massed, or cone-bearing cypresses—
Juppiter's own tall wood, or a grove sacred to Diana.
Our panic prompted us to pay out the sheets and run for it,*
Whatever the course might be, scudding before the wind.
Yet Helenus had warned not to attempt the passage
Between Scylla and Charybdis, there being on either side
So narrow a margin of safety. Well, in the end we resolved
To put about. But just then we caught a northerly wind
Slanting from Cape Pelorus; so on we went past the rocks at
Pantagias' mouth, the Megarian bay, and low-lying Thapsus.
Such places along the coast Achemenides pointed out to us,
Retracing now the route he had come with unlucky Ulysses.

   Over against wave-worn Plemyrium there's an island
Athwart the gulf of Syracuse, an isle the ancients named
Ortygia. According to legend, Alpheus, the river of Elis,
Once drove a secret passage hither, beneath the sea-bed,
To mingle at Arethusa's fount with waters of Sicily.
As instructed, we worship the patron spirits of the place; then
     on past
The marshy mouth of Helorus with its most fertile soil.
Next, we skirt Pachynus—a place of high rocks and jutting
Reefs; and now, far off, is Camarina,* which fate said
Must never be reclaimed, and the Geloan plains,
And Gela, which is named after its own wild river.

Then Acragas*on its crag shows from afar its great walls—
A town renowned one time for its mettlesome breed of
   horses.
The wind blows fair, and we leave palm-fringed Selinus
   behind
To skirt Lilybaeum's*waters, tricky with reefs submerged.
After which, we put in at port Drepanum, a landfall
Of little joy; for here, after so many storms weathered,
I lost, alas, my father, him who had lightened my cares
And troubles—lost Anchises. Oh, best of fathers, to leave me
Here, sick-hearted, when you had survived—yet all for
   nothing—
Such dangers! The seer, Helenus, though many horrors he
   warned of,
Never predicted this grief, nor did the sinister Celaeno.
This was the last agony, the turning-point of my long course.
From there Providence took me and drove me upon your
   coasts.
   So, while all the others intently listened, Aeneas
Recounted his heaven-sent trials and told about his wander-
   ings.
Now he stops talking and falls silent, his story done.

BOOK IV

But now for some while the queen had been growing more
    grievously love-sick,
Feeding the wound with her life-blood, the fire biting within
    her.
Much did she muse on the hero's nobility, and much
On his family's fame. His look, his words had gone to her
    heart
And lodged there: she could get no peace from love's dis-
    quiet.
    The morrow's morn had chased from heaven the dewy
    darkness,
Was carrying the sun's torch far and wide over earth,
When, almost beside herself, she spoke to her sister, her
    confidante:—
    Anna, sister, why do these nerve-racking dreams haunt
    me?
This man, this stranger I've welcomed into my house—
    what of him?
How gallantly he looks, how powerful in chest and shoulders!*
I really do think, and have reason to think, that he is heaven-
    born.
Mean souls convict themselves by cowardice. Oh, imagine
The fates that have harried him, the fight to a finish he
    told of!
Were it not that my purpose is fixed irrevocably
Never to tie myself in wedlock again to anyone,
Since that first love of mine proved false and let death cheat
    me;
Had I not taken a loathing for the idea of marriage,
For him, for this one man, I could perhaps have weakened.
Anna, I will confess it, since poor Sychaeus,* my husband,

Was killed and our home broken up by my brother's mur-
       derous act,
This man is the only one who has stirred my senses and
       sapped
My will. I feel once more the scars of the old flame.
But no, I would rather the earth should open and swallow me
Or the Father of heaven strike me with lightning down to the
       shades—
The pale shades and deep night of the Underworld—before
I violate or deny pure widowhood's claim*upon me.
He who first wedded me took with him, when he died,
My right to love: let him keep it, there, in the tomb, for ever.
   So Dido spoke, and the rising tears flooded her bosom.
Anna replied:—
                    You are dearer to me than the light of day.
Must you go on wasting your youth in mourning and solitude,
Never to know the blessings of love, the delight of children?
Do you think that ashes, or ghosts underground, can mind
       about such things?
I know that in Libya, yes, and in Tyre before it, no wooers
Could touch your atrophied heart: Iarbas*was rejected
And other lords of Africa, the breeding-ground of the great.
Very well: but when love comes, and pleases, why fight
       against it?
Besides, you should think of the nations whose land you have
       settled in—
Threatening encirclement are the Gaetuli, indomitable
In war, the Numidians (no bridle for them), the unfriendly
       Syrtes;
On your other frontier, a waterless desert and the far-raging
Barcaei.*I need not mention the prospect of Tyrian aggression,
Your brother's menacing attitude.
I hold it was providential indeed, and Juno willed it,
That hither the Trojan fleet should have made their way. Oh,
       sister,
Married to such a man, what a city you'll see, what a kingdom

Established here! With the Trojans as our comrades in arms,
What heights of glory will not we Carthaginians soar to!
Only solicit the gods' favour, perform the due rites,
And plying our guest with attentions, spin a web to delay
    him,
While out at sea the winter runs wild and Orion is stormy,
While his ships are in bad repair, while the weather is un-
    acquiescent.
    These words blew to a blaze the spark of love in the queen's
    heart,
Set hope to her wavering will and melted her modesty's
    rigour.
So first they went to the shrines, beseeching at every altar
For grace: as religion requires, they sacrificed chosen sheep to
Ceres, giver of increase, to Phoebus, and to the Wine-god;
To Juno, chief of all, for the marriage-bond is her business.
Dido herself, most beautiful, chalice in hand, would pour
Libations between the horns of a milk-white heifer, and
    slowly
Would pace by the dripping altars, with the gods looking on,
And daily renew her sacrifice, poring over the victims'
Opened bodies*to see what their pulsing entrails signified.
Ah, little the soothsayers know! What value have vows or
    shrines
For a woman wild with passion, the while love's flame eats
    into
Her gentle flesh and love's wound works silently in her
    breast?
So burns the ill-starred Dido, wandering at large through the
    town
In a rage of desire, like a doe pierced by an arrow—a doe
    which
Some hunting shepherd has hit with a long shot while un-
    wary
She stepped through the Cretan woods, and all unknowing
    has left his

Winged weapon within her: the doe runs fleetly around the
    Dictaean*
Woods and clearings, the deathly shaft stuck deep in her
    flank.
Now she conducts Aeneas on a tour of her city, and shows
    him
The vast resources of Carthage, the home there ready and
    waiting;
Begins to speak, then breaks off, leaving a sentence un-
    finished.
Now, as the day draws out, she wants to renew that first feast,
In fond distraction begs to hear once again the Trojan
Story, and hangs on his words as once again he tells it.
Then, when the company's broken up, when the moon is
    dimming
Her beams in turn and the dipping stars invite to sleep,
Alone she frets in the lonely house, lies down on her bed,*
Then leaves it again: he's not there, not there, but she hears
    him and sees him.
Or charmed by his likeness to his father, she keeps Ascanius
Long in her lap to assuage the passion she must not utter.
Work on the half-built towers is closed down meanwhile;
    the men
Of Carthage have laid off drilling, or building the wharves
    and vital
Defences of their town; the unfinished works are idle—
Great frowning walls, head-in-air cranes, all at a standstill.
   Now as soon as Juppiter's consort perceived that Dido was
    mad
With love and quite beyond caring about her reputation,
She, Juno, approached Venus, making these overtures:—
   A praiseworthy feat, I must say, a fine achievement you've
    brought off,
You and your boy; it should make a great, a lasting name for
    you—
One woman mastered by the arts of two immortals!

It has not entirely escaped me that you were afraid of my city
And keenly suspicious of towering Carthage's hospitality.
But how will it all end? Where is our rivalry taking us?
Would it not be far better, by arranging a marriage, to seal
A lasting peace? You have got the thing you had set your
          heart on:
Dido's afire with love, wholly infatuated.
Well then, let us unite these nations and rule them with equal
Authority. Let Dido slave for a Trojan husband,
And let the Tyrians pass into your hand as her dowry.
     Venus, aware that this was double-talk by which
Juno aimed at basing the future Italian empire
On Africa, countered with these words:—
                              Senseless indeed to reject
Such terms and prefer to settle the matter with you by
          hostilities,
Provided fortune favour the plan which you propose.
But I'm in two minds about destiny, I am not sure if Juppiter
Wishes one city formed of Tyrians and Trojan exiles,
Or would approve a pact or miscegenation between them.
You are his wife:*you may ask him to make his policy clearer.
Proceed. I will support you.
                         Queen Juno replied thus:—
     That shall be my task. Now, to solve our immediate prob-
          lem,
I will briefly put forward a scheme—pray give me your
          attention.
Aeneas and his unfortunate Dido plan to go
A-hunting in the woods tomorrow, as soon as the sun
Has risen and unshrouded the world below with his rays.
On these two, while the beaters are scurrying about and
          stopping
The coverts with cordon of nets, I shall pour down a darkling
          rain-storm
And hail as well, and send thunder hallooing all over the
          sky.

Dispersing for shelter, the rest of the hunt will be cloaked in
     the mirk:
But Dido and lord Aeneas, finding their way to the same cave,
Shall meet. I'll be there: and if I may rely on your goodwill,
There I shall join them in lasting marriage, and seal her his,
With Hymen*present in person.
                                   Venus made no opposition
To Juno's request, though she smiled at the ingenuity of it.
So now, as Aurora*was rising out of her ocean bed
And the day-beam lofted, there sallied forth the élite of
     Carthage:
With fine-meshed nets and snares and the broad hunting
     lances
Massylian riders galloped behind a keen-nosed pack.
The queen dallies: the foremost Carthaginians await her
By the palace door, where stands her horse, caparisoned
In purple and gold, high-spirited, champing the foam-flecked
     bit.
At last she comes, with many courtiers in attendance:
She wears a Phoenician habit, piped with bright-coloured
     braid:
Her quiver is gold, her hair bound up with a golden clasp,
A brooch of gold fastens the waist of her brilliant dress.
Her Trojan friends were there too, and young Ascanius
In high glee. But by far the handsomest of them all
Was Aeneas, who came to her side now and joined forces
     with hers.
It was like when Apollo leaves Lycia,* his winter palace,
And Xanthus river to visit Delos, his mother's home,
And renew the dances, while round his altar Cretans and
     Dryopes
And the tattooed Agathyrsi are raising a polyglot din:
The god himself steps out on the Cynthian range,* a circlet
Of gold and a wreath of pliant bay on his flowing hair,
The jangling weapons slung from his shoulder. Nimble as he,
Aeneas moved, with the same fine glow on his handsome face.

When they had reached the mountains, the trackless haunt
    of game,
Wild goats—picture the scene!—started from crags up above
    there,
Ran down the slopes: from another direction stags were
    galloping
Over the open ground of a glen, deserting the heights—
A whole herd jostling together in flight, with a dust-cloud
    above it.
But young Ascanius, proud of his mettlesome horse, was
    riding
Along the vale, outstripping group after group of hunters,
And praying hard that, instead of such tame quarry, a froth-
    ing
Boar might come his way or a sand-coloured mountain lion.
  At this stage a murmur, a growling began to be heard
In the sky: soon followed a deluge of rain and hail together.
The Trojan sportsmen, their Carthaginian friends and the
    grandson
Of Venus, in some alarm, scattered over the terrain
Looking for shelter. Torrents roared down from the
    mountain-tops.
Now Dido and the prince Aeneas found themselves
In the same cave. Primordial Earth and presiding Juno
Gave the signal. The firmament flickered with fire, a wit-
    ness
Of wedding.* Somewhere above, the Nymphs cried out in
    pleasure.
That day was doom's first birthday and that first day was the
    cause of
Evils: Dido recked nothing for appearance or reputation:
The love she brooded on now was a secret love no longer;
Marriage, she called it, drawing the word to veil her sin.
    Straight away went Rumour through the great cities of
    Libya—
Rumour, the swiftest traveller of all the ills on earth,

Thriving on movement, gathering strength as it goes; at the
    start
A small and cowardly thing, it soon puffs itself up,
And walking upon the ground, buries its head in the cloud-
    base.
The legend is that, enraged with the gods, Mother Earth
    produced
This creature, her last child, as a sister to Enceladus*
And Coeus*—a swift-footed creature, a winged angel of ruin,
A terrible, grotesque monster, each feather upon whose body—
Incredible though it sounds—has a sleepless eye beneath it,
And for every eye she has also a tongue, a voice and a pricked
    ear.
At night she flits midway between earth and sky, through the
    gloom
Screeching, and never closes her eyelids in sweet slumber:
By day she is perched like a look-out either upon a roof-top
Or some high turret; so she terrorizes whole cities,
Loud-speaker of truth, hoarder of mischievous falsehood,
    equally.
This creature was now regaling the people with various
    scandal
In great glee, announcing fact and fiction indiscriminately:
Item, Aeneas has come here, a prince of Trojan blood,
And the beauteous Dido deigns to have her name linked with
    his;
The couple are spending the winter in debauchery, the whole
    long
Winter, forgetting their kingdoms, rapt in a trance of lust.
Such gossip did vile Rumour pepper on every mouth.
Not long before she came to the ears of king Iarbas,
Whispering inflammatory words and heaping up his resent-
    ment.
  He, the son of Ammon*by a ravished African nymph,
Had established a hundred shrines to Jove in his ample
    realm,

A hundred altars, and consecrated their quenchless flames
And vigils unceasing there; the ground was richly steeped in
Victims' blood, and bouquets of flowers adorned the portals.
He now, driven out of his mind by that bitter blast of rumour,
There at the altar, among the presences of the gods,
Prayed, it is said, to Jove, with importunate, humble en-
    treaty:—
  Almighty Jove, whom now for the first time the Moorish
    people
Pledge with wine as they banquet on ornamental couches,
Do you observe these things? Or are we foolish to shudder
When you shoot fire, O Father, foolish to be dismayed
By lightning which is quite aimless and thunder which growls
    without meaning?
That woman who, wandering within our frontiers, paid to
    establish
Her insignificant township, permitted by us to plough up
A piece of the coast and be queen of it—that woman, reject-
    ing my offer
Of marriage, has taken Aeneas as lord and master there.
And now that philanderer,* with his effeminate following—
His chin and oil-sleeked hair set off by a Phrygian bonnet—
That fellow is in possession; while we bring gifts to your
    shrine.
If indeed you are there and we do not worship a vain myth.
  Thus did Iarbas pray, with his hands on the altar; and
    Jove
Omnipotent, hearing him, bent down his gaze upon Dido's
City and on those lovers lost to their higher fame.
Then he addressed Mercury,* entrusting to him this errand:—
  Go quick, my son, whistle up the Zephyrs and wing your
    way
Down to the Trojan leader, who is dallying now in Carthage
Without one thought for the city which fate has assigned to
    be his.
Carry my dictate along the hastening winds and tell him,

Not for such ways did his matchless mother guarantee him
To us, nor for such ends rescue him twice*from the Greeks;
Rather, that he should rule an Italy fertile in leadership
And loud with war, should hand on a line which sprang from
    the noble
Teucer and bring the whole world under a system of law.
If the glory of such great exploits no longer fires his heart
And for his own renown he will make no effort at all,
Does he grudge his son, Ascanius, the glory of Rome to be?
What aim, what hope does he cherish, delaying there in a
    hostile
Land, with no thought for posterity or his Italian kingdom?
Let him sail. That is the gist. Give him that message from me.
  Jove spake. Mercury now got ready to obey
His father's command. So first he bound on his feet the
    sandals,
The golden sandals whose wings waft him aloft over sea
And land alike with the hurrying breath of the breezes. Then
He took up his magic wand (with this he summons wan
    ghosts
From Orcus*and consigns others to dreary Tartarus,*
Gives sleep or takes it away, seals up the eyes of dead men).
Now, with that trusty wand, he drove the winds and threshed
    through
The cloud-wrack; descried as he flew the peak and pre-
    cipitous flanks of
Atlas, that dour mountain which props the sky with his
    summit—
Atlas,*his pine-bristled head for ever enwrapped in a bandeau
Of glooming cloud, for ever beaten by wind and rain;
Snow lies deep on his shoulders, and watercourses plunge
    down
That ancient's chin, while his shaggy beard is stiff with ice.
Here first did Mercury pause, hovering on beautifully-
    balanced
Wings; then stooped, dived bodily down to the sea below,

Like a bird which along the shore and around the pro-
, montories
Goes fishing, flying low, wave-hopping over the water.
Even so did Mercury skim between earth and sky
Towards the Libyan coast, cutting his path through the
.winds,
On his way from that mountain giant, Atlas, his mother's
sire.
As soon as his winged feet had carried him to the shacks
there,
He noticed Aeneas superintending the work*on towers
And new buildings: he wore a sword studded with yellow
Jaspers, and a fine cloak of glowing Tyrian purple
Hung from his shoulders—the wealthy Dido had fashioned it,
Interweaving the fabric with threads of gold, as a present to
him.
Mercury went for him at once:—
                              So now you are laying
Foundations for lofty Carthage, building a beautiful city
To please a woman, lost to the interests of your own realm?
The king of the gods, who directs heaven and earth with his
deity,
Sends me to you from bright Olympus: the king of the gods
Gave me this message to carry express through the air:—
What do you
Aim at or hope for, idling and fiddling here in Libya?
If you're indifferent to your own high destiny
And for your own renown you will make no effort at all,
Think of your young hopeful, Ascanius, growing to man-
hood,
The inheritance which you owe him—an Italian kingdom,
the soil of
Rome.
        Such were the words which Mercury delivered;
And breaking off abruptly, was manifest no more,
But vanished into thin air, far beyond human ken.

Dazed indeed by that vision was Aeneas, and dumb-
  founded:
His hair stood on end with terror, the voice stuck in his
  throat.
Awed by this admonition from the great throne above,
He desired to fly the country, dear though it was to him.
But oh, what was he to do? What words could he find to get
  round
The temperamental queen? How broach the matter to her?
His mind was in feverish conflict, tossed from one side to the
  other,
Twisting and turning all ways to find a way past his dilemma.
So vacillating, at last he felt this the better decision:—
Sending for Mnestheus, Sergestus and brave Serestus, he
  bade them
Secretly get the ships ready, muster their friends on the
  beach,
Be prepared to fight: the cause of so drastic a change of plan
They must keep dark: in the meanwhile, assuming that
  generous Dido
Knew nothing and could not imagine the end of so great a
  love,
Aeneas would try for a way to approach her, the kindest
  moment
For speaking, the best way to deal with this delicate matter.
  His comrades
Obeyed the command and did as he told them with cheerful
  alacrity.
  But who can ever hoodwink a woman in love? The queen,
Apprehensive even when things went well, now sensed his
  deception,
Got wind of what was going to happen. That mischievous
  Rumour,
Whispering the fleet was preparing to sail, put her in a
  frenzy.
Distraught, she witlessly wandered about the city, raving

Like some Bacchante* driven wild, when the emblems of
    sanctity
Stir, by the shouts of Hail, Bacchus! and drawn to Cithaeron
At night by the din of revellers, at the triennial orgies.
Finding Aeneas at last, she cried, before he could speak:—
    Unfaithful man, did you think you could do such a dread-
        ful thing
And keep it dark? yes, skulk from my land without one word?
Our love, the vows you made me—do these not give you
    pause,
Nor even the thought of Dido meeting a painful death?
Now, in the dead of winter, to be getting your ships ready
And hurrying to set sail when northerly gales are blowing,
You heartless one! Suppose the fields were not foreign, the
    home was
Not strange that you are bound for, suppose Troy stood as
    of old,
Would you be sailing for Troy, now, in this stormy weather?
Am I your reason for going? By these tears, by the hand you
    gave me—
They are all I have left, today, in my misery—I implore you,
And by our union of hearts, by our marriage hardly begun,
If I have ever helped you at all, if anything
About me pleased you, be sad for our broken home, forgo
Your purpose, I beg you, unless it's too late for prayers of
    mine!
Because of you, the Libyan tribes and the Nomad chieftains
Hate me, the Tyrians are hostile: because of you I have lost
My old reputation for faithfulness—the one thing that could
    have made me
Immortal. Oh, I am dying! To what, my guest, are you
    leaving me?
'Guest'—that is all I may call you now, who have called you
    husband.
Why do I linger here? Shall I wait till my brother, Pygmalion,
Destroys this place, or Iarbas leads me away captive?

If even I might have conceived a child by you before
You went away, a little Aeneas to play in the palace
And, in spite of all this, to remind me of you by his looks, oh
   then
I should not feel so utterly finished and desolate.
   She had spoken. Aeneas, mindful of Jove's words, kept his
      eyes
Unyielding, and with a great effort repressed his feeling for
   her.
In the end he managed to answer:—
                              Dido, I'll never pretend
You have not been good to me, deserving of everything
You can claim. I shall not regret my memories of Elissa*
As long as I breathe, as long as I remember my own self.
For my conduct—this, briefly: I did not look to make off
   from here
In secret—do not suppose it; nor did I offer you marriage
At any time or consent to be bound by a marriage contract.
If fate allowed me to be my own master, and gave me
Free will to choose my way of life, to solve my problems,
Old Troy would be my first choice: I would restore it, and
   honour
My people's relics—the high halls of Priam perpetuated,
Troy given back to its conquered sons, a renaissant city,
Had been my task. But now Apollo and the Lycian*
Oracle have told me that Italy is our bourne.
There lies my heart, my homeland. You, a Phoenician, are
   held by
These Carthaginian towers, by the charm of your Libyan
   city:
So can you grudge us Trojans our vision of settling down
In Italy? We too may seek a kingdom abroad.
Often as night envelops the earth in dewy darkness,
Often as star-rise, the troubled ghost of my father, Anchises,
Comes to me in my dreams, warns me and frightens me.
I am disturbed no less by the wrong I am doing Ascanius,

Defrauding him of his destined realm in Hesperia.

What's more, just now the courier of heaven, sent by
    Juppiter—

I swear it on your life and mine—conveyed to me, swiftly
    flying,

His orders: I saw the god, as clear as day, with my own eyes,

Entering the city, and these ears drank in the words he
    uttered.

No more reproaches, then—they only torture us both.

God's will, not mine, says 'Italy'.

    All the while he was speaking she gazed at him askance,

Her glances flickering over him, eyes exploring the whole
    man

In deadly silence. Now, furiously, she burst out:—

    Faithless and false! No goddess mothered you, no
    Dardanus*

Your ancestor! I believe harsh Caucasus begat you

On a flint-hearted rock and Hyracanian* tigers suckled you.

Why should I hide my feelings? What worse can there be to
    keep them for?

Not one sigh from him when I wept! Not a softer glance!

Did he yield an inch, or a tear, in pity for her who loves him?

I don't know what to say first. It has come to this,—not Juno,

Not Jove himself can view my plight with the eye of justice.

Nowhere is it safe to be trustful. I took him, a castaway,

A pauper, and shared my kingdom with him—I must have
    been mad—

Rescued his lost fleet, rescued his friends from death.

Oh, I'm on fire and drifting! And now Apollo's prophecies,

Lycian oracles, couriers of heaven sent by Juppiter

With stern commands—all these order you to betray me.

Oh, of course this is just the sort of transaction that troubles
    the calm of

The gods.* I'll not keep you, nor probe the dishonesty of your
    words.

Chase your Italy, then! Go, sail to your realm overseas!

I only hope that, if the just spirits*have any power,
Marooned on some mid-sea rock you may drink the full cup
   of agony
And often cry out for Dido. I'll dog you, from far, with the
   death-fires;
And when cold death has parted my soul from my body, my
   spectre
Will be wherever you are. You shall pay for the evil you've
   done me.
The tale of your punishment will come to me down in the
   shades.
   With these words Dido suddenly ended, and sick at heart
Turned from him, tore herself away from his eyes, ran
   indoors,
While he hung back in dread of a still worse scene, although
He had much to say. Her maids bore up the fainting queen
Into her marble chamber and laid her down on the bed.
   But the god-fearing*Aeneas, much as he longed to soothe
Her anguish with consolation, with words that would end her
   troubles,
Heavily sighing, his heart melting from love of her,
Nevertheless obeyed the gods and went off to his fleet.
Whereupon the Trojans redoubled their efforts, all along
The beach dragging down the tall ships, launching the well-
   tarred bottoms,
Fetching green wood to make oars, and baulks of un-
   fashioned timber
From the forest, so eager they were to be gone.
You could see them on the move, hurrying out of the
   city.
It looked like an army of ants when, provident for winter,
They're looting a great big corn-heap and storing it up in
   their own house;
Over a field the black file goes, as they carry the loot
On a narrow track through the grass; some are strenuously
   pushing

The enormous grains of corn with their shoulders, while others marshal
The traffic and keep it moving: their whole road seethes with activity.
Ah, Dido, what did you feel when you saw these things going forward?
What moans you gave when, looking forth from your high roof-top,
You beheld the whole length of the beach aswarm with men, and the sea's face
Alive with the sound and fury of preparations for sailing!
Excess of love, to what lengths you drive our human hearts!
Once again she was driven to try what tears and entreaties
Could do, and let love beggar her pride—she would leave no appeal
Untried, lest, for want of it, she should all needlessly die.
　Anna, you see the bustle down there on the beach; from all sides
They have assembled; their canvas is stretched to the winds already,
And the elated mariners have garlanded their ships.
If I was able to anticipate this deep anguish,
I shall be able to bear it. But do this one thing, Anna,
For your poor sister. You were the only confidante*
Of that faithless man: he told you even his secret thoughts:
You alone know the most tactful way, the best time to approach him.
Go, sister, and make this appeal to my disdainful enemy:—
Say that *I* never conspired with the Greeks at Aulis* to ruin
The Trojan people, nor sent squadrons of ships against Troy;
I never desecrated the ashes of dead Anchises,
So why must Aeneas be deaf and obdurate to my pleading?
Why off so fast? Will he grant a last wish to her who unhappily
Loves him, and wait for a favouring wind, an easier voyage?

Not for our marriage that was do I plead now—he has for-
　　sworn it,
Nor that he go without his dear Latium and give up his
　　kingdom.
I ask a mere nothing—just time to give rein to despair and
　　thus calm it,
To learn from ill luck how to grieve for what I have lost, and
　　to bear it.
This last favour I beg—oh, pity your sister!—and if he
Grants it, I will repay him; my death shall be his interest.
　　Such were her prayers, and such the tearful entreaties her
　　　agonized
Sister conveyed to Aeneas again and again. But unmoved by
Tearful entreaties he was, adamant against all pleadings:
Fate blocked them, heaven stopped his ears lest he turn
　　complaisant.
As when some stalwart oak-tree, some veteran of the Alps,
Is assailed by a wintry wind whose veering gusts tear at it,
Trying to root it up; wildly whistle the branches,
The leaves come flocking down from aloft as the bole is
　　battered;
But the tree stands firm on its crag, for high as its head is
　　carried
Into the sky, so deep do its roots go down towards Hades:
Even thus was the hero belaboured for long with every
　　kind of
Pleading, and his great heart thrilled through and through
　　with the pain of it;
Resolute, though, was his mind; unavailingly rolled her tears.*
　　But hapless Dido, frightened out of her wits by her destiny,
Prayed for death: she would gaze no more on the dome of
　　daylight.
And now, strengthening her resolve to act and to leave this
　　world,
She saw, as she laid gifts on the incense-burning altars—
Horrible to relate—the holy water turn black

And the wine she poured changing uncannily to blood.

She told no one, not even her sister, of this phenomenon.

Again, she had dedicated a chantry of marble within

The palace to her first husband; held it in highest reverence;

Hung it with snow-white fleeces and with festoons of greenery:

Well, from this shrine, when night covered the earth, she seemed

To be hearing words—the voice of that husband calling upon her.

There was something dirge-like too, in the tones of the owl on the roof-top

Whose lonely, repeated cries were drawn out to a long keening.

Besides, she recalled with horror presages, dread forewarnings

Of the prophets of old. Aeneas himself pursued her remorselessly

In dreams, driving her mad; or else she dreamed of unending

Solitude and desertion, of walking alone and eternally

Down a long road, through an empty land, in search of her Tyrians.

Just so does the raving Pentheus*see covens of Furies and has the

Delusion of seeing two suns in the sky and a double Thebes:

Just so on the stage does Orestes, the son of Agamemnon,

Move wildly about while his mother pursues him with torches and black snakes,

And at the door the avenging Furies cut off his retreat.

   So when, overmastered by grief, she conceived a criminal madness

And doomed herself to death, she worked out the time and method

In secret; then, putting on an expression of calm hopefulness

To hide her resolve, she approached her sorrowing sister with these words:—

I have found out a way, Anna—oh, wish me joy of it—
To get him back or else get free of my love for him.
Near Ocean's furthest bound and the sunset is Aethiopia,
The very last place on earth, where giant Atlas pivots
The wheeling sky, embossed with fiery stars, on his shoulders.
I have been in touch with a priestess from there, a Massylian,*
    who once,
As warden of the Hesperides' sacred close, was used to
Feed the dragon which guarded their orchard of golden
    apples,
Sprinkling its food with moist honey and sedative poppy-
    seeds.
Now this enchantress claims that her spells can liberate
One's heart, or can inject love-pangs, just as she wishes;
Can stop the flow of rivers, send the stars flying backwards,
Conjure ghosts in the night: she can make the earth cry out
Under one's feet, and elm trees come trooping down from
    the mountains.
Dear sister, I solemnly call to witness the gods and you whom
I love, that I do not willingly resort to her magic arts.
You must build up a funeral pyre high in the inner court-
    yard,
And keep it dark: lay on it the arms which that godless man
Has left on the pegs in our bedroom, all relics of him, and the
    marriage-bed
That was the ruin of me. To blot out all that reminds me
Of that vile man is my pleasure and what the enchantress
    directs.
  So Dido spoke, and fell silent, her face going deadly white.
Yet Anna never suspected that Dido was planning her own
    death
Through these queer rites, nor imagined how frantic a mad-
    ness possessed her;
Nor feared any worse would happen than when Sychaeus
    had died.
So she made the arrangements required of her.

When in the innermost court of the palace the pyre had
    been built up
To a great height with pinewood and logs of ilex, the queen
Festooned the place with garlands and wreathed it with
    funereal
Foliage: then she laid on it the clothes, the sword which
    Aeneas
Had left, and an effigy of him; she well knew what was to
    happen.
Altars were set up all round. Her hair unloosed, the en-
    chantress
Loudly invoked three hundred deities—Erebus, Chaos,
Hecate,* three in one, and three-faced Diana, the virgin.
She had sprinkled water which came, she pretended, from
    Lake Avernus;*
Herbs she had gathered, cut by moonlight with a bronze
    knife—
Poisonous herbs all rank with juices of black venom;
She had found a love charm, a gland*torn from the forehead
    of a new-born
Foal before its mother could get it.
Dido, the sacramental grain in her purified hands,
One foot unsandalled, her dress uncinctured, stood by the
    altars
Calling upon the gods and the stars that know fate's secrets,
Death at her heart, and prayed to whatever power it is
Holds unrequited lovers in its fair, faithful keeping.
    Was night. All over the earth, creatures were plucking the
    flower
Of soothing sleep, the woods and the wild seas fallen quiet—
A time when constellations have reached their mid-career,
When the countryside is all still, the beasts and the brilliant
    birds
That haunt the lakes' wide waters or the tangled under-
    growth
Of the champain, stilled in sleep under the quiet night—

Cares are lulled and hearts can forget for a while their travails.
Not so the Phoenician queen: death at her heart, she could not
Ever relax in sleep, let the night in to her eyes
Or mind: her agonies mounted, her love reared up again
And savaged her, till she writhed in a boiling sea of passion.
So thus she began, her thoughts whirled round in a vicious
   circle:—
   What shall I do? Shall I, who've been jilted, return to my
      former
Suitors? go down on my knees for marriage to one of the
   Nomads
Although, time and again, I once rejected their offers?
Well then, am I to follow the Trojan's fleet and bow to
Their lightest word? I helped them once. Will that help me
   now?
Dare I think they remember with gratitude my old kindness?
But even if I wished it, who would suffer me, welcome me
Aboard those arrogant ships? They hate me. Ah, duped and
   ruined!—
Surely by now I should know the ill faith of Laomedon's*
   people?
So then? Shall I sail, by myself, with those exulting mariners,
Or sail against them with all my Tyrian folk about me—
My people, whom once I could hardly persuade to depart
   from Sidon—
Bidding them man their ships and driving them out to sea
   again?
Better die—I deserve it—end my pain with the sword.
Sister, you started it all: overborne by my tears, you laid up
These evils to drive me mad, put me at the mercy of a foe.
Oh, that I could have been some child of nature and lived
An innocent life, untouched by marriage and all its troubles!
I have broken the faith I vowed to the memory of Sychaeus.
   Such were the reproaches she could not refrain from
      uttering.

High on the poop of his ship, resolute now for departure,
Aeneas slept; preparations for sailing were fully completed.
To him in a dream there appeared the shape of the god,
    returning
Just as he'd looked before, as if giving the same admoni-
    tions—
Mercury's very image, the voice, the complexion, the yellow
Hair and the handsome youthful body identical:—
    Goddess-born, can you go on sleeping at such a crisis?
Are you out of your mind, not to see what dangers are brew-
    ing up
Around you, and not to hear the favouring breath of the
    West wind?
Being set upon death, her heart is aswirl with conflicting
    passions,
Aye, she is brooding now some trick, some desperate deed.
Why are you not going, all speed, while the going is good?
If dawn finds you still here, delaying by these shores,
You'll have the whole sea swarming with hostile ships, there
    will be
Firebrands coming against you, you'll see this beach ablaze.
Up and away, then! No more lingering! Woman was ever
A veering, weathercock creature.
                              He spoke, and vanished in the darkness.
Then, startled by the shock of the apparition, Aeneas
Snatched himself out of sleep and urgently stirred up his
    comrades:—
    Jump to it, men! To your watch! Get to the rowing
    benches!
Smartly! Hoist the sails! A god from heaven above
Spurs me to cut the cables, make off and lose not a moment:
This was his second warning. O blessed god, we follow you,
God indeed, and once more we obey the command joy-
    fully!
Be with us! Look kindly upon us! Grant us good sailing
    weather!

Thus did Aeneas cry, and flashing his sword from its
    scabbard,
With the drawn blade he severed the moorings. The same
    sense of
Urgency fired his comrades all; they cut and ran for it.
The shore lay empty. The ships covered the open sea.
The oarsmen swept the blue and sent the foam flying with
    hard strokes.

And now was Aurora, leaving the saffron bed of Tithonus,*
Beginning to shower upon earth the light of another day.
The queen, looking forth from her roof-top, as soon as she
    saw the sky
Grow pale and the Trojan fleet running before the wind,
Aware that the beach and the roadstead were empty, the
    sailors gone,
Struck herself three times, four times, upon her lovely breast,
Tore at her yellow hair, and exclaimed:—
                     In god's name! shall that foreigner
Scuttle away and make a laughing-stock of my country?
Will not my people stand to arms for a mass pursuit?
Will some not rush the warships out of the docks? Move,
    then!
Bring firebrands apace, issue the weapons, pull on the oars!
What am I saying? Where am I? What madness veers my
    mind?
Poor Dido, the wrong you have done—is it only now coming
    home to you?
You should have thought of that when you gave him your
    sceptre. So this is
The word of honour of one who, men say, totes round his
    home-gods
Everywhere, and bore on his back a doddering father!
Why could I not have seized him, torn up his body and
    littered
The sea with it? finished his friends with the sword, finished
    his own

Ascanius and served him up for his father*to banquet on?
The outcome of battle had been uncertain?—Let it have
    been so:
Since I was to die, whom had I to fear? I should have
    stormed
Their bulwarks with fire, set alight their gangways, gutted the
    whole lot—
Folk, father and child—then flung myself on the conflagra-
    tion.
O sun, with your beams surveying all that is done on earth!
Juno, the mediator and witness of my tragedy!
Hecate, whose name is howled by night at the city cross-
    roads!
Avenging Furies, and you, the patrons of dying Elissa!—
Hear me! Incline your godheads to note this wickedness
So worthy of your wrath! And hear my prayer! If he,
That damned soul, must make port and get to land, if thus
Jove destines it, if that bourne is fixed for him irrevocably,
May he be harried*in war by adventurous tribes, and exiled
From his own land; may Ascanius be torn from his arms;
    may he have to
Sue for aid, and see his own friends squalidly dying.
Yes, and when he's accepted the terms of a harsh peace,
Let him never enjoy his realm or the allotted span,
But fall before his time*and lie on the sands, unburied.
That is my last prayer. I pour it out, with my lifeblood.
Let you, my Tyrians, sharpen your hatred upon his children
And all their seed for ever: send this as a present to
My ghost. Between my people and his, no love, no alliance!
Rise up from my dead bones,* avenger! Rise up, one
To hound the Trojan settlers with fire and steel remorse-
    lessly,
Now, some day, whenever the strength for it shall be granted!
Shore to shore, sea to sea, weapon to weapon opposed—
I call down a feud between them and us to the last genera-
    tion!

These things she said; then tried to think of every ex-
pedient,
Seeking the quickest way out of the life she hated.
Briefly now she addressed Barce, the nurse of Sychaeus,
Her own being dust and ashes, interred in her native land:—
Dear nurse, please will you get my sister, Anna. She must
Hasten to purify herself with living water, and fetch
The cattle, tell her—the atonement offerings, as directed;
Then let her come. And do you go and put on the holy head-
band.
These rites to Jove of the Underworld, duly made ready and
started,
I mean to go through with now, and put an end to my
troubles,
Committing to the flames the funeral pyre of that Trojan.
She spoke. The nurse hurried off with senile officiousness.
But Dido, trembling, distraught by the terrible thing she was
doing,
Her bloodshot eyes all restless, with hectic blotches upon
Her quivering cheeks, yet pale with the shade of advancing
death,
Ran to the innermost court of the palace, climbed the lofty
Pyre, frantic at heart, and drew Aeneas' sword—
Her present to him, procured once for a far different purpose.
Then, after eyeing the clothes he had left behind, the
memoried
Bed, pausing to weep and brood on him for a little,
She lay down on the bed and spoke her very last words:—
O relics of him, things dear to me while fate, while heaven
allowed,
Receive this life of mine, release me from my troubles!
I have lived,* I have run to the finish the course which fortune
gave me:
And now, a queenly shade, I shall pass to the world below.
I built a famous city, saw my own place established,
Avenged a husband, exacted a price for a brother's enmity.

Happy I would have been, ah, beyond words happy,
If only the Trojan ships had never come to my shore!
   These words; then, burying her face in the bed:—

                              Shall I die unavenged?
At least, let me die. Thus, thus! I go to the dark, go gladly.
May he look long, from out there on the deep, at my flaming
      pyre,
The heartless! And may my death-fires signal bad luck for his
      voyage!
   She had spoken; and with these words, her attendants saw
      her falling
Upon the sword, they could see the blood spouting up over
The blade, and her hands spattered. Their screams rang to
      the roofs of
The palace; then rumour ran amok through the shocked city.
All was weeping and wailing, the streets were filled with a
      keening
Of women, the air resounded with terrible lamentations.
It was as if Carthage or ancient Tyre should be falling,
With enemy troops breaking into the town and a conflagration
Furiously sweeping over the abodes of men and of gods.
Anna heard it: half dead from extreme fear, she ran through
The crowd, tearing her cheeks with her nails, beating her
      breast
With her fists, and called aloud by name on the dying
      woman:—
   So this was your purpose, Dido? You were making a dupe
      of me?
That pyre, those lighted altars—for me, they were leading to
      this?
How shall I chide you for leaving me? Were you too proud to
      let your
Sister die with you? You should have called me to share your
      end:
One hour, one pang of the sword could have carried us both
      away.

Did I build this pyre with my own hands, invoking our family
    gods,
So that you might lie on it, and I, the cause of your troubles,*
    not be there?
You have destroyed more than your self—me, and the lords
And commons and city of Sidon. Quick! Water for her
    wounds!
Let me bathe them, and if any last breath is fluttering*from
    her mouth,
Catch it in mine!

             So saying, she had scaled the towering pyre,
Taken the dying woman into her lap, was caressing her,
Sobbing, trying to staunch the dark blood with her own dress.
Dido made an effort to raise her heavy eyes,
Then gave it up: the sword-blade grated against her breast
    bone.
Three times she struggled to rise, to lift herself on an elbow,
Three times rolled back on the bed. Her wandering gaze
    went up
To the sky, looking for light: she gave a moan when she
    saw it.
    Then did almighty Juno take pity on her long-drawn-out
Sufferings and hard going, sent Iris*down from Olympus
To part the agonized soul from the body that still clung to it.
Since she was dying neither a natural death nor from others'
Violence, but desperate and untimely, driven to it
By a crazed impulse, not yet had Proserpine*clipped from
    her head
The golden tress, or consigned her soul to the Underworld.
So now, all dewy, her pinions the colour of yellow crocus,
Her wake a thousand rainbow hues refracting the sunlight,
Iris flew down, and over Dido hovering, said:—
    As I was bidden, I take this sacred thing, the Death-god's
Due: and you I release from your body.
                 She snipped the tress.
Then all warmth went at once, the life was lost in air.

BOOK V

Meanwhile Aeneas held his fleet on its course through the
    deep sea
Undeviating, and clove the waves that were gloomed by a
    North wind.*
He looked back at Carthage's walls; they were lit up now by
    the death-fires
Of tragic Dido. Why so big a fire should be burning
Was a mystery: but knowing what a woman is capable of
When insane with the grief of having her love cruelly dis-
    honoured,
Started a train of uneasy conjecture in the Trojans' minds.
   The ships being now well out to sea, no further sight of
Land in the offing, nothing but sea and sky all round them,
An indigo-coloured rain cloud stood overhead, the pre-
    cursor
Of gloom and storm, and the sea's face darkened with
    shuddering catspaws.
Palinurus, the steersman, high on the afterdeck, exclaimed:—
   My god! What does this pack of cloud in the sky portend?
Father Neptune, what have you in store for us?
                      Then he ordered
His comrades to make all fast and strain at the stalwart oars,
And sailing his ship closer-hauled to the wind, he spoke
    again:—
   Great-hearted Aeneas, not even if Juppiter guarantees it,
Have I any hope of making Italy in such weather.
The wind has changed, and is blowing abeam: the West looks
    black—
A gale is getting up there, clouds are gathering densely.
I am certain we cannot sail in the teeth of that storm, or
    make

Enough way against it. Since fortune's too strong for us, we
   should give in,
Change course at her direction. The coasts of your brother
   Eryx*
Are safe, and not far off, I think, and the harbours of Sicily,
Let me but remember the stars I steered by, last time we
   sailed there.
   Aeneas the true replied:—
                              I agree. I have seen for some time that
The wind so requires and you have been making no head-
   way against it.
Pay off on this other course, then. What land could be more
   welcome,
Where would I rather get these battered ships to port,
Than the place where my Trojan friend, Acestes,* is still
   living
And the bones of my father, Anchises,* lie in the lap of
   earth?
   When he had spoken, they turned for port; the sails drew
      well
In the West wind from astern and the fleet raced over the
   rough sea,
Until, elated, they brought up on the sandy beach they knew.
   Afar, from a high hill-top, Acestes marvelled to see
His friends' ships bearing toward his coast: he went to meet
   them,
A rough-looking man with his javelins and the pelt of the
   Libyan she-bear
He wore—Acestes, son of a Trojan dame and the river
Crimisus. Thinking now of the Trojan blood in his veins
He congratulates them on their return, genially plies
   them
With rustic plenty, comforts the tired travellers with good
   cheer.
   On the morrow, at early dawn, when the bright day had
      sent

The stars packing, Aeneas summoned his men from their
        bivouacs
Along the shore to a meeting, stood on a dune and addressed
        them:—
    Proud Dardans,* you who trace your lineage from the high
        gods,
Twelve months have passed, a year has almost come full
        circle
Since we interred the remains, the bones of my own sainted
Father, and consecrated an altar to him in sorrow.
And now, unless I'm mistaken, the day is near which will
        always
Be bitter and sacred to me—such was your will, you gods.
Were I spending it as an exile among the Gaetulian Syrtes,*
If it came upon me in mid-Aegean or in Mycenae,
I would keep that day with anniversary vows and solemn
Cortege, loading the altars with the gifts that are proper to
        them.
But now—and I'm quite sure it's with the design and ap-
        proval of heaven—
We're actually close to the spot where my father's ashes and
        bones
Are buried, we have been brought to enter this friendly
        harbour.
Come then, let us all with cheerful hearts honour the festival:
Pray we for favourable winds: may he grant me, my city
        founded,
Yearly to hold these rites at a shrine dedicated to him.
Like a good son of Troy, Acestes is contributing
Two head of oxen for every ship. Invite to the feast
Our own home-gods and the ones whom our host, Acestes,
        worships!
What's more, if the ninth dawn from now, with her rays un-
        shrouding
The earth below her, should bring a fine day for us to enjoy,
I shall hold a Trojan Games:* a regatta, first, for the ships;

Then let the champion runners, and those who take the arena
Confident in their skill at throwing the javelin or archery;
Those, too, that boldly challenge with the rawhide boxing
    gloves—
Let them all come forward, eager to win the palm of the
    victor.
Now silence, all, for the rites, and garland your heads with
    greenery!
    So saying, Aeneas put on a wreath of his mother's myrtle.
Helymus did the same, and the ripe-aged Acestes
And young Ascanius; the rest of the men there followed suit.
Then from the place of meeting, with a great crowd about
    him,
Thousands of them, Aeneas moved on to the burial mound.
Here, in a ceremonial libation, he poured on the earth*
Two goblets of wine unwatered, two of fresh milk, and two
Of victims' blood; and scattering bright-coloured blossoms,
    he spoke:—
    I greet you again, my hallowed sire! Greetings, ye ashes,
Spirit and shade of the father I rescued from Troy in vain!
It was not allowed I should have you with me upon my quest
    for
Italy, our destined home, and that mysterious Tiber.
    So much he had said, when a giant snake*came slithering
    out from
Under the shrine. It had seven great rolling coils. Inoffensive,
It now encircled the barrow, sliding between the altars:
Upon its back was a sheen, a dapple of blueish markings
And of gold-glinting scales, like the shimmer of many
    colours
A rainbow lays on the dark cloud, refractions from the sun-
    light.
Aeneas was awed by the sight. The snake now, dragging its
    gradual
Length among the bowls and polished wine-cups, tasted
The sacramental meats, then harmlessly went back under

The burial mound again, leaving the altars he'd fed from.
Heartened by this, Aeneas resumed the rites he'd begun
In Anchises' honour, not sure if that snake should be deemed his father's
Familiar or the genius of the place: as the rites require,
He sacrificed two sheep, two swine and two black heifers;
Poured out wine from the bowls, invoked the spirit of noble
Anchises, invoked his phantom, a revenant from death's domain.
His comrades too—each man as his means permitted—with high hearts
Brought offerings, made sacrifice of bullocks, loaded the altars;
While others in turn set up cauldrons and, stretched at their ease,
Roasted the meat upon spits over the charcoal embers.
   The day was come they had so looked forward to—the ninth day,
Dawning fine and calm, brought on by the Sun-god's horses.
Attracted by the name and prestige of famous Acestes,
Crowds of people were coming in holiday spirits from all round,
To stare at Aeneas' men, and some to take part in the Games.
First were the prizes displayed, for all to see, in the middle
Of the arena—tripods for sacrifice, green garlands,
Palm-wreaths, the winners' awards, with pieces of armour, and clothing
Purple-dyed, and gold and silver weighed out in talents.
A fanfare, blown from a mound at the centre, opened the Games.
The first event was a rowing race, for which four galleys
Equally matched, and chosen from the whole fleet, were entered.
The speedy *Whale*, with its lively crew, was commanded by Mnestheus—
Soon to be Mnestheus of Italy and found the Memmian clan*:

Gyas was skipper of the *Chimaera*, a huge vessel,

Big as a town, which its Dardan crew propelled with triple-
banked

Oars—three tiers of them, one staggered over another:

Sergestus, from whom the Sergian family*gets its name,

Shipped in the great *Centaur*: Cloanthus had the sea-blue

Scylla—from him is descended your family, Roman
Cluentius.*

  Well out at sea, right opposite this spindrift-tossing shore,

There is a rock, submerged and thumped by a heavy swell

At times when the wintry nor'-westers blot out the stars from
the sky:

In a calm, it's a quiet place, lifting above still water

A flat top, where the gulls love to perch and bask in the sun-
shine.

Here Aeneas erected an ilex, leaves and all,

As a seamark for the mariners, to show them where they must
turn,

And rounding it, row back the length of the course again.

Then they drew lots for position: the masters, up on the
afterdecks,

Noticeable from afar in their gold and purple finery;

The rest of the crews wearing garlands of poplar leaves,

Their shoulders bare and shining with the oil they had
applied.

They get to the rowing thwarts, their arms are braced on the
oars;

Tensely they wait the starting signal, hearts drained of blood,

Leaping and pounding with nervousness and the lust for
victory.

Then a clear trumpet-call was given. In a flash, the four
ships

Were over the starting-line. The bosuns' calls beat out,

White with foam is the water churned up by those strong arms
pulling.

Side by side they furrow the sea, whose face is all

Convulsed and troughed by the oars and the trident-like
   bows of the galleys.
Not at such headlong speed, in a race for two-horse chariots,
Do the cars leap forth from the starting-box and burn up the
   track, when wildly
The charioteers have shaken their rippling reins hard over
The necks of the bolting horses and are leaning right for-
   ward to lash them.
Now the woods all resound with applause, with the shindy of
   backers
Yelling their favourites on, and the shouting is bandied
   around
The hills that shut in the shore as it strikes them and echoes
   back.
Amidst that hurly-burly, Gyas gets out in front
Of the ruck and leads the others: Cloanthus is lying second—
His crew are better together, but the weight of their pine-built
   ship
Handicaps them. At an equal distance behind these two,
The *Whale* and the *Centaur* struggle, jockeying for a lead;
Now the *Whale* has it, now the big *Centaur* spurts and passes
   her,
Now, neck and neck they are rowing, both, their bows dead
   level
And their long keels together cutting the briny deep.
When they were nearing the rock and close to the turning-
   point,
Gyas, who at the half-way mark was still ahead,
Loudly hailed Menoetes, the coxswain of his galley:—
   Why are you keeping so far out to starboard? Steer in!
   Port rudder!
Hug the rock's edge! I want the port-side oar-blades to
   graze it!
Let the rest of them keep to deep water!
                              He spoke: but Menoetes, fearing
Some hidden reef, turned further away to the open sea.

Where are you wandering? I've told you, make for the
  rock, Menoetes!
Gyas shouted him back on his course. But that moment he
  saw
Over his shoulder Cloanthus in the inside berth and closing
  him.
He, to port of Gyas, scrapes through between Gyas' ship
And the surf-roaring rock-face; and all at once he has passed
The leader, rounded the sea-mark, and won into safe water.
Then was young Gyas pierced to the quick by extreme
  chagrin,
And tears rolled down his cheeks: forgetting decorum,
  blind to
His crew's safety, he seized the unenterprising Menoetes
And heaved him bodily overboard from the afterdeck,
Then taking the tiller himself, as master and coxswain both,
Cheered on his men and ruddered the galley closer inshore.
But heavy with age, his soaked clothes weighing him down,
  Menoetes
Struggled at last to the surface from the bottom of the sea,
  and dripping
Clambered up the rock and sat down on its dry top.
The Trojans laughed at the sight of him going overboard,
  swimming,
And now they laugh to see him spew up the brine from his
  stomach.
This event cheered the two last captains, Sergestus and
  Mnestheus:
They had a possible hope now to catch up with Gyas and
  pass him.
Nearing the rock, Sergestus draws just ahead; but there is no
Daylight yet between his ship and Mnestheus'—he only leads
By half a length, the *Whale*'s bows are pressing him hard
  amidships.
Mnestheus, moving among his crew, in the waist of the
  galley,

Encourages them:—

            Now for a spurt! Quicken the stroke now!
You fought at Hector's side. I chose you to be my comrades
In the last days of Troy. Now let us see the strength,
The valour of heart you showed among the Gaetulian*quick-
    sands,
In the Ionian sea and the hard-running waves off Malea.*
I do not aim at the first place now, or strive to be winner,
Although—— But let victory go to the crew for whom
    Neptune intends it!
To come in last *would* be a disgrace: don't fail so badly,
My friends! Avoid such a scandal!

                So, with the utmost exertion
They pulled; and the bronze poop throbbed at their tre-
    mendous strokes,
And the sea whisked by beneath them: their bodies, their
    bone-dry mouths
Shook as their breath came faster: they ran rivers of sweat.
An accident, pure chance gave Mnestheus the honour he
    wanted:
For, while Sergestus edges his prow towards the rock
In a frantic attempt to get through on the inside, the space
    there being
Too narrow,* his ship unluckily grounds on a jutting reef.
The rock was jarred, the oars smashed on its jagged edge
As they struck it; the impact lifted the bows and wedged them
    fast.
The crew, cursing aloud this hold-up, leapt to their feet,
With iron-tipped poles and sharp-pointed quants struggling
    to push off
The galley, and salvaging the splintered oars from the sea.
But Mnestheus, heartened and braced in nerve by this bit of
    luck,
At a high rate of striking, the wind at his back, made for
The sea that sloped before him, raced on through the open
    water.

Just as a pigeon, startled and suddenly flushed from the cave
Where her home, her darling nest is hidden deep in the rock,
Goes flying over the fields—first a loud, terrified clapping
Of wings as she breaks from cover, then through the noise-
    less air
She fluently skims her way, gliding without a wing-beat:
So Mnestheus went, so the *Whale* ran rapidly over the last
    lap
Of the course, so was she carried on by her own momentum.
First she leaves Sergestus behind, high and dry on the reef,
In the shoal water, struggling to back off, vainly shouting
For help, and taking a lesson in rowing with broken oars.
Next, she is after Gyas and his huge, ponderous ship,
Chimaera, which falls away, through lack of her proper
    helmsman.
And now, as they near the finish, Cloanthus alone is left:
In chase of him, Mnestheus goes all out—a tremendous
    spurt.
Then was the din redoubled; the spectators all to a man
Cheered on the pursuer; crash after crash of applause
    thundered.
One crew was impelled by the shame of losing a prize they
    had all but
Gained for their own, and would give their lives for its glory;
    the other
Was fired by success—they could do it because they believed
    they could do it.
And now they had drawn level and well might win the prize,
But that Cloanthus,* stretching his palms out to the sea,
Poured forth a prayer and invited the gods to strike a bar-
    gain:—
   You gods, you emperors of the sea, whose waters I race on,
Gladly upon this shore will I offer up at your altars
A sleek white bull, in discharge of my vow, presenting its
    entrails
To the salt waves and making libation of wine as well.

He spoke; and from deep under water was heard by the
    whole company
Of Nereids and of Phorcus and by the sea-nymph Panopea;
And father Portunus*himself pushed the ship on its way
With a huge hand, so that it sped to the shore swifter than
    wind
Or a flying arrow, and buried itself deep in the harbour.
Now the son of Anchises, calling them all around him
In the usual way, proclaimed, through a loud-voiced herald,
    Cloanthus
The winner, and placed on his head a garland of green bay
    leaves;
Then gave him first choice of the prizes presented for each of
    the crews—
Namely, three bullocks, with wine, and a heavy talent of silver.
Special awards were made to the actual captains next:
The victor received a cloak wrought of gold thread, with a
    double
Key-patterned border of rich Meliboean*purple around it;
Woven upon it was Ganymede,* hunting on leafy Ida
With his javelin, hunting down swift stags—you could
    almost see him
Panting, the nimble boy; he was pictured, too, being snatched
    up
Aloft from Ida in the claws of Juppiter's fast-flying eagle—
His aged guardians are raising their impotent hands to
    heaven,
His dogs are furiously barking up at the sky above them.
Next, the captain whose stout heart had won him the second
    place
Was given for his own—a handsome thing and a safeguard in
    battle—
A corselet made of smooth gold chain mail, triple-meshed,
That Aeneas himself had stripped from the corpse of
    Demoleos, vanquished
In combat beneath the walls of Ilium, near Simois' torrent.

The servants, Phegeus and Sagaris, were staggering under
    the weight of
Its intricate mesh, could hardly shoulder it; yet Demoleos,
Wearing it, used to pursue at a run the Trojans he'd routed.
For third prize, Aeneas put up a pair of copper cauldrons
And two bowls, fashioned of silver, with designs in high relief.
Now all the recipients were moving away, showing off their
    prizes,
With purple ribbon strung through the garlands upon their
    temples,
When Sergestus, who'd worked himself off that cruel rock
    with great skill
And trouble, oars lost, one tier of them quite disabled, was
    bringing
His vessel ingloriously to port, amid general laughter.
As often occurs when a snake has been caught on the hump
    of a high road,
A bronze wheel running across it, or a wayfarer smashing it
    hard with
A stone and leaving it there, crushed and half dead, the
    serpent
Makes futile attempts to escape, wriggling its long body—
Part of it still defiant, eyes blazing, the neck reared upright
And hissing; while part of it, crippled by injury, drags,
Lashing itself into knots and writhing back on its own
    coils.
Something like this was the oarage working that sluggish
    vessel:
However, she made sail too and fetched into port under full
    sail.
Aeneas, pleased that the ship was not wrecked and his friends
    had got back
Safely, presented Sergestus with the reward he had promised.
His personal prize was a slave girl, skilled in Minerva's
    tasks*—
Pholoë, of Cretan stock, with twin sons at her breast.

This event being decided, true-hearted Aeneas now
Moved off to a grassy plain which lay with wooded hills
All round it—the valley forming a natural amphitheatre
And race-track. Hither, a great throng about him, repaired
     the hero
And sat down on a dais amid the assembled crowds.
Here, for whoever might wish to compete in a running race,
He set up prizes—awards to stimulate their rivalry.
Competitors came flocking, Sicilians and Trojans together:
Nisus and Euryalus*were first—
Euryalus outstanding in beauty and bloom of youth,
Nisus renowned for his pure love of his friend: they were
     followed
By prince Diores, a young man of Priam's noble stock;
After him, side by side, Salius and Patron,*the one
Acarnanian, the other Arcadian, of a Tegaean family:
Next were two young Sicilians, Helymus and Panopes,
Expert foresters both, attendants on old Acestes;
And many besides, less known to fame, their names not
     mentioned.
Aeneas gathered them round him, and spoke to them now
     like this:—
   Give me your cheerful attention, take to heart what I'm
     saying.
None of you will depart without a present from me.
I shall give to every man, as a token of honour, a pair of
Gnossian*arrow-heads, made of bright-polished steel, and an
     axe
Chased with silver, to carry away. The first three to finish
Get prizes as well, and a garland of pale-green olive to wear.
For the winner there is a horse, finely caparisoned:
For second place, an Amazon's quiver filled with Thracian
Arrows, slung upon a broad belt gold-embossed,
And fastened by a buckle set with a polished gem:
He who comes third may be pleased to take this Argive
     helmet.

After this speech, they took up position. The starting
  signal
Was given. In a flash they are off and sprinting along the
  track
Like a ragged rain-cloud, keeping their eyes fixed on the
  finish.
Now Nisus, going faster than wind or a winged thunderbolt,
Shoots to the lead and draws right away from the ruck of the
  runners.
Next to him, but next with a long distance between them,
There follows Salius; and then, some way behind him,
Euryalus lies third.
Euryalus is being chased by Helymus: but Diores
Is right at Helymus' shoulder, running there stride for stride
And grazing his heel—if only the course were a little longer,
He'd get ahead and leave him fighting for a place.
Now the race was almost over; the spent runners
Were nearing the tape, when Nisus had the misfortune to
  slip
In a greasy patch of blood which lay on the course and
  made its
Grass surface slippery (bullocks, it chanced, had been
  slaughtered there).
Here the young man, already flushed with victory, could not
Keep his footing on the ground; he teetered, and fell head-
  long
Face down in the filthy slime and the blood of the sacrificed
  animals.
Yet, even so, he remembered Euryalus, his dear friend;
Rose from the slippery mess, got in the way of Salius
And sent him spinning, tumbling down on the clotted earth.
Euryalus now darted by, and thanks to his friend's act,
Ran in first, and flew on to wild cheering, a popular winner.
Helymus came in next: Diores took the third place.
Salius at once, before the whole crowd in the huge amphi-
  theatre

And the elders who sat in the best seats, loudly objected,
    claiming
He'd been done out of the prize by foul play, and ought to be
    given it.
Popular feeling sided with Euryalus*—there was also
His manly distress, and that worth which is made the more
    winning by good looks.
Diores backed him too, with appeals to the public: Diores
Had got a place, but in vain—there would be no third prize
For him, if the first prize were handed over to Salius.
Then father Aeneas proclaimed:—
                      Your prizes, my lads, are assured you:
No one is changing the order of the first three who finished.
But I may show my regret for an innocent friend's downfall.
  So saying, he gave Salius the skin of a great Gaetulian
Lion—a weighty thing with its shock of hair and its gilt
    claws.
Now Nisus remarked:—
                  If you give such rewards to losers and feel
So sorry for those who have come a cropper, what suitable
    prize
Have you got for me? After all, I'd have won the victor's
    crown
If I had not been baulked by the same bad luck as Salius.
  While he was speaking, Nisus displayed his face and limbs
Fouled with the slimy filth. Then good Aeneas laughed at
    him
And ordering a shield to be brought (Didymaon's work, it
    had hung once
By the gateway of Neptune's temple*and been torn down by
    the Greeks),
Presented it to the excellent youth, a prize of value.
  Later, the races finished and the prizes all distributed,
Now, said Aeneas, if any has courage and speed of reaction,
Let him step forward and put on the gloves for a boxing
    match.

For this contest Aeneas set up a couple of prizes:
The winner would get a garlanded bullock with gilded horns,
The loser console himself with a sword and a fine-looking
  helmet.
They didn't wait long, for at once Dares stood forth in all
  his
Powerful bulk; a deep murmur came from the crowd as he
  rose:
He—no others dared—used to take Paris on;
He it was, at the tomb where mighty Hector sleeps,
Who met the champion Butes,* a mountain of a man, when
  he came
To Troy (Butes was of the Bebrycian clan of Amycus),
Knocked him out, laid him dying upon the tawny sand.
Such was the Dares who now put himself in a challenging
  posture,
Exhibiting his broad shoulders, leading with left and right
As he pounded the air and indulged in a bout of shadow-
  boxing.
An opponent for him was sought: but, from that whole
  gathering,
Not one man had the nerve to come forward and put on the
  gloves.
So, thinking he'd get the prize by default, Dares exultantly
Stepped right up to Aeneas and, without further preamble
Seizing the bullock by a horn with his left hand, spoke as
  follows:—
    Goddess-born, if no one dares enter the ring against me,
What am I waiting for? How long am I to be kept here?
Let me take my award!
                        Then all the Trojans unanimously
Called out, saying the man should be given the guaranteed
  stake.
But at this point Acestes sternly reproved Entellus,*
Who happened to be sitting next him upon the grassy
  mound:—

Entellus, you were once the bravest of heroes: but now!—
Are you going to sit there tamely and let such a prize be won
Without a blow? Where now is Eryx, your heaven-born
     instructor?—
We are foolish, it seems, to take pride in him. And what of
     your own
Sicily-wide reputation? the trophies that hang in your house?
     Entellus replied:—
                    It is not that my love of fame, of glory,
Has yielded to cowardice. No, but I'm getting old and
     sluggish;
My reactions are slower, my blood runs cooler, my strength
     is burnt out.
If I had now what I once had—what that exhibitionist
     yonder
So brashly relies on—if only I had my youth again,
By god, I'd need no inducement, no prizes of beautiful
     bullocks,
To enter the ring! But to hell with prizes!
                              Entellus spoke;
Then hurled into the ring a pair of enormously heavy
Boxing gloves,* which the fast-footed Eryx was used to wear
When he was fighting, their tough hide laced tight over his
     forearms.
Petrified were the spectators; for seven huge ox-hides had
     gone to
Those terrible gloves, lead and iron had been sewn in to
     harden them.
Dares himself, above all, stood aghast, shrank back and
     refused
To fight. Great-hearted Aeneas was turning this way and
     that
The gloves, testing their weight and the numerous layers of
     their bindings.
Then did Entellus, the veteran, utter these words from his
     heart:—

What would you say if you'd seen the gloves which great
  Hercules used
In the ring, or the fatal bout that took place on this very
  shore?
These are the ones which belonged to Eryx, your own
  brother:
Look, you can still see the marks of blood and of brains upon
  them!
With these he stood up to great Hercules.* I too have often
  worn them
In my best days, when the blood ran strong in my veins,
  before
Envious age began to sprinkle my head with grey hair.
But if Dares the Trojan refuses to meet these weapons,
If that is Aeneas' ruling, approved by my backer, Acestes,
Let's fight upon level terms. I'll forgo the gloves of
  Eryx;
So don't be frightened, Dares—just take off those Trojan
  gloves!
  So saying, he doffed the double-folded cloak from his
  shoulders;
The mighty joints of his limbs, the mighty bones and thews
  were
Revealed, and he took up his stand, a giant, in the arena.
Then the son of Anchises, presiding, had gloves of equal
  weight
Brought out, so the combatants' fists were bound with
  identical weapons.
Now straight away they both went into their fighting posi-
  tions,
Up on their toes, up with their fists, cool and undaunted.
Heads held high and well back, to keep out of reach of a
  punch,
Hand to hand they were sparring, and warming up to the
  business.
Dares relied upon his youth and his faster footwork;

Entellus' strength was his massive physique, but his legs
    were slow
And shaky, and soon he was breathing heavily, out of condi-
    tion.
Many punches are thrown by both of them, missing their
    target;
Many get home on the hollow ribs or beat a tattoo on
The mighty chests: against ear and temple their fists go
    flickering
Constantly out, and their cheek-bones are rattled by heavy
    punches.
Entellus stands solidly rooted, not changing his stance, avoid-
    ing
Blows by weaving and carefully watching his enemy's move-
    ments.
Dares, like one who assaults with siege-works a towering city
Or skirmishes round some mountain redoubt he is blockad-
    ing,
Tries here and there for an opening, reconnoitres with expert
    skill,
And launches attacks from every angle, but all to no purpose.
Now, rising to his full height, Entellus signalled and swung
An overarm hook with his right; his nimble opponent saw it
Coming all the way, and quickly side-stepped out of trouble.
The force of the blow was spent on thin air—and worse,
    Entellus,
Losing his balance, with all his heavyweight bulk went
    crashing
Heavily to earth; so a pine tree, eaten out by age,
Might have fallen, its roots wrenched up, on Ida or Ery-
    manthus.*
Trojans and Sicilians leapt to their feet in solicitude:
Amid the hubbub, Acestes got to Entellus first
And with compassion helped his veteran friend to rise.
But the hero, far from being slowed or unnerved by his
    fall,

Went back to the fight more aggressively, more violent now
　　because
He was seeing red. The humiliation, and with it the sense that
His courage was unimpaired, kindled his strength: im-
　　petuously,
Battering Dares with lefts and rights, he sent him reeling
All round the ring. No pause, no respite: thick as a hail-
　　storm
Rattling on roofs, came the punches Entellus threw, as he
　　pounded
Dares and spun him about with a two-fisted attack.
Aeneas refused to let the murderous fray go on—
Entellus was blind with rage, like a killer, and must be
　　stopped;
So he called an end to the bout, saving the punch-drunk
　　Dares
From further punishment, and spoke a few words to console
　　him:—
　Poor chap, can you not see that to go on now would be
　　madness?
That you have lost the ascendancy, and how the gods have
　　turned
Against you? Give in to their will.
　　　　　　　　　　　　At his word, the contest is over.
Dares is led away to the ships by his loyal friends,
All groggy, knees sagging, legs trailing behind him, his head
　　lolling
From side to side, and spitting teeth and clotted blood
Out of his mouth. Then they're called up to take the sword
　　and helmet
On his behalf, leaving the bullock and palm for Entellus.
The victor, in highest spirits, overjoyed with his bullock,
　　exclaims:—
　O goddess-born, and all you Trojans, let this inform you
What strength of body I had in my young days, and also
From what a fate you have rescued and are preserving Dares.

With these words, Entellus placed himself in front of the
    bullock,
His prize for the bout, which was standing nearby, drew back
    his right fist
And brought it hard down from full height just between the
    horns
Of the beast: that blow smashed into its skull and dashed the
    brains out.
Sprawling, quivering, lifeless, down on the ground the brute
    fell.
Over its corpse Entellus spoke, and with great emotion:—
    Eryx, this better life instead of the death of Dares
I give you; and now, a champion lays down his gloves, his
    science.
    Immediately after this, Aeneas called upon those who
Wished to compete at archery, announced the prizes; and
    then
He had a mast unshipped from Serestus' great galley
And erected. A dove was tied, fluttering, with cord passed
    through
A hole in the high masthead, as a target for the arrows.
The competitors gathered, and tossed their lots into a helmet
Of bronze. Hippocöon's number was drawn out first, amid
    cheers
From his fanciers—Hippocöon, son of Hyrtacus: next
In the order of shooting was Mnestheus—he who had just
    now won
A prize in the rowing race, and wore a green garland of olive.
Eurytion drew third turn; a brother he was of the famous
Pandarus*who, on a day long ago, being bidden to break
The truce, had shot the first arrow into the Grecian ranks.
Last, from the bottom of the helmet, Acestes' lot came up—
Yes, he would have a go at this strenuous, young man's sport.
Then, putting forth their strength, each in his own measure,
They bent and strung their bows, and drew shafts from the
    quivers.

The son of Hyrtacus shot the first arrow, his bowstring
    twanging;
It sped through the air with a sound like the whine of a whip-
    lash, then
It was home, stuck fair and square in the tough wood of the
    mast.
The mast quivered, the dove was all one terrified flurry
Of wings, and a roar of applause broke out across the arena.
Now Mnestheus took up position eagerly, drew back the
    bowstring
For a high shot, then aimed the arrow and sighted along it.
He was unlucky, failing to hit the bird itself
With his shaft, but cutting in two the knotted, hempen cord
Which had tied its foot and held it dangling down from the
    masthead;
The dove sped off to the fleecy clouds in the sky. Quickly
Eurytion, who'd been ready, bow bent and arrow nocked,
For some time, breathed a vow to his brother Pandarus,
And marking the dove up there in the blue, exultantly
    clapping
Its wings, he shot, and transfixed it before it could reach
    cloud cover.
Stone-dead the dove came down, leaving its life in the regions
Of air—came tumbling down with the arrow still stuck
    through it.
Acestes alone was left, and the prize already won:
However, he aimed his arrow up at the sky, so that all could
Witness a veteran's skill and hear the strong tone of his
    bow.
A startling phenomenon*was seen now—one of the utmost
Significance for the future: huge events were to show
Its meaning, and frightening seers one day would declare
    what it omened.
The shaft, as it sped among the streaming clouds, took fire,
Blazing a trail in the sky, then burnt itself out and vanished
Into thin air: thus, often, a star dislodges itself

From heaven and shoots across it, trailing a long-haired
    flame.
Sicilians and Trojans alike were amazed, and in two minds
    about it:
They prayed to the Powers above: Aeneas himself accepted
The omen favourably, put his arms round the elated
Acestes, loaded him with a splendid present, and spoke:—
    Sire, take this. The great lord of Olympus has given clear
        signs
That he wishes you to receive an extra-special award.
You shall have this prize, as it were from old Anchises in
    person—
This bowl, engraved with figures: it was originally
Presented to my father by Thracian Cisseus,* a notably
Fine present, for a keepsake and token of deep friendship.
    When he had spoken, Aeneas put on Acestes' head
The wreath of green laurel, and publicly named him the first
    prize-winner.
Good-natured Eurytion grudged him not the premier
Award, although it was he himself who had shot the bird
    down.
Next after him for a prize was the man who had severed the
    cord;
And last, the one who had pierced the mast with his flying
    arrow.
But father Aeneas, before the archery match was over,
Called Epytus' son to his side, the guardian and chief atten-
    dant
Of young Ascanius, and confidentially whispered these
    words:—
    Off you go, and tell Ascanius, if he is ready
With the boys' squadron now and the riders are all in forma-
    tion,
To lead them on and give us his martial display, in honour
Of his grandfather.
                    Aeneas ordered the crowd, which had been

Encroaching upon the arena, to move back and leave it
    empty.
Now the boys ride in, before the eyes of their fathers,*
In perfect dressing, a brilliant sight on their bridled horses—
Sicilians and Trojans greet them with murmurs of admira-
    tion.
They wear on their hair*ceremonial garlands of leaves, well
    trimmed,
And each of them carries a couple of steel-tipped, cornel-
    wood lances;
Some have a polished quiver slung over the shoulder; high
    up on
The breast and round the neck lies the flexible golden torque.
Three troops compose the squadron, and three troop-majors
    ride
In front, each of them followed by a detachment of twelve
    boys:
The three troops, each with its leader, make a most gallant
    show.
The first was led, on this ceremonial parade, by a little
Priam, named after his grandsire, the noble son of Polites,
Destined to breed Italians: he rode on a Thracian horse—
An animal with white markings, the pasterns showing white
As it paced, and white the forehead it carried high. Next
    came
Atys, from whom the Latin Atii*trace their descent—
Young Atys, who was a special friend of Ascanius.
Ascanius himself, the best-looking of all of them, led the
    third troop,
Riding upon the Tyrian horse that Dido had trustingly
Given him, as a token of love, to remind him of her.
The rest of the boys were mounted upon Sicilian horses
Lent by Acestes.
As they rode shyly on, the Trojans clapped, in delight at
The spectacle, tracing family likenesses in the boys' features.
When they had proudly passed in review before the eyes of

Their relatives and the rest, and were drawn up ready, the
    signal
Was given by Epytides from a distance—a shout and whip-
    crack.
The three troops now broke up, each into its two detach-
    ments,
Which wheeled apart and then, at the word of command,
    again
Came galloping back and charged one another with lances
    levelled.
Next, they staged a new set of manœuvres and counter-
    manœuvres,
Keeping their relative positions, each group, while perform-
    ing their maze of
Evolutions—a mimic engagement of mounted troops:
Now they turn their backs in flight, now wheel and charge
With lance in rest, and now ride peacefully, file by file.
It was like the fabled Labyrinth*constructed in mountainous
    Crete—
A maze of unbroken walls, with thousands of blind alleys
To keep the venturer guessing and trick him, so that the
    right path
Into the heart of the maze was a puzzle to find or retrace.
Just like this were the tracks made by the complex manœuvres
Of the boys, as they wove their patterns of sham flight or
    sham encounter,
Moving as dolphins move when they gambol among the
    waves,
Through the Carpathian*and Libyan seas sportively swim-
    ming.
This kind of cavalry tournament Ascanius, when he was
    building
The walled town of Alba Longa, first introduced to the early
Latins, and taught them to follow its ceremonial routine
Just as he'd done when a boy, with the Trojan boys of his
    squadron.

The Albans taught their children; and finally Rome herself
Received the tradition and kept it to honour her ancestors.
We call it 'the Trojan Game', and the squadrons are named
   after Troy.
Thus far, the Sports in honour of the sainted Anchises.
   At this point, fickle Fortune changed sides and turned
      against them
For, while they perform the rites at the tomb with various
   contests,
Iris*has been despatched from heaven by Saturnian Juno,
On the wings of a favouring wind, to the Trojan fleet: the
   goddess
Has certain designs; unappeased as yet is her old resentment.
Unseen by any, the virginal Iris speeds to earth,
Sliding along the curve of a rainbow of many colours.
She observes the vast assembly, and then, scanning the shore,
Sees the deserted harbour, the ships left unattended.
But, by themselves, at a distance, upon a lonely beach
The Trojan women lamented Anchises' death, and weeping
Gazed out on the deep together. Alas, such a wearisome
   waste of
Water still to be travelled—that was the cry of them all.
They yearn for a home; they are sick of the sea and endless
   voyaging.
Iris, who was an expert at trouble-making, put off now
Her heavenly mien and raiment, went quickly amongst them
   and joined
The group of Trojan matrons, transformed into the likeness
Of Beroe, the aged wife of Tmarian*Doryclus,
A dame of good family who had once had position and
   children:—
   Pity it is that we were not dragged by the Greek soldiers
To death under our own walls during the war! Unlucky
People, for what catastrophe is fortune saving you up?
Now wanes the seventh summer*since the destruction of
   Troy,

And still over land and water we roam, over a world of
Unharbouring rocks, as we steer by the stars and around the
    wide seas
From wave to wave chase after that will-o'-the-wisp, Italy.
Here's the land of a brother, Eryx. Here's hospitable Acestes.
Who stops us laying our walls here, giving our people a
    home?
Dear Troy! Dear home-gods, why were you rescued from
    the foe,
If Troy-town's walls*are to be for ever a dream? if nowhere
I am to see a Xanthus, a Simois, rivers of Hector?
Quick! Help me then to burn these ships that bring no luck!
There came to me, as I slept, the phantom of our prophetic
Cassandra*: she gave me a burning torch, it seemed, and said,
Here find your Troy. Here is your home. It is time for
    action—
Such prodigies brook no delay. Look at these four altars
To Neptune! He furnishes us with fire and the will to use it.
  So saying, as ring-leader, Iris violently snatched up a
    dangerous
Firebrand, swung back with her right hand strongly, waved
    it aloft, then
Hurled it. The Trojan women lost their good sense, and
    awoke to
A phantasy world. One of their number, the oldest, Pyrgo,
The nurse of so many royal children of Priam, called out:—
  Ladies, this is not Beroe! This is not the Trojan wife of
Doryclus, I tell you! Look at the signs of heavenly
Grace that she bears! the fire in her eyes! Mark well her spirit,
Her countenance, the timbre of her voice, and the way she
    walks!
Why, it was only just now that I left Beroe behind,
Ailing, and fretting because she alone could take no part in
The ceremonies nor bring the offerings due to Anchises.
  Thus Pyrgo spoke.
The ladies were in two minds at first, eyeing the ships

With malicious glances, torn between their piteous craving
For the land they were in and the call of the land promised by
    destiny.
But now, spreading her wings, the goddess took off from
    earth,
Describing a rainbow arc under the clouds as she flew.
Then indeed, amazed at the miracle, driven by a frenzy,
All crying out, they ransack the nearby houses for flame:
Some strip the altars,* to hurl greenery, twigs, torches
Onto the ships. The Fire-god gallops in full career
Over the thwarts, the oars, the poops of painted pinewood.
Now to Anchises' tomb and the crowded stands of the sports
    ground
Eumelus brought the news that the fleet was on fire: the
    spectators
Could see for themselves the black ashes eddying up in a
    smoke cloud.
At once Ascanius, just as he was when blithely command-
    ing
The mounted display, galloped off with great presence of
    mind to the riotous
Ship-stead, leaving his breathless trainers far behind.
    What weird madness is this? My poor good Trojan ladies,
What, oh what were you after? No enemy, no Greek camp
But your own future goes up in smoke. Look, it is I, your
Ascanius! he said, and threw down at their feet the clattering
    helmet
Which he had worn when leading his boys in the sham fight.
Aeneas hurried up now, and with him the mass of the Trojans.
But the scared women broke and fled in every direction
Over the shore, running for woods or caves—anywhere
To hide, ashamed to be seen after what they had done, them-
    selves
Again and knowing their kin, now Juno's spell was broken.
Not in the least though, for that, did the flames of the con-
    flagration

Slacken their unquenched violence: between the wet planks,
    the caulking
Smouldered and gave off greasy smoke; and the heat slowly
Ate its way down through the hulls, consuming them like a
    cancer,
So that all efforts to put out the fire with water were useless.
Then god-fearing Aeneas rent his garments and called
Aloud on the gods for help, stretching his palms out to
    heaven:—
    Almighty Jove, if you do not yet abhor each one of
Us Trojans, if as of old in your loving-kindness you have
    some
Regard for men's sufferings, grant that our fleet may escape
    this fire now,
And save, O Father, save our frail hopes from destruction!
Or else, if there's nothing left for it and this is what I deserve,
Let your lightning send us straight to perdition here and now!
    Scarce were the words out when the sky grew dark and
    there came
A cloudburst, a storm of unparalleled violence: hill and dale
Were rocked by thunderclaps; all the firmament was one
    avalanche
Of driving rain, one blackness of cloud piled up by the South
    wind.
The hulls were brimmed by that downpour, the half-burnt
    timbers soaked,
Until the fires were all extinguished, and the ships—
All but four of them—had been saved from complete destruc-
    tion.
    But lord Aeneas, hard hit by this most cruel disaster,
Was full of anxiety, and his mind kept oscillating
Between two thoughts—should he settle down in Sicily here
And forget his destiny, or struggle on towards Italy?
Then did the aged Nautes*—he whom Pallas Athene
Had singled out as a pupil to learn her lore and be famed for it
(Him she favoured with explanations of what a god's

Great wrath should mean, and what the scheme of the fates
    demanded)—
He now addressed to Aeneas these words of consolation:—
  Goddess-born, let us follow our destiny, ebb or flow.
Whatever may happen,* we master fortune by fully accept-
    ing it.
Acestes now—he's a Dardan, and of divine lineage:
Make him a partner in your plans; I think he'll agree.
Detail to him the crews of the burnt-out ships, and any
Who have lost heart in your great enterprise and your
    fortunes:
Let the oldest men fall out, the women who are sick of voyag-
    ing,
And any weaker vessels you have, ones daunted by danger—
Weed them out, they are spent, let them make a walled home
    here;
If he permits the name, they shall call their city Acesta.*
  Aeneas was much disturbed by the words of his aged
    friend;
All the more he was pulled this way and that by his worries.
And when dark night, upwheeling, possessed the sky, there
    came
To him in a vision, gliding down through the gloom, his
    father
Anchises' figure, which at once urgently spoke:—
  My son, dearer to me than life when life was mine,
My son, much wrought upon by the fate of Ilium,
At Jove's command I am come here—Jove who repulsed the
    fire
From your ships, and showered down pity from heaven in
    the nick of time.
Follow the excellent advice which aged Nautes
Gives you. Choose out warriors, the bravest of heart, and lead
    them
To Italy: for tough and primitive are the people*
That you will have to subdue in Latium. First, however,

Death's kingdom you must enter, and traversing the vale of
Avernus,* come to meet me, my son. I dwell not with
The damned in Tartarus or the purgatorial spirits,
But with the happy throngs of the Blessed in Elysium.
Here, when you've sacrificed*many black sheep, the chaste
    Sibyl shall bring you.
Then shall you learn where your home is to be, and your
    people's destiny.
Farewell now. Dewy night drives on at mid-career,
And close I feel the breath of dawn's coursers, come to part us.
    These words: then he vanished, like a wisp of smoke, into
    thin air.
So quickly gone? Aeneas cried: gone from me whither?
Whom do you flee? Who fences you off from my embrace?
So saying, Aeneas stoked up the fire, the sleepy embers,
Paid reverence to Troy's patron spirit, and to Vesta
Time-hallowed, with offerings of ritual corn and clouds of
    incense.
    Immediately then he summoned his friends, Acestes first,
To inform them of Jove's command, his own dear father's
    injunctions,
And of the firm decision which now at last he had come to.
No time was lost in debating it. Acestes gave his consent.
They enrolled the women for the colony, off-loaded the men
    who wanted
To stay there—persons with no great hankering after glory.
The remainder renewed the thwarts, made good the timbers
    charred
By fire on the ships, and fitted them out with new oars and
    rigging—
Few in number they were, but in high heart for warfare.
Meanwhile Aeneas traced with a plough the city's cir-
    cumference,
Allotted the sites, and named one quarter of the town
    'Ilium',*
Another 'Troy'. The Trojan Acestes was glad to be king of it,

Appointed a court, gave laws to an assembled parliament.

Then, on the skyey peak of Mount Eryx,* was founded a shrine

To Idalian*Venus, while for the sepulchre of Anchises

A priest was ordained and a sacred grove planted all round it.

Nine days now the whole people have spent in feasting and paying

Sacrifice on the altars: the waves are lulled by gentle

Breezes; a South wind, steadily blowing, invites them to sea again.

Over the salient shore goes up a great noise of weeping:

Embracing each other, they try to make night and day last longer.

Those women, those very men who, before, had shrunk from the venomous

Face of the sea and could not abide even the thought of it

Wanted to go now, were willing to bear every ordeal of travelling.

These did the good Aeneas console with kindly words,

And weeping, gave them into the care of their cousin, Acestes.

Then he had three bull-calves sacrificed to Eryx

With a lamb to the Storm-gods, and ordered the ships to weigh anchor in turn.

Himself, a garland of well-trimmed olive about his temples,

He stood high up in the bows, holding a bowl from which he

Cast wine over the salt waves, and with it the votive entrails.

A freshening off-shore wind drove them upon their course.

Eagerly rowed the mariners, sweeping the sea with long strokes.

While this was doing, Venus, anxious of heart, approached

Neptune and unburdened herself of a grievance, thus:—

The heavy wrath of Juno, the grudge she implacably cherishes,

Force me to have recourse to every kind of entreaty.

She is softened neither by time nor by any propitiations,

Unswayed by the ruling of Jove or by fate, still active against
  us.
It is not enough for her infamous hatred to have devoured
The heart of the Phrygians, Troy, and made its survivors run
A whole gamut of retribution: she hunts down the very ashes
Of the dead city. She'd best have good reason for such
  vindictiveness.
You are my witness, Neptune, what a wild riot of waters
She raised but now in the Libyan sea,* what a hell she brewed
  up
Employing the storm-winds of Aeolus. She failed in her pur-
  pose. But this
She actually dared to do in your province.
Then, just think, she wickedly worked on the Trojan women
To burn the ships, a foul deed! And thus she has forced
  Aeneas,
Fleet gone, to leave his friends behind in a foreign country.
All I ask now is that you should give the remnant a safe
Sea passage up to Laurentine Tiber—if indeed
What I ask is lawful, and there is the home which the Fates
  have granted them.
    Then spoke Saturn's son,* the emperor of the deep:—
Every right you have to rely on me, the ruler
Of ocean, where you were born.* I have earned your con-
  fidence, too,
For often have I quelled the mad fury of wind and sea.
Also on land—I call to witness Xanthus and Simois*—
I have looked after your Aeneas. When Achilles
Pursued the panicking Trojans and crushed them against
  their walls,
When he dealt death to thousands till the choked rivers
  groaned with
Corpses, and Xanthus could not find or wind his way
To the sea, even then I carried off in a hollow cloud
Aeneas, who faced Achilles in a combat where neither the
  gods

Nor the combatants were equally matched—I did it, though
My will was to root up the perjured Troy*I had built with my
    own hands.
So fear no more: as then, my attitude is unaltered.
He shall get safe to the harbour of Cumae: you have your
    wish.
One only shall you miss, one shall be lost at sea,
One life must be surrendered for many lives.
    When he had gladdened the goddess' heart with these
        comforting words,
Her father put the gold yoke*on his horses, fastened the foam-
    ing
Bridles on the spirited creatures and freely shook out the
    reins.
Lightly skims the dark-blue chariot over the sea's face:
The waves go down, beneath those roaring wheels the steep
    swell
Turns to a calm, the storm-clouds fleet from the wastes of the
    sky.
Then come his retainers, diverse in appearance*—prodigious
    whales,
The antique school of Glaucus, Palaemon the son of Ino,
With the fast-swimming Tritons and all the flotilla of
    Phorcus;
On the left are Thetis and Melite and maiden Panopea,
Nesaea, too, and Spio, Thalia and Cymodoce.
    Aeneas had been in suspense; but his mood changed now,
        and a calm joy
Thrilled through his heart. He gave orders that all the masts
    should at once
Be stepped and the sails broken out from the yards. The crews
    all set
Their mainsheets, and all together slanted the lofty yard-
    arms
This way or that, to keep the sails filled, as the breeze shifted
To port or starboard quarter. A fair wind bore them on.

They were sailing in close column, with Palinurus ahead
In the lead, the rest being ordered to shape their course by his.
And now the dewy night had nearly come to its half-way
Mark in the heavens: the mariners, sprawled on the hard
    benches
Beside their oars, were all relaxed in solacing quiet.
Just then did Sleep*come feathering down from the stars
    above,
Lightly displacing the shadowy air, parting the darkness,
In search of you, Palinurus, carrying death in a dream
To your staunch heart. Now, taking the shape of Phorbas, the
    Sleep-god
Perched up there in the stern-sheets and rapidly spoke these
    words:—

Palinurus, son of Iasus, the seas are bearing the ships on,
Steadily blows the breeze, and you have a chance to rest.
Lay your head down, and take a nap; your eyes are tired with
Watching. I will stand your trick at the helm for a little.

Palinurus could hardly raise his heavy eyes, but he
    answered:—

Are you asking me to forget what lies behind the pacific
Face of the sea and its sleeping waves? to trust this devil?
What? Shall I leave Aeneas to the mercy of tricky winds—
I who, time and again, have been taken in by a clear sky?

While he spoke, Palinurus kept a good grip on the tiller—
By no means would he release it—and a steadfast gaze on the
    stars.
But look! over his temples the god is shaking a bough
That drips with the dew of Lethe*, the drowsy spell of Stygian
Waters. And now, though he struggles, his swimming eyes
    are closing.
As soon as, taken off guard, he was relaxed in unconscious-
    ness,
The god, leaning down over him, hurled him into the sea
Still gripping the tiller; a part of the taffrail was torn
    away:

As he fell, he kept calling out to his friends, but they did not
 hear him.
Up and away skywards the Sleep-god now went winging.
Safe as before, the fleet was scudding upon its course—
Nothing to fear, for Neptune had guaranteed a safe passage.
And now, racing on, they were near the rocky place of the
 Sirens,*
Dangerous once for mariners, white with the bones of many;
From afar the rasp of the ceaseless surf on those rocks could
 be heard.
Just then Aeneas became aware that his ship was yawing
Badly, her helmsman missing; he brought her back on to
 course
In the night sea, and deeply sighing, stunned by the loss of his
 friend, said:—
  O*Palinurus,* too easily trusting clear sky and calm sea,
You will lie on a foreign strand, mere jetsam, none to bury
 you.

BOOK VI

Thus spoke Aeneas, in tears, then gave the ships their head,
And at long last they slid to the shores of Euboean Cumae.*
The bows are swung round to face the sea, the vessels made
    fast with
The biting hook of their anchors, and the sheer sterns are
    lining
The beach. Now, full of excitement, the heroes tumble out
On the Hesperian shore: some look for the seeds of fire
Hidden in veins of flint, some scour the woods, the tangled
Haunts of wild beasts, for fuel, and point to the springs they
    have found.
But the god-fearing Aeneas made for the shrine where Apollo*
Sits throned on high, and that vasty cave—the deeply-
    recessed
Crypt of the awe-inspiring Sibyl, to whom the god gives
The power to see deep and prophesy what's to come.
Now they passed into Diana's grove and the gold-roofed
    temple.
    The story is that Daedalus,* when he escaped from Minos,
Boldly trusting himself to the air on urgent wings,
An unprecedented mode of travel, went floating northwards
Until he was lightly hovering above the Cumaean hilltop.
Here he came first to earth, hung up his apparatus
Of flight as a thanks-offering to Phoebus, and built a great
    temple.
On its door was depicted the death of Androgeos*; also the
    legend
Of how the Athenians, poor souls, were forced to pay yearly
    tribute
With seven of their sons—the scene when the lots had just
    been drawn.

Facing this, there's a bas-relief; with Crete rising out of the
 waves;
Pasiphae, cruelly fated to lust after a bull,
And privily covered; the hybrid fruit of that monstrous
 union—
The Minotaur, a memento of her unnatural love:
Here's the insoluble maze constructed by Daedalus;
Yet, sympathizing with Ariadne*in her great passion,
He gives her himself the clue to the maze's deceptive wind-
 ings,
And guides with a thread the blind steps of Theseus. In the
 artifact
Icarus too would have had a prominent place, if his father's
Grief had allowed: but twice, trying to work the boy's fall
In gold, did Daedalus' hands fail him. They'd have perused
The sculptured tale right through, but that Achates, who
 had
Been sent ahead, arrived with the priestess of Phoebus and
 Trivia,*
Deiphobe, daughter of Glaucus. She now addressed
 Aeneas:—
 This is no time for poring over those works of art.
Just now you would do best to sacrifice seven bullocks
That have not been yoked, and as many properly chosen
 sheep.
 She addressed Aeneas; and he promptly performing the
 rites she
Requested, the priestess summoned them into the lofty
 temple.
 There's a huge cave* hollowed out from the flank of
 Cumae's hill;
A hundred wide approaches it has, a hundred mouths
From which there issue a hundred voices, the Sibyl's
 answers.
They had reached its threshold when, time it is to ask your
 destiny,

The Sibyl cried, for lo! the god is with me. And speaking,
There by the threshold, her features, her colour were all at
    once
Different, her hair flew wildly about; her breast was heaving,
Her fey heart swelled in ecstasy; larger than life she seemed,
More than mortal her utterance: the god was close and
    breathing
His inspiration through her:—

                        What? Slow to pay your vows
And say your prayers, Aeneas of Troy? Yet only then
Will the spell work and the doors open,

                              she cried, and again
Fell silent. An icy shudder ran through their very bones
And Aeneas poured out a prayer from the bottom of his
    heart:—
  O Phoebus, often you pitied the load Troy had to bear;
You it was who guided the hand and the Trojan arrow
Of Paris against Achilles*; you were the guide I followed
Into so many seas, lapping great lands, and through
Remote Massylian*peoples, the fields the Syrtes fringe:
And now, at long last, we have caught the elusive shores of
    Italy.
Let Troy's ill luck, that has dogged us so far, follow no
    further.
Ye too, gods and goddesses all, who could not bear
Ilium and the great fame of the Dardans, it is proper now
For you to spare the Trojans. And, O most holy Sibyl,
Foreseer of future things, grant—I but ask for the kingdom
Owed by my destiny—grant that we Trojans may settle in
    Latium,
We and our wandering gods, the hard-driven deities of
    Troy.
Then will I found a temple*of solid marble to Phoebus
And Trivia, appointing festival days in Phoebus' honour.
You too shall have your holy place*in the realm to be,
Where I shall deposit the oracles, the mystic runes you utter

For my own people, ordaining a priesthood*to their service,
O gracious one. But do not commit your sayings to leaves,
Lest they become the sport of whisking winds and are
    scattered:
Speak them aloud, I pray.

                                    Aeneas made an end now.
But the Sibyl, not yet submissive to Phoebus, there in her
    cavern
Prodigiously struggled, still trying to shake from her brain
    the powerful
God who rode her: but all the more he exhausted her foam-
    ing
Mouth and mastered her wild heart, breaking her in with a
    firm hand.
And now the hundred immense doors of the place flew open
Of their own accord, letting out the Sibyl's inspired re-
    sponses:—
    O you that at last have done with the dangers of the deep
(Yet graver ones await you on land), the Trojans shall come
To power in Lavinium—be troubled no more about this—
But shall not also be glad that they did. Wars, dreadful wars
I see, and Tiber foaming with torrents of human blood.
You will not escape a Simois, a Xanthus*there, a Greek
Encampment; Latium has a new Achilles*in store for you,
He too a goddess' son: nor yet shall the Trojans anywhere
Be rid of Juno's vendetta. Ah then, in your extremity,
What tribes, what townships of Italy shall you not sue for
    aid!
Once more it's an alien bride,* a foreign marriage that's
    destined
To cause such terrible harm to the Trojans.
But never give way to those evils: face them all the more
    boldly,
Using what methods your luck allows you. The way of salva-
    tion
Begins where you'd least expect it, stems from a Greek city.*

Thus from her sanctum spoke the Cumaean Sibyl, pro-
nouncing
Riddles that awed them; her voice came booming out of the
cavern,
Wrapping truth in enigma: she was possessed; Apollo
Controlled her, shaking the reins and twisting the goad in
her bosom.
As soon as her ecstasy ebbed and her raving mouth was silent,
The hero Aeneas began to speak:—

        Maiden, there's nothing
New or unexpected to me in such trials you prophesy.
All of them I have forecast, worked out in my mind already.
I have one request: since here is reputed to be the gateway
Of the Underworld and the dusky marsh from Acheron's*
overflow,
May it befall me to go into my dear father's
Presence—open the hallowed gates and show me the way!
Him through the flames, through a thousand pursuing
missiles I rescued
Out of the enemy's midst and bore him away on these
shoulders:
He voyaged with me, enduring sea after sea, enduring
All menace of sea and storm, weak as he was—great ordeals
Beyond his strength, exceeding the normal lot of old age.
Yes, and he himself most earnestly bade me, more than once,
To come to you here and make this appeal. I pray you, kind
one,
Take pity on father and son. You have the power: it was not
For nothing that Hecate*put you in charge of the grove of
Avernus.
Orpheus,* with only the tuneful strings of a Thracian lyre
To aid him, could conjure forth the ghost of his wife; Pollux,*
Who, turn about, shares life and death with his mortal
brother,
Constantly comes and goes this way; I need not mention
Theseus*or Hercules;*I too am descended from great Jove.

Thus he was making petition, his hands upon the altar,
When the Sibyl began to speak:—

O child of a goddess' womb,
Trojan son of Anchises, the way to Avernus is easy;
Night and day lie open the gates of death's dark kingdom:
But to retrace your steps, to find the way back to daylight—
That is the task, the hard thing. A few, because of Jove's
Just love, or exalted to heaven by their own flame of good-
ness,
Men born from gods, have done it. Between, there lies a
forest,
And darkly winds the river Cocytus*round the place.
But if so great your love is, so great your passion to cross
The Stygian waters twice and twice behold black Tartarus,
If your heart is set on this fantastic project,
Here's what you must do first. Concealed in a tree's thick
shade
There is a golden bough*—gold the leaves and the tough
stem—
Held sacred to Proserpine: the whole wood hides this bough
And a dell walls it round as it were in a vault of shadow.
Yet none is allowed to enter the land which earth conceals
Save and until he has plucked that gold-foil bough from the
tree.
Fair Proserpine ordains that it should be brought to her
As tribute. When a bough is torn away, another
Gold one grows in its place with leaves of the same metal.
So keep your eyes roving above you, and when you have
found the bough
Just pull it out: that branch will come away quite easily
If destiny means you to go; otherwise no amount of
Brute force will get it, nor hard steel avail to hew it away.
Also—and this you know not—the lifeless corpse of a friend*
Is lying unburied, a dead thing polluting your whole expedi-
tion,
While you are lingering here to inquire about fate's decrees.

Before anything else, you must give it proper burial and
     make
Sacrifice of black sheep: only when you are thus
Purified, shall you see the Stygian groves and the regions
Untreadable to the living.
                              She spoke, then closed her lips.
Aeneas, eyes downcast, countenance full of sorrow,
Moved off, leaving the cave, pondering much in his heart
On the cryptic issues the Sibyl had raised. Loyal Achates
Walked with him, his gait heavy beneath the same load of
     trouble.
Many were the conjectures they threw out, one to the other,
As to which of their dead friends the Sibyl had meant, and
     whose body
Must be interred. Now when they drew near the beach, they
     saw there
The body of Misenus, cut off by cruel death—
Misenus, son of Aeolus, whom none had excelled in firing
The warrior passions of men with thrilling trumpet calls.
He had been a comrade of mighty Hector, at Hector's side
Had fought and won great fame as a trumpeter and a spear-
     man.
After Achilles had defeated Hector and killed him,
This valiant hero, Misenus, attached himself to Dardan
Aeneas' company, following now no lesser a man.
But today, as he sent his horn's notes ringing over the sea,
Most rashly challenging the gods to a musical contest,
Jealous Triton*caught him off guard—if we may credit
The story—and plunged him down in the surf among those
     rocks.
Now they were all standing around him, lamenting loudly,
Not least the good-hearted Aeneas. And now at once they
     hasten
Weeping to carry out the Sibyl's instructions, piling
Timber up with a will for a towering funeral altar.
Into the age-old forest, where only wild things lurk,

They go: spruces are felled, the holm oak rings with axe
    blows,
Wedges are used to split ash logs and the cleavable wood
Of oaks, immense rowans are rolled down from the heights.
Aeneas himself, in the middle of these activities,
Carrying the same tools as they, encouraged his friends.
But also, sad at heart, gazing up at the huge forest,
He brooded; and then he uttered his thoughts aloud in a
    prayer:—
    If only I might glimpse that golden bough on its tree
In the great wood this very moment! for all that the Sibyl
Said about you, Misenus, was true, too sadly true.
    The words were hardly out when it befell that two doves
Came planing down from above before his very eyes
And alighted upon the green turf. The hero recognized
His mother's birds.* His heart leapt up and he said a prayer:—
    Show me the way, if way there is! Oh, wing your flight
To that part of the forest where the precious bough over-
    shadows
The fruitful soil. Do not forsake me, heavenly mother,
At this most crucial hour!
                    He spoke; stopped in his tracks
To note what signs they gave and in what direction they'd
    move.
Now the doves, as they fed, flitted on from spot to spot, but
    never
So far ahead that one who followed lost sight of them.
Then, when they came to the mouth of foul-breathing
    Avernus,*
Swiftly they soared, went gliding through the soft air and
    settled,
The pair of them, on a tree, the wished-for place, a tree
Amid whose branches there gleamed a bright haze, a dif-
    ferent colour—
Gold. Just as in depth of winter the mistletoe blooms
In the woods with its strange leafage, a parasite on the tree,

Hanging its yellow-green berries about the smooth round
    boles:
So looked the bough of gold leaves upon that ilex dark,
And in a gentle breeze the gold-foil foliage rustled.
Aeneas at once took hold of the bough, and eagerly breaking
It off with one pull, he bore it into the shrine of the Sibyl.
Meantime upon the shore the Trojans were still lamenting
Misenus, and paying the last rites to his oblivious dust.
First they laid resinous wood, and upon it sections of oak
    trees
To build the pyre up high; the sides of the pyre were wattled
With sombre-foliaged boughs; in front they planted funereal
Cypresses, and his shining arms adorned its top.
Some lit fires beneath the cauldrons, and boiled water;
They washed and anointed the corpse of their friend, so cold
    in death.
All were lamenting. When they had wept him, they laid on
    the bier
His body, covering it with purple drapes and the dead man's
Own clothing. The bearers lifted the bier onto the pyre,
A melancholy office, and in the traditional manner
Averting their eyes, applied the lighted torches. The pile of
Offerings burned—the incense, the meat, the libations of oil.
Now when the ashes had fallen in and the flames died down,
They quenched the remains, the thirsty embers, with wine;
    and collecting
The bones, Corynaeus put them away in a casket of bronze.
He then moved round his comrades three times, bearing pure
    water;
Aspersing them with drops he shook from a branch of fruitful
Olive, he purified them, and spoke the farewell words.
Aeneas the true now raised over his friend a massive
Tomb, laying on it the man's own arms, his oar and his
    trumpet,
Beneath that high headland which takes its name from him,
Misenum, and preserves his fame unto all ages.

This done, Aeneas hastened to follow the Sibyl's directions.
A deep, deep cave*there was, its mouth enormously gaping,
Shingly, protected by the dark lake and the forest gloom:
Above it, no winged creatures could ever wing their way
With impunity, so lethal was the miasma*which
Went fuming up from its black throat to the vault of heaven:
Wherefore the Greeks called it Avernus, the Birdless Place.
Here the Sibyl first lined up four black-skinned bullocks,
Poured a libation of wine upon their foreheads, and then,
Plucking the topmost hairs from between their brows, she placed
These on the altar fires as an initial offering,
Calling aloud upon Hecate, powerful in heaven and hell.
While other laid their knives to these victims' throats, and caught
The fresh warm blood in bowls, Aeneas sacrificed
A black-fleeced lamb to Night, the mother of the Furies,*
And her great sister, Earth, and a barren heifer to Proserpine.
Then he set up altars by night to the god of the Underworld,
Laying upon the flames whole carcases of bulls
And pouring out rich oil over the burning entrails.
But listen!—at the very first crack of dawn, the ground
Underfoot began to mutter, the woody ridges to quake,
And a baying of hounds was heard through the half-light:
    the goddess was coming,
Hecate.*The Sibyl cried:—
                                        Away! Now stand away,
You uninitiated ones, and clear the whole grove!
But you, Aeneas, draw your sword from the scabbard and fare forth!
Now you need all your courage, your steadfastness of heart.
    So much she said and, ecstatic, plunged into the opened cave mouth:
Unshrinking went Aeneas step for step with his guide.
    You gods who rule the kingdom of souls! You soundless shades!

Chaos, and Phlegethon!*O mute wide leagues of Night-
. land!—
Grant me to tell what I have heard! With your assent
May I reveal what lies deep in the gloom of the Underworld!
   Dimly through the shadows and dark solitudes they
     wended,
Through the void domiciles of Dis,* the bodiless regions:
Just as, through fitful moonbeams, under the moon's thin
    light,
A path lies in a forest, when Jove has palled the sky
With gloom, and the night's blackness has bled the world of
    colour.
See! At the very porch and entrance way to Orcus*
Grief and ever-haunting Anxiety make their bed:
Here dwell pallid Diseases, here morose Old Age,
With Fear, ill-prompting Hunger, and squalid Indigence,
Shapes horrible to look at, Death and Agony;
Sleep, too, which is the cousin of Death; and Guilty Joys,
And there, against the threshold, War, the bringer of Death:
Here are the iron cells of the Furies, and lunatic Strife
Whose viperine hair is caught up with a headband soaked in
    blood.
   In the open a huge dark elm tree spreads wide its im-
    memorial
Branches like arms, whereon, according to old wives' tales,
Roost the unsolid Dreams,* clinging everywhere under its
    foliage.
Besides, many varieties of monsters*can be found
Stabled here at the doors—Centaurs and freakish Scyllas,
Briareus with his hundred hands, the Lernaean Hydra
That hisses terribly and the flame-throwing Chimaera,
Gorgons and Harpies, and the ghost of three-bodied Geryon.
Now did Aeneas shake with a spasm of fear, and drawing
His sword, offered its edge against the creatures' onset:
Had not his learned guide assured him they were but in-
    corporeal

Existences floating there, forms with no substance behind
  them,
He'd have attacked them, and wildly winnowed with steel
  mere shadows.
  From here is the road that leads to the dismal waters of
  Acheron.
Here a whirlpool boils with mud and immense swirlings
Of water, spouting up all the slimy sand of Cocytus.
A dreadful ferryman looks after the river crossing,
Charon*: appallingly filthy he is, with a bush of unkempt
White beard upon his chin, with eyes like jets of fire;
And a dirty cloak draggles down, knotted about his shoulders.
He poles the boat, he looks after the sails, he is all the crew
Of that rust-coloured wherry which takes the dead across—
An ancient now, but a god's old age is green and sappy.
This way came fast and streaming up to the bank the whole
  throng:
Matrons and men were there, and there were great-heart
  heroes
Finished with earthly life, boys and unmarried maidens,
Young men laid on the pyre before their parents' eyes;
Multitudinous as the leaves that fall in a forest
At the first frost of autumn, or the birds that out of the deep
  sea
Fly to land in migrant flocks, when the cold of the year
Has sent them overseas in search of a warmer climate.
So they all stood, each begging to be ferried across first,
Their hands stretched out in longing for the shore beyond the
  river.
But the surly ferryman embarks now this, now that group,
While others he keeps away at a distance from the shingle.
Aeneas, being astonished and moved by the great stir, said:—
  Tell me, O Sibyl, what means this mustering at the river?
What purpose have these souls? By what distinction are
  some
Turned back, while other souls sweep over the wan water?

To which the long-lived Sibyl uttered this brief reply:—
O son of Anchises' loins and true-born offspring of heaven,
What you see is the mere of Cocytus, the Stygian marsh*
By whose mystery even the gods, having sworn, are afraid
    to be forsworn.
All this crowd you see are the helpless ones, the unburied:
That ferryman is Charon: the ones he conveys have had
    burial.
None may be taken across from bank to awesome bank of
That harsh-voiced river until his bones are laid to rest.
Otherwise, he must haunt this place for a hundred years
Before he's allowed to revisit the longed-for stream at last.

    The son of Anchises paused and stood stock still, in deep
Meditation, pierced to the heart by pity for their hard
    fortune.
He saw there, sorrowing because deprived of death's fulfil-
    ment,
Leucaspis and Orontes,* the commodore of the Lycian
Squadron, who had gone down, their ship being lost with all
    hands
In a squall, sailing with him the stormy seas from Troy.

    And look! yonder was roaming the helmsman, Palinurus,*
Who, on their recent voyage, while watching the stars, had
    fallen
From the afterdeck, thrown off the ship there in mid-passage.
A sombre form in the deep shadows, Aeneas barely
Recognized him; then accosted:—

                Which of the gods, Palinurus,*
Snatched you away from us and made you drown in the mid-
    sea?
Oh, tell me! For Apollo, whom never before had I found
Untruthful, did delude my mind with this one answer,*
Foretelling that you would make your passage to Italy
Unharmed by sea. Is it thus he fulfils a sacred promise?
    Palinurus replied:—

                The oracle of Phoebus has not tricked you,

My captain, son of Anchises; nor was I drowned by a god.*
It was an accident: I slipped, and the violent shock
Of my fall broke off the tiller to which I was holding firmly
As helmsman, and steering the ship. By the wild seas I swear
That not on my own account was I frightened nearly so
    much as
Lest your ship, thus crippled, its helmsman overboard,
Lose steerage-way and founder amid the mountainous
    waves.
Three stormy nights did the South wind furiously drive me
    along
Over the limitless waters: on the fourth day I just
Caught sight of Italy, being lifted high on a wave crest.
Little by little I swam to the shore. I was all but safe,
When, as I clung to the rough-edge cliff top, my fingers
    crooked
And my soaking garments weighing me down, some bar-
    barous natives
Attacked me with swords, in their ignorance thinking that I
    was a rich prize.
Now the waves have me, the winds keep tossing me up on the
    shore again.
So now, by the sweet light and breath of heaven above
I implore you, and by your father, by your hopes for growing
    Ascanius,
Redeem me from this doom, unconquered one! Please
    sprinkle
Dust on my corpse—you can do it and quickly get back to
    port Velia:*
Or else, if way there is, some way that your heavenly
    mother
Is showing you (not, for sure, without the assent of deity
Would you be going to cross the swampy Stygian stream),
Give poor Palinurus your hand, take me with you across the
    water
So that at least I may rest in the quiet place, in death.

Thus did the phantom speak, and the Sibyl began to speak
    thus:—
This longing of yours, Palinurus, has carried you quite
    away.
Shall you, unburied, view the Styx, the austere river
Of the Infernal gods, or come to its bank unbidden?
Give up this hope that the course of fate can be swerved by
    prayer.
But hear and remember my words, to console you in your
    hard fortune.
I say that the neighbouring peoples, compelled by portents
    from heaven
Occurring in every township, shall expiate your death,
Shall give you burial and offer the solemn dues to your
    grave,
And the place shall keep the name of Palinurus*for ever.

Her sayings eased for a while the anguish of his sad heart;
He forgot his cares in the joy of giving his name to a region.

So they resumed their interrupted journey, and drew near
The river. Now when the ferryman, from out on the Styx,
    espied them
Threading the soundless wood and making fast for the bank,
He hailed them, aggressively shouting at them before they
    could speak:—
Whoever you are that approaches my river, carrying a
    weapon,
Halt there! Keep your distance, and tell me why you are
    come!
This is the land of ghosts, of sleep and somnolent night:
The living are not permitted to use the Stygian ferry.
Not with impunity did I take Hercules,*
When he came, upon this water, nor Theseus, nor Pirithous,
Though their stock was divine and their powers were
    irresistible.
Hercules wished to drag off on a leash the watch-dog of
    Hades,

Even from our monarch's throne, and dragged it away
      trembling:
The others essayed to kidnap our queen from her lord's bed-
      chamber.
   The priestess of Apollo answered him shortly, thus:—
   There is no such duplicity here, so set your mind at rest;
These weapons offer no violence: the huge watch-dog*in his
      kennel
May go on barking for ever and scaring the bloodless dead,
Proserpine keep her uncle's house, unthreatened in chastity.
Trojan Aeneas, renowned for war and a duteous heart,
Comes down to meet his father in the shades of the Under-
      world.
If you are quite unmoved by the spectacle of such great faith,
This you must recognize—
                        And here she disclosed the golden
Bough which was hid in her robe. His angry mood calms
      down.
No more is said. Charon is struck with awe to see
After so long that magic gift, the bough fate-given;
He turns his sombre boat and poles it towards the bank.
Then, displacing the souls who were seated along its benches
And clearing the gangways, to make room for the big frame
      of Aeneas,
He takes him on board. The ramshackle craft creaked under
      his weight*
And let in through its seams great swashes of muddy water.
At last, getting the Sibyl and the hero safe across,
He landed them amidst wan reeds on a dreary mud flat.
   Huge Cerberus,* monstrously couched in a cave confront-
      ing them,
Made the whole region echo with his three-throated bark-
      ing.
The Sibyl, seeing the snakes bristling upon his neck now,
Threw him for bait a cake of honey and wheat infused with
Sedative drugs. The creature, crazy with hunger, opened

Its three mouths, gobbled the bait; then its huge body
    relaxed
And lay, sprawled out on the ground, the whole length of its
    cave kennel.
Aeneas, passing its entrance, the watch-dog neutralized,
Strode rapidly from the bank of that river of no return.

At once were voices heard, a sound of mewling and wailing,
Ghosts of infants*sobbing there at the threshold, infants
From whom a dark day stole their share of delicious life,
Snatched them away from the breast, gave them sour death
    to drink.
Next to them were those condemned to death on a false
    charge.
Yet every place is duly allotted and judgement is given.
Minos,* as president, summons a jury of the dead: he hears
Every charge, examines the record of each; he shakes the
    urn.
Next again are located the sorrowful ones who killed
Themselves, throwing their lives away, not driven by guilt
But because they loathed living: how they would like to be
In the world above now, enduring poverty and hard trials!
God's law forbids: that unlovely fen with its glooming water
Corrals them there, the nine rings of Styx corral them in.
Not far from here can be seen, extending in all directions,
The vale of mourning—such is the name it bears: a region
Where those consumed by the wasting torments of merciless
    love
Haunt the sequestered alleys and myrtle groves that give
    them
Cover; death itself cannot cure them of love's disease.
Here Aeneas descried Phaedra and Procris,* sad
Eriphyle showing the wounds her heartless son once dealt
    her,
Evadne and Pasiphae; with them goes Laodamia;
Here too is Caeneus, once a young man, but next a woman
And now changed back by fate to his original sex.

Amongst them, with her death-wound still bleeding, through
the deep wood
Was straying Phoenician Dido. Now when the Trojan leader
Found himself near her and knew that the form he glimpsed
through the shadows
Was hers—as early in the month one sees, or imagines he
sees,
Through a wrack of cloud the new moon rising and glimmer-
ing—
He shed some tears, and addressed her in tender, loving
tones:—
   Poor, unhappy Dido, so the message was true that came
to me
Saying you'd put an end to your life with the sword and were
dead?
Oh god! was it death I brought you, then? I swear by the
stars,
By the powers above, by whatever is sacred in the Under-
world,
It was not of my own will, Dido, I left your land.
Heaven's commands, which now force me to traverse the
shades,
This sour and derelict region, this pit of darkness, drove me
Imperiously from your side. I did not, could not imagine
My going would ever bring such terrible agony on you.
Don't move away! Oh, let me see you a little longer!
To fly from me, when this is the last word fate allows us!
   Thus did Aeneas speak, trying to soften the wild-eyed,
Passionate-hearted ghost, and brought the tears to his own
eyes.
She would not turn to him; she kept her gaze on the ground,
And her countenance remained as stubborn to his appeal
As if it were carved from recalcitrant flint or a crag of marble.
At last she flung away, hating him still, and vanished
Into the shadowy wood where her first husband, Sychaeus,*
Understands her unhappiness and gives her an equal love.

None the less did Aeneas, hard hit by her piteous fate,
Weep after her from afar, as she went, with tears of com-
    passion.
  Then he passed on the appointed way. They came to the
    last part
Of Limbo, the place set apart for men famous in war.
Here Tydeus*met him, here that warrior of high renown
Parthenopaeus, here the pale spectre of Adrastus;
Then those for whom lamentation had risen on earth—the
    fallen
Fighters of Troy; Aeneas groaned aloud when he saw those
Long ranks of death—Glaucus, Medon, Thersilochus,
The three sons of Antenor, Polyphoetes the priest of Ceres,
Idaeus,*still with the arms he bore, the chariot he drove once.
To right and left the spirits press thickly around Aeneas.
Not enough just to have seen him once—they want to detain
    him,
To pace along beside him and find out why he has come there.
But the Greek generals and the regiments of Agamemnon,
When they beheld his armour glinting through the gloom,
Were seized with fear and trembling; some turned tail,
    even as
In the old days*they had run for their ships; some uttered a
    wraith of
A war cry—they tried to shout, but their wide mouths only
    whimpered.
  Just then Aeneas caught sight of Deiphobus,*his whole body
A mass of wounds, most horribly mangled about the face—
The face and both the hands, head mutilated with ears
Torn off, and the nose lopped—a barbarous disfigurement.
The moment he'd recognized that shrinking creature who
    covered
His ghastly wounds, Aeneas burst out in familiar tones:—
  Deiphobus, great fighter, descended from high-born
    Teucer,
Who was it chose to inflict such atrocious punishment on you?

Who could go to such lengths against you? On Troy's last
  night
I heard a rumour that, worn out with killing and killing
  Greeks,
You had sunk down on a huge indiscriminate heap of dead
  bodies.
Then, myself, I erected by the Rhoetean*shore
A cenotaph for you, and thrice invoked your spirit aloud.
Your name and a trophy mark the spot; yourself I could not
Find to inter in your native soil before I departed.
  The son of Priam replied:—
                        Dear friend, you neglected nothing;
All that was needed you've done for Deiphobus and his shade.
My destiny and the destructive nature of that Lacaenian*
Woman brought me to this: it was she who gave me these
  souvenirs.
You remember how we spent that last night in rejoicings,
In a fools' paradise; too well, no doubt, you remember it.
When the horse of doom had cleared at a bound the battle-
  ments
Of Troy, bearing an armed detachment within its belly,
That woman faked a dance, led the Trojan women around,
Yelling in Bacchanal orgy; under cover of which herself
With a blazing torch in her hand signalled the Greeks from
  our citadel.
I, worn out by our ordeals and leaden with sleep, was lying
In my unlucky bedroom under a coverlet
Of deep, delicious rest, very like the peace of death.
Meantime that nonpareil wife of mine removed all the arms
  from
Our house, yes, even my trusty sword from beneath my
  pillow;
Then called Menelaus inside, opened the door to him,
  hoping—
Vile thing—to make a wonderful present of me to her lover
And thus erase the stigma of her old wicked doings.

No more of this: they burst into the bedroom; Ulysses was
  with them,
Promoter and compère of crimes. Ye gods, may such deeds
  recoil
On the Greeks, if my prayer for revenge is made with a clear
  conscience.
But tell me now in turn, what chance has brought you here
Alive. Were you compelled by your wanderings on the ocean,
Or a command from heaven? Or what fate irks you, that you
  should
Enter this joyless, sunless abode, these vague, vexed regions?
 So they conversed, till Aurora, driving her rosy chariot,
Had passed the midway point of the sky in her flying course;
And indeed they might have used up all the allotted time thus,
Had not his guide, the Sibyl, spoken a few words of warn-
  ing:—
  Night comes apace, Aeneas; yet we spend the hours in
  grieving.
Here is the spot where the way forks, going in two direc-
  tions;
The right-hand leads beneath the battlements of great Dis,
And is our route to Elysium*; the left-hand takes the wicked
To Tartarus, their own place, and punishment condign.
  Deiphobus said:—
        Great Sibyl, do not be angry with me.
I will leave you, return to the shades and make their number
  complete.
Fare on, Aeneas, our pride, and with better luck than mine!
 Thus he spoke, and speaking, turned on his heel and went.
 Aeneas looked back on a sudden: he saw to his left a cliff
Overhanging a spread of battlements, a threefold wall about
  them,
Girdled too by a swift-running stream, a flaming torrent—
Hell's river of fire, whose current rolls clashing rocks along.
In front, an enormous portal, the door-posts columns of
  adamant,

So strong that no mortal violence nor even the heaven-
  dwellers
Could broach it: an iron tower stands sheer and soaring
  above it,
Whereon Tisiphone*sits, wrapped in a bloodstained robe,
Sleeplessly, day-long, night-long, guarding the forecourt
  there.
From within can be heard the sounds of groaning and brutal
  lashing,
Sounds of clanking iron, of chains being dragged along.
Scared by the din, Aeneas halted; he could not move:—
  What kinds of criminals are these? Speak, lady! What
    punishments
Afflict them, that such agonized sounds rise up from there?
  Then the Sibyl began:—
                          O famous lord of the Trojans,
No righteous soul may tread that threshold of the damned:
But, when Hecate appointed me to the Avernian grove,
She instructed me in heaven's punishments, showed me all.
Here Rhadamanthus*rules, and most severe his rule is,
Trying and chastising wrongdoers, forcing confessions
From any who, on earth, went gleefully undetected—
But uselessly, since they have only postponed till death their
  atonement.
At once Tisiphone, the avenger, scourge in hand,
Pounces upon the guilty, lashing them, threatening them
With the angry snakes in her left hand, and calls up her
  bloodthirsty sisters.
Then at last the hinges screech, the infernal gates
Grind open. Do you see the sentry, who she is,
Posted over the forecourt? the shape that guards the thres-
  hold?
Within, there dwells a thing more fierce—the fifty-headed
Hydra,*with all its black throats agape. Then Tartarus
Goes sheer down under the shades, an abyss double in
  depth

The height that Olympus stands above a man gazing sky-
  ward.
Here Earth's primeval offspring, the breed of Titans,* who
Were hurled down by Jove's lightning, writhe in the bottom-
  less pit.
Here have I seen the twin sons of Aloeus,* the gigantic
Creatures who sought to pull down heaven itself with their
  own
Bare hands, and to unseat Jove from his throne above.
Salmoneus* too have I seen undergoing the rigorous sentence
Imposed when he mimicked the thunder and lightning of
  Jove almighty:
Drawn by a four-horse team and shaking a lighted torch,
He would go through Greece exulting, even through the
  middle of Elis
City, claiming the homage due to the gods alone—
Madman, to copy the nonpareil lightning, the thunderstorm
With a rumble of bronze wheels and a clatter of hard-hoofed
  horses!
But the Father almighty, among his serried storm clouds,
  launched
A weapon—no torches, no smoky light of farthing dips
Was this—and hurled the blasphemer down with the wind
  of its passage.
Tityos* too, the nursling of Earth who mothers all,
Was to be seen, his body pegged out over a full nine
Acres, a huge vulture with hooked beak gnawing for ever
His inexhaustible liver, the guts that are rich in torment,
Pecking away for its food, burrowing deep through the body
It lives in, and giving no rest to the always-replenished vitals.
Need I mention the Lapithae, Ixion or Pirithous?*
Over them, always about to fall and looking as if it were
Falling, a black crag hangs:* banqueting couches gleam with
Golden legs, raised high, and feasts of regal opulence
Are set before damned eyes; but the chief of the Furies,
  reclining

Nearby, forbids them to stretch out their hands for the food;
　she leaps up,
Menacing them with her lifted torch, and shouts like thunder.
Here are those who in life hated their own brothers,
Or struck their parents; those who entangled their depen-
　dants
In fraudulent dealing; and those who sat tight on the wealth
　they had won,
Setting none aside for their own kin—most numerous of all
　are these;
Then such as were killed for adultery, took part in militant
　treason,
Men who made bold to break faith with their masters:—all
　such await
Punishment, mewed up here. And seek not to know what
　punishment,
What kind of destined torment awaits each one in the Pit.
Some have to roll huge rocks;*some whirl round, spread-
　eagled
On spokes of wheels: the tragic Theseus*sits, condemned to
Spend eternity in that chair: the poor wretch, Phlegyas,*
Admonishes all, crying out through the mirk in solemn
　avowal,
Be warned by me! Learn justice, and not to belittle the gods!
One sold his country for gold, putting her under the yoke of
Dictatorship, and corruptly made and unmade her laws;
One entered the bed of his daughter, forced an unholy
　mating:
All dared some abominable thing, and what they dared they
　did.
No, not if I had a hundred tongues, a hundred mouths
And a voice of iron, could I describe all the shapes of wicked-
　ness,
Catalogue all the retributions inflicted here.
Thus spoke the long-lived priestess of Phoebus, then added
　this:—

But come, resume your journey, finish the task in hand!
Let us go quickly on. I can see the bastions, forged in
The Cyclops'*furnaces, and the arch of the gateway yonder,
Where we are bidden to put down your passport, the golden
     bough.
     She had spoken. Side by side they went the twilight way,
Rapidly covering the space between, and approached the
     gateway.
Aeneas stopped at the entrance, sprinkled himself with
     holy
Water, and placed the bough right at the doorway there.
     Now this was done at last, and Proserpine had her offer-
     ing,
They went on into the Happy Place, the green and genial
Glades where the fortunate live, the home of the blessed
     spirits.
What largesse of bright air, clothing the vales in dazzling
Light, is here! This land has a sun and stars of its own.
Some exercise upon the grassy playing-fields
Or wrestle on the yellow sands in rivalry of sport;
Some foot the rhythmic dances and chant poems aloud.
Orpheus,* the Thracian bard, is there in his long robe,
To accompany their measures upon the seven-stringed lyre
Which he plucks, now with his fingers, now with an ivory
     plectrum.
Here is the ancient line of Teucer, a breed most handsome,
Great-hearted heroes born in the happier days of old,
Ilus, Assaracus, and Dardanus,* founder of Troy.
From afar Aeneas marvelled at the arms, the phantom
     chariots.
Spears stood fixed in the ground, everywhere over the plain
Grazed the unharnessed horses. The pleasure those heroes
     had felt,
When alive, in their arms and chariots, the care they had
     taken to pasture
Their sleek horses—all was the same beyond the tomb.

Aeneas noticed others to left and right on the greensward
Feasting and singing a jovial paean in unison
Amidst a fragrant grove of bay trees, whence the river
Eridanus*springs, to roll grandly through woods of the world
    above.
Here were assembled those who had suffered wounds in
    defence of
Their country; those who had lived pure lives as priests; and
    poets
Who had not disgraced Apollo, poets of true integrity;
Men who civilized life by the skills they discovered, and men
    whose
Kindness to other people has kept their memory green—
All these upon their temples wore headbands white as snow.
Now the Sibyl addressed the company dotted about there,
And specially Musaeus,* for round him a large group
Gazing up at him as he towered head and shoulders above
    them:—
   Tell me, you blessed spirits, and you, most honoured poet,
Whereabouts can we find Anchises? We have come here,
Crossing the great rivers of the Underworld, to see him.
   So did Musaeus make reply with these few words:—
   None of us has a fixed abode: we dwell in shady
Groves, we make our beds on river-banks, reside in
Watersweet meadows. But if your heart's desire is such,
Then climb this rise and I'll set your feet on an easy path.
   He spoke, and leading the way, showed them the luminous
    plains
Extending below them. Now they went down from the
    uplands.
   Deep in a green valley stood father Anchises, surveying
The spirits there confined before they went up to the light of
The world above: he was musing seriously, and reviewing
His folk's full tally, it happened, the line of his loved children,
Their destinies and fortunes, their characters and their deeds.
Now, when he saw Aeneas coming in his direction

Over the grass, he stretched out both hands, all eagerness,
And tears poured down his cheeks, and the words were
tumbling out:—
So you have come at last? The love that your father relied
on
Has won through the hard journey? And I may gaze, my
son,
Upon your face, and exchange the old homely talk with you?
Thus indeed I surmised it would be, believed it must happen,
Counting the days till you came: I was not deceived in my
hopes, then.
Over what lands, what wide, wide seas you have made your
journey!
What dangers have beset you! And now you are here with me.
How I dreaded lest you should come to some harm at
Carthage!*
Aeneas replied:—
                    Your image it was, your troubled phantom
That, often rising before me, has brought me to this place.
Our ships are riding at anchor in the Tyrrhene sea. Oh, let me
Take your hand and embrace you, father! Let me! Withdraw
not!
Even as he spoke, his cheeks grew wet with a flood of tears.
Three times he tried to put his arms round his father's neck,
Three times the phantom slipped his vain embrace—it was
like
Grasping a wisp of wind or the wings of a fleeting dream.
Now did Aeneas descry, deep in a valley retiring,
A wood, a secluded copse whose branches soughed in the
wind,
And Lethe*river drifting past the tranquil places.
Hereabouts were flitting a multitude without number,
Just as, amid the meadows on a fine summer day,
The bees alight on flowers of every hue, and brim the
Shining lilies, and all the lea is humming with them.
Aeneas, moved by the sudden sight, asked in his ignorance

What it might mean, what was that river over there
And all that crowd of people swarming along its banks.
Then his father, Anchises, said:—
                  They are souls who are destined for
Reincarnation; and now at Lethe's stream they are drinking
The waters that quench man's troubles, the deep draught of
    oblivion.
Long, long have I wanted to tell you of these and reveal them
Before your eyes, to count them over, the seed of my seed,
That you might the more rejoice with me in the finding of
    Italy.
  But, father, must it be deemed that some souls ascend
    from here
To our earthly scene? re-enter our dull corporeal existence?
Why ever should so perverse a craving for earth possess
    them?
  I will tell you, my son, certainly; I will not keep you in
    doubt,
Answered Anchises, and then enlarged on each point suc-
    cessively:—
  First, you must know that the heavens, the earth, the
    watery plains
Of the sea, the moon's bright globe, the sun and the stars
    are all
Sustained by a spirit within; for immanent Mind,* flowing
Through all its parts and leavening its mass, makes the uni-
    verse work.
This union produced mankind, the beasts, the birds of the
    air,
And the strange creatures that live under the sea's smooth
    face.
The life-force of those seeds is fire, their source celestial,
But they are deadened and dimmed by the sinful bodies they
    live in—
The flesh that is laden with death, the anatomy of clay:
Whence these souls of ours feel fear, desire, grief, joy,

But encased in their blind, dark prison discern not the
    heaven-light above.
Yes, not even when the last flicker of life has left us,
Does evil, or the ills that flesh is heir to, quite
Relinquish our souls; it must be that many a taint grows
    deeply,
Mysteriously grained in their being from long contact with
    the body.
Therefore the dead are disciplined in purgatory, and pay
The penalty of old evil: some hang, stretched to the blast of
Vacuum winds; for others, the stain of sin is washed
Away in a vast whirlpool or cauterized with fire.
Each of us finds in the next world his own level: a few of us
Are later released to wander at will through broad Elysium,
The Happy Fields; until, in the fullness of time, the ages
Have purged that ingrown stain, and nothing is left but pure
Ethereal sentience and the spirit's essential flame.
All these souls, when they have finished their thousand-year
    cycle,
God sends for, and they come in crowds to the river of Lethe,
So that, you see, with memory washed out, they may revisit
The earth above and begin to wish to be born again.

    When Anchises had finished, he drew his son and the Sibyl
Into the thick of the murmuring concourse assembled there
And took his stand on an eminence from which he could scan
    the long files
Over against him, and mark the features of those who passed.
    Listen, for I will show you your destiny, setting forth
The fame that from now shall attend the seed of Dardanus,
The posterity that awaits you from an Italian marriage—
Illustrious souls, one day to inherit our Trojan name.
That young man there—do you see him?—who leans on an
    untipped spear,
Has been allotted the next passage to life, and first of
All these will ascend to earth, with Italian blood in his
    veins;

He is Silvius,* an Alban name, and destined to be your last
    child,
The child of your late old age by a wife, Lavinia, who shall
Bear him in sylvan surroundings, a king and the father of
    kings
Through whom our lineage shall rule in Alba Longa.
Next to him stands Procas, a glory to the Trojan line;
Then Capys and Numitor, and one who'll revive your own
    name—
Silvius Aeneas,* outstanding alike for moral rectitude
And prowess in war, if ever he comes to the Alban throne.
What fine young men they are! Look at their stalwart bearing,
The oak leaves that shade their brows—decorations for
    saving life!
These shall found your Nomentum, Gabii and Fidenae,*
These shall rear on the hills Collatia's citadel,
Pometii, and the Fort of Inuus, Bola and Cora—
All nameless sites at present, but then they shall have these
    names.
Further, a child of Mars shall go to join his grandsire—
Romulus,* born of the stock of Assaracus by his mother,
Ilia. Look at the twin plumes upon his helmet's crest,
Mars' cognizance, which marks him out for the world of
    earth!
His are the auguries, my son, whereby great Rome
Shall rule to the ends of the earth, shall aspire to the highest
    achievement,
Shall ring the seven hills with a wall to make one city,
Blessed in her breed of men: as Cybele,* wearing her turreted
Crown, is charioted round the Phrygian cities, proud of
Her brood of gods, embracing a hundred of her children's
    children—
Heaven-dwellers all, all tenants of the realm above.
Now bend your gaze this way, look at that people there!
They are *your* Romans. Caesar is there and all Ascanius'
Posterity, who shall pass beneath the arch of day.

And here, here is the man, the promised one you know of—
Caesar Augustus, son of a god, destined to rule
Where Saturn*ruled of old in Latium, and there
Bring back the age of gold: his empire shall expand
Past Garamants*and Indians to a land beyond the zodiac
And the sun's yearly path, where Atlas the sky-bearer pivots
The wheeling heavens, embossed with fiery stars, on his
    shoulder.
Even now the Caspian realm, the Crimean country
Tremble at oracles of the gods predicting his advent,
And the seven mouths of the Nile are in a sweat of fear.
Not even Hercules*roved so far and wide over earth,
Although he shot the bronze-footed deer, brought peace to
    the woods of
Erymanthus, subdued Lerna with the terror of his bow;
Nor Bacchus,* triumphantly driving his team with vines for
    reins,
His team of tigers down from Mount Nysa, travelled so far.
Do we still hesitate, then, to enlarge our courage by action?
Shrink from occupying the territory of Ausonia?*
Who is that in the distance, bearing the hallows, crowned
    with
A wreath of olive? I recognize—grey hair and hoary chin—
That Roman king*who, called to high power from humble
    Cures,
A town in a poor area, shall found our system of law
And thus refound our city. The successor of Numa, destined
To shake our land out of its indolence, stirring men up to
    fight
Who have grown unadventurous and lost the habit of victory,
Is Tullus. After him shall reign the too boastful Ancus,
Already over-fond of the breath of popular favour.
Would you see the Tarquin kings, and arrogant as they,
    Brutus*
The avenger, with the symbols of civic freedom he won back?
He shall be first to receive consular rank and its power of

Life and death: when his sons awake the dormant conflict,
Their father, a tragic figure, shall call them to pay the extreme
Penalty, for fair freedom's sake. However posterity
Look on that deed, patriotism shall prevail and love of
Honour. See over there the Decii, the Drusi, Torquatus
With merciless axe, Camillus with the standards he recovered.*
See those twin souls,* resplendent in duplicate armour: now
They're of one mind, and shall be as long as the Underworld holds them;
But oh, if ever they reach the world above, what warfare,
What battles and what carnage will they create between them—
Caesar descending from Alpine strongholds, the fort of Monoecus,
His son-in-law Pompey lined up with an Eastern army against him.
Lads, do not harden yourselves to face such terrible wars!
Turn not your country's hand against your country's heart!
You, be the first to renounce it, my son of heavenly lineage;*
You be the first to bury the hatchet! . . .
That one shall ride*in triumph to the lofty Capitol,
The conqueror of Corinth, renowned for the Greeks he has slain.
That one shall wipe out Argos and Agamemnon's Mycenae,
Destroying an heir of Aeacus,* the seed of warrior Achilles,
Avenging his Trojan sires and the sacrilege*done to Minerva.
Who could leave unnoticed the glorious Cato, Cossus,
The family of the Gracchi, the two Scipios—thunderbolts
In war and death to Libya; Fabricius, who had plenty
In poverty; Serranus, sowing his furrowed fields?*
Fabii, where do you lead my lagging steps? O Fabius,*
The greatest, you the preserver of Rome by delaying tactics!
Let others* fashion from bronze more lifelike, breathing images—
For so they shall—and evoke living faces from marble;

Others excel as orators, others track with their instruments
The planets circling in heaven and predict when stars will
    appear.
But, Romans, never forget that government is your medium!
Be this your art:—to practise men in the habit of peace,*
Generosity to the conquered, and firmness against aggressors.
    They marvelled at Anchises' words, and he went on:—
    Look how Marcellus*comes all glorious with the highest
Of trophies, a victor over-topping all other men!
He shall buttress the Roman cause when a great war shakes it,
Shatter the Carthaginian and rebel Gaul with his cavalry,
Give to Quirinus the third set of arms won in single combat.
    Aeneas interposed, seeing beside Marcellus
A youth of fine appearance,* in glittering accoutrements,
But his face was far from cheerful and downcast were his
    eyes:—
    Father, who is he that walks with Marcellus there?
His son? Or one of the noble line of his children's children?
How the retinue murmurs around him! How fine is the young
    man's presence!
Yet is his head haloed by sombre shade of night.
    Then father Anchises began, tears welling up in his eyes:—
    My son, do not probe into the sorrows of your kin.
Fate shall allow the earth one glimpse of this young man—
One glimpse, no more. Too puissant had been Rome's stock,
    ye gods,
In your sight, had such gifts been granted it to keep.
What lamentations of men shall the Campus Martius*echo
To Mars' great city! O Tiber, what obsequies you shall see
One day as you glide past the new-built mausoleum!
No lad of the Trojan line shall with such hopeful promise
Exalt his Latin forebears, nor shall the land of Romulus
Ever again be so proud of one she has given birth to.
Alas for the sense of duty, the old-time honour! Alas for
The hand unvanquished in war! Him would no foe have met
In battle and not rued it, whether he charged on foot

Or drove his lathering steed with spurs against the enemy.
Alas, poor youth! If only you could escape your harsh fate!
Marcellus you shall be. Give me armfuls of lilies
That I may scatter their shining blooms and shower these
  gifts
At least upon the dear soul, all to no purpose though
Such kindness be.
                          So far and wide, surveying all,
They wandered through that region, those broad and hazy
  plains.
After Anchises had shown his son over the whole place
And fired his heart with passion for the great things to come,
He told the hero of wars he would have to fight one day,
Told of the Laurentines*and the city of Latinus,
And how to evade, or endure, each crisis upon his way.
  There are two gates of Sleep*: the one is made of horn,
They say, and affords the outlet for genuine apparitions:
The other's a gate of brightly-shining ivory; this way
The Shades send up to earth false dreams that impose upon us.
Talking, then, of such matters, Anchises escorted his son
And the Sibyl as far as the ivory gate and sent them through it.
Aeneas made his way back to the ships and his friends with
  all speed,
Then coasted along direct to the harbour of Caieta.
Bow-anchors out, the ships are lining the shore with their
  sterns.

BOOK VII

Caieta*too, who was nurse to Aeneas, when she died
Gave Italy's coast undying fame: for even now
The place where she rests is preserved by her legend, she has
    an epitaph
In a place-name of great Hesperia—no small glory.
When the ever-faithful Aeneas has paid her the last rites
And heaped a burial mound above her, the deep sea now
Being calm, he weighed from harbour and set course under
    sail.
The wind blew steadily on into the night, a bright moon
Favoured their voyage, its radiance dancing upon the water.
Soon they were skirting close by the shore of Circe's*land
Where that luxurious daughter of the Sun, her song for ever
Thrilling through spell-protected groves, in her proud palace
Burns fragrant cedarwood during the night to see by,
While the rattling shuttle runs through the gossamer warp.
From this place could be heard through the small hours the
    groaning
Roars of angry lions resentful at their captivity;
Bristly boars and bears were heard from the enclosures
Furiously raging, and wolf-like creatures howling—
Men they had once been, but the terrible goddess had turned
    them
Into beast faces, things on all fours, with her magic herbs.
So, lest the god-fearing Trojans touched at that fiendish
    coast,
And putting in there, suffered the same weird transformation,
Neptune, filling their sails with a wind from the right quarter,
Got them away and past the surf that boils inshore.
   Now was the sea's face blushing with dawn rays, and in
       heaven

Rosily charioted shone crocus-yellow Aurora,
When the wind dropped—all of a sudden not one breath
Was blowing—and the oars toiled in water slow as syrup.
Now, looking forth from the deep, Aeneas sighted a big wood:
Through this wood the genial stream of Tiber*flowing,
Yellow with racing eddies that stir up sand galore,
Debouches into the sea. Around and above, bright-plumaged
Birds whose habitat is the river banks and channel
Charmed the air with their song, flitted about the wood.
Aeneas ordered his squadron to change course towards the
     land.
Soon in high spirits he entered the shady mouth of the river.
  Come, Muse of Love,* let me rehearse the kings, the
     phase of
History, and the conditions that reigned in antique Latium
When first that expedition arrived upon the beaches
Of Italy: I'll recall what first led to the war there.
Speak through me, then, Spirit of Song! Grim wars I'll
     tell of,
And battlefronts, and princes courageous unto death,
The levies of the Etruscans, aye, all Hesperia mustered
In arms. A grander train of events is now before me,
A grander theme I open. An old man now, Latinus*
Was king of the towns and country, his reign being long and
     peaceful.
He was the son, we are told, of Faunus*and the Laurentian
Nymph, Marica: Faunus was son of Picus, who called
Saturn his father—yes, Saturn originated their line.
Latinus, by fate's decree, had no son now; his male
Succession was no more, cut off in the bloom of first youth.
One daughter he had, sole prop of his house and heir of his
     ample
Estate, a girl fully budded now and ripe for marriage.
Many sought her hand, from all over Latium, from all
Italy: the handsomest by far of these wooers was Turnus*—
He had the prestige of a splendid pedigree and the backing

Of the queen, who had set her heart on getting him as a son-
    in-law:
But various alarming portents from heaven were proving an
    obstacle.
There grew in the central court of the palace a laurel tree,
Its leafage holy and held in reverence for many years,
Which king Latinus was said to have found there, when he
    first
Established the city, and dedicated the tree to Phoebus,
Using its name to christen his colonists the Laurentes.*
A strange thing happened now: a tight-packed swarm of bees
Came loudly humming through the limpid air, and settling
Upon the top of that tree, they interlocked their feet;
Next moment a swarm was hanging down from the green
    bough.
At once the soothsayer cried:—
                        I see a stranger coming.
Men are coming from where the bees came—coming to settle
Where the bees have settled, this fortress their seat of empire.
    Apart from this, while the maiden Lavinia stood beside
Her father, who with ritual taper was lighting the altar—
Sinister thing—they beheld her long hair set on fire
And all her head-dress burning with crackling flames; they
    saw
Those queenly tresses ablaze, ablaze her coronet
Of precious stones: before long, enshrouded in golden-
    glowering
Smoky flame, she was fountaining sparks all over the palace.
It was counted, of course, as a dreadful, miraculous mani-
    festation:
The maiden herself, they foretold, was singled out for a
    famous
Destiny, but for the people it meant a widespread war.
    The king, greatly disturbed by this portent, goes to visit
The oracle of Faunus, his prophet father, and questions
The grove where Albunea*towers over the forest, resounding

With hallowed cascade and darkly exhaling a deadly vapour.
Here the Italian tribes, all the Oenotrians, go for
Advice in times of perplexity: hither the priestess brings
The offerings, and couched at dead of night on the fleeces
Of the sheep sacrificed there, she woos slumber; and then
Visions appear to her, shapes are floating strangely about
    her,
And in her ears are many voices—she is conversing
With deity, addressing the powers of the nether regions.
This was where Latinus now went to consult the oracle;
After the ritual sacrifice of a hundred wool-bearing sheep
He lay down and reclined upon the hides, the outspread
Fleeces: and at once from the depths of the wood a voice
    came:—
    Seek not, my son, to marry your daughter to a man of
The Latin race. Embark not upon a native alliance.
From abroad shall sons-in-law come, to wed our women and
    make
Our name illustrious: to their descendants the whole
Spinning globe shall be a footstool and an empire—
All that the sun looks down on, even to the ends of the earth.
    The oracle of his father, Faunus, the counsel given
Thus in the stilly night, Latinus kept not secret;
But rumour had already flown it far and wide
Throughout the towns of Ausonia, when the Trojan expedi-
    tion
Lay with their vessels moored to the grassy bank of the Tiber.
    Aeneas, his lieutenants and fair Ascanius
Sat themselves down beneath the boughs of a tall tree
To have a meal. Now it happened—Juppiter prompted the
    action—
They laid the viands on flat cakes of meal about the grass,
Using those cereal mats to heap the fruits of the earth on.
Well, when they'd eaten all the rest, being still hungry,
It befell that they turned their attention to the slender cakes
    of meal:

With hands and teeth they were broaching incontinent those
    round cakes
(Symbol of destiny) and devouring their broad sections,
When 'Goodness, we're eating our tables*too!' Ascanius cried
Joking. Just that. But that was enough; for his words pro-
    claimed
The beginning of the end of their trials: as such, his father at
    once
Seized upon them, and struck by their god-sent meaning,
    would have no more said,
But cried himself on the instant:—

                  O promised land of my destiny,
All hail! And all hail to you, ye gods of Troy, for you spoke
    truth!
Here is our home, this is our country. I recall now
My father Anchises*bequeathed me this secret of fate, saying,
When you are come to a strange shore and compelled by
    hunger,
Food running short, to devour your tables, that is the time
To look for a home in your weariness, that is the place—mark
    well—
To choose a site and begin to work hard on a fortified settle-
    ment.
This was the hunger he spoke of, this the last ordeal awaiting
    us,
Putting a term to our deadly perils.
Come therefore, at sunrise in high heart let us spread out all
    ways
From the harbour, let us explore the interior and investigate
What manner of men live here and where their cities are
    sited.
Now offer libations from bowls to Juppiter, offer a prayer to
My father Anchises, and set forth a good supply of wine.
    After these words Aeneas, twining about his temples
A leafy bough, invoked the genius of the place, and Earth,
First of deities; called on the Nymphs and the still unknown

Rivers; then called on Night and the rising Stars of Night,
Juppiter, patron of Ida,* the Phrygian Mother next;
Called on his parents, one in heaven, one in the Underworld.
Now from a clear sky did the Father almighty thunder
Three times, and his own hand showed forth a cloud from
    heaven,
A cloud that blazed and quivered with dartings of golden
    light.
A rumour spread like magic among the rank and file,
That the day had come at last to found their promised city.
Exhilarated by so splendid an omen, they eagerly
Started the feast again, set wine and crowned the bowl.
  When the next day had dawned and its early beams were
    lighting
The earth, they went out in parties to reconnoitre the land,
Its city, shores and frontiers. Here, they found, was the
    pool of
Numicius'*spring, here Tiber, here dwelt the stalwart Latins.
Then did Aeneas send out to the stately town of the king
A hundred ambassadors, chosen from every rank in his
    company,
Garlanded all with olive branches,* Athene's emblem,
Bidden to take the king presents and to ask peace for the
    Trojans.
At once they set off on their mission, hastening towards the
    palace.
Aeneas himself traced out the walls with a shallow trench,
And breaking the ground, threw up a rampart and battle-
    ments as for
A military encampment, round his first home there on the
    coast.
Now, their journey accomplished, his emissaries drew near
The walls and could see the towers and high roofs of the
    Latins.
In front of the town were boys, and youths in their first
    flower, practising

Horsemanship and training chariot teams on the campus,
Or bending the lively bow, or the tough javelin hurling
Strenuously, and challenging one another at running or
     boxing.
Just then a rider brought to the ears of the long-lived king
A message that some mighty men, in unfamiliar
Livery, had arrived. He orders them to be summoned
To the great hall, and awaits them there on the throne of his
     fathers.
A stately hall there was on the city's heights, a huge place
Of a hundred soaring columns, the palace once of Laurentian
Picus: it stood in a grove dark with ancestral dread.
Here, to have fortunate reigns, their kings must be crowned
     and display first
The symbols of office: this temple was senate house and
     scene of
Religious banquets alike; here, when a ram had been sacri-
     ficed,
Elders were used to sit down at the long, refectory tables.
Here too, in a row, were standing the statues of their fore-
     fathers,
Carved from old cedarwood—Italus*; father Sabinus,
The planter of vines, with a pruning-knife held in his carven
     hand;
Ancient Saturn, and Janus*facing-both-ways—all stood
Near to the entrance, with other kings from the earliest days
And heroes who had suffered wounds in defence of their
     country.
Numerous trophies, too, were displayed on the sacred
     portals—
Chariots captured in war, battle-axes with curving blades,
Helmet crests, huge bars from the gates of ransacked cities,
Javelins and shields, and beaks removed from warships.
There, holding the augur's staff,*arrayed in a short toga
Purple-striped, the holy shield on his left arm, sat
Picus,*tamer of horses: vainly lusting to bed with him,

Golden Circe had used her wand and her magic potions,
And turned him into a bird, into a pied woodpecker.
Such was the holy shrine, the ancestral hall within which
Latinus sat enthroned and summoned the Trojans to him.
When they had entered his presence, he began, and peace-
    ably spoke:—
  Trojans—oh yes, your city and line are not unknown to us,
We'd heard of you before you sailed this way—pray tell me
What you would have. What motive, what need has brought
    your ships
So many leagues of blue sea to these Ausonian*shores?
Did you mistake your course, or were you driven off it
By gales—for such things often happen to men on the high
    seas—
That you have sailed into the estuary and lie at anchor?
Anyway, feel you are welcome; and know that we, the Latins,
Are children of Saturn, depend on no penal system for equity,
Keeping from wrong of our own free will in the time-
    honoured, golden
Rule of that god. I indeed remember, though time has
    dimmed
The legend, Auruncan elders telling how Dardanus
Was born here, and hence migrated to the towns of Phrygian
    Ida
And into Thracian Samos, which men call Samothrace*now.
His beginnings were here, in the Tuscan home of Corythus*:
    now
He has his throne in the golden palace of the star-glistering
Heavens, and adds one more to the altars of the gods.
  Latinus had spoken: Ilioneus then made reply as follows:—
  O king, illustrious son of Faunus, no black storm,
No heavy seas it was that drove us to your country,
Nor did we err in our course through misreading the stars or
    the landmarks.
By common consent, of our own volition, have we come to
Your city, being cast out from our empire, once the greatest

The sun could see as it travelled from the very east of the sky.
Jove was the first of our line: the Dardan people boasts of
Jove as their ancestor: our king, Trojan Aeneas,
Who sent us to you, was born of the most high stock of Jove.
How terrible a storm, unleashed from cruel Mycenae,*
Burst over the plains of Ida; how destiny compelled
A war between East and West, the collision of Europe and
    Asia:—
All have heard this: it is known in remotest lands where
    Ocean
Breaks on the earth's rim, known where the tyrant sun
    cuts off
From us the dwellers in tropical countries about the equator.
That storm swept Troy away. We voyaged on sea after sea:
Now we but ask a small, inoffensive plot for our home-gods
Here on the coast, with water and air that are free to all men.
We shall not disgrace your kingdom; to receive us will bring
    you great honour
Amongst mankind and win undying gratitude from us;
Ausonia will never regret having taken Troy to her bosom.
By the destiny of Aeneas I swear it, and his strong right arm
Trusty alike in friendship or war to whoever has tried it,
Many the peoples, the nations have willingly sought for
    alliance
And union with us; so do not look down on us because now
It is we who make the petition and offer the olive branch.
At heaven's express command, fate's bidding, we sought out
Your land. From here Dardanus took his origin: hither
Apollo recalls us, strictly enjoining that we come back
To Tuscan Tiber and the sacred pools of Numicius' spring.
Aeneas offers you, too, these gifts—small tokens of
Our old prosperity, relics we saved from burning Troy:
A chalice of gold which his father, Anchises, used for liba-
    tions;
And these, Priam's regalia when he gave laws in the old
    way

To his assembled peoples—a sceptre, a royal diadem,
And vestments wrought by the ladies of Ilium.
   Latinus received this speech of Ilioneus with a gaze
Steadily fixed on the ground; he remained motionless, thinking
Hard, his eyes restive. It was not so much that the royal purple-
Embroidered robe and the sceptre of Priam influenced the king,
As that his mind was absorbed by the thought of his daughter's marriage
And deeply pondering the oracle Faunus had given him.
This, he reflected, must be the man from abroad who is meant
By the fates to become my son-in-law and to be partner in
My sovereignty: from him shall stem that future breed,
Excelling in courage, whose might is to master the whole world.
At last, much elated, he said:—
                      May the gods forward our project
And fulfil their revelation! You shall have what you ask for, Trojan.
Nor do I slight these presents. As long as I'm king, you shall not
Be lacking in fertile land, and Troy as of old shall be prosperous.
Let but Aeneas come here in person; if such is his need
For us, if he's eager to join us in amity and be called
Our ally, he must not be shy of meeting friends face to face.
For me, a part of the bargain it is to shake hands with your sovereign.
Do you take back, in reply, this commission of mine to Aeneas.
I have a daughter, whom neither my sire's most arcane oracle
Nor heaven's will, expressed in many portents, permits to marry

A man of her own people: rather, they presage, for Latium
Is destined a prince consort from overseas, and his blood shall
Exalt our name to the skies. I believe it's Aeneas that fate
    means,
And if there's any truth in my intuition, accept him.

   Thus spoke the king; and then chose out from the three
    hundred
Beautifully-groomed horses which stood in his lofty stables.
For each of the envoys, there and then, he bade to be brought
A courser caparisoned in crimson-embroidered trappings:
Their chests were hung with parures of gold, and gold-
    embroidered
Their housings were, and red-gold the bits they champed in
    their mouths.
To the absent Aeneas he sent a chariot and two horses
Of pedigree divine, breathing fire from their nostrils;
They came of that mixed breed which the sorceress, Circe*,
    had raised
To her father, the Sun, when she stole his stallions and put
    them to a mare.
Now, with these words and gifts from Latinus, did the Trojan
Envoys return, proudly mounted, bearers of peace.

   But look! from Argos, city of Inachus,* now returning
And well on her way through the sky, the vindictive consort
    of Juppiter
Saw from the air above Pachynus*in Sicily,
At a great distance, Aeneas triumphant, his fleet all there.
She notes they have disembarked from their ships and are
    busily building
Habitations already, feeling quite safe in that land.
Bitter resentment checked her. Shaking her head, she burst
    out:—

   Ah, those obnoxious Trojans, whose destiny so conflicts
    with
The destinies of my peoples! Could they perish on Ilium's
    plains?

Be kept in captivity when they'd been captured? be burnt to
    ashes

In blazing Troy? Not they! Through fire and steel they
    found

A way of escape. I think my deity must be spent

And supine, or else my rancour is sleeping from sheer satiety.

Yet, when they'd been hurled out of their country, I was not
    slow to

Persecute them in their exile and oppose every stage of their
    voyage.

Against the Trojans I spent all the might of sea and sky.*

What use to me were the Syrtes, Scylla, engulfing Charyb-
    dis?

The Trojans are snug in Tiber's channel, their hoped-for
    haven,

Snapping their fingers at ocean and me. Yet Mars had the
    power to

Destroy the giant brood of the Lapithae; Jove himself

Gave over to the wrath of Diana time-honoured Calydon.*

What had the Lapithae done, or Calydon, to deserve it?

Yet I, the great consort of Jove, who have left nothing un-
    tried,

Who have stooped to every expedient against him, am a
    failure—

Beaten by Aeneas. Well, if my powers are not great enough,

I shall not hesitate—that's sure—to ask help wherever

Help may be found. If the gods above are no use to me,
    then I'll

Move all hell. From his Latin kingship I may not bar him;

The fates are firm that he shall marry Lavinia: so be it.

What I can do is to postpone these great events, to delay
    them,

And to wreak havoc upon the peoples of both the kings.

They shall pay with their lieges' lives the price for becoming
    related;

And you, Lavinia—Italian and Trojan blood shall be your

Marriage portion, and War your bridesmaid. Not only Hecuba*
Shall have conceived a firebrand, brought forth a fire-raising bridegroom:
No, Venus' son is the same—a second Paris, whose wedding-
Taper shall be a funeral torch to resurgent Troy.

  When she had spoken, Juno came down to earth, horrific,
And haled forth from the infernal regions, the home of the terrible
Deities, Allecto,* maker of grief, who revels
In war, in open and underhand violence, in damaging quarrels.
Even her father, Pluto, and her hellish sisters loathe
That fiend, Allecto, so manifold her aspects and so ferocious
Each form she takes, such a nest of vipers swarms in her black hair.
Now Juno began to speak, whetting this creature's appetite:—
  Maiden, daughter of Night, do me this favour—it's your kind—
This service, so that our honour and reputation may not be
Diminished, so that the Trojans fail to wheedle Latinus
By means of this marriage or to take possession of Italy.
You can set brothers of one mind at one another's throats,
Torment a home with hatred, bringing your whips and destructive
Firebrands to lash the house: you have a thousand titles,
A thousand tricks for making mischief. Stir up your teeming
Ideas! Disrupt the peace they have made! Sow seeds of war!
Let them wish for weapons, demand them and use them, all in an instant.

  At once Allecto went, steeped in her viperish venom,
And sought out first the high walls of the Laurentine monarch*
In Latium. There she pickets Amata's quiet threshold—
The queen, whose motherly heart is seething with grief and chagrin

Over the Trojans' coming and the marriage with Turnus
    cancelled.
On her the fiend now casts a serpent, one of her snake-blue
Tresses, and thrusts it into her bosom, deep into her heart,
So that the queen may discharge through the household its
    maniac infection.
Gliding between her dress and her smooth breasts, that
    serpent
Coils—she feels not its touch nor notices it in her mad-
    ness—
Breathing its morbid breath into her: swelling, it turns
Into a golden necklace, into the head-dress binding
Her hair, and its pendant ribbon, and slithers over her body.
Now, while that moist and magic contagion was but beginning
To work upon her mind and twine her bones with fire,
The queen, whose thoughts were not yet wholly possessed
    by the flame in
Her breast, quite gently spoke, as soft-hearted mothers do,
Greatly distressed by the thought of her daughter wedding
    a Trojan:—
    Father, must our Lavinia be wed to a Trojan, an outcast?
Have you no feeling for her? no sense of your own interests?
No pity for her mother?—that false-hearted pirate will
    leave me
As soon as a fair wind blows, and sail away with my daughter.
It's Paris all over again—just so did Paris steal into
Sparta, then carried Ledaean Helen away to Troy.
What of your solemn pledge? the love you had in the old
    days
For your own people? the promise given so often to Turnus,
Your kinsman? If it is settled our son-in-law must be
Of foreign extraction—if thus your father, Faunus, enjoins
    you—
I say that any land which is separate from ours and auto-
    nomous
Is in fact foreign, and this was what the oracle meant.

Now Turnus, if we go back to the origin of his family,
Is Mycenaean, descended from Inachus and Acrisius.

   But when she saw these arguments had no effect on Latinus
And he was firmly opposed; when the serpent's frenzying
      poison
Had worked its way into her marrow and spread all over her
      being;
Then, overwrought by monstrous hallucinations, the poor
      queen
Went uncontrollably raving, beside herself, round the city.
Just so it is that a top goes spinning under the whip lash—
A top that boys, absorbed in their play, whip round an empty
Court in a great circle: driven by the lash, it moves
Round and round, gyrating: puzzled, in childish amazement
The boys hang over it there and gape at the top's revolutions,
Livelier at every blow. So fast and furious the queen was
Driven right through the city among the inflammable popu-
      lace.
What's more, pretending to hear the call of Bacchus (a
      greater
Evil this, and launched her forth on a wilder madness),
She flew to the woods, hid her daughter among the forested
      hills,
To cheat of his bride the Trojan, or at least delay the marriage.
Hail, Bacchus! she shrieked: you alone are worthy of the
      maid,
She kept shouting; for you she takes up the soft-leafed
      thryrsus, and you
She follows in the dance, and to you is vowed the tress she is
      growing!
The rumour flew fast: a mass hysteria swept the housewives,
A burning compulsion to go and find new dwellings some-
      where.
They have left their homes, they are baring neck and hair to
      the breeze;
Some of them fill the air with whimpering cries, dress up in

Fawn-skins, and carry staves all twined about with vine-
  shoots.
Amongst them, holding aloft a blazing torch, the hectic
Queen is chanting a marriage song for her daughter and
  Turnus:
Her bloodshot eyes are rolling: harshly all of a sudden
She cries:—
      Mothers of Latium, listen, wherever you are!
Do you feel in your duteous hearts any kindness for poor
  Amata?
Does any care for a mother's rights still prick your con-
  science?
Then loose your hair from the headband and join the revels
  with me!
  So with the scourge of Bacchus Allecto, who was every-
  where
Among the trees, in the wild-beast coverts, chivvied the
  queen.
  When it was clear that the queen's first injection of madness
  was strong enough,
And that Latinus' purpose and household were thoroughly
  shaken,
The louring Allecto mounted at once on her sombre wings
And made for the walls of hot-headed Turnus—the city
  which men say
Danaë*founded and colonized with her Acrisians, when she
Was driven that way by the South wind. Our ancestors called
  the place
Ardea; though it retains the great name of Ardea still,
Its best days are far behind it. Here, in the lofty palace,
Turnus was taking his rest at the mid-hour of night.
Allecto now sloughed off her grim looks and diabolical
Form, changing herself to the likeness of an old crone,
Uncannily furrowing her brow with wrinkles; she assumed
White hair and a headband, wreathed her head with a chaplet
  of olive:

So, as the aged priestess of Juno's temple, Calybe,
Coming before the young man's eyes, she spoke as follows:—
    Turnus, will you tolerate that all your efforts should run
To waste, the dominion you've worked for pass into the
        hands of foreigners?
The king denies you your bride and the marriage-portion
        you've bought with
Bloodshed: an alien now is called in to be his successor.
Go then, you laughing-stock, face dangers, mow down the
        Tuscans,*
Ensure peace for the Latins!—this is the thanks you get.
Indeed, almighty Juno appeared in person and bade me
Speak to you even thus, while you lay in the quiet of night.
Up, then! Take heart of grace! Mobilize the army! March
Out of the gates to war! Those Trojan ships and leaders
That occupy our beautiful river—burn them to ashes!
These are orders from the heavenly powers. Let king
        Latinus,
Unless he agree to stand by his word and allow your mar-
        riage,
Suffer for it, and discover what Turnus is like as an enemy.
    Here the young man in his turn began to speak, deriding
Her prophecy:—
                    I am not, as you seem to think, unaware that
A fleet has sailed into the Tiber; the news did come to my
        ears.
Do not be such an alarmist, I beg you. Queen Juno is not
Indifferent to me and mine.
As for you, mother—it's old age, clogging the mind and
        impairing its
Sense of reality, that haunts you with bogey-man worries,
And scares your prophetic soul with delusions of civil war.
Your job's to look after the temple and the images of the
        gods:
Leave making of war and peace to men, whose business is
        warfare.

These words of Turnus made Allecto explode into anger.
As the young prince still spoke, a sudden palsy shook him,
And his eyes went stiff with fear; for the Fury, hissing-snake-
    tressed,
Was hideously revealed at her full height. She rolled
Her flaming eyes, she flung him back as he tried to falter
A few more words; two snakes stood up like horns on her
    head,
And she cracked her whip, and spoke again, her mouth like
    a mad dog's:—
    So! My mind is clogged? Old age, impairing my sense of
Reality, scares me with delusions of civil war?
Look at me, then! I am come from the place where the Furies
    are.
War and death I bear in this hand.
So saying, she hurled an incendiary brand at Turnus, which
    buried
Itself deep in his heart, blazing and pitchily smoking.
Extreme terror awoke him from sleep; a sweat broke out
All over the young man's body, soaked him from head to
    foot.
Madly yelling for arms, by his bed, through his house he
    hunts for them;
Crazy with bloodlust he is, with the criminal mania for fight-
    ing,
Still more, with resentment. So, when a fire of wood, loud
    crackling,
Is stoked up high beneath the belly of a boiling cauldron,
The water dances in the heat; within the cauldron the water
Seethes and fumes, bubbling, spitting up foam, till it cannot
Contain itself any more and a cloud of dense steam rises.
Breaking the peace, then, Turnus ordered his army com-
    manders
To get on a war footing and march against king Latinus:
Italy must be protected, the foe thrown back from its
    frontiers;

He would be more than a match for Trojans and Latins
    together.
So Turnus proclaimed, and called the gods to witness his
    vow.
The Rutuli*spur one another on to war with enthusiasm,
Some being stirred by the youthful, handsome presence of
    Turnus,
Some by his royal lineage, some by his notable deeds.
    While Turnus inspired his people with the spirit of aggres-
    sion,
Allecto sped to the Trojans upon her hellish wings,
Hatching a new scheme, spying out the place where hand-
    some
Ascanius, with snares and hounds, was hunting near the sea-
    shore.
Here, the devilish hag cast a sudden frenzy upon
Those hounds, touching their nostrils with a familiar scent,
So that they ran in full cry after a stag: the beginning
Of trouble this was, for it kindled to war the hearts of the
    countryfolk.
There was a stag, a most noble creature, with high-branched
    antlers,
Which had been taken away from its mother, when young,
    and kept
As a pet by the boys of Tyrrheus and Tyrrheus himself, the
    warden
Of the royal herds, who had charge of the pastures through-
    out the kingdom.
Silvia, the boys' sister, had taught the beast to obey her,
Looked after it, used to adorn it with soft-leafed garlands
    wreathed
About its antlers, and groom it, and bathe it in fresh spring
    water.
The stag was meek to her touch and trained to its master's
    table:
It used to rove the woods; but at night, however late it was,

Always could find its own way home to the well-known door.
This creature the hot-foot hounds of Ascanius now started
While it was far from home—by turns, so it happened, float-
    ing
Down a river and cooling itself on the verdurous bank.
Ascanius, too, was immensely keen to get so glorious
A prize. He bent his bow and shot an arrow. Luck
Was with him, his aim was true. The shaft streaked from the
    bowstring,
Viciously whirring, to pierce the stag through flank and belly.
Wounded, the animal ran*to hide in the well-known home-
    stead,
Crept sobbing into its stall there, covered with blood, and
    filled
The place with pathetic cries like some beseeching creature.
Silvia, the sister, striking her arms in grief, was the first
To call for help, and her call brought the tough countrymen
    round her.
They—for that virulent Fury lurked in the quiet woods—
Were with her quicker than thought, brandishing fire-
    hardened stakes
Or bludgeons of knotty wood; whatever came first to hand
As they angrily groped for a weapon, served them as such.
    Now Tyrrheus,
Panting with rage, snatched up an axe—just then, so it
    happened,
He was splitting an oak into four with wedges—and mustered
    his men.
From aloft the fell Fury could see that this was the moment
    for mischief:
She flew to the steep-pitched roof of the shippon, and perch-
    ing upon it
Blew the rustic alarum, a blast on a crooked horn,
With the full force of her demon lungs; the sound rang on,
Shaking the woods to their roots, through the deep forest
    baying:

The lake of Diana*heard it afar, the Nar heard it—

That sallow, sulphurous river, the springs of Velinus
heard it;

Terrified mothers clutched their babies to their breasts.

Then, ah then, how swift to answer the summoning call

Of that sinister horn, snatching up their arms, the hardy
countrymen

Gathered from far and wide. The warriors of Troy at the
same time

Poured through the gates of their camp and hurried to help
Ascanius.

The two sides face each other. This is no village brawl now

To be fought out with rugged shillelaghs and fire-toughened
stakes:

With steel, with two-edged steel they join issue; all over the
field

Darkly bristles a crop of drawn swords; their bronze accoutre-
ments

Fling the sun's challenge back, send flashes of light up-
wards.

So, in a rising wind, white horses begin to appear

On the sea's face; then little by little the sea gets rougher,

The waves steeper, until the sea is all mountains and valleys.

Now in the front rank Almo, he who had been the eldest

Of Tyrrheus' sons, was laid low, hit by a whirring arrow:

Deep in his throat was the wound; the arrow stuck there and
choked

With blood the fluent passageway of the voice, the frail life.

Around him were many corpses, old Galaesus amongst
them,

Most upright of men and the biggest landowner once in
Ausonia,

Killed while trying to mediate between the combatants:

Five flocks of bleating sheep he had owned, five herds of
cattle

He pastured, and a hundred ploughs worked on his land.

While they fought over the plain there, with neither side
   prevailing,
Allecto, her promise fulfilled now she had given the war
Its baptism of blood and opened its first encounter with kill-
   ings,
Took leave of Hesperia; wheeling up and away through the
   airs of
Heaven, she addressed queen Juno in tones of insolent
   triumph:—
   See, discord has been brought to fruition in stern war!
Try telling them to be friends and to make a pact of peace
Now that I've splashed the Trojans with blood of Ausonian
   men!
This too will I add to my feats, if I am assured of your
   backing—
I'll drag the neighbouring peoples into the war by spread-
   ing
Rumours, and kindle their passions with the mad lust for
   battle,
So that they all come in and the whole country's at war.
Juno replied:—
               We have plenty enough of alarm and aggression.
The reason for war is established; already they're fighting
   bitterly.
An accident started the quarrel, but bloodshed now has con-
   firmed it.
Let that so wonderful son of Venus, let king Latinus
Celebrate thus the marriage they have arranged between
   them!
The Father, supreme lord of Olympus, would not be pleased*
To find you trespassing too freely here on high.
Away, then! Whatever else may befall in this conflict, I
Myself will deal with it.
                    Thus the daughter of Saturn spoke.
And Allecto, the Fury, spreading her wings that hissed with
   serpents,

Made for her home in the Underworld, leaving the height of
    heaven.
There is a place in the heart of Italy, under the mountains,
A well-known spot whose fame is told of in many countries—
The Vale of Amsanctus.* On either side, steep, wooded slopes
Darken this vale with dense foliage, and down its middle
A watercourse rumbles, eddying and clucking among the
    rocks.
Here can be seen an awesome cave and the vents of the dread-
    ful
Underworld; a great chasm formed by the upthrust of
    Acheron
Yawns, emitting a plague-breath: into it now disappeared
The hateful Fury, relieving earth and sky of her presence.
But the royal daughter of Saturn was still giving the war
Its finishing touches. The shepherds all broke from the field
    of battle
And hurried into the city, bearing their dead with them—
Young Almo and Galaesus, who was horribly disfigured.
There they supplicated the gods and appealed to Latinus.
Turnus was present, amid their angry complaints at the
    bloodshed
Redoubling his threats. The Trojans are called in to rule us,
    he shouted;
Our blood's to be mingled with Phrygian; I am debarred
    from the palace.
Next they whose womenfolk, possessed by Bacchus, were
    roving
The trackless woods in their coven (great too was Amata's
    influence)
Gathered together and clamoured importunately for war.
Accursed war they will have, at once, flying in the face of
Omens and oracles, impelled by a power malign.
A belligerent mob surrounds the palace of Latinus:
He like a sea-cliff stands, resistant, inexpugnable;
Like a sea-cliff that, when a comber comes crashing against it,

Stands in its massive bulk unmoved, with the wave-pack
    yelping
Below it; about the reefs and the foaming rocks the sea howls
Impotent; seaweed is dashed on its flanks, flung streaming
    back again.
But when he saw he had no power to quell their purblind
Demand and all was going merciless Juno's way,
Latinus made many appeals to the gods, to the deaf, blind
    heavens:—
  Oh! We are pounded by doom, adrift at the storm's mercy!
It is you, poor souls, who will pay in your own blood for this
    sacrilege.
Yours is the guilt, Turnus; punishment most severe is
In store for you: too late shall you turn to the gods with
    prayer.
My rest is assured; I am right at the mouth of the haven, with
    nothing
To lose but a peaceful death.
                              Latinus said no more,
But shutting himself in his palace, relinquished the reins of
    government.
  There was a custom of old in Latium, religiously
Kept up by the Alban townships, and now a tradition
    observed by
Rome, mistress of empire, when first she prepares for battle,
Whether she goes to make war, with all its tears, on the Getae,
The Arabs or the Hyrcanians, or to march further east
Against the Indians, or get back her standards from the
    Parthians.
There are twin gates of War*—that is their name; the religion
And terrible indwelling presence of Mars have sanctified
    them.
A hundred bronzen bolts and bars of durable iron
Secure them: Janus keeps his perpetual watch by the en-
    trance.
When the Senate has made a final decision for war,

The Consul, grand in Quirinal robe*caught up with the
    Gabine
Cincture, himself opens these gates on their grinding
    hinges,
In person proclaims war; the soldiers take up his cry
And the bronze trumpets blare together in hoarse accord.
After this manner Latinus was now told to declare
War on Aeneas' people and open the joyless gates.
But the good old king would not touch them: turning away
    in revulsion
From such a shocking duty, he buried himself from sight.
Then did the queen of heaven glide down, and with her own
    hand
Roughly push open those resisting doors, dash wide
Upon their turning hinges the iron gates of war.
Indifferent before and lethargic, Ausonia now caught fire.
Some ready themselves to march as infantry; others are
    mounted
On tall steeds and kick up a galloping dust: all clamour to
    fight.
What burnishing now of shields and javelin points with rich
    fat
Until they shine again! What whetting of battle-axes!
Their hearts are stirred to hear the trumpets and troop the
    colours.
Five great towns establish workshops for the production
Of new armaments—powerful Atina, haughty Tibur,
Ardea, Crustumerium, and turreted Antemnae.*
Here they are fashioning helms to protect the head, manu-
    facturing
Wicker frames for shields, hammering out bronze breast-
    plates,
And working polished leg-guards from malleable silver.
To this has come their pride in share and sickle, to this
The plough's prestige. In the furnace they temper their
    father's swords again.

Now the trumpets sound; the word goes out for war.
One man hurriedly takes his helmet from store; another
Yokes his neighing horses, slips on the shield, the cuirass
Of triple-meshed gold chainmail, and straps his trusty sword
    on.
  Muses, throw Helicon*wide now! Inspire me to tell the
    tale,
To sing of the chieftains aroused to war, the ranks that
    followed
Each chieftain, packing the plains, the manhood that even in
    those days
Our bountiful Italy bloomed with, the martial array that
    blazed there!
For you are divine, you remember it all, you can recount it—
All that for me has become the faint whisper of antique story.
  The first to arm his men and enter the war was Mezentius,*
A Tuscan exile, a man embittered and irreligious.
Beside him marched his son, Lausus,* who far excelled
All others in personal beauty except for Laurentine Turnus.
Lausus, the tamer of steeds, the mighty hunter, was leading
A thousand men from the town of Agylla—an enterprise
Doomed to disaster. Well he deserved to live under a better
Régime and to have a better father than Mezentius.
  After these came the handsome son of handsome Hercules,
Aventinus:* on the greensward he showed off his prize-
    winning horses
And chariot bearing the victor's palm; he wore on his shield
His father's blazon—the snake-clad Hydra,* and a hundred
    serpents.
Him upon the woody Aventine hill a priestess,
Rhea, brought privily forth to the light of day, when she
A mortal had lain with a demigod, the champion from
    Tiryns, Hercules,
Who, after killing Geryon,* came to the Laurentine land
And dipped his Iberian cattle in the waters of Tuscany's
    Tiber.

His men bore javelins and stabbing-spears into battle,
For they fought with the tapering spearhead and the short
   Sabine blade.
Aventinus himself, on foot, swathed in a great big
Lion-skin, shaggy and terribly bristling its hair, the white
   fangs
Grinning above his head, entered the royal palace
Like that, all hairy, the garment of Hercules over his shoulders.

   Next, twin brothers marched from the walled city of Tibur*
Where lived a people named after their brother, Tiburtus—
Catillus and mettlesome Coras they were, warriors born in
Argos, and moving now in the van where the fire is hottest:
Even as when two Centaurs, born of the clouds, descend
From some high mountain-top, galloping rapidly down from
Homole or snow-capped Othrys,* and the great forest yields to
Their passage as they career and crash through the under-
   growth.

   Caeculus* too was there, the founder of Praeneste,
The king who men throughout the ages have believed
Was son of Vulcan, born among flocks and herds, and found
On the hearth. A yeoman regiment came straggling on behind
   him—
Warriors who dwelt in high Praeneste, or the Gabine district
Where Juno is worshipped, or by the cold Anio, or in the
   stony
Hernican brooklands; men whom fertile Anagnia reared
Or the river Amasenus. Not all of them had armour,
Shields or clattering chariots: most of them used slings
With bullets of light-grey lead, while some carried a pair of
Javelins: they wore brown-coloured caps of wolf-skin
As covering for their heads; the left foot, taking the weight of
The slinger's stance, was naked, the right being shod with
   rawhide.

   Messapus,* tamer of horses, the seed of Neptune—he
Whom no man might lay low with fire or steel—now calling
All of a sudden to arms his tribes that had long been torpid

And lost the habit of fighting, took up the sword again.
They lived on Fescennae's jagged skyline, at Falerii
The just, in the fields of Flavinium, or the hill-country of
    Soracte,
By the lake and mountain of Ciminus, in the woodland of
    Capena.
Evenly dressed they marched, singing their chieftain's glory:
So it is when snow-white swans come winging away
From their feeding ground through a whey of cloud, their
    necks strain forward
Uttering rhythmic cries, and the watermeads of Caÿster*
Sound and resound.
No one would ever have thought it a multitude all made up
Of armoured files, but rather a cloud of birds overhead
Driving to land from over the deepsea with husky cries.

   See next how Clausus comes, of the old pure Sabine blood,
Leading a mighty host, and he a host in himself—
Clausus from whom are descended the Claudian clan*and
    family,
Widespread in Latium now since Rome was shared with the
    Sabines.
With him, a big Amitérnian detachment, and men from
    historic
Cures, and all from Eretum and olive-growing Mutusca;
Citizens of Nomentum, dwellers in the Rosean district
Around Velinum, in craggy Tetrica, Mount Severus,
Casperia, Foruli, and by the river Himella;
Those who drink from Tiber and Fabaris, those whom frigid
Nursia sent, with Ortine hordes and tribes of Latium;
Men whom the flood of Allia*(ill-omened name!) sequesters:
In multitude like the waves that sweep the Libyan sea
When raging Orion sinks down below the wintry waters,
Thick as the ears of corn that bake in the orient sunshine
Over the plain of Hermus*or the yellow prairies of Lycia*
Shields clang, and the earth trembles with men marching in
    step.

Next, Agamemnon's son, Halaesus,* who hated every-
    thing
Trojan, harnessed his chariot team and brought to Turnus
Post-haste a thousand warlike clans—hoers of the wine-rich
Massic country, men whom their fathers had sent from the
    hills
Of Aurunca, men who had come from the nearby Sidicine
    plains,
Men who hailed from Cales, men who lived by the shallow
Volturnus river; and with them, Oscan levies and warlike
Saticulans. Their weapons were missiles with rounded
    handles
Which they were used to throw with whippy thongs attached:
A targe protected their left side; a scimitar was carried for
    close work.
    Then Oebalus must not go unhonoured and unsung—
Oebalus whom, it is said, Telon begat on the nymph
Sebethis, when he was king of Teleboean Capreae,
Advanced now in years. But his son, not content with his
    father's frontiers,
Even at this time held sway, further afield, over
Sarrastian tribes and the plains which the river Sarnus
    irrigates,
Over the dwellers in Rufrae, Batulum, rural Celemna,
And the dwellers below the town of apple-growing Abella,*
Whose practice it was to hurl boomerangs, Celtic-fashion:
Their head-pieces were made of bark stripped from the cork
    tree;
Their light shields plated with bronze glittered, their bronze
    swords glittered.
    The mountainy district of Nursae*sent forth to the war
    Ufens,
Who had a high reputation as a successful fighter:
His clan, the Aequi, living on a thin soil and hardened
By constant hunting over the woodlands, excelled in tough-
    ness.

Armed to the teeth they are when they till the ground, and
    they never
Tire of carrying off new plunder, living on loot.

   Again, from the Marruvian*tribe there came a priest,
His helmet adorned with a favour of fruitful olive leaf,
Sent by his chieftain, Archippus: this hero's name was
    Umbro:
He had a remarkable talent for hypnotizing by spell
And touch the serpent kind, all evilly-breathing snakes;
He was able to charm their anger and cure their bites with his
    skill.
But his art was powerless to heal the wound he got from a
    Trojan
Spearpoint; neither his soporific spells nor the simples
He'd gathered on Marsian hills availed him when he was
    wounded.
The grove of Angitia wept him; Fucinus, glassy-watered,
All limpid lakes lamented him.

   The son of Hippolytus, too, most beautiful, went to the
    wars—
Virbius,* a fine young man, sent by his mother, Aricia,
Who'd brought him up near the shore of the lake in Egeria's
    wood
Where stands an altar to Diana, rich and reverenced.
The legend is that Hippolytus, after he'd been laid low
By his stepmother's plotting and, torn to bits by bolting
    horses,
Had slaked with blood his father's vengeance, rose to the
    starry
Firmament and breathed the air of heaven, brought back
To life by Diana's love and the herbs of Aesculapius.*
But then the Father almighty, wroth that a mortal being
Should rise to light and life from the shades of underground,
Hurled down to hell with a levin-stroke from his hand this
    son
Of Phoebus, who had discovered so potent an art of healing.

But Diana was kind and hid Hippolytus in a secret
Place, removing him to the grove of the nymph Egeria,*
Where he should live out his days a solitary unknown
In Italian woods, having changed his name and become
 Virbius.
Wherefore to this day horses are not allowed near Diana's
Temple or sacred wood, because horses, scared by a sea
 beast,
Had spilt Hippolytus once and his chariot on the shore.
His son, for all that, was now driving fiery horses
Upon the level plain and racing to war in a chariot.
  Turnus himself, of magnificent build, bearing his weapons
Moved amongst the leaders, a head higher than they.
Upon his triple-crested, tall helmet a Chimaera*
Was rampant, breathing out volcanic fire from its jaws;
The bloodier waxed the battle, the more did that creature
 appear to
Roar and rage, to go berserk and shoot forth glowering
 flames.
But on his polished shield was blazoned in gold the image
Of Io,* now changed to a heifer, with horns uplifted, and
 rough-haired—
A potent symbol; also her guardian, Argus, and Inachus
Her father, pouring out his stream from a graven pitcher.
At Turnus' heels there followed a cloud of infantry, packing
The plain with their armoured columns—Argive warriors
 marching,
Auruncan levies, Rutuli, old-established Sicani,
Sacranian files and the painted bucklers of the Labicans;
Men who ploughed Tiber's vales, and the sacred coastland
 about the
Numicius; men who worked with the plough the Rutulian
 hills
And the promontory of Circe; men from the parts round
 Anxur
Where Jove is patron, men from the greenwoods of Feronia,

The fenlands dark of Satura, and the deep combes where
  Ufens
Cold-running winds its way down and plunges into the sea.
  Beside all these there came from the Volscian nation
    Camilla*
Leading a cavalry column, squadrons petalled with bronze:
A warrior maid, her woman's hand unaccustomed to
    womanly
Tasks—to the distaff, the basket of wool; a girl, but hardy
To face the horrors of battle and to catch up with the winds.
She could have skimmed along the blades of an unmown
    corn-crop
Without so much as bruising their tender ears as she ran:
She could have flitted over the waves of a swelling sea
Without so much as wetting the quicksilver soles of her feet.
From field and cottage the young came running, the house-
    wives gathered
To stare at this Camilla and marvel as she went by,
Gaping, struck with amazement to see how nobly sat
The cloak of royal crimson on her smooth shoulders—see
The gold clasp in her hair, the Lycian quiver she carried
And the spear-shaft of country myrtle with its warhead.

BOOK VIII

When Turnus hoisted the ensign of war from the Laurentine*
Citadel, and the trumpets blared out their husky calls;
When Turnus lashed his mettlesome horses and clashed his
    weapons,
Instantly men were excited: the alarm brought about a
    feverish
Uprising and leaguing-together in Latium: war hysteria
Gripped the youth. Now first their commanders, Messapus
    and Ufens
And the god-mocker, Mezentius, combed the country all
    round
For troops, so that the fields were stripped of labourers every-
    where.
Next was Venulus sent to the city of great Diomedes*
To ask his aid and tell him that Trojans had planted them-
    selves
In Latium, Aeneas had come with a fleet, bringing in Troy's
    vanquished
Home-gods, claiming that destiny demanded he should be
    king there;
Many tribes, what's more, were joining the cause of the
    Dardan
Hero, whose reputation was spreading all over the country:
What purpose lay behind this undertaking, or what
Aeneas hoped would result from a war, if fortune blessed him,
Would be clearer to Diomed than it was to Latinus or
    Turnus.
    So things went in Latium. Aeneas, seed of Laomedon,
Seeing them so, was much agitated by surging worries,
His mind in feverish conflict, tossed from one side to the
    other,

Twisting and turning all ways to find a way past his dilemma;
As when, in a bronze basin, the quivering water reflects
A sunbeam or the round of the radiant moon, a light
Goes glancing hither and thither, now shooting up from the
     water
And jigging upon the fretted ceiling over your head.
It was night, and throughout the earth deep slumber lay
     upon
All weary creatures, lay on bird and beast alike.
Bedded upon the river-bank under the chilly vault
Of heaven, his heart much exercised by sombre thoughts
About war, Aeneas at last yielded himself to sleep.
Before his face there appeared now, rising amidst the leaves of
The poplars out of that pleasant river, its deity, old
Tiberinus*: a veil of grey and gauzy stuff was draped
About him, a coronal of reeds shadowed his brow.
He spoke to Aeneas, relieving his troubled heart like this:—
     O prince of divine lineage, who out of the enemy's clutches
Bring Troy town back to us,* preserving it for all time;
O long-awaited in the Laurentine land, in Latium,
Here your appointed home is, the resting place for your gods.
Do not give up, or be frightened by threats of war. The
     swelling
Anger of heaven has abated.
Even now, lest you think all this but a baseless fiction of sleep,
You shall find lying beneath the oaks on the river-bank
A great white sow,* with a litter of thirty new-born piglets
White as she, clustered at the teats of their sprawling mother.
Here is the site for your city, sure terminus of your travails.
And this is the sign that, when thirty years roll by, Ascanius
Shall found the white town, Alba,* the city of shining name.
I prophesy certainties. Now pay heed while I tell you briefly
How you may best unravel the urgent problem before you.
Arcadians, a people descended from Pallas,* followers now
Of king Evander in peace and war, having chosen a site
Within this country, have built a township on the hills

And named it Pallanteum after their ancestor, Pallas.
This people wages war persistently with the Latins:
Make a treaty with them, and get them onto your side.
I for my part will conduct you straight up my waterway
That, rowing against the current, you may achieve a passage.
Rise up then, goddess-born, and with the waning stars
Make solemn prayer to Juno, avert her menacing wrath
By vows and supplication. To me you may do honour
When you're successful. I, whom you see with ample stream
Lipping these banks and flowing through these rich farm-
      lands—I am
Caerulean Tiber, the river most beloved by the gods.
Here's my broad home; my source emerges among tall cities.

      Thus the River-god spoke, then sank out of sight deep into
His watery home. Aeneas awoke from night and dreaming,
Rose up, beheld the light of the orient sun in the sky,
Held out in solemn oblation his hands which cupped some
      water
Scooped from the stream, and uttered these heartfelt words
      to heaven:—
   Nymphs, Laurentine nymphs, you fountain-heads of
      rivers,
And you, O father Tiber, you and your hallowed stream,
Bless Aeneas, keep him from harm at this long last!
Wherever the secret springs of your being, and wherever
You issue forth in majesty, since you have shown compassion
For my hard trials, you shall be always graced with homage
And offerings from me, horned River,* king of Italian waters.
Only be with me, confirm your revelation directly!

      Such were Aeneas' words: then he chose a couple of galleys
Out of his fleet, manned them and issued the crews weapons.

      But look!—a prodigy startling, amazing for them to view—
Among the trees there, shining, the same white hue as her
      litter,
Sprawled on the verdant bank, for all to behold, a sow.
To Juno, mightiest Juno, god-fearing Aeneas then

Led mother and young to stand at the altar, and sacrificed
them.
All that night the Tiber smoothed down its popply stream
And the current beneath its quietened surface came to a
standstill,
So that the face of the waters was flat as a gentle pool
Or a calm mere, and rowing cost no strenuous effort.
So with the river helping they sped on the trip they had
started.
The well-tarred ships glide on; waters and woods admire
A spectacle new to them—shields of warriors shining
Afar down the river and painted hulls floating upon it.
All night and the following day the Trojans rowed without
respite,
Up the long loops of the river, under the shade of diverse
Trees, through the green reflection of woods in the glass-
calm water.
The blazing sun had climbed to the midway of heaven
When they saw in the distance walls, a citadel, and a few
Scattered roofs: Rome's dominion* has since exalted that
place
To the skies; but then Evander was lord of a meagre
realm.
Quickly the Trojans steered to the bank and approached the
settlement.
  It happened that day the Arcadian king was holding a
festival
Honouring Hercules, heir of Amphitryon,* and the gods
In a grove outside the city. With him his son, Pallas,
The younger notables all and the plain-living senators
Burnt incense, while the warm blood of victims steamed at the
altars.
Now when they saw the tall ships come gliding up amid
The trees, through the wood's dim vistas, and the oars
quietly moving,
Alarmed by so unexpected a sight, they started up from

The banquet as one man. But Pallas, undaunted, forbade
 them
To leave the rites unfinished; seizing a weapon, he hurried
Towards the Trojans and hailed them from a vantage-point
 at a distance:—
 Strangers, whither away, taking a route so strange to you?
Who are you? Where do you come from? Do you bring peace
 or war?
 Then, where he stood high up on the poop, Aeneas
 answered,
Holding out in his hand an olive branch, emblem of peace:—
 We are sons of Troy that you see here, and no friends to the
 Latins
Who have driven us out of their land by a cynical act of
 aggression.
We're looking for king Evander. Tell him a deputation
Of Trojan leaders has come to plead for his alliance.
 Pallas, struck with awe by so famous a name, called out:—
 Come ashore, whoever you are, sir. Come, and talk to my
 father
Yourself. Do us the honour of being a guest in our house.
 He extended a welcoming hand and clasped Aeneas' right
 hand.
Leaving the river-bank they went forward into the wood.
Before long, Aeneas was making a friendly speech to the
 king:—
 Best of the sons of Greece, it is fortune's will that to you
I should come for a favour, extending the formal olive branch.
I do so without misgivings, although you are an Arcadian,
A leader of Greeks, and related by blood to the twin Atridae.*
My own merit, the sacred oracles of the gods,
The kinship between our fathers, your own far-reaching
 fame
Have bound me to you, and I follow the bidding of fate most
 gladly.
Dardanus,* the progenitor and founder of Ilium's city,

Born, as the Greeks maintain, of Electra, daughter of Atlas,
Sailed to our Teucrian land: yes, Electra's father was mighty
Atlas, who holds aloft on his shoulders the heavenly firma-
    ment.
Now Mercury is your father—Mercury whom fair Maia
Conceived and bore upon the snowy peak of Cyllene.
But Maia, if we believe at all the tales we have heard,
Was begotten by Atlas, the Atlas who props the starry sky.
So both of our families stem from the same original source.
Relying on this, I launched no professional-diplomatic
Overtures, to make a compact with you: I have come
In person to ask your aid and have put my life in your hands.
We are bitterly menaced in war by that same Daunian people*
Which persecutes you: they believe they have only to drive
    us out
And nothing will stop them from subjugating the whole of
    Hesperia
And getting control of the Adriatic and Tuscan seaboards.
Let us exchange guarantees. My men are stout-hearted
    fighters,
And their morale is high; as soldiers, their deeds speak for
    them.
    Thus spoke Aeneas. The king for some time had been
    watching intently
His face and eyes, scrutinizing the whole man while he talked.
Now he replied briefly:—
                    Most glad am I, bravest of Trojans,
To welcome and get to know you. How vividly you remind
    me
Of your great father Anchises in speech, in accent and
    feature!
For I remember how Priam, Laomedon's son, when he
    travelled
To visit his sister Hesione's kingdom,* *en route* for Salamis,
Came on from there and crossed the borders of cold Arcadia.
I was a young man then, in the first flush of youth:

I used to hero-worship your Trojan chiefs and their prince,
The son of Laomedon; but taller than any, strode
Anchises. I recollect in boyish enthusiasm
Longing to speak to the hero and shake him by the hand.
I went up to him, eagerly brought him into the city of
      Pheneus.*
He gave me, when he left, a very fine quiver containing
Lycian arrows,* a gold-embroidered scarf, and a pair of
Golden bridles which now are owned by my son, Pallas.
And so, the hand you ask for in friendship—here, it is yours!
Tomorrow, as soon as the earth grows light, I will send you
      away
With an escort to gladden your heart, and will aid you from
      my resources.
Meantime, this annual feast which we cannot rightly defer—
Since you have come here as friends, do us the kindness of
      sharing it
With us, begin straight away to get used to the board of your
      comrades.
    So saying, he has the dishes and wine cups put back, which
      had been
Removed, and himself arranges the Trojans on grassy seats,
Inviting Aeneas, as guest of honour, to take his place on
A maple chair which is draped with the shaggy pelt of a lion.
Then picked young men and the priest of the altar, promptly
      attentive,
Bring on the roast meat of bulls, and baskets loaded high with
Cereal food expertly prepared, and serve the wine.
Aeneas and his Trojan comrades all are feeding
On a whole chine of beef, and the meat left from the sacrifice.
    Hunger being satisfied, the desire for eating checked now,
King Evander began:—
                              These solemn ceremonies,
This ritual feast, this altar hallowed by deity were not
Imposed on us by some fanciful heresy regardless
Of older gods. We keep up these rites, Aeneas, in honour

Of one who saved us from cruel danger and well deserves
   them.
Look at that scarp up there, that overhanging rock face!
See the wide scatter of boulders! How desolate stands the
   mountain
Abode, with the crags that have toppled down, gigantic
   debris!
Once a cavern was there, deeply recessed in the hill-side,
Impervious to the sun's rays: its occupant was a half-human,
Horrible creature, Cacus; its floor was for ever warm with
New-spilt blood, and nailed to its insolent doors you could
   see
Men's heads hung up, their faces pallid, ghastly, decaying.
This ogre was the son of Vulcan; as he moved
In titan bulk, he breathed out his father's deadly flame.
But to us too, in our longing that help would some day come,
Time brought deliverance, aid divine. For the great avenger
Hercules came, in the glory of having slain and despoiled
Triform Geryon; victorious, he drove this way
His great bulls, and his herds were thronged by our marshy
   river.
Cacus, beside himself with lunatic greed, so that nothing
Crooked or criminal should remain undared, unattempted,
Rustled four bulls of surpassing build out of the steadings,
And with them as many heifers, very fine creatures. These,
To ensure that they left no tracks pointing the way they had
   gone,
He dragged by their tails backwards into his cave, reversing
The trail, and hid his plunder deep in the sunless rock there.
A searcher would find no clues leading him to the cave.
Well, when the time had come for Hercules to move on
His herds from the pasturage they had cropped down, as he
   was going,
His oxen plaintively mooed at leaving the place, our hills
And woods all rang with the lowings of the departing herd.
Just then one of the heifers, corralled within that desolate

Cavern, bellowed in answer, betraying Cacus' plot.
Then, bitterly galled, the son of Alcides*erupted in furious
Anger: seizing his weapons, his heavily-knotted club,
He made hot-foot for the top of that mountain, right up there.
Then. did our folk for the first time see Cacus thoroughly
    frightened,
With panic in his eyes: he was off in a flash and running
Towards his cave like the wind; fear gave wings to his feet.
Now he had shut himself in there by breaking the iron chains,
His father's handiwork, which held a huge rock poised,
So that it fell, blocking and reinforcing the entrance
Like a portcullis: next moment Hercules, wild with rage,
Was there, looking this way and that to find a possible way in,
Grinding his teeth. Three times all over Mount Aventine
He scoured in furious anger; three times he vainly went for
That rock barricade; three times sank down in the valley,
    exhausted.
There stood a tapering needle of flint, sheer upon all sides,
Which soared up out of the cave's roof, dizzily high to
    view—
A convenient place for carrion birds to lodge their nests in.
This pinnacle leaned from the ridge at an angle over the
    stream
To its left: Hercules threw his whole weight against its right
    side,
Shook it, wrenching it loose from its deep-rooted base; then
    suddenly
Pushed: at that push a crack like thunder rang through the
    wide sky,
The river-banks leapt apart, the river recoiled in terror.
But the den of Cacus, his whole great castle, unroofed, was
    now
Visible, the dark cavern revealed to its inmost depths.
It was as if the earth, violently fissured and yawning
Right to its depths, should uncover the regions of hell, the
    spectral

Domain unloved by the gods, and you could peer into the
    abyss
From above and see the ghosts there flinch at the gush of day-
    light.
As Cacus, caught in his rocky chamber, startled and shocked
By the unexpected torrent of light, was uncouthly roaring,
Hercules showered down arrows upon him, then anything
That would do to pelt him with—boughs and immense
    boulders.
Cacus, seeing no other escape from his predicament,
Belched a great cloud of smoke (you may well be amazed at
    this part of
The story), so that a smoke-screen went rolling over his lair,
Blotting out everything from sight, and the cave was all one
Thick, black, fog-bound night, shot through with glares of
    flame.
Hercules lost all restraint, in his fury at this: he hurled him-
    self
Down through the fire with a headlong leap, to the point
    where the smoke
Rolled thickest and billowed about the huge cave in eddying
    black clouds.
He laid hands on the ogre, who vainly was vomiting flame
Through the mirk, got a quick hold, knotted him double, and
    throttled him
So that his eyes started, a haemorrhage came in his dry throat.
At once the doors were torn open and the dark den exposed,
Bringing to light the cattle which Cacus had stolen, the loot
He'd had to disgorge, while his own grotesque carcase was
    dragged
Out by the heels. Our people could never be done with gazing
At the bestial creature—his terrible eyes, his face, the
    bristling
Hair on his breast, the extinct volcano of his gullet.
Since then these rites have been practised, this day kept holy
    by grateful

Posterity, headed by its founder, Potitius,*and by
The Pinarian family, wardens of the worship of Hercules.
This altar, which he himself set up in the grove here, always
Shall be for us, in name and in truth, the Ara Maxima.
Come then, my friends, do honour to such heroic feats!
Garland your hair with leaves, solemnly raise the wine cups,
Call on the gods we share now, and freely offer libation!
   Evander had spoken: the shade of silver-green poplar, an
     emblem
Of Hercules, twined his hair—a circlet of leaves with a
     pendant;
The consecrated chalice was in his right hand. At once
With a will they all made libation and put up a prayer to the
     gods.
   Evening the while drew nearer, hastening down the sky:
So now the priests went forth, Potitius at their head,
Robed in hides, their traditional vestment, and carrying
     torches.
Renewing the feast, they brought on welcome offerings to
     furnish
A second banquet, and piled the altars with loaded dishes.
The Salii*too, their temples enwreathed with poplar leaves,
Stood by at the kindled altars, ready to sing—one choir
Of young men, one of older; who now rehearsed in song
The feats and fame of Hercules:*—how as a babe he strangled
Two snakes, the first of the monsters raised up in his path by
     his stepmother;
How he tore, stone from stone, two cities renowned in
     war,
Troy and Oechalia*; how, at the will of that same stepmother,
Hostile Juno, he went through a thousand heavy labours
For king Eurystheus.* Invincible hero, you killed the cloud-
     born
Centaurs, Hylaeus and Pholus, you killed the monster of
     Crete,
You killed the huge great lion in the Nemaean den.

You daunted the river Styx, and the watch-dog of Hell
    couched on
A pile of half-gnawed bones within its blood-stained cave.
Nothing you saw could affright you, not even Typhoeus him-
    self—
That towering, armoured Titan. You did not lose your nerve
    when
The heads of the Lernaean*dragon encircled you like a mob.
All hail, true son of Jove, new splendour in the pantheon!
Graciously grant your favouring presence to us, your wor-
    shippers!
Such was the paean they sang in his honour, crowning it with
A passage about fire-breathing Cacus himself and his cavern.
The woods all rang with their singing, the hills echoed it back.

  As soon as the sacred rites had been completed, they went
Home to the town in a body. The aged king, as he walked,
Kept his son and Aeneas beside him for company,
Whiling away the road in talk on various subjects.
Aeneas was looking around him with unforced admiration,
Enthralled by the scenes they passed through, eagerly asking
    questions
And hearing the stories behind those monuments of past ages.
Then king Evander, the founder of Rome's citadel, said:—
  These woods were once the home of indigenous fauns and
    nymphs,
And of men who had sprung from hard-wood oaks,*who had
    no settled
Way of life, no civilization: ploughing, the forming of
Communal reserves, and economy were unknown then.
They lived on the produce of trees and the hard-won fare of
    the hunter.
The first thing was that Saturn*came hither from Olympus,
An exile deprived of his kingdom, fleeing the power of Jove.
He made a united nation of this intractable folk
Scattered among the hills, gave laws to them, chose the
    name of

Latium*—a word suggesting the safe refuge he had found
  here.
His reign was the period called in legend the Golden Age,
So peacefully serene were the lives of his subjects. It lasted
Till, little by little, the time grew tarnished, an age of baser
Metal came in, of mad aggression and lust for gain.
Ausonian hordes*and tribesmen from Sicily arrived then,
And more than once the land of Saturn resigned its name.
Tyrants arose, for example the harsh, huge-bodied Thybris*
From whom, in later days, our Italian river was called
The Tiber, and lost its original name, which used to be
  Albula.
I myself, an exile seeking the ocean's uttermost
Verge, at the will of all-powerful Fortune, of inescapable
Destiny settled here: I had followed the solemn warnings
My mother, the nymph Carmentis,* gave me, inspired by
  Apollo.
  He finished; and going a little way onward, was able to
    point out
The altar and the Carmental gate, as Romans call it,
Which were set up of yore to honour the nymph, Carmentis,
Prophetic seeress, the first to foretell how great would be
Aeneas' line, how glorious the town of Pallanteum.
Next he showed a large grove, which later the active Romulus
Called a Retreat,* and a cave on the cold hill-side—the
  Lupercal,*
Named in Arcadian fashion after Lycaean Pan.
He pointed out also the sacred wood of Argiletum,*
Explained how his guest, Argos, had died, showing the very
Spot. From here he took them along to the Tarpeian site
And the Capitol,* golden today, but then a tangle of thicket.
Even at that time the timorous countrymen went in awe of
The god-haunted feel of the place, trembled at wood and
  rock.
Evander remarked:—
                        This wood, this hill with its leafy crest

Some god inhabits; though which, we cannot be sure. The
    Arcadians
Believe they have witnessed great Jove himself, seen him
    repeatedly
Shaking his dark aegis and summoning up the storm clouds.
Now look at those ruined walls: there used to be two towns
    there,
And what you see are the relics, the monuments of a past age.
Janus built a citadel here, there Saturn built one;
This was called the Janiculum,* that other the Saturnian.
    Conversing thus together, they approached the un-
    pretentious
Dwelling of Evander: cattle were everywhere, lowing
In what is now the Forum of Rome and the elegant Ship-
    Place.*
Arrived at the palace, the king said:—

                          Hercules stooped to enter
This door: this humble palace received the conquering hero.
Have the courage, my guest, to despise possessions: train
    yourself,
As he, to be worthy of godhead: don't be intolerant of poverty.
    Evander, with these words, led tall Aeneas beneath
The roof of his simple dwelling, and gave him a couch of
    leaves
With a coverlet made from the skin of a Libyan bear, to
    sleep in.
    Night came down, enfolding the earth in her dusky wings.
Venus, her mother's heart alarmed, as well it might be,
Perturbed by the threats and the fierce uprising of the
    Laurentines,
Spoke to her husband, Vulcan,* as they lay in their gold bed-
    chamber,
Breathing into the words all her divine allurement:—
    While Argive kings assaulted in war the foredoomed
    stronghold
Of Pergamum, the towers destined to fall in flames,

I asked no help of you for my unhappy people,
Made no demands on your skill and resource as a forger of
     weapons:
I did not care to put you to work that was bound to be wasted,
Dearest husband, although I owed a great debt to the sons of
Priam, and often had grieved at the ordeal Aeneas was suffer-
     ing.
Now, at the will of Jove, he has set foot in Italy:
Yet it is now that I'm asking a deity whom I reverence
For arms, appealing to you on my son's behalf. You were
     moved by
The tears of Thetis*once, and the tears of the wife of Tithonus.
See, what peoples are mustering, what cities have barred
     their gates
And are sharpening weapons against me, to exterminate those
     I love!
   Since Vulcan complied not at once, the goddess softly
     embraced him
In snowdrift arms, caressing him here and there. Of a sudden
He caught the familiar spark and felt the old warmth darting
Into his marrow, coursing right through his body, melting
     him;
Just as it often happens a thunderclap starts a flaming
Rent which ladders the dark cloud, a quivering streak of fire.
Pleased with her wiles and aware of her beauty, Venus could
     feel them
Taking effect. Vulcan, in love's undying thrall, said:—
   You need not delve in the past for persuasions. What has
     become of
Your trust in me, my goddess? If you had brought me your
     troubles
That other time, then too I could rightfully have armed the
     Trojans;
For neither the Father almighty nor fate's decrees forbade
That Troy should stand or Priam survive another ten years.
And now, if your purpose is to make all ready for warfare,

Any effort that's mine to give in the exercise of my craft,
Whatever can be done with iron and molten alloys,
All work of furnace and bellows—nay, plead no more; why
　　need you
Cast doubt upon your influence over me?

　　　　　　　　　　　　　　　Thus saying,
He gave his wife the love he was aching to give her; then he
Sank into soothing sleep, relaxed upon her breast.

　　As soon as he'd woken, rested, requiring to sleep no longer,
In the small hours when night was waning (the time when the
　　housewife,
Who must eke out a slender livelihood with her loom
And distaff, pokes the drowsy embers upon the hearth,
Making night too a work-time and keeping her maids
　　employed
At the long shift by lamp-light, so that her married life
And the bringing up of her little sons be not endangered),
Just so, and active as she at that very hour, did the Fire-lord
Rise from his downy bed and go to his ironworks.
Between the Sicilian coast and Aeolian Lipare*there's an
Island, whose cliffs, sheer-rising, jet out smoke from their
　　crannies:
Deep within it are vaults, a rumbling volcanic cavern
Scooped out by the action of the Cyclops' fires; you can
　　hear
The clang of hard blows on the anvils, the roaring when
　　masses of ore
Are smelted within, and a throbbing blast of flame from the
　　furnaces.
Here is Vulcan's place; the island is called Vulcania.
Hither now the Fire-god repaired from heaven above.
The Cyclops were hard at work in this underground iron-
　　foundry—
Brontes and Steropes, Pyracmon*stripped to the buff.
They manufactured a thunderbolt, such as the Father of
　　heaven

Shoots down in such great numbers at earth from all over
    the sky:
Part of it was already streamlined, part unfinished.
They had given it three fins of twirling sleet, and three
Of cloudburst, three of russet fire and three of stormwind.
Now they were putting in as components frightening flashes,
The noise that creates panic, the piercing flames of wrath.
Elsewhere, a job was being hurried on for Mars—a chariot
With swift wheels, such as he rides in to rouse up men and
    nations.
Some busily burnished the aegis* Athene wears in her
    angry
Moods—a fearsome thing with a surface of gold like scaly
Snake-skin, and the linked serpents and the Gorgon herself
    upon
The goddess' breast—a severed head rolling its eyes.
    Put all that work aside, pack in the jobs you're engaged
    on,
You Cyclops of Mount Aetna,* and turn your attention to
    this—
The making of arms for a hot-blooded hero! Now there is
    need for
Your strength, your speediest work and your master-
    craftsmanship.
Get bustling on it at once!
                    That was all Vulcan said:
Quickly they set to the business, shared out the tasks among
    them
Equally. Rivers of molten bronze and gold are flowing;
The deadly steel is smelted in an immense furnace.
They fashion a shield of heroic size, to withstand by itself
Every missile the Latins can use, welding seven rounds of
    metal
One on another to make it. Some pump away at the bellows,
Drawing in air and expelling it; some dip the hissing metal
In troughs. The cavern groans under the stress of anvils.

They raise their arms with the powerful alternate rhythm of
    cranks,
They keep the iron-ore turning in the close grip of their tongs.
  While on Aeolian shores*the lord of Lemnos was hurrying
Forward this work, Evander was roused from his humble
    dwelling
By the genial light and the dawn song of birds beneath his eaves.
The old man got out of bed, clothed himself in a tunic,
And laced the Tyrrhene clogs on his feet; then shouldered a
    baldric
So that his sword of Tegea*could hang at his side, and threw
A panther-skin over his left shoulder to dangle behind him.
Two dogs, his bodyguard, preceded him as he stepped
Through the doorway, and went with their master on his
    errand.
He made for the private room where his guest, Aeneas, was
    lodged,
For he'd not forgotten their talk, the old hero, or what he had
    promised.
Aeneas too was up and about that early morning:
Achates walked at his side; at Evander's, his son Pallas.
The four of them met, shook hands, then retired to an inner
    room
Where they could sit and at last converse together freely.
The king began:—
    Great captain of the Teucrians*—believe me, I'll never
    admit
The cause of Troy is lost, or its hope of dominion, while you
Are alive—though our reputation is high, we are short in the
    sinews
Of war to aid you, confined as we are on this side by the Tiber,
Hard pressed on that by the Rutuli,*whose arms clang round
    our walls.
But I propose to bring to your side a confederation
Of rich and numerous peoples: an unforeseen chance has
    offered

This reinforcement. It must have been fate that brought you
    here.
Not far away lies Caere,* a populous city, founded
On ancient rock: a tribe from Lydia, renowned in war,
Settled it long ago upon a hill of Etruria.
For many years they flourished; but there rose a king,
    Mezentius,*
Who with insolent tyranny and cruel force oppressed them.
I will not enlarge on that despot's brutish acts or his damnable
Massacres—may the gods keep such things for himself and
    his breed!
Why, he would even have live men bound to dead bodies,
Clamping them hand to hand and face to face—a horrible
Method of torture—so that they died a lingering death
Infected with putrefaction in that most vile embrace.
At last the townsfolk could stand it no more: they rose in arms
Against the criminal maniac, besieged him in his palace,
Put his friends to the sword and set the place alight.
But Mezentius somehow escaped through the slaughter into
    Rutulian
Territory, and asked his guest-friend, Turnus, for protection.
So all Etruria has risen in righteous anger, demanding
His extradition for punishment, or else they'll make war at
    once.
Thousands they are, Aeneas, and I'll put you at their head:
You see, their invasion fleet is serried along the shore
And they're clamouring to advance, but an aged seer restrains
    them,
Uttering fate's decree:—You crack troops of the Etruscans,
You flower and chivalry of an ancient people, your honest
Indignation, your just wrath at Mezentius spur you against
The foe: but no Italian may lead a team of such fighters
As you. You must find a foreign commander. At this, the
    Etruscan
Army, awed by the warning of heaven, settled back on the
    plain there.

Tarchon*himself has sent me ambassadors with the royal
Crown and sceptre, offering the insignia of his power
If I will go to their camp and take over command of the
    Etruscans.
But I cannot accept it; for I am outworn with years, old age
Has chilled my blood and withered my aptitude for adventure.
I'd encourage my son to go, were it not that he inherits
Italian blood from his mother, a Sabine. But you are the right
    man
In age and race, fate's chosen, the one the divine Will calls
    for:
Go then, most valiant leader of Trojans and of Italians.*
Besides, you shall have my son here, my hope and consola-
    tion,
Pallas, that under your tuition he may be trained
In soldiering, the rough work of war—to endure its rigours,
And watching your deeds, to model himself on you from the
    start.
Him will I give two hundred Arcadian horsemen, the flower
    of
Our youth, and Pallas shall give you two hundred in his own
    name.
    He had barely finished speaking. Aeneas, son of Anchises,
And his confidant, Achates, their eyes downcast, were reflect-
    ing
Sadly on the hard trials before them, and long would have
    done so
But that Venus sent them a sign out of the clear sky.
All of a sudden the heavens shook with a flash of lightning
And thunder pealed: it seemed as if the whole universe sud-
    denly
Tottered and Etruscan trumpets*were bawling above them.
They looked up: again and again a terrific crash resounded.
Up there among the fleecy clouds in the fair-weather sky
Were arms, red-glinting and thunderously clashing through
    the clear air.

The rest were stunned with amazement: but the Trojan hero
    heard
In the sound his divine mother keeping a promise she'd given.
So then he exclaimed:—

                  My friend, do not, oh, do not ask
What issue these portents may bring! They're a call from
    above, and the call is
For me. My goddess mother foretold she would send this
    sign
If war was looming close, and would come to my help through
    the air
With arms of Vulcan's making.
Ah, what terrible slaughter awaits the Laurentines now!
What a price you will pay me, Turnus! How many shields and
    helmets
And corpses of gallant men shall the Tiber roll beneath
Its waves! Now let them clamour for war and break their
    treaties.
  When he'd said this, Aeneas got up from where he was
    sitting,
And at once rekindling the drowsy fire on the altar of Hercules,
Cheerfully paid his respects to the guardian of the house
And its humble gods, as he'd done on the previous day.
    Evander
Sacrificed duly chosen sheep, and the Trojans likewise.
Then Aeneas returned to the ships, where the rest of his
    comrades were,
And selected the bravest of them to accompany him upon
His military mission; while the remainder floated
Effortlessly down the glass-calm river, borne by
Its current, to tell Ascanius how it fared with his father and
    the rest.
The Trojans on their way to the Etruscan camp were
    furnished
With horses; for Aeneas a specially fine one, housed in
The tawny skin of a lion with glittering, gilded claws.

The news was quickly spread abroad through the little
 township
That men were riding post-haste to the Etruscan king.
In apprehension, the mothers pray harder; fear walks closer
In peril's train, and the spectre of war looms larger now.
Then did Evander, weeping uncontrollably, cling to
The hand of his departing son, Pallas, and say:—
 If Juppiter would only restore those bygone years*
And the man I was when under Praeneste's walls I laid
The front rank low and triumphantly burnt the piled-up
 shields!
Yes, and with this right hand I despatched to Hades king
 Erulus*—
He whom his mother, Feronia, had given at birth three lives
(Frightening it is to relate), and three sets of equipment;
Thrice over he had to be slain, yet on that day my strong hand
Took all his lives away and thrice despoiled him of armour.
The man I was then would not have been torn from you now,
 my dear son,
That's sure; nor would Mezentius ever have heaped such
 insults
On me, his neighbour, with all those killings he ruthlessly
Has perpetrated, depriving my town of so many citizens.
Ye heaven-dwellers, and you, great ruler of the gods,
Juppiter, have compassion for an Arcadian king
And hear a father's prayer, I implore you: if your will
And fate's it is to keep my Pallas safe and sound for me,
If I am living to see him again, again to be with him,
Then let me live; for that, I can bear any burden. But if
Fortune means something I dare not speak of to happen to
 him,
Let me be rid of my bitter existence this very moment
Before anxiety becomes certainty, and hope dies
In the known event—yes now, as I hold you, dear lad, my
 last
Lone joy, or ever some terrible tidings should hurt my ears.

So, at their final parting, the old man spoke from his heart;
Then he collapsed, and his servants carried him into the
    house.
And now the gates had been opened and the horsemen had
    sallied forth,
Aeneas with his close friend, Achates, among the leaders;
Next, other Trojan princes; Pallas himself was riding
In the middle of the column, his tunic and blazoned armour
    conspicuous—
Just like the Morning Star, beloved by Venus above all
The stars of heaven, when it rises from bathing in ocean
    deeps, and
Puts forth its holy light from the sky and melts the darkness.
On the city wall stand the mothers, trembling; their eyes
    follow
Those squadrons—flashes of bronze and a dust cloud rolling
    about them.
The armoured horsemen, taking a short cut, pick their way
Through brushwood; then loud shouts are heard as, all in a
    body,
With clatter of hammering hooves they go galloping over
    the dry flats.
There's an extensive woodland near the cool stream of Caerè,
Reverenced by all around in the faith of their fathers:
    encircled
By hills, that wood of dark green fir-trees lay in a hollow.
The legend is that the ancient Pelasgians,* the first settlers
Of Latium in the old days, had dedicated the wood
And a festival day to Silvanus,* the god of fields and cattle.
Not far from here were Tarchon and his Etruscans, camped in
A good defensive position; and now from the hills above
They could see the whole of his army, their tents all over the
    plain.
Aeneas, leading his chosen combat brigade, soon entered
The camp: his tired men saw to their horses and then their
    own comfort.

Venus, divinely shining among the dark clouds, descended
Bringing her presents: when she had seen from afar Aeneas
On the other side of a cool stream in a secluded dell,
She offered herself to his view quite unexpectedly, saying:—
   Look! Here are the presents my consort promised. All his
      science
Has gone to their making. Now you need not shrink from
      challenging
Haughty Laurentines and hot-headed Turnus to battle, my
      son.
   With these words, the Cytherean* went into her son's
      embrace:
The radiant arms she had propped up against an oak, before
      him.
Aeneas, overjoyed by her gifts and the glory of them,
Eyed each piece, couldn't have enough of gazing: in wonder
He took them up with his hands, in his arms, examining
      each—
The formidable helmet with plumes like fountains of fire,
The sword that would deal out doom, the breastplate of hard
      bronze,
Massive and ruddy-coloured, like to some louring cloud
When it catches fire from the rays of the sun and glows afar;
Then the burnished greaves of gold-alloy inlaid with high-
      carat
Gold, and the spear, and the shield's miraculous workman-
      ship.
Upon this shield the Fire-god, with knowledge of things to
      come,
Being versed in the prophets, had wrought events from Italian
      history*
And Roman triumphs; upon it appeared the whole line that
      would spring from
Ascanius' stock, and the wars they would fight in, one by
      one.
He had depicted the mother wolf as she lay full length in

The green-swarded cave of Mars, with the twin boy babies*
    fondling
And suckling at her udders, fearlessly nuzzling their dam;
She, her graceful neck bent sideways and back, is caressing
Each child in turn with her tongue, licking them into shape.
Nearby he had pictured the Sabine women* so uncere-
    moniously
Snatched from among the crowds around the arena at Rome
During the Great Games; then the war that immediately
    came,
Between Romulus' people and Tatius's hard-living Sabines.
Next, these same two kings, their quarrel laid aside,
Are standing at Jove's altar, armed, with bowls in their hands,
Ratifying a treaty by the sacrifice of a sow.
Near this was the scene where chariots, driven apart, had
    torn
Mettus*to pieces (but you should have kept to your word,
    Alban!)—
Tullus is dragging away the remains of that false-tongued
    man
Through a wood, and the brambles there are drenched with
    a bloody dew.
Again, you could see Porsenna*telling the Romans to take
    back
The banished Tarquin, and laying strenuous siege to Rome,
While the sons of Aeneas took up the sword for freedom's
    sake:
He was pictured there to the life, pouring out threats and wild
    with
Chagrin, seeing that Cocles*dared to break down the bridge
And Cloelia had slipped her fetters and was swimming across
    the river.
At the top of the shield, Manlius,* warden of the Tarpeian
Fortress, stood before the temple, guarding the Capitol—
The palace, just built by Romulus, being shown with a rough
    thatched roof.

Here too a silvery goose went fluttering through a golden
Colonnade, honking out an alarum, that the Gauls are on us:
Under the cover of a dark night, lucky for them, the Gauls
Creep closer through the brushwood, some have already scaled
The citadel's heights: their clothing and hair were done in
    gold;
The stripes on their cloaks are gleaming; about their fair-
    skinned throats
Are necklaces fastened; each of them brandishes two Alpine
Spears in his hand, and carries a tall, narrow shield for pro-
    tection.
Vulcan had also embossed the dancing Salii*and naked
Luperci, their head-dresses bound with wool, and the shields
    that fell from
Heaven*: a solemn procession of virtuous ladies*was moving
In cushioned carriages through the city. Elsewhere the deep
    gates
Of hell were represented, the domicile of the damned
And the torments they suffer—Catiline*hangs from the edge
    of a terrible
Precipice, shrinking away from the faces of Furies above him:
But the righteous are set apart, with Cato as their law-giver.
Among these subjects extended a wide and swelling sea;
It was done in gold, yet it looked like the blue sea foaming
    with white-caps:
Dolphins, picked out in silver, were cart-wheeling all around,
Lashing the face of the deep with their tails and cleaving the
    water.
Centrally were displayed two fleets of bronze, engaged in
The battle of Actium*; all about Cape Leucas you saw
Brisk movement of naval formations; the sea was a blaze of
    gold.
On one side Augustus Caesar, high up on the poop, is leading
The Italians*into battle, the Senate and People with him,
His home-gods and the great gods: two flames shoot up from
    his helmet

In jubilant light, and his father's star dawns over its crest.
Elsewhere in the scene is Agrippa*—the gods and the winds
    fight for him—
Prominent, leading his column: the naval crown with its
    miniature
Ships' beaks, a proud decoration of war, shines on his head.
On the other side, with barbaric wealth and motley equip-
    ment,
Is Anthony, fresh from his triumphs in the East, by the
    shores of the Indian
Ocean; Egypt, the powers of the Orient and uttermost Bactra
Sail with him; also—a shameful thing—his Egyptian wife.*
The fleets are converging at full speed, the sea is all churned
    and foaming
As the oarsmen take their long strokes and the trident bows
    drive on.
They manœuvre for sea-room: you'd think the Cyclades isles
    were unmoored
And afloat, or mountains were charging at mountains, to see
    those massive
Galleys on one side attacking the turreted ships of the
    other.
Volleys of flaming material and iron missiles fly thick
And fast; a strange new slaughter reddens the plains of
    Neptune.
In the midst, Cleopatra rallies her fleet with Egyptian timbrel,*
For she cannot yet see the two serpents of death behind her.
Barking Anubis,* a whole progeny of grotesque
Deities are embattled against Neptune and Minerva
And Venus. Mars is raging in the thick of the fight, his figure
Wrought from iron, and ominous Furies look on from above;
Here Discord strides exulting in her torn mantle, and she is
Followed by Bellona*wielding a bloodstained scourge.
Viewing this, Apollo*of Actium draws his bow
From aloft: it creates a panic; all the Egyptians, all
The Indians, Arabians and Sabaeans now turn tail.

You could see the queen Cleopatra praying a fair wind, making

All sail, in the very act of paying the sheets out and running.

The Fire-god had rendered her, pale with the shadow of her own death,

Amid the carnage, borne on by the waves and the westerly gale;

And, over against her, the Nile, sorrowing in all its length,

Throws wide the folds of its watery garment, inviting the conquered

To sail for refuge into that blue, protective bosom.

But Caesar has entered the walls of Rome in triumphal procession,*

Three times a victor; he dedicates now a thanks-offering immortal

To Italy's gods—three hundred great shrines*all over the city.

The streets resound with cheering, rejoicing and merrymaking:

In all the temples women are chanting, altars are lit up;

At the foot of the altars lie the bodies of sacrificed bullocks.

Caesar, enthroned in the marble-white temple*of dazzling Apollo,

Inspects the gifts from the nations and hangs them up on the splendid

Portals: subjected tribes pass by in a long procession—

A diversity of tongues, of national dress and equipment.

Here Vulcan had represented the Nomads,* the flowing robes of

Africans, here the Leleges, Carians, Gelonian bowmen;

Some carry a picture of Euphrates, its waters pacified;

There go the Morini,* furthest of men, the branching Rhine,

The Scythians untamed, the Araxes*fretting about its bridge.

Such were the scenes that Aeneas admired on the shield of Vulcan

His mother gave him. Elated by its portrayal of things

Beyond his ken, he shouldered his people's glorious future.

BOOK IX

Now while Aeneas was thus engaged in a far-distant
Part of the country, Saturnian Juno sent down Iris
From heaven to the fiery Turnus. He, as it happened, was
    then
Taking his ease in the hallowed vale of Pilumnus,* his fore-
    father.
Rose-lipped Iris,* daughter of Thaumas, thus addressed
    him:—
   Turnus, what none of the gods would dare to promise,
       however
You prayed, has been brought about by the mere passage of
    time.
Aeneas, leaving his fleet, his friends and his settlement,
Has gone afar to the Palatine kingdom, the home of Evander;
Nay more, he has made his way to remote Etruscan cities,
Is gathering armed levies among the Lydian*yeomen.
Why hesitate? Now is the time to call for horses and chariots.
Move fast! Make a surprise attack on his camp and cap-
    ture it!
   So she said; then soaring to heaven on balanced wings,
Blazed a rainbow trail beneath the clouds as she flew.
Turnus recognized her divinity, raised his two hands
Heavenwards, and sent these words after the fleeting god-
    dess:—
   Iris, glory of the sky, who was it conveyed you, cloud-
       borne,
Down to me here on earth? How came this sudden bright-
    ness
Up there? For I can see the firmament roll apart
And the vagrant stars unveiled. I acknowledge the sign, who-
    ever

You are that call me to battle.

                       Turnus, with these words, went to
The waterside, scooped up water out of the brimming stream,
And offered many prayers and vows to the gods above.

  Soon his whole army was marching across the open plains,
A mass of chargers, a mass of gold-embroidered apparel:
Messapus is marshalling the advance guard, Tyrrhus' sons
The rear, while the main body is under the command of
    Turnus,
Who rides there fully armed, a head higher than all;
Even as Ganges or Nile, all seven tranquil branches,
Silently rise in flood, and then withdrawing from the low
    lands
Their fertilizing water, return to their channels again.
Now did the Trojans see, as they looked forth, a dust cloud
Suddenly formed, a darkness mounting above the plain.
Caicus was first to spy it from the rampart and raise the
    alarum:—

  Hey there! What is that body looms up in a gloom of dust?
To arms! Jump to it! Issue the weapons! Man the walls!
The enemy is upon us!

                  There were loud shouts as the Trojans
Came hurrying in through all the gates and lined the battle-
    ments.
Aeneas, that excellent soldier, had instructed them so to do,
Before he left: if such an emergency should arise
In his absence, they must not risk deploying to fight in the
    open,
Only defend the camp from behind the ramparts' protection.
So now, though rage and humiliation tempt them to mix it,
They secure the gates, just as Aeneas had told them, take
    cover
Inside the turrets, ready their weapons and wait the foe.
Turnus, who'd shot ahead of his cumbrously-moving column
With a bodyguard of twenty picked horsemen, got to the
    camp

Unexpectedly soon: the Thracian charger he rode had mark-
    ings
Of white, and he wore a helmet of gold with blood-red plume.
Will any of you be the first, lads, with me against the foe to—
Watch me! he cried; and hurled a javelin into the blue,
A prelude of battle, then stately advanced out on the field.
His companions acclaimed it with cheers and followed him
    with bloodcurdling
War-cries: they were amazed at the Trojans' inactivity,
Amazed that such warriors did not come out on the open
    plain
And there oppose them, but huddled in the camp. Im-
    patiently Turnus
Rode this way and that round the walls, seeking a way in
    where none was.
Just as a wolf that lurks near to some crowded sheepfold,
Howling around the pens, with rainstorms driving upon him,
And late at night—meanwhile the lambs safe under their
    mothers
Bleat and bleat—the wolf in a fury of exasperation
Snarls at the prey he cannot reach, for long-sharpening,
    grinding
Hunger has driven him wild and his throat is parched for
    blood:—
Just so did Turnus gaze at the camp's fortifications
With mounting rage: his chagrin burned him right to the
    bone
As he cast about for some way to get at the Trojans, dislodge
    them
From their besieged emplacements and tumble them out in
    the open.
Their fleet, which lay concealed close to one flank of the
    camp,
Protected all round by earth-works and the river itself, he
    now
Moved against; told his exulting men to bring incendiaries;

Snatched up a blazing pine-torch himself in his hot excite-
  ment.

How they went to it then! The presence of Turnus inspired
  them.

Soon the hearths had been stripped, and every soldier was
  armed with

A smoking firebrand: the resinous torches were spouting up

To the sky a mirky glare which gave off volleys of sparks.

  What deity was it, O Muses, averted that merciless blaze

From the Trojans? Who drove away so fierce a fire from their
  ships?

Tell me! The proofs are deep-buried in the past, but the tale
  is undying.

At the time when, in Phrygian Ida,* Aeneas was beginning

To build a fleet and preparing to venture forth on the deep
  sea,

Cybele* herself, mother of the gods, is said to have made

This appeal to mighty Juppiter:—

                              Grant me, my son, what I ask—

What your dear mother asks who helped you to power in
  Olympus.

I had a forest of pine trees, cherished for many a year,

A plantation high up on the mountain, dusky with glooming
  spruces

And maple wood: men used to bring me offerings there.

This did I gladly give to the Dardan* prince, when he needed

A fleet; but now a dreadful anxiety gnaws and troubles me.

Banish my fears: let a mother's prayer be so far efficacious

That neither hurricanes nor any other stress of voyaging

Vanquish those ships; may they find it a blessing they came
  from my mountain.

  Her son, who turns the heavenly constellations, replied:—

What would you bend the fates to? What is this you are ask-
  ing, my mother,

For those ships? May vessels built by mortal hands have
  immortals'

Privilege? or Aeneas go, sure of immunity,

Through hazards whose issue is unsure? No god has the
    power to grant that.

No, when they've accomplished their task and lie at journey's
    end

One day in Italian harbour, such ships as escape the sea

And carry the Dardan hero to the Laurentine land

I shall relieve of their mortal shape, and command they
    become

Goddesses of the great deep,* like Doto, Nereus' child,

And Galatea, who cleave the foaming sea with their breasts.

   So Juppiter spoke; and then by the stream of his Stygian
    brother,*

The banks where boiling pitch flows in a black maelstrom,
    he nodded,

Confirming his promise: the nod caused all Olympus to
    tremble.

   So now that promised day was here, the allotted time

Fulfilled by the Fate-spinners. Cybele now was warned, by
    the outrage

Turnus intended, to ward off the fire from her sacred ships.

First did a strange light blaze upon their eyes, and a huge
    cloud

Was seen to career across the sky from the eastwards, loud
    with

The crashing of Cybele's cymbals:* a voice that awed them
    broke

From the cloud and fell about the ears of Trojans and
    Rutuli:—

   Teucrians, do not trouble yourselves to defend my ships!

Put by your weapons! For Turnus shall sooner burn up the
    sea

Than those blessed ships of mine. Go forth, enfranchised
    barques,

As goddesses of the sea. The Mother bids you.

                       At once

Each vessel snapped the moorings that held her stern to the
    bank,
And all, burying their beaks in the water, plunged deep down
Like dolphins. Soon they surfaced again, but—wonder of
    wonders—
Each was a maiden now as they coursed over the sea—
Each ship that had been lying, bronze-beaked, along the
    shore.
   The Rutuli*were dumbfounded: Messapus himself was
    terrified;
His horses reared in panic; the river, harshly growling,
Checked its flow—yes, Tiber recoiled from the deep sea
    then.
But the fiery Turnus did not lose confidence—far from it,
He spoke to raise their spirits, he even rebuked his men:—
   This portent is pointed *against* the Trojans, Jove himself
Has removed their usual stand-by: their ships are not staying
    to face
Rutulian fire and steel. Well, the seaways are closed to the
    Teucrians,
And that was their only escape route; one-half of the world
    is lost them,
While we have command of the land, since in their thousands
    the tribes of
Italy have flocked to arms. I am not in the least dismayed by
This or that god-given ruling of destiny they may boast of:
The Fates and Venus have had their pay-off, in that the
    Trojans
Have reached our fertile land of Ausonia. I too have oracles
Backing me; I am to root out this damnable race with the
    sword
In revenge for their stealing my bride—a resentment not only
    the sons of
Atreus can feel; others may take up arms for the same cause.
Let the Trojans say, It's enough to have once been ruined:
    I say

It should be enough to have sinned once and then to loathe
    well nigh all
The feminine sex. It's quaint how a rampart between, a
    delaying
System of trenches—frail barricades against death—have
    given them
Courage and confidence! Have they not seen Troy's battle-
    ments,
Built by the hand of Neptune,* collapse into the flames?
But you, my storm troops, which of you is ready to hack his
    way
At my side through the rampart and break into their flustered
    defences?
I don't need arms from Vulcan, or a thousand ships, before
I'll fight the Trojans. Let all the Etruscans flock to their side
This very minute. The foe need fear no cowardly theft
Of Athene's image,* in darkness, with the sentries up on the
    citadel
Murdered: nor are we going to hide in a horse's dark paunch.*
By day, from the open, I mean to fire their walls' perimeter.
I'll make them realise they're not dealing with Danaans*or
    with
Pelasgian troops, such as Hector fought off till the tenth year.
For the present, since the better part of to-day is over,
You shall have the rest to recuperate, set up by the knowledge
    that so far
You have done well, the assurance that I am preparing for
    battle.
    Messapus was given charge now of watching the enemy's
    gates
With pickets and lighting a ring of fires around the perimeter.
Fourteen Rutulian officers were picked for the duty—to
    keep
Watch on the camp; each led a detachment, a hundred strong,
In golden glittering accoutrements with red plumes on their
    helmets.

Briskly they pass to and fro, relieved and relievers; they
     sprawl on
The grass to take their wine, tilting the bowls of bronze.
Brightly shine the watch-fires; the watchers keep awake
By gaming through the night.
     The Trojans, standing to arms on the ramparts above,
     looked down at
These operations. In a bustle of alarm they tested the bars of
Their gates, and laid out gangways communicating between
The strongpoints, carrying arms as they did so. Mnestheus
     and gallant
Serestus urged on this work—the two whom Aeneas had
     chosen
To be field commanders and civil governors in case of
     emergency.
Their whole force manned the walls, drawing lots for the
     points of danger,
And mounted guard in turn, each at his post as ordered.
     One gate was held by Nisus,*that most aggressive of fighters:
He was Hyrtacus' son, and had come from the hunting
     grounds of Ida
To follow Aeneas; a lightning shot with arrow or javelin.
Euryalus was beside him, his friend; no man of Aeneas,
No wearer of Trojan arms was handsomer than he—
That lad with the bloom of youth on his unshaven cheeks.
These two were one in love; they would charge into battle
     together:
To-night they were doing sentry-duty at the same gate.
Nisus said:—
               Is it God that makes one burn to do brave things,
Or does each of us make a god of his own fierce passion to do
     them?
For long I've been itching to hurl myself into a fight, or
     venture
Some notable deed; inaction and calm do not appeal to me.
Look at the confidence the Rutuli have in their fortunes:

Far apart glimmer their watch-fires; unstrung by wine and
sleep

They are prostrate; all is silence down there. Well, listen to
what I'm

Debating in my mind, the idea that comes to me now.

Everyone, commons and councillors alike, has been saying
that we must

Send for Aeneas, send men with official news of what's
happened.

If they promise you the reward I shall ask (for myself the
glory

Of the deed is enough), I believe, under cover of yonder high
ground,

I can find a way through to the fortified town of Pallanteum.*
  Euryalus was dazed, struck by the same great zest

For glory: at once he spoke to his eager friend, like this:—
  Nisus, you wouldn't fight shy of having me as your comrade

In such an adventure? Could I let you go into danger without
me?

Not so did my father, the veteran soldier Opheltes, teach me,

Who brought me up in the midst of the Argive terror, the
ordeal

Of Troy: nor, during our friendship, have I done aught to
make you doubt me,

As I followed great-heart Aeneas wherever his destiny led us.

I am no clinger to life, not I, but rather one

Who believes it were well exchanged for the renown you
aim at.

  Nisus replied:—

                      I had no such fears about you, I swear it:

That would be wrong indeed. May Jove (or however we
should name him

Who looks on these things with favour) restore me to you
triumphant.

But if, as so often happens in desperate affairs like this,

Some accident or god should send my plans awry,

I would like you to survive me; you're young, with your life
    before you.
May there be one to rescue my corpse from the fray, or
    ransom it,
And, in our fashion, inter it—or, if some chance should pre-
    vent that,
To build a handsome cenotaph and to bring offerings there.
Nor do I want to cause your poor mother such terrible anguish,
Dear lad, who alone of Troy's elderly women would have no
Truck with Acestes' city*but bravely came on with you here.
  But Euryalus made answer:—
                   It's no use your bringing out all these
Arguments, for my mind is made up and you cannot shift me.
Let us get down to it quickly.
                  At once he awoke the guard, who
Relieved them and took their watch. Leaving his post, he
    walked
At the side of Nisus, his friend, and they went to look for the
    prince.
  All other living creatures on earth were asleep, their
    worries
Dissolved in sleep, their minds oblivious of toil and trouble:
But the high command of the Trojans, the flower of the
    people, were holding
A conference on the critical state of affairs, discussing
What they should do and whom they should send to report
    to Aeneas.
Leaning upon their long spears, with shields on their arms,
    they stand
In the centre of the camp's parade-ground. Euryalus and
    Nisus
Come hurrying up and eagerly beg an immediate audience:
An important matter, they say—well worth the interruption
Ascanius greeted the impatient pair, told Nisus to speak.
He began like this:—
               Gentlemen, please give a kindly hearing

To what we propose, and do not dismiss it as coming from
    men
So junior to you. Relaxed by drinking and sleep, the Rutuli
Are silent all. We have noticed a possible place for a stealthy
Break-out: it lies by the seaward gate where two ways fork.
The ring of watch-fires is broken there, some being extin-
    guished,
Others all smoke. If you'll let us make use of this bit of luck
To go in quest of Aeneas to fortified Pallanteum,
You'll soon see us back again—and laden with spoils, having
    done
Great execution on the foe. We shall not mistake our way,
    either;
For we have sighted that town from below in the valley
    coverts
Where often we go hunting, and have got to know the whole
    river.
    Then spoke the aged Aletes, a man of mature judgement:—
    Gods of our fathers, beneath whose protection Troy
    remains always,
You cannot, for all that has happened, intend to destroy us
    completely
When you have brought us young men of such spirit and such
    a resolute
Character—
    Even as he spoke, he put his arms round their shoulders
And gripped their hands, with the tears rivering down his
    cheeks:—
    My lads, what recompense can I think of for you, that's
    at all
Worthy of an enterprise so glorious? The first and fairest
Reward will come from heaven and your own virtue: in
    addition,
Aeneas the true will repay you promptly, and also Ascanius
Whose life is before him, who's never forgetful of noble
    service.

Ascanius at once took it up:—

Why, yes! I adjure you—I whose
Salvation lies in my father's return—adjure by the great gods
Of home, the first family god of Assaracus*and the shrine of
Revered Vesta: my fortunes, my every hope for the future,
I lay in your hands, Nisus. Bring back my father, oh, let me
See him again! If he comes, all our dejection goes.
I will give two goblets made of silver and richly encrusted
With figures—my father took them as spoils at the sack of
    Arisba*
Also a pair of tripods, two full talents of gold,
And an antique bowl—a present from Carthaginian Dido.
But if it befalls that we win the war and become masters
Of a conquered Italy, so that I portion out the spoils—
You saw the horse which Turnus was riding, and his golden
Armour—that same horse, that shield and the red-plumed
    helmet
I shall set aside; consider them yours, my reward to you,
    Nisus.
Besides, my father shall give you twelve women of choicest
    beauty
And as many male captives, too, each with his own equip-
    ment;
In addition to these, you shall have the private estates of
    Latinus.
Now, Euryalus, for you: I admire you greatly, and I am
Not far behind you in age; so I take you now to my heart—
You shall be my friend and share my fortunes, whatever they
    are.
I shall never seek renown for myself without you beside
    me:
Whether in peace or war, I shall put the utmost reliance
On you for word and deed.

Euryalus made answer:—
You shall never be disillusioned by my falling away from
So brave a beginning as this: let only my luck stay good

And not turn sour on me. But, apart from what you have
    given,
I beg one boon: my mother, a lady of Priam's ancient
Lineage, would not remain behind in the land of Ilium
Or settle in Acestes' township, poor soul, but has travelled
    with me.
I am leaving her now—she knows naught of these dangers I
    have to face,
Whatever they are—without saying good-bye, because (I
    swear it
By Night and your own right hand) her tears would be sure
    to unman me.
Helpless she'll be, and lonely; I implore you, befriend and
    console her.
If I know I can count on you for this, I shall go the more
    bravely
To meet what I have to meet.
                       Deeply touched by his words,
The Trojans shed some tears; especially fair Ascanius,
At the image of filial love thus printed upon his mind.
Then he began, like this:—
    All shall be done as befits your great enterprise, I assure
    you.
Indeed I will be a son to your mother, and she shall become
Creusa*in all but name: much kindness is coming to her
Who bore such a son. Whatever the consequences of your
    action—
By my own head, which my father was wont to swear by,
    I swear it—
All that I've promised to give you if you return successful,
The same shall hold good for your mother and for your kin
    always.
    So Ascanius spoke, in tears. Then he unslung from his
    shoulder
The gold-hilted sword which Lycaon of Gnossos had
    fashioned with wonderful

Workmanship and had fitted with an ivory sheath for carry-
ing.

Mnestheus presented to Nisus the shaggy skin of a lion,

While good Aletes exchanged his own helm for the helmet
of Nisus.

At once, full-armed, the pair moved off: the Trojan leaders

Escorted them to the gate, old and young in a body,

With prayers for their safety. Ascanius, who had a grown
man's sense

Of responsibility and an old head on young shoulders,

Gave them many commissions to take to his father. But all
was

Whirled aloft by the winds, atomized, went for nothing.

Sallying out, they crossed the earthworks and made
through the dark night

Towards the fatal camp—fatal for them, though first

They would be death to many. All over the grass they see

Bodies asprawl in drunken sleep, chariots parked by

The shore, men lying amidst the harness and wheels, a litter

Of weapons and wine-cups together. Nisus began to say:—

Euryalus, we must risk it. Now is our opportunity.

Here lies our route. You must guard me and keep a look-out
all behind us,

On the alert for any who tries to attack from the rear.

I'm going to make havoc here, and hack a broad path for
your feet.

These words he whispered, no more; and at once he thrust
with his sword at

The haughty Rhamnes, who chanced to be lying nearby on
a great heap

Of rugs, his broad chest heaving in slumber—he was a king

Himself, but also the prophet most favoured by king Turnus:

Now, his prophetic gifts could not avert his doom.

Then Nisus killed three attendants who lay, off guard, at his
side

Among their weapons, with Remus' squire and his charioteer

Whom he found at the horses' feet, and severed their lolling
   heads:
Next he beheaded their master, Remus, and left his trunk ,
Throbbing out jets of blood like sobs; the warm, wet blood
Darkened his couch and the ground. Lamyrus, Lamus he
   slew,
And young Serranus—a man of exceptional looks, who'd
   begun
The night with an orgy of gaming and now was lying com-
   pletely
Insensible from wine; well for him, if he'd gone on
Gambling all night, protracted his play into the morning.
So does a famishing lion, driven by insensate hunger,
Run amok through the crowded sheepfolds, mauling and
   dragging
The meek sheep, mute with terror, and roars from his blood-
   stained mouth.
No less was the damage done by Euryalus; unlagging
In fury, he surprised and killed Fadus, Herbesus, Rhoetus,
Abaris, and many others who lay in his path unconscious.
Rhoetus was actually awake, a witness of all this,
But in extreme terror was crouching behind a big wine-
   jar;
His enemy got him full in the breast at close quarters,
   just as
He rose, drove the sword right through him, withdrew it in
   spouts of blood.
Rhoetus poured out his life, all crimson; dying, he coughed up
Blood and wine: the other pressed on with his stealthy killing.
Now he was nearing the lines of Messapus, where he could
   see
The watch-fire burning low and the horses, properly
   tethered,
Browsing upon the grass. At this moment Nisus, aware that
His friend was being carried too far by bloodlust, called out
   to him:—

Let's stop! It will be light soon, and light is no friend
to us.

We have taken toll enough, we have cut a swathe through the
enemy.

They had to leave behind a wealth of solid silver

Accoutrements, of drinking bowls and magnificent carpets.

The ornaments Rhamnes had worn on his breast, and his
gold-studded baldric—

They were presents, originally, sent to Remulus of Tibur*

By the rich Caedicus, to obtain his friendship, in absence;

Remulus on his death-bed bequeathed them to his grandson,

Then they became the battle spoils of the Rutuli—these did

Euryalus whip off and put over his own strong shoulders,

A short-lived prize: he donned Messapus' well-fitting helmet

With its gay plume. Then they left the camp and made for
safety.

Meanwhile a cavalry force sent ahead from the Latin city,

While the rest of the army remained, in formation, upon the
plain,

Were on their way, carrying despatches to king Turnus—

Three hundred, with modern equipment, under command of
Volscens.*

Now they were nearing the camp, almost beneath its ram-
parts,

When they saw at a distance the pair turning off by a path to
their left hand,

Euryalus being betrayed by the helmet he'd thoughtlessly
clapped on

Reflecting the moonbeams among the glimmering shades of
night.

That sight was not lost on them. From the head of the
column cried Volscens:—

Halt, there! What is your business? Who are you that carry
arms,

And where are you off to?

               The pair made no reply to this challenge

But hurried on into the wood, hoping the darkness would
    save them.
The horsemen, knowing the place well, stationed themselves
    at the crossways
On either hand, and cordoned the wood to stop each exit.
That wood was an unkempt tangle of bushes and black holm-
    oaks
Right through, and everywhere thickly overgrown with
    brambles:
Here and there showed their path among a confusion of dim
    tracks.
Euryalus, who was hampered by the weight of his spoils, un-
    sighted
And hindered by the branches, in fright lost his direction.
Nisus got clear away; forgetting his friend, he had slipped
The foe and reached the place which later was called Alba,*
After Albanus, but then housed the royal herds of Latinus,
When, halting, he looked back—in vain, for his comrade was
    not behind him:—
    Euryalus, my poor dear friend, where did I leave you?
Where shall I look for you, should I retrace all my ravelled path
Through that bewildering wood?
                         At once he turns back; and carefully
Following the trail he'd made, roves through the hushed
    thickets.
Soon he can hear horses and the din that means a pursuit.
Not long now before a loud cry comes to his ears,
And he sees his friend whom, tricked by the mazy wood and
    the darkness,
Bemused by their sudden attack, the whole mob has pounced
    on and now
Is dragging away, overpowered, frantically, vainly struggling.
What can Nisus do? What weapons or strength can avail him
To rescue the lad? Or shall he just hurl himself to destruction
Upon their swords, to die quickly and honourably of his
    wounds?

On the instant he draws back his arm, with spear poised ready
  to throw,
And looking up at the moon above, he says this prayer:—
  Goddess, be with me and help me in what I have to do,
Latona's child, supremest of stars and warden of woodlands!
If ever my father Hyrtacus brought offerings to your altar
On my behalf; if I've honoured you with the spoils of the chase,
Hung them within your dome or on your hallowed roof-
  top—
Grant me to rout this mob, and speed my weapons un-
  erringly!
  Then, putting all his body into the throw, he hurled
The spear. It flew with a swish through the shadowy night
  and struck
Sulmo, whose back was turned, from behind: the shaft broke
  there,
But the splintered wood drove on, piercing the wall of the
  heart.
Spouting warm blood from his breast, Sulmo went rolling;
  the chill of
Death came upon him; his flanks heaved with long-drawn
  gaspings.
His comrades looked round them everywhere. Nisus, the
  more aggressive
For this, was poising another weapon above his ear-tip.
With the foe quite at a loss, it went right through both
  temples
Of Tagus, and warmly weltering stuck in the brain it trans-
  fixed.
Volscens, unable to see the assailant anywhere,
Or what direction to charge in, was bloody-hearted with
  rage:—
  All right! In the meantime *you* shall pay the account for
  these two
With your own life-blood,
                he cried; and instantly, drawing his sword,

He went for Euryalus. Then, frightened out of his wits,
Nisus gave a yell—he could not any longer
Remain concealed by the darkness or stand such terrible
    anguish:—
  Here! I am standing here! I did it! Oh, Rutuli, turn your
Weapons on me! It was all my doing. He couldn't have
    harmed you
Or tried to. I swear it by heaven and the all-seeing stars.
Only he loved too well a friend who has brought him bad luck.
    So Nisus spoke. But the sword, violently thrust, had
        passed through
The ribs, and while he yet spoke, was boring a hole in the
    white breast.
Euryalus rolled over, dying: the blood ran down
His beautiful limbs, and his neck dropped feebly onto one
    shoulder.
So, when its stalk is cut by the ploughshare, a shining flower
Grows limp and dies, or poppies droop down their heads
    upon
The languid stems when the weight of a shower is too much
    for them.
But Nisus went straight in at the foe: he was after Volscens
And nobody else; nothing would stop him getting at Volscens.
Closely hemming him round on this side and that, they
    struggle
To fight him off: but he presses forward all the more furiously
Whirling his sword in arcs of lightning, until he has slashed it
Full in the screaming face of Volscens, and dying, slain him.
Then, riddled with wounds, he throws himself down over
    his lifeless
Friend, and there at last grows still in the calm of death.
Ah, fortunate pair! if my poetry has any influence,
Time in its passing shall never obliterate your memory,
As long as the house of Aeneas dwell by the Capitol's move-
    less
Rock, and the head of the Roman family keeps his power.

Now the victorious Rutuli stripped the spoils from the
    bodies
And weeping carried the lifeless Volscens into their camp.
Lamentation waxed there when they found Rhamnes dead
And so many of their best men, like Numa and Serranus,
Killed in the same massacre. A crowd collected around
The dead and dying, the spot where the ground was warm
    and reeking
With the late slaughter, and blood ran like rivers foaming in
    spate.
The spoils were identified—Messapus' glittering helmet
And the breast adornments of Rhamnes, recovered with so
    much effort.

And now was Aurora,* leaving the saffron bed of Tithonus,
Beginning to shower upon earth the light of another day.
As soon as the sun was risen and there was light to see by,
Turnus, in full armour, whipped up his men to fight:
Each captain mustered for battle his bronze-accoutred
    company,
All with their anger whetted by tales of the night's doings.
What's more—a shocking sight—impaled on spears, up-
    lifted,
And followed by the shouting Rutuli were the heads of
Euryalus and Nisus.
On the left flank of their ramparts, the right being well pro-
    tected
By the river, the tough troops of Aeneas took up position;
They man the system of trenches or stand on the turrets
    above,
In low spirits and shocked to see the impaled heads—
Those too familiar faces, alas, dripping with black gore.

Meantime winged Rumour, flitting over the shaken
    encampment,
Came with post-haste news and swooped to the ears of the
    mother
Of Euryalus. Poor woman, her bones suddenly turned

To ice, the shuttle*was dashed from her hands, the thread
  unwound.
A pathetic figure, she darted out, wailing and keening,
Tearing her hair, and frantically made for the walls, the front
  line of
Defenders; she was regardless of the men stationed there
Or the danger of flying missiles. Loudly now she lamented:—
  Oh, Euryalus, to see you like this! How could you leave me
Desolate—oh, heartless—you, the solace of my sere
Old age? And to think that you went on so dangerous a
  mission
Without your poor mother being allowed to say farewell to
  you!
O god! you are lying, a prey to the dogs and birds of Latium,
On alien soil! And I, your mother, have not brought you—
Your body—to burial, not closed the eyes nor washed
The wounds, nor wrapped you in the robe I had been busily
  working
For you, by day and night, to distract my old mind from its
  troubles.
Where shall I seek you? In what place are lying your mutilated
Body, your severed limbs? Is this all of yourself you bring
  me
Back—this head? Was it this I journeyed by land and sea
  for?
Rutuli, if you have any human feelings, oh, kill me!
Turn all your weapons upon me! Let me be the first to die!
Or else may the Father of heaven take pity on me, and finish
This life I hate, striking me down with his fire to Hades,
Since I've no other way to end my cruel existence.
  Her wailing shook their hearts: a general groan of sorrow
Went up: they were benumbed, and had lost all spirit for
  fighting.
As she was fanning their grief, by the orders of Ilioneus
And the bitterly weeping Ascanius, Idaeus and Actor lifted
Her up in their arms and carried her back into her dwelling.

Then did the brazen tongue of the trumpet utter afar
Its terrible call: war-cries went up, and the whole sky
    bellowed.
Under a driving, tight-fitting roof of shields the Italians
Charged, essaying to fill in the trenches and break through
    the breastwork.
Some of them tried to get in by scaling the walls on ladders
At a point where the ring of defenders was thinnest and day-
    light showed
Between their spaced-out bodies. In reply, the Trojans rained
All kinds of missile and thrust down with tough pikes at the
    attackers,
Being trained by long experience of siege to defend their
    battlements.
Ponderous, deadly rocks they pitched down, too, in an effort
To shatter that armoured column; but these, beneath their
    compact
Casemate of shields, were in good shape to take whatever
    might come down.
But now they failed: for where the great press of assailants
    threatened,
The Trojans rolled up an enormous boulder and tipped it
    over,
Which falling burst through the casemate of shields, knocked
    down the Rutuli
Like ninepins. The latter, though brave men, were now less
    keen to engage in
Such a blind, head-on assault; so they tried to drive the
    defenders
Off the ramparts by sniping.
On another sector Mezentius, ferocious of aspect, brandished
Etruscan torches, attacked with smoking incendiaries;
While Messapus, tamer of horses, a son of Neptune, hacked
    through
The palisade and shouted for ladders to scale the battlements.
    Calliope, I pray that the Muses inspire my song,

To tell what execution the sword of Turnus now wrought
    there,
What deaths; what men each fighting-man despatched to
    Hades.
I pray you unroll with me the spacious map of the battle.
For you are divine, you remember it all, and can recount it.
  There stood, in a key position, a turret tall and sheer,
And linked with gangways aloft. This the Italians were
    struggling
With all their might to storm, putting all their skill to its over-
    throw;
While for their part the Trojans fought back, volleying stones,
Keeping up a heavy fire of arrows through its embrasures.
At the head of his men, Turnus now hurled a lighted fire-dart
Which stuck in the tower's side, blazing: fanned by the wind,
    it rapidly
Spread fire all over the planking, consumed the door it was
    lodged in.
Alarm and confusion seized the defenders within; they
    sought to
Escape their doom, but in vain. Jammed together, they
    pressed back
To the side of the tower that was free from fire: but suddenly,
    bodily
The tower collapsed and fell with a crash that resounded to
    heaven.
Half dead they were pitched to the ground, the huge mass of
    the tower avalanching
Upon them, impaled by their own weapons, with splinters
    of tough wood
Spitting their bodies through. Helenor and Lycus alone
Just managed to scramble clear: Helenor, a man in the
    prime of
Youth, was the natural son of the Lydian king by a slave from
Licymna, who'd sent him to fight at Troy, though forbidden
    —a light-armed

Swordsman, with no reputation in war, no device on his
     shield.
As soon as he saw that he was hemmed in by the hordes of
     Turnus—
A ring of Latin troops, rank upon rank, around him—
Like some wild beast, walled in by a thick cordon of hunters,
Which furiously snarls at their weapons, and knowing she's
     doomed, with a great spring
Hurls herself to her death upon the hunting spears,
Even so did the young man charge right into the press of the
     foe,
Where he saw their weapons were thickest, as one who was
     bound to die.
But Lycus, being much swifter a runner, made good his
     escape
Through all the hostile arms as far as the rampart; and
     now
He was struggling to grip its parapet and clutch the hands of
     his comrades.
But Turnus, who'd been in hot pursuit and had hurled a
     weapon,
Triumphantly taunted him thus:—
                              You half-wit, did you really
Think you could give us the slip?
                         Then he seized the man as he clung there
And tore him off; a large piece of the wall came away with
     him.
It was like when the war-bird of Jove*has seized a hare or a
     snow-white
Swan in its crooked talons and soars aloft to its eyrie;
Or the wolf of Mars has snatched from the fold a lamb which
     its mother
Looks for with long-drawn bleatings. On the whole front the
     din
Crescendoed, the foe running in and bridging the trenches
     with rubble,

While some of them tossed incendiaries up at the wall-tops
  above.
With a rock as big as a chunk of mountain, Ilioneus
Now felled Lucetius, who was close to the gate with a fire-
  brand:
Emathion was killed by Liger, Corynaeus by Asilas—
Liger good with his spear, Asilas at long-range bowshots:
Ortygius went down to Caeneus, who then was killed by
  Turnus;
Turnus as well slew Itys, Clonius, Dioxippus, Promulus,
Sagaris, and Idas who stood in defence of a turret.
Capys killed Privernus, who had just received a flesh wound
From the spear of Themilla: he foolishly let go his shield and
  clapped
His hand to the wound; so now the flighted arrow of Capys
Pinned his hand to his left side, and deeply penetrating
Buried its point in his lungs and gave him a mortal wound.
The son of Arcens stood, conspicuous in his armour
And finely-embroidered tunic of a bright Spanish rust-red:
A handsome fellow he was—had grown up in the woods of his
  mother
About Symaethus*river, where stands the Palici's rich
And reverenced altar: him, then, his father Arcens had sent.
Downing his spears, Mezentius now whirled his buzzing
  sling
Three times around his head on a tense thong, then shot;
And the scorching bullet struck that warrior clean in the fore-
  head,
Splitting it open, and laying him out full length on the
  ground.
  This, so legend tells, was the first time that Ascanius
Fired in war the arrows with which he'd been used to
  terrorize
Swift-running game: a shot of his struck down the gallant
  Numanus,
Whose surname was Remulus; this man had recently taken

In marriage the younger sister of Turnus. Today he was
    strutting
In front of the Latin lines, yelling out remarks—some proper,
Some not, to record; his royal alliance had given him
A swelled head—showing off his giant physique, and shout-
    ing:—
    You men of twice-captured Troy,* aren't you ashamed to be
      once more
Besieged and cooped up in your ramparts? skulking from
    death behind battlements?
Look at the heroes who make war to win them brides from
    our people!
What god—or what lunatic impulse—has dragged you to
    Italy?
You'll find no Atridae here, no double-talking Ulysses.
We are brought up hard from birth; we take our children
    young to
The river and harden them in the painful, ice-cold water.
Our boys go hunting all night and tirelessly rove the forests:
The taming of horses, and archery practice, to them are
    pastimes.
Our young men, inured to hard work and an austere way of
    living,
Tame the soil with hoes or rock cities in battle
We live with steel in our hands; reversing the spear, we use it
To belabour the backs of our oxen. Not even old age, that
    cramps others,
Weakens our mental powers or impairs our physical vigour:
Though our hair be grey, we put on the helmet, and never
    lose
Our gusto for carrying off fresh plunder and living upon it.
But you, in your dresses embroidered with yellow and loud
    purple,
You with the hearts of loafers, you devotees of dancing,
With frilly sleeves to your tunics, and bonnets kept on by
    ribbons!—

You Phrygian women*(for Phrygian men you are not), run
    away
To mount Dindymus,* where the double-mouthed pipe
    tweedles for addicts!
The timbrels and Berecynthian fife of Cybele call you.
Leave fighting to men, I advise you; relinquish sword-play
    to others.
    Ascanius found this fellow's bragging and loud-mouthed
    frightfulness
Intolerable. So, drawing back his bowstring of horse-gut
With arrow noeked, he took up his stance, with his arms
    extended
Wide, having first uttered a prayer and a vow to Jove:—
    Almighty Jove, grant me success in this brave venture!
I in return will bring to your temple a yearly offering
And set up at your altar a bullock with gilded horns—
A snow-white bullock standing as many hands high as its
    mother,
One old enough to butt with its horns and paw the ground.
    The Father heard his prayer: from a clear tract of sky
He thundered upon the left: simultaneously twanged the fatal
Bow, and the arrow sped from the string with a terrible whirr
To pass through the head of Remulus, its point transfixing
    the hollow
Temples:—
        Now go and mock good men with insolent words!
The men of twice-captured Troy send this reply to the
    Rutuli.
    No more did Ascanius say. The Trojans hailed his feat
With a cheer, and shouted for joy; their morale was raised
    sky-high.
Now it happened that long-haired Apollo, throned on a
    cloud, was looking
Down from the regions of air at the Italian lines
And the settlement; then he spoke to the triumphant
    Ascanius:—

More power to your young valour, my son! You're going
    the right way
To starry fame, O god-born and sire of gods to be!
Rightly all destined foes shall be quelled by the house of
    Assaracus.
Troy is not big enough for you.
                       Thus did he say; then launched
Himself from the heights of heaven, and brushing aside the
    breezes,
Made his way to Ascanius. He now took on the appearance
Of aged Butes—a man who had formerly been the squire
And trusted household guard of Trojan Anchises; later
Aeneas made him Ascanius' personal aide. Apollo
Came as the living image of this old man—the same voice,
Complexion and white hair, the same fierce-clashing
    accoutrements—
And to the fiery-spirited prince addressed these words:—
    Son of Aeneas, let it suffice to have killed Numanus
And come off scot-free yourself. Great Apollo has granted
    you this first
Distinction, and is not jealous you've won it with his own
    weapon.
But take no more part in the fighting, young prince.
                         So Apollo began;
But while he was yet speaking, he went from the sight of men,
Vanishing into the distance before their eyes, into thin air.
The Trojan commanders recognized him for a god,* and his
    arms
Divine, catching the noise of his quiver which rattled as he
    flew.
So they used the god's authority to deter Ascanius
From further fighting, keen though he was, and themselves
    returned
To the combat, risking their lives at the deadly breach of
    danger.
Now the din rises along the walls, over all the defences:

They are aiming the vicious bows, and spinning the spears.
    The ground
Is one great litter of missiles: the shields and the rounded
    helmets
Ring with their blows: the fray swells to a bitter climax.
It was wild as the storm that comes from the West, at the time
    of the rainy
Goat-stars,* flailing the earth; or the gales that go racing sea-
    wards
Pelting with hail, when Juppiter, terrible in the South wind,
Bursting the clouds above us, unleashes tornadoes of water.
    Pandarus and Bitias, sprung from Alcanor of Ida,
Reared by the dryad*Iaera in Juppiter's sacred wood—
Young men as tall as their native pine trees and mountains—
    these two,
Confident in their weapons, threw open the gate which their
    general
Had given them to guard, positively inviting the foe to enter
The ramparts; while they, swords drawn, flaunting the
    plumes on their tall heads,
Stood just inside, to left and right, in front of a turret.
So by some flowing river—by the banks of the Po, it might be,
Or Athesis' genial waters—twin oaks stand, head in air,
Soaring up side by side, raising their leafy crowns
Into the sky, their tops dizzily nodding. The Rutuli,
Seeing a gateway open, made a concerted rush for it.
But, the next minute, Quercens, handsomely-armed
    Aquicolus,
Tmarus the impetuous and Haemon the scion of Mars,
With all their detachment, were either routed and running
    away
Or had laid down their lives right in that very entrance.
Then did the hearts of the combatants kindle to fiercer rage;
The Trojans, rallying, concentrated at that point, willing
To mix it and make extensive sallies beyond their walls.
    Now Turnus, who was fighting ferociously and creating

Havoc elsewhere on the field, received a despatch—the
    Trojans,
Flushed with the losses they'd just inflicted, had thrown a
    gate open.
He left the work in hand, and moved by prodigious anger,
Charged at the Trojan gate and those insolent brothers who
    fought there.
Antiphates first (for he was there in the forefront) Turnus
Felled with a javelin-throw—Antiphates, bastard son of
Sarpedon by a woman of Thebes: the cornel-wood lance
Flew through the soft air, went home in the stomach just
    under his tall
Chest; the darkly-gaping wound spouted a torrent
Of blood, and the lung it was lodged in warmed its iron point.
Then Turnus slew Meropes and Erymas, then Aphidnus;
Then Bitias, whose eyes were blazing, whose mind was
    berserk—
But not with a javelin—no javelin would have killed him.
A heavy projectile came catapulted and screeching at him,
Travelling like a meteor: the reinforced, bull's-hide shield,
The trusty cuirass and its two layers of golden chainmail,
    could not
Withstand that weapon; Bitias' giant frame fell crashing.
Earth groaned, and his mighty shield came clattering down
    upon him.
That fall was like when a stone pier, constructed from huge,
    shaped blocks
Of masonry and built out into the sea in the bay of
Baiae,* near Cumae, collapses: the wall of it falls away,
    dragging
A mass of rubble behind, slaps the water and sinks to the
    bottom;
The sea is all in a welter, black sludge oozes up to the surface:
That impact shakes to the core Prochyta and the bedrock
Of Inarime*beneath which, at Jove's bidding, Typhoeus was
    buried.

At this, the War-god Mars lent extra courage and strength
To the Latins, applying his sharpest stimulus to their
    hearts,
But loosing the spirit of Flight and Panic among the Tro-
    jans.
The Latins gather their forces, for now they can get to grips
    with
The foe, and the god of battle possesses them.
Pandarus, when he saw his brother laid low, and realized
How the engagement was going, the momentous turn it had
    taken,
Putting his broad shoulders to the gate, with a convulsive
Effort swung it shut upon its hinges, leaving
Many of his comrades in desperate action outside the battle-
    ments.
Others he locked in with him as they came streaming back,
But fatally failed to notice the Rutulian leader amongst
    them,
Yes, breaking into the settlement: he'd actually locked him
    in there—
As bad as putting a tiger in with a helpless flock.
At once a new light blazed from the eyes of Turnus, and
    dreadfully
Clashed his armour; the blood-red plumes on his helmet
    quivered;
His shield gave off bright shimmers, like lightning. Aeneas'
    men
In sudden consternation recognize that detested
Visage, those giant limbs. Now the immense Pandarus,
Burning with vengefulness for his brother's death, leaps
    forward
And cries:—
        This is not the palace that goes with Amata's*daughter
As dowry. Nor is it Ardea, your native town, you're shut
    up in.
This is an enemy camp, and you'll never get out of it, Turnus.

But Turnus, quite unflustered, smiling a little, replied:—
Come on, then, if you've courage enough! Come on and
    fight!
You can tell Priam later you met a second Achilles.
    He spoke. Pandarus summoned all his strength and hurled
A spear, its shaft rugged with knots and the unpeeled bark.
The winds received it: Saturnian Juno was there to deflect it
From Turnus' body: the weapon stuck harmlessly in the
    door:—
    But you'll not escape this weapon I wield in my strong right
    hand.
I'm not a man who misses or leaves his opponent a whole
    skin,
    Said Turnus; then, rising on tiptoe, he whirled his sword
    aloft, and
Brought the blade down between his enemy's temples,
    splitting
The young man's forehead and face in half, a hideous
    gash.
There was a crash as the young giant came to the ground:
Dying, he lay stretched out, his limbs unstrung and his
    armour
Spattered with blood and brains from the head that was
    slashed in two
And sagging away to left and right over each shoulder.
The Trojans, panicking wildly, turned, scattered and ran.
And if only the conquering Turnus*had had the presence of
    mind
To break open the bars of the gate and let his own comrades
    in,
That day would have been the end of the war and the Trojan
    nation.
But he was fighting-mad; the blood lust drove him on
Against his adversaries.
First he caught Phaleris, and Gyges whom he had ham-
    strung;

Then, snatching up their spears, he hurled them at the
    backs of
The fleeing enemy: Juno supplied him with strength and
    courage.
Now he killed Halys too, and Phegeus, whose shield he
    pierced;
And while the defenders fought on the walls, unaware of his
    presence,
He killed Alcander, Halius, Noemon and Prytanis.
Lynceus came at him next, calling up his comrades; but
    Turnus,
The rampart on his right, lashed out with his flickering
    sword
And got him; his head, swept off by that one short-arm blow,
Tumbled and lay at a distance, still helmeted. Amycus next,
That mighty hunter, was slain—none was so adept as he
In the business of impregnating the tips of weapons with
    poison;
Then Clytius, son of Aeolus, and Cretheus, beloved by the
    Muses—
Cretheus, the Muses' darling, whose heart was given for ever
To song and the lyre, to plucking the tuneful strings, who
    sang
For ever about war-horses, battles, heroic deeds.
    When news of the losses their men were suffering came
    at last to
The Trojan generals, Mnestheus and fiery Serestus arrived,
To see their people scattered and the foe within the gates.
So Mnestheus shouted:—
               Where do you think you're running away to?
What other refuge have you? What battlements but these?
My lads, is one man going to make such a killing all over
The settlement—one man who is trapped in our ramparts—
    and get
Away with it? one who has sent so many of our best to
    perdition?

You cowards, aren't you ashamed? Have you no pride, no
        feeling
For our distressful country, our ancient gods, and Aeneas?
    Stung by his words, the Trojans closed up their ranks and
        stiffened
Resistance. Little by little Turnus gave back from the on-
        slaught
Towards the river, that part of the wall which the Tiber
        bounded.
Made more aggressive by this, the Trojans pressed in on him,
        shouting
And concentrating their forces; so will a crowd of men harry
A savage lion with spears levelled; the brute, in alarm,
Backs away, murderous-minded, viciously glaring; his rage
And his courage forbid him to turn tail; but equally, much as
He'd like to, he cannot drive a path through those men with
        their weapons.
Just so did Turnus give ground. He was in a fix, but his move-
        ments
Were quite unflurried; his fighting blood was on the boil still.
Yes, even then he had twice gone in at the thick of the foe,
Driven them twice in headlong confusion all round the
        ramparts.
But the whole garrison came running to form up against
        him.
Saturnian Juno dared not lend him the strength to oppose
        them,
Not now, for Juppiter sent Iris flying down
From on high with a very brusque command to his sister and
        consort—
There will be trouble if Turnus leaves not the Trojan's
        encampment.
And so that warrior found his shield less sure to protect him,
His sword-arm flagging: volleys of missiles from every angle
Were snowing him under. The helmet upon his temples rang
        with

Incessant blows, its strong bronze cracked open by fusillades
of

Stones, and the plumes torn away from its crest: his shield's
boss could not

Stand up to the battering: led by Mnestheus, who fought
like a fury,

The Trojans redoubled their fire. Then Turnus was bathed
in sweat

Which ran—he had not a moment's breathing-space—dirty
and sticky

All over him, and he panted heavily, sick with exhaustion.

At last he hurled himself, full-armed as he was, at one leap

Into the river below. Its yellow tide received him

As he plunged in, and bearing him up on its gentle waters,

Washed the blood off and restored him in high heart to his
friends.

BOOK X

Now a new day threw open the halls of almighty Olympus,
And a council was called by the Father of heaven, the ruler of
    mankind,
To meet in his sky palace where, from the heights, he sur-
    veyed
All earth, the Trojan encampment and the peoples of
    Latium.
They passed to their seats in the great hall, and Jove it was
    who spoke:—
  Great heaven-dwellers, why have you reversed the deci-
    sion
Agreed on? What is the meaning of such unruly contentious-
    ness?
I had forbidden that Italy should meet the Trojans in war.
Do you brawl in spite of my veto? What agency has frightened
This side or that into taking up arms and provoking a conflict?
A time will come when it's right to fight—do not be pre-
    mature—
One day when barbarous Carthage*shall open a way through
    the Alps
And roll a tide of disaster up to Rome's very towers.
Then will strife and hatred, then will all violence be lawful.
Have done now! Give your whole-hearted assent to the pact
    I've decreed.
  So Juppiter briefly declared. But golden Venus in answer
Spoke at some length:—
  Father, eternal Power over men and men's affairs—
What other power is there which I can now entreat?—
Do you mark how the Rutuli are exulting? how Turnus goes
Through the fray, charioted and conspicuous? how he
    speeds,

Puffed up with triumph? The ring of their ramparts no
　　longer protects

The Trojans: no, they are battling within the gates, on the
　　high-built

Parapets of the earthworks, and flooding the moat with
　　blood.

Aeneas is far away, and knows nothing of this. Will you never

Allow the siege to be lifted? Once more an enemy threatens

Troy town—this baby Troy—and a second army assails us:

Once more from Aetolian Arpi is Diomed*moving against

The Trojans. I well believe I too am not done with being
　　wounded—

Your child—and till then this war of mortals will not be over.

If it's without your leave and against your will that the
　　Trojans

Made for Italy, let them expiate their sins, and withhold

Your succour from them: but if they were following out the
　　solemn

Commands of the gods and the dead, why is anyone now
　　permitted

To cancel what you have ordered and to rewrite their destiny?

Need I bring up again the burning of their fleet*on the shore

Of Eryx? or the suborning against them of the Storm-king*

And his wild winds from Aeolia? or the mission that Iris*was
　　sent on?

Now Juno is dredging up the Underworld—a province

Hitherto unexplored—and has suddenly loosed Allecto*

On the earth, to spread delirium through the Italian towns.

Empire means nothing to me now: that was something we
　　hoped for

While luck was with us. Let them you prefer to win be the
　　winners.

If there's no place on earth which your hard-hearted wife

Will ever concede to the Trojans, I implore you, sire, by the
　　smoking

Ruins of fallen Troy, let Ascanius be released

Unharmed from the battlefield, O let my grandson survive it.
Aeneas may be tossed on unknown waters—so be it—
Pursuing whatever path Fortune has found for him:
I ask but to preserve, to withdraw his son from the fatal
Fight. I possess Amathus, Mount Paphus, and Cythera,
And a shrine in Idalia*: here let him live out his days, un-
  known
To fame¦ laying down his arms. Command, if you will, that
  Carthage
Crush Italy, hold her down with supreme power: there shall
  be no
Opposition from Ascanius. What was the use in escaping
The horrors of war, slipping out between the Argive fires,
Running the gamut of peril through seas and desolate lands,
When the Trojans are still in search of a second Troy in
  Latium?
Better, I think, to have settled amongst his own country's
  expiring
Ashes, upon the soil where Troy stood. Father, I beg you,
Give Xanthus and Simois*back to my piteous Trojans, grant
  them
To tread out the doom of Troy a second time!

Then queen Juno,

Inspired by strong passion, spoke up:—

Why do you force me to break

My profound silence, to tear the skin from my grief and
  expose it?
Has any mortal man or any god compelled
Aeneas to be the aggressor and attack the ruler of Latium?
'At the bidding of fate he came to Italy': very well—
Though Cassandra's*ravings it was that moved him. But
  did *I*
Ask him to quit the settlement or trust his life to the
  winds?
To leave his camp and the focal point of the war in a boy's
  charge?

Undermine the Etruscans' loyalty? make trouble among
    peaceful tribes?
Was he driven to this treacherous policy by a god, or some
    ruthless compulsion
Of mine? How does Juno, or Iris' mission, come into it?
Shocking, you say, that Italians should ring your baby Troy
With fire, and Turnus should set foot on his own native
    soil—
Turnus, grandson of Pilumnus,* son of the nymph Venilia.
Well, what of the Trojans spreading fire and havoc in
    Latium?
Oppressing a land not theirs and driving off plunder? choos-
    ing
Whom they shall wed, and abducting betrothed girls from
    their lovers?
Pretending to offer peace while their ships bristle with
    weapons?
You may filch your Aeneas* out of the grip of the Greeks,
Stretching a veil of cloud, thin air, in defence of your hero.
You may transform his vessels* into as many sea-nymphs:
But if I help the Italians at all, that is a crime.
'Aeneas is far away, unknowing of this': let him stay so.
You possess Paphus, Idalium, lofty Cythera: well then,
Why do you meddle with hot-tempered folk who are spoiling
    for battle?
Are you saying it's I who am trying to capsize the leaky cause
Of Troyland? I? Not the one who threw the pitiable Trojans
To the Greeks? What started Europe and Asia rising in arms
Against each other?* Whose thieving hand broke down their
    peace?
Was I responsible for the Dardan philanderer ransacking
Sparta? Did I give him weapons, or kindle a war with his
    lust?
Then was the time to have feared for your people: too late
    now you rise with
Unjustified grievances, spattering futile insults upon me.

Such was Juno's plea; it got a mixed reception
From the heaven-dwellers, who raised a buzz like the sound
    in a forest
When a wind is getting up among the branches, gustily,
Sulkily murmuring, warning sailors of gales to come.
Then the almighty Father, the first lord of the universe,
Uttered; and as he spoke, the high places of heaven fell silent,
Earth shook to its foundations, and the firmament was still;
The West winds held their breath, the sea smoothed out its
    face:—
Now take my words to heart, and let them not be forgotten.
Since it was not permitted that the Italians should come to
Terms with the Teucrians,* and your dispute allows of no
    ending,
This day, whatever the fortune each warrior has and the
    hope
He pursues, be he Trojan or Rutulian, I shall make no dis-
    tinction—
Whether the camp is besieged through the destiny of the
    Italians,
Or a fault inherent in Troy, or the taking of bad advice.
I do not exempt the Rutuli. The selfhood of each shall deter-
    mine
His effort and how it fares. I am king to all, and impartial.
Fate will settle the issue.
                    By the stream of his Stygian brother,*
The banks where boiling pitch flows in a black maelstrom,
    he nodded,
Confirming his promise: the nod caused all Olympus to
    tremble.
That was the end of the conference. Juppiter rose from his
    golden
Throne, and the heaven-dwellers escorted him to his own
    place.
   Meantime the Rutuli pressed hard on the gates all round,
Doing great execution, encircling the walls with fire,

While Aeneas' men were hemmed in behind their ramparts
    and had
No hope of getting away. They stood, dispirited, helpless,
In the turrets, and manned the ring of their walls with
    thinning forces.
Asius, son of Imbrasus, Thymoetes, son of Hicetaon,
The two Assaraci, with Castor and aged Thymbris,
Were in the forefront: beside them stood Clarus and
    Themon, the two
Brothers of Sarpedon, who came from mountainous Lycia.
There, lifting a huge boulder, a sizeable chunk of mountain,
With a superhuman effort, is Acmon of Lyrnesus—
A giant like Clytius, his father, and his brother Menestheus.
With javelins and stones the defenders are fighting bitterly,
Shooting incendiaries and fitting arrow to bowstring.
Among them, see! the Dardan lad, special favourite of Venus
And looking it too, his noble head uncovered, Ascanius
Glows like some jewel set in yellow gold, which graces
The wearer's neck or hair; like ivory which an artist
Has inlaid upon boxwood or terebinth-wood from Oricum
He shines: his hair is falling loose about his milk-white
Neck, and is gathered above by a circlet of pliant gold.
Ismarus, you too your great-hearted clansmen saw
As you steeped arrows in poison and fired with unerring
    aim—
High-born Ismarus from Maeonia, where they till
Fertile fields irrigated by the gold-bearing river Pactolus.*
Mnestheus was there as well, raised to the heights by the
    glory
Of beating Turnus off just now from the high-built ramparts;
And Capys, from whom the town in Campania*gets its name.
  So they were all engaged in the exacting struggle
Of war. And now, at midnight, Aeneas was ploughing the
    seas.
On leaving Evander and entering the Etruscan camp, he
    presented

Himself before their king, told him his name and nation,
The aid he sought and the offer he brought; acquainted him
Of the forces Mezentius had won to his side, and the violent
    reactions
Of Turnus; warned him what need there was for reciprocal
    trust
If the king's own affairs were to prosper, and added a plea.
    Tarchon
Struck a treaty at once, joining forces with him. The Etruscan
Army embarked: heaven was with them and fate's embargo
Lifted, now they followed a foreign commander. Aeneas'
Ship led the line; on its prow were Phrygian lions* sur-
    mounted
By Ida, most dear to the Trojan refugees, for a figurehead.
Here was stationed the hero Aeneas, calculating
The changeful factors of war. Pallas stayed close at his left
    side,
Inquiring about the stars by which they steered through the
    dark night,
Then asking Aeneas to tell his adventures on land and sea.
    Now, Muses, throw Helicon* wide and inspire my poetry
        to speak of
The host that followed Aeneas from the Etruscan shore
Upon that night, manning the ships which rode the seaways.
    Massicus led a squadron, sailing in his bronze-beaked
        vessel,
The *Tiger*; his contingent, a thousand strong, had come from
Clusium and the town of Cosae; their arms were a deadly
Bow and a light-weight quiver of arrows slung over the
    shoulder.
Grim Abas came too, his whole detachment in glittering
    armour,
A gilded image of Apollo gleaming upon his poop:
Populonia had given him six hundred of her sons,
Expert fighters all;* Ilva had furnished three hundred—
That isle so rich in mines of inexhaustible iron.

Third came Asilas, a medium between mankind and the gods,
A master at divining*from the entrails of sacrificed beasts,
The stars in the sky, the songs of birds, the presage of
    lightning:
He hurried to war a thousand spearmen in close formation;
Etruscan Pisa,* whose founders had come from the river
    Alphaeus,
Had raised them for him to command. Then followed the
    handsome Astyr,
Confident in his charger and many-coloured accoutrements.
Three hundred more, who were all of one mind in their wish
    for battle,
Came from their homes in Caere, from the country around
    the Minio,
The ancient town of Pyrgi and malarial Gravisca.*

   I must not pass over Cinyras, most valiant leader in war
Of the Ligurians,* or Cupavo with his small force
And swan's plumes waving above his crest—a symbol of his
    father's
Transformation, and thus a reproach to Cupid and Venus;
The legend being that his father, Cycnus,* in grief for beloved
Phaethon,* was consoling his sorrowful heart with song
Beneath the shady leaves of poplars, once Phaethon's sisters,
When he took on soft plumage, yes, snow-white as old age,
And left the earth behind and sang his way to the stars.
His son was sailing now with a band of other young men,
Oaring onwards a great ship, the *Centaur*, which trod the
    waves
In towering bulk, its figurehead threatening the water below
With a huge rock, its long keel furrowing through the deep-
    sea.

   There too was Ocnus, who'd whipped up a force from his
    native land:
He, the son of the Tuscan river and the seeress Manto,
Founded the city of Mantua* and gave it his mother's
    name—

Mantua, rich in its forefathers, who were not all of the same
  stock:
Three clans it had, each clan ruling over four townships,
With Mantua, by reason of its Etruscan blood, as the capital.
Five hundred from here had taken up arms against Mezen-
  tius:
They sailed in warships following a figurehead of the river
Mincius wreathed with the grey-green rushes of Lake
  Benacus.
Aulestes drove wallowing on, his hundred men tugging
  hard at
The sweeps and thrashing the waves; the sea's face foamed as
  they churned it:
His ship was the giant *Triton*, the sound of whose conch
  affrighted
The dark-blue water; its dipping figurehead was the hairy
Trunk of a man to the waist, below the belly a great fish;
The water foamed and gurgled under that monster's breast.
So many the chosen princes who sailed in thirty ships
Cutting the sea with their bronze prows, to the relief of the
  Trojans.
  And now had the daylight gone from the sky, and the gentle
    moon's
Night-riding horses were pacing half-way across the heavens.
Aeneas, whose anxiety allowed him no rest, was doing
A trick at the helm and handling the sheets himself on the
  ship's stern,
When, in mid-passage, a marvel—an argosy of his own ones
Came to meet him; the nymphs, the ships that kindly Cybele
Had turned into nymphs and bidden to have a divine power in
The deep, came swimming up abreast, cleaving the waves,
As many as once had been moored by their bronze beaks to
  the shore.
From afar they knew the hero, and dancing wreathed around
  him.
Cymodoce, the one who was most skilled at speaking,

Followed behind, and gripping the stern with her right hand, raised up

Her body, while her left hand silently paddled the water.
Then she startled him, saying:—

                         Are you on the alert, Aeneas,

O heaven-descended? Awake! Pay out the sheets! Run free!
It is we, your fleet, your barques built from the pinewood of holy

Mount Ida, but now we are sea-nymphs. When treacherously the Italian

Attacked us with fire and steel, we had to hurry and break
Your moorings, though we hated to do it. All over the sea
We've been looking for you. The Mother took pity and changed us into

What you now see, to be goddesses, living our lives in the deep.'

But your son, Ascanius, beleaguered within the walls and entrenchments,

Is heavily under fire from the furiously fighting Italians.
By now the Arcadian cavalry, with a stiffening of Etruscans,
Are at the rendezvous. Turnus is firmly resolved to prevent them

Linking with the besieged, to intercept and attack them
With his own squadrons. Up, then, and when the dawn comes, order

Your comrades at once to be roused to arms, and take the invincible

Gold-rimmed shield which the Lord of Fire himself has given you!

Tomorrow's light—these are no empty words I am speaking,
Do not suppose it—shall see the Italians slaughtered in great heaps.

  So saying, and dropping away, she gave the tall poop a push with

Her right hand—an expert propulsion. The ship fled over the waves

Faster than any javelin or wind-swift arrow could fly.

The other ships crowded on speed when they saw it. Trojan Aeneas

Was mystified and astonished, yet the omen heartened him greatly.

Gazing up at the vault of heaven, he uttered a short prayer:—

 O gracious lady of Ida,* mother of the gods, who rejoice in

Dindymus, turreted cities, lions harnessed in couples,

Be now my guide in the battle! Be near and divinely prosper

This omen! Be with your Phrygian sons, O goddess, and bless them!

  No more did he say; but even as he spoke, the returning day

Was streaming back in full flush of light, routing the darkness.

Now for a start he ordered his men to ready themselves—

Their hearts and equipment—for combat, and to obey his signals.

And now, as he stood high up in the stern-sheets, Aeneas held

His Trojans and their encampment in view: so he lifted his shield with

His left hand and made it flash. The Dardans upon the walls there

Raised a great shout; their fighting spirit revived at this new hope,

Their fire was redoubled: so it is when under the dark clouds

The cranes flying back to the Strymon* announce their approach, and trail their

Bugling cries as they swim through the air ahead of the South wind.

But Turnus and the Italian commanders thought it a strange thing

Until, looking round, they saw ships backing up to the beach

And the whole sea one swarm of vessels running towards them.

The peak of Aeneas' helmet was blazing, flame poured from
　　its lofty
Crest, and the golden boss of his shield spurted huge flashes:
It was as when on some cloudless night you see a comet
Glowing, blood-red and ominous, or the fiery Dog-star
　　rising
Which glooms the sky with sinister light and carries with it
Drought and pestilence to suffering humanity.
Yet the gallant Turnus' confidence was unimpaired—he
　　reckoned
To occupy the beaches before them and beat off the landing-
　　forces.
He spoke to raise their spirits, he even rebuked his men:—
　　This is what you have hoped and prayed for—to break
　　　them in hand-to-hand combat!
Brave men have the very spirit of war in their hands. Let each
　　of you
Now remember his wife and his home, remember the
　　great
And glorious deeds of our fathers. We'll meet the foe right
　　at the sea's edge
While he's in a flurry, just disembarking, his foothold pre-
　　carious.
Fortune always fights for the bold.
　　So Turnus spoke; then considered whom he should lead
　　in this onset
And whom he could delegate to carry on with the siege.
　　Meanwhile Aeneas was landing his men by assault gang-
　　ways
From the high sterns of the ships. Many watched for the
　　backwash
Of a swell that had spent its violence, then boldly jumped
　　into the shallows;
Others slid down the oars. Tarchon, eyeing the beaches,
Noticed a point where no shoals were heaving and roaring
　　with breakers,

But the seas ran up and spread out over the shore, unbroken,
And quickly changed course towards it, crying out to his
    comrades:—
  Now then! Rise to the stroke! Row hard, my gallant lads!
Lift the ships! Hurl them forward! Let's make a gash with
    our bows in
That enemy land! Let our keel gouge out a trough for itself
    there!
I don't care if the ship breaks up on the foreshore yonder
Once we have got a grip on the land.
                                        As soon as Tarchon
Had shouted these words, his crews all tugged on the oars
    together
And ran their ships in a smother of spray at the Latin shore
Until the bows were lodged on dry land and the keels wedged
    there,
Undamaged all—all except Tarchon's ship: this galley,
Striking a shoal, ran aground on the ridge of a treacherous
    sandbank
Where she hung balanced awhile, see-sawing and slapping
    the waves,
Then broke her back, tipping out her crew into the water;
Splintered oars and floating thwarts got in their way,
And the waves' backwash sucked at their feet as they struggled
    shorewards.
  Turnus reacted with speed and decision, aggressively
    throwing
His whole force at the Trojans, blocking the beach against
    them.
Trumpets rang out. Aeneas led the assault on the yeoman
Ranks—an auspicious start for the fray, mowed down the
    Latins
And killed Theron, a giant of a man, who had had the nerve
To attack him: Aeneas' sword pierced a joint of his bronze
    corselet,
The tunic stiff with gold, and mortally opened his side.

Next he slew Lichas, who had been ripped from the womb of
　　his dead
Mother, and consecrated to Phoebus*because, as a babe,
He'd survived that perilous knife. Nearby, Aeneas put down
To death tough Cisseus and huge Gyas, who were laying
　　about them
With clubs: no use to them now was the weapon of Hercules,*
　　though,
Nor their own strength, nor the spirit of Melampus, their
　　father, who'd been
The companion of Hercules during all his difficult labours
On earth. Now, see! while Pharus is boasting aloud like a
　　novice,
Aeneas hurls a javelin right into his bawling mouth.
Cydon too, the golden down of youth on his cheek still,
Poor Cydon, who'd come here to be with Clytius, his latest
　　love,
Would have fallen pitiably to the Trojan's sword and lain
　　there
Oblivious of all his youthful loves,* his ruling passion,
Had not his brothers, the offspring of Phorcus, interposed
Themselves in a solid body; seven they were, and seven
Spears they threw, some of which glanced harmlessly off
　　from Aeneas'
Helmet and shield, while the rest were deflected by guardian
　　Venus
So as merely to graze him. He now called out to his close
　　friend, Achates:—
　Pile me up weapons here! Each one I throw shall find its
Billet in an Italian, each weapon that once on the plains of
Ilium lodged in a Greek.
　　　　　　　　Then, snatching up a great spear,
He hurled it: that flying spear whacked through the bronze
　　of Maeon's
Shield, shattered his breastplate, shattered the breast as
　　well.

Alcanor goes to support his brother, holds up with his right
　　arm
The tottering Maeon; a spear drives through that arm, and
　　onward
Goes streaking still upon its bloody course, but Alcanor's
Arm is lifelessly dangling by the sinews from his shoulder.
Now Numitor, pulling out the spear from his brother's body,
Aimed it at Aeneas; but this time it was not allowed to
Strike its target—it merely grazed the thigh of Achates.
Now Clausus, from Cures, came up, all confident in his
　　youthful
Physique, and hit Dryops under the chin—a long shot with
　　a hardwood
Spearshaft, which went deep in, transfixing his throat and
　　at one stroke
Depriving him of voice and life itself: so Dryops
Struck the ground with his forehead and vomited up thick
　　gore.
Clausus laid low, as well, one way or another, three Thracians
Of the exalted line of Boreas,* and three whom their father,
Idas, had sent from their native Ismarus. Now Halaesus
Ran up with his Auruncans; Messapus, the son of Neptune,
Renowned for his chargers, arrived in support. Each army
　　strains
In turn to dislodge the other. The battle rages on Italy's
Very doorstep. As in high heaven the opposing winds
Battle with one another, equal in strength and spirit,
Wind to wind, cloud to cloud, wave to wave locked and un-
　　yielding;
Doubtful the issue—one long thrust and counterthrust,
　　neither
Side budging. Just so did the ranks of Troy and Latium clash
Together, foot to foot, man to man locked in the mêlée.

　　But on another sector, where a torrent had scattered about
The terrain, rolling boulders and bushes torn up from its
　　banks,

Pallas observed his Arcadians turn tail and the Latins pur-
        suing:
The broken ground here had led them for once to dismount
        from their horses,
But they were not accustomed to fighting on foot. So he tried
        the one thing
Left him to try in such a grave situation, and sought to
Revive their morale with a mixture of pleading and harsh
        rebuke:—
  Where are you running to, men? I call on you—by your
        brave deeds,
By the name of your king Evander, by the wars we have won,
        by my own
Ambition which now is stirring to rival my father in glory—
Don't put any hopes on retreating! We must break our way
        through the foe
With cold steel. There, where they mass against us in greatest
        numbers,
Is the route by which our dear country bids you and me to
        return to her.
No gods are after us: we are men, hard pressed by enemies
Who also are men, with two hands and mortal lives, like us.
Look! that great barrier of sea cutting us off, and no room
Left for flight now! What shall it be—the sea, or Troy?
  With these words, Pallas hurled himself into the thick of
        the foe.
First to confront him was Lagus, led by unfair fate to
The encounter. Him, as he wrenched up a stone of immense
        weight,
Pallas hit with a spear-throw, nailing him just where the
        spine
Is joined to the ribs on either side, then started to pull
        out
His spear, which was stuck in the bone. Hisbo, who hoped to
        get him
While he was stooping, failed: as he ran in, full of rage

At the bitter death of his comrade, and reckless, Pallas was
    ready
And struck first, burying his sword in the lungs distended
    with anger.
Next he went for Sthenius, and Anchemolus, a man of
Rhoetus' ancient line,* who had lain with his own stepmother.
Larides and Thymber fell too on Italian soil:
They were twin brothers, exactly alike, the sons of Daucus—
Their parents could not tell them apart, and with happy
    affection
Mistook them. But Pallas now created a dreadful difference
Between them, for his sword swept off the head of Thymber,
While Larides—his severed right hand groped to find
Its owner, the half-alive fingers twitching, clutching at the
    sword-hilt.
The Arcadians, stung by Pallas' rebuke and witnessing these
Outstanding feats, now charged at the foe in shame and anger.
Then Pallas picked off Rhoeteus as he whirled past in a two-
    horse
Chariot. Ilus won a certain reprieve by that;
For Pallas had aimed his strong spear at Ilus from a distance,
But Rhoeteus received it, coming between as he fled from the
    gallant
Teuthras and his brother Tyres; he pitched from the chariot
And drummed upon the Italian ground with his heels, dying.
Just as, in summer-time, when the winds he has prayed for
    have risen,
A shepherd may light fires at intervals over the heathland;
All of a sudden the interspaces catch fire, an unbroken
Line of crackling flame is spread across the broad acres;
He sits and reviews the exultant flames like a conqueror:
Even so did the brave hearts of Pallas' men all rally and weld
Into one, and they backed him up. But that quick-moving
    fighter, Halaesus,
Came forward to meet them, crouching tensely behind his
    shield.

He killed Ladon, Pheres and Demodocus; his flashing

Sword lopped off the right hand of Strymonius, who was
    making

A thrust at his throat; he struck Thoas in the face with a
    stone,

Smashing the skull into fragments spattered with blood and
    brains.

His father, presageful of fate, had hidden Halaesus in a forest;

But when he was old, near death, his eyes glazing and
    whitening,

The Fate-spinners laid their hands upon him, and made him
    a victim

To Evander's weapons. Pallas now went for Halaesus, first
    praying:—

  O father Tiber, grant this spear which I poise to throw

Good luck! May it find its way through the stubborn heart
    of Halaesus!

Your sacred oak shall be graced with the armour I strip from
    him.

  The god gave ear to this prayer. Halaesus, who was shield-
    ing

Imaon, alas uncovered his own breast to Pallas' weapon.

  But Lausus,* who was a major factor in war, allowed

No panic amongst his men at Pallas' killings. He first slew

Abas, who'd been a problem baffling the opposition

And holding them up. Many Arcadians went down and
    Etruscans,

Trojans too—warriors the Greeks had not destroyed.

Equal in force and leadership, the armies close. Support
    troops

Press up to strengthen the front line: so thick the mêlée, they
    can hardly

Move weapon or hand. Here Pallas strains*and shoves, here
    Lausus

Struggles to meet him: the two are of much the same age,
    and both

Uncommonly handsome; but fate had forbidden that they
 should ever
Return to their own homelands. The ruler of great Olympus
Did not, however, allow these two to confront each other:
Their fates await them—how near!—at the hands of greater
 foes.
  Meanwhile Turnus was warned by his guardian sister to
 hurry
To Lausus' aid; so he cut through the fray in his speeding
 chariot.
When he got there, he called out:—
                              You can stop fighting now.
I am going alone against Pallas: he is my meat, and mine
Alone. I wish his father was here to witness the duel.
  He spoke; and his comrades withdrew from the field of
 battle, as bidden.
But when the Rutulians moved back, young Pallas, amazed
 by that arrogant
Order, stood tongue-tied a moment, surveying the mighty
 bulk of
Turnus, and truculent, looking him up and down at a dis-
 tance,
Then he hurled back these words in the teeth of that haughty
 prince:—
  I shall soon be renowned for winning the arms of an enemy
 general
Or dying a glorious death: my father can take either.
To hell with your threats!
                          So saying, he moved out onto the field.
The blood of his Arcadians grew chill, and their hearts numb.
Leaping down from his chariot, Turnus prepares for close
 combat
On foot. As a lion who has espied, from some high point of
Vantage, far off on the plain a bull spoiling for battle,
He bounds forward; yes, that was what Turnus' oncoming
 looked like.

Pallas, as soon as he reckoned his foe was in range of a spear-
    cast,
Was first to move, hoping that luck would side with one who
    dared
To take on a powerfuller man, and praying thus to high
    heaven:—
    Hercules, I implore you,* by the welcome my father gave
    you,
The table you shared, though a stranger, help me in this great
    enterprise!
Let Turnus, dying, behold me strip off his bloodstained
    armour,
And let his closing eyes acknowledge me as his conqueror!
    Hercules heard the lad. He repressed a terrible groan
That rose from deep in his heart, gave way to hopeless tears.
Then the Father of heaven spoke these kindly words to his
    son:—
    Every man's hour is appointed. Brief and unalterable
For all, the span of life. To enlarge his fame by great deeds
Is what the brave man must aim at. Beneath Troy's lofty
    battlements
Fell many sons of the gods; aye, there Sarpedon*among them
Fell, who was my son. Turnus too is summoned
By his fate, and is nigh to the destined finish of his life.
    So Juppiter spoke, then averted his eyes from the land of
    Italy.
But Pallas hurled a spear, putting all his strength behind it,
And plucked his sword, flashing, out of the hollow scabbard.
That skimming spear went home high up, where shield and
    armour
Protect the shoulder, and actually piercing the rim of the
    shield,
Just managed to graze in the end the mighty body of Turnus.
Turnus now gave himself plenty of time to poise and aim at
Pallas his steel-tipped, oaken spear; as he threw it, he
    shouted:—

Watch out, and see if my spear does not go deeper than his
   went!
Pallas' shield, for all its layers of iron and bronze,
For all the protective layers of bull's hide that reinforced it,
Was broken through in the centre by the impact of Turnus'
   quivering
Spearpoint, which drove on to pierce the breastplate and then
   the breast.
Pallas wrenched out the weapon warm from the wound: it
   was no good;
His blood and his life ebbed, through the same channel, at
   once.
Hunched over the wound, he fell, his armour clanging above
   him—
Fell with his bleeding mouth to the enemy soil, dying.
Turnus straddled above him and spoke:—
   Remember well what I say, you Arcadians, and tell your
      king
I send him back his Pallas, a dead man; Evander deserved it.
What compensation there is in a tomb, what comfort in burial,
He can have. He'll find he has paid dear enough for making
   friends with
Aeneas.
         So saying, he pressed his left foot hard on the back of
The corpse, and tore off the sword-belt, a thing of immense
   weight,
Engraved with a legendary crime*—that family of brothers
   foully
Murdered upon their wedding-night, the bed-chambers
   swimming in blood;
Eurytus' son, Clonus, had worked it in rich gold chasing.
This belt was now taken by Turnus for spoils, and delighted
   his heart.
Ah, mind of man, so ignorant of fate, of what shall befall him,
So weak to preserve moderation when riding the crest of
   good fortune!

For Turnus a time is coming*when he'd give anything
To have left Pallas unharmed, and will loathe this day and
the spoils
It brought him. But Pallas' comrades clustered around him, laid
His corpse on a shield and bore it away, lamenting and weep-
ing.
What grief, what pride his father would feel at his home-
coming!
Today had been his baptism in war, today his end;
Still, he had left behind him a trail of Italian dead.
   This calamity came to the ears of Aeneas now, not as a
rumour
But through an official message to tell him his allies were
right on
The brink of disaster, were broken and needed succour
immediately.
Mowing down all who stood in his way, like a demon he
carved out
A broad swathe with his sword through the foe; his objective
was Turnus,
Insolent from his last killing. He seemed to see Pallas,
Evander,
The banquet—the first he'd been welcomed to here in this
land as a stranger,
The hands he had clasped—to see them before him. So now
he captured
Alive four warrior sons of Sulmo and four whom Ufens
Had reared, designing to sacrifice them*to the ghost of Pallas
And sprinkle his funeral pyre with the blood of these captive
youths.
Next in his anger he tried a long spear-shot at Magus,
Who ducked adroitly, so that the vibrant projectile flew over
him,
Then clutching the knees of the Trojan, babbled out prayers
for mercy:—

By the shade of your sire and by all your hopes for Ascanius'
    future,
I implore you, don't kill me, preserve me for my son's sake
    and my father's!
There's a fine palace, it's mine, and deep below it are buried
Talents of chased silver; I've plenty of gold, too—wrought
And unwrought gold. The Trojans don't have to depend
    upon killing
Me to win the day: one life will not make any difference.
    Magus had spoken. Aeneas gave him his answer, thus:—
    Those many talents of silver and gold you tell me about—
Keep them for your children! Such courteous bargains in
    war
Turnus was first to abjure, just now, when he killed Pallas.
That's what my father Anchises thinks, and my son Ascanius.
    So saying, Aeneas gripped the man's helmet in his left
    hand,
Bent his head back, while he pleaded, and drove the sword
    home in his throat
Up to the hilt. Nearby was Haemon's son, a priest of
Apollo and Trivia, wearing the wreath and sacred headband,
Resplendent from head to foot in his dress and distinctive
    accoutrements.
Him did Aeneas meet on the field, send flying and strike
    down,
Then, standing over him, killed him, palled him in darkness:
    Serestus
Collected and bore off the dead man's arms, as a trophy for
    Mars.*
Now the enemy ranks were stiffened by Caeculus, a man
Of Vulcan's line, and by Umbro who came from the Marsian
    hills.
Aeneas stormed against them. His sword lopped off the left
    arm
Of Anxur, and with that arm the round shield fell to the
    ground.

Anxur had just said something big, thinking his prowess

Would equal his boasting; maybe he was building castles in
the air

And had seen every prospect of living to a ripe old age.

Next moment, in glittering armour, Tarquitus bounded
forth,

The son of the nymph Dryope, by Faunus,* lord of the wood-
lands,

And stood in the path of the raging Aeneas; who, drawing
his spear back,

Pinned Tarquitus' ponderous shield to his corselet with a
thrust:

Then, as he begged for mercy, uselessly babbling, Aeneas

Struck off his head, sent it rolling, and pushing away the
still warm

Trunk of the man, stood above it, saying these pitiless
words:—

Lie there, you terrible warrior! Your lady mother shall
never

Inter you, commit your remains to the tomb of your ancestors.

You're for the carrion birds; or else you'll be chucked in the
sea

For the waves to dispose of, the hungry fishes to suck your
wounds.

At once he went in chase of Antaeus and Lucas, front-rank

Soldiers of Turnus, brave Numa, and the ginger-haired
Camertes

Whose father was generous Volscens, the biggest of all Italian

Landowners, and governed Amyclae,* where no one might
sound the alarum.

Even as Aegaeon,* whom legend relates to have had a hundred

Arms and hands, to have breathed out fire from fifty mouths
and

Fifty chests, to have fought against Juppiter's thunderbolts

With fifty identical shields clanging and fifty swords,

Just so did Aeneas, once he had whetted his steel with blood,

Storm over the battlefield irresistibly. Look, how he goes at
Niphaeus' four-horse chariot—head-on at him and his
　　　horses!
They, when they see his giant strides and hear him bellowing
Hideous threats, wheel round in panic and bolt away
Towards the shore with the chariot, tipping their master out
　　　of it.
Meantime Lucagus charges into the fray on his chariot
Drawn by two white horses, his brother Liger beside him
As driver, and he himself whirling his sword with furious
　　　purpose.
Aeneas could not abide the way they came charging at full
　　　pelt;
Made for them; stood in their path, a giant, his spear at the
　　　ready.
Liger cried:—
　　These aren't the horses of Diomed*or Achilles' chariot
　　　before you!
You aren't on the plains of Troy! No, this very spot is now
　　　going
To see the end of the war, and of you!
　　　　　　　　　　　　They were flung to the winds—
Those crazy words of Liger. The Trojan hero's reply was
Not to reply in words, but to hurl his spear at the enemy.
Lucagus, leaning right forward and lashing the horses on
With the flat of his sword, now took up position for combat,
　　　his left foot
Advanced: as he did so, Aeneas' spear passed through the
　　　rim
Of his shining shield, at the bottom, then penetrated his left
　　　groin:
He was knocked out of the chariot, and rolled on the ground,
　　　dying.
Aeneas the true addressed these bitter words to his victim:—
　　Lucagus, you're not betrayed by your chariot horses'
　　　running

Too slowly, or shying away from some bodiless enemy
        shadow:
It's you who abandoned them, jumping down from the
        wheels. So saying,
He gripped the horses' bridles. Poor Liger slid down from
        the chariot,
And quite unnerved held out imploring hands to Aeneas:—
        Sir Trojan, have pity, I beg you, and spare my life—I
        entreat you
By your own soul, by the parents who gave the world such a
        great man!
        He'd have gone on beseeching, but Aeneas broke in:—
        Your language
Was different just now. You're to die. Brothers should stick
        together.
        Then he broached the heart of Liger, the crypt of life, with
        his blade.
Such were the killings done all over the field by the Dardan
Leader, who stormed like a river in spate or a black cyclone.
Finally prince Ascanius and the Trojan garrison made
A successful sortie from their encampment. The siege was
        lifted.
        Meanwhile, uninvited, Juppiter spoke to Juno:—
        Sister and most beloved consort of mine, it's Venus,*
Just as you thought—you were not mistaken in so thinking—
Who buoys up the Trojan cause; it is not their own resilient
Strength, their warlike temper and steadiness under fire.
        Juno meekly replied:—
                                My fairest husband, why
Do you tease me? I am sick-hearted, and overawed by your
        stern words.
If my love had the influence on you that once it had,
And still should have, you would surely not refuse this to
        Juno,
You the all-powerful—that I might at least convey my
        Turnus

Out of the battle and keep him unscathed for Daunus, his
    father.
As it is, let him die and atone with his patriot blood to the
    Trojans—
Although he can trace his origin back to the gods (for
    Pilumnus*
Was his grandfather's grandsire), although he has often
    loaded
Your altars with a wealth of offerings, a lavish hand.
    To her, the lord of Olympus on high made this brief
    answer:—
    If it's a short reprieve from death, a mere breathing-space
For one who is doomed, that you ask; if you realize fully my
    meaning;
You may snatch Turnus away to escape his impending fate
For a little. So far I may indulge you. But if your petition
Conceals some further demand on my goodwill, if you
    imagine
The war's result is being changed or affected, your hopes are
    vain.
    And Juno replied, in tears:—
                                    What if your will should grant
What your words grudge, and long life be assured, after all,
    for Turnus?
As it is, though he's done no wrong, a hard end awaits him,
    or else I am
Wide of the mark. Would rather I were deluded by empty
Fears, and you—as you can—might think again, alter your
    policy!
    When she had spoken, Juno at once came down from the
    heights of
Heaven, cloud-enshrouded, riding upon the storm,
And made for the Trojan lines and Laurentine camp. Out of
    thin mist
She supernaturally fashioned a strengthless and insubstantial
Wraith,* to look like Aeneas—a miracle apparition;

Hung it with Trojan weapons, faking the shield and the
    plumed
Helmet the hero wore; endowed it with lifelike tongue,
An automaton's speech; and made it mimic the gait of Aeneas.
It resembled the phantom figures that flit, they say, after
    death,
Or the dream-images that seem real when we are sleeping.
Well, that figure gleefully stalked out in front of the fighters,
Provoking the foe with its weapons, uttering loud taunts.
Turnus went for it, hurled from a distance a whirring spear
At the phantom, which, wheeling about, retreated from him.
    Then Turnus
Really believed that Aeneas had shirked a fight and was
    running.
Bemused by this, he began to nourish unjustified hopes:—
    Aeneas, where are you off to? Don't welsh on your mar-
    riage contract!
I'll give you the land you have crossed the seas to find—six
    feet of it.
    Turnus, shouting these words, and brandishing his sword,
    pursued,
Not knowing that what so thrilled him was only a *doppel-
gänger*.
Now it happened a ship was lying, moored to the lofty side of
A rocky mole, with its gangway and rope-ladders all in posi-
    tion—
The ship which had brought king Osinius here from the
    shores of Clusium.
This way the apparition of fleeing Aeneas hastened
And plunged into hiding. Turnus, following swift on its
    heels,
Surmounted all obstacles and bounded across the high gang-
    way.
The instant he was aboard, Juno cut the cables
And whisked out the unmoored vessel upon a receding
    wave.

But Aeneas kept challenging the man who had vanished to
    fight him:
Many the foes he slew as he scoured the field after Turnus.
Then did his double, that tissue of air, try to hide no longer,
But soaring aloft was soon absorbed into the dark clouds.
Turnus, far out at sea now, was driven on by the gale:
He had no idea of the truth, no gratitude for his deliverance;
Kept looking back; stretched out both hands to heaven in
    prayer:—
  Father almighty, do I deserve to incur so grave
A reproach? to be punished so sorely? Was this your will and
    your judgement?
Where and from what am I being taken? I cannot fathom
This running away, its means or its end. How can I face
Laurentum again, my town and stronghold? What of the
    men who
Followed my flag, all left to die?—such a death, I can't speak
    of it,
I'm so ashamed—all scattered now, I can see them and hear
Their groans as they fall. What am I to do? What grave would
    be deep enough
Now to hide my dishonour? Oh, rather, you winds, take pity
And dash this vessel on rock or reef—from my heart I
    implore you—
Pile it up on some merciless quicksand, anywhere
Beyond the ken of my people, the reach of my shameful
    story!
  So Turnus spoke, and his mind was all one surge and back-
    wash—
Whether to fling himself on his sword in desperation
At such a disgrace, and drive the cruel blade through his
    ribs,
Or throw himself into the deepsea and try to swim back to
    the shore
Of the bay, so he might once more wade in at the Trojan
    soldiers.

Three times he began to attempt either alternative; three times
Great Juno held him back, and, pitying him, prevented it.
Onwards he went through the deep, with wave and current behind him,
Until he brought up at the ancient town of his father, Daunus.
Meanwhile, prompted by Juppiter, Mezentius* dashingly took
Turnus' place in the fight and attacked the exultant Teucrians.
The Etruscans closed in upon him: with all their hatred, with all
Their fire-power they concentrated on him, on him alone.
He, like some rocky cliff that juts out into the wild sea,
Exposed to the tempests' fury and the full force of the waves,
Outstaying the threats, the concerted violence of sea and sky,
Standing immovable there—so Mezentius stood, and laid low
Hebrus, son of Dolichaon, Latagus, fleet-footed Palmus:
Latagus he got with a stone, a regular chunk of
Mountain, full in the mouth and face; while Palmus he hamstrung
And left to wallow disabled, giving his armour to Lausus
To wear on his own person and stick the plumes on his helmet.
He killed Evanthes, too, a Phrygian, and Mimas,
The friend and coeval of Paris, born to his mother, Theano,
And his father, Amycus, on the same night that Hecuba,
Pregnant with fire,* gave birth to Paris: Paris, he sleeps
In his native soil; but Mimas is buried, a stranger, in Italy.
Now, like a boar which the hounds have driven down from the mountains,
Snapping at his heels—a boar that has sheltered for years on pine-crowned
Vesulus,* or one that has skulked in the Laurentine fenland
Feeding upon the reed beds—but now it is in the toils of

The hunters, at bay, ferociously snorting, its shoulders
    bristling,
And none of them has the nerve to get his blood up and go
    closer,
But from a safe distance they assail it with yells and missiles—
Just so, of all who cherished a righteous wrath at Mezentius,
Not a single one had the courage to draw his sword and close
    with him;
No, they stood off, shouting, hurling weapons, baiting him.
But he, undaunted, unflurried, turned all ways to confront
    them,
Setting his teeth, while the spears bounced off his back like
    raindrops.
From the ancient township of Corythus*had come a man of
    Greek origin,
Acron a refugee, who had left his betrothed there, unwed
    still.
Mezentius spotted him far off in the thick of the battle, wear-
    ing
His lady's favours—a purple garment and plumes of crim-
    son.
Then, like a famishing lion which pads to and fro through the
    jungle,
As often happens, compelled by crazed hunger, and when he
    has marked down
Some timorous goat, it may be, or a stag with its antlers
    pricked up,
Exults, huge jaws agape, hair standing on end, and crouches
Over the kill, claws deep in the flesh, his ravenous muzzle
Horribly steeped with gore—
Just so did Mezentius eagerly spring right into the thick of
The foe, and felled poor Acron, who dying drummed with his
    heels
On the darkening ground and stained with his blood the
    broken spear.
Mezentius now would not cheapen himself by killing Orodes,

Who was running away, with a spear-cast, a wound in the
    back: instead,
He ran to cut off and meet him face to face, confronted him,
Mastered him, not by underhand means, but hand to hand.
Then he planted his foot on the fallen, strained at his spear,
    and cried:—
    Comrades, here lies Orodes, one of our tallest obstacles!
    His friends took up the cry of triumph with one great
    shout.
But the dying Orodes said:—
                        My death will be avenged.
You have not long to rejoice in your triumph, whoever you
    are;
For a like fate awaits you, the same earth shall cover you later.
    Now Mezentius, smiling but angry too, replied:—
    Die then! Leave my future to the father of gods and king
Of mortals!
        With these words, he plucked his spear from the body.
Unkind repose, the iron sleep weighed down Orodes'
Eyes: his eyelids closed for everlasting night.
Caedicus slew Alcathous, Sacrator slew Hydaspes,
Rapo slew Parthenius and the very powerful Orses;
Messapus slew Clonius and Erichaetes, the son of Lycaon—
The one while he lay on the ground, his bridleless steed
    having stumbled,
The other in combat on foot. Agis, the Lycian, had ridden
Forward; but Valerus, skilled in the fighting mode of his
    fathers,
Unhorsed him. Thronius fell to Salius, he to Nealces
Famed both for javelin work and the arrow that kills at a
    distance.
    Now the hard hand of the War-god was dealing out im-
    partially
Death and agony: either side had its ups and downs,
Its killings and fallen, alike; but neither dreamed of retreat-
    ing.

In the halls of Jove*the gods felt pity for all that pointless
Fury, to think that men should inflict such pains on their
    fellows.
Saturnian Juno and Venus sat, well apart, looking down
Where pale Tisiphone*raged among the embattled armies.
But now Mezentius, shaking his mighty spear, strode forth
Over the field like some tornado. As great Orion*
Moves forward, cleaving his way, with his feet treading the
    floor
Of the deepest mid-ocean, his shoulders overtopping the
    waves;
Or, when he's carrying back from the hills some venerable
    ash tree,
Walking upon the ground he buries his head in the cloud-
    base—
So, with his giant weapons, Mezentius advanced.
On the other side Aeneas, seeing him there in the long
Column, went out to meet him. Mezentius, undismayed,
Awaited his heroic foe, stood firm and massive:
Then, judging by eye the moment Aeneas would come within
    spear-range:—
  May this right hand, which is god to me,* and this spear I
    am poising
Bring me luck now! Lausus, I'll clothe you in armour stripped
    from
This brigand's corpse; you shall be a living trophy, I vow,
Of my victory over Aeneas.
                              He spoke. At long range his spear
Went whistling, but ricocheted from the shield of Aeneas to
    pierce
Good Antores, who stood nearby, between his thigh and his
    ribs—
Antores, a friend of Hercules, who had come on a mission
    from Argos,
Attached himself to Evander and settled in a town of Italy.
Felled by a weapon meant for another, he now gazed up at

The sky, and his last moments were filled with thoughts of
    dear Argos.
Aeneas the true then hurled his spear, which went through
    the convex
Triple-bronze face of the shield, its layers of linen, its inner-
    most
Backing composed of threefold bull's-hide, and lodged low
    down
In Mezentius' groin; but it failed to drive home deep. So
    Aeneas,
Elated to see his enemy bleeding, promptly drew
His sword from its scabbard and went for the dazed man with
    furious energy.
Lausus, seeing this happen, groaned deeply in sympathy
For his beloved father, and tears rolled down his cheeks.
How could I pass over in silence the heroic action of Lausus
And the hard death befell him?—he's worthy of fame, and we
May credit such deeds because long tradition allows us to
    do so.*
Mezentius was giving ground, crippled and sorely en-
    cumbered,
With his enemy's spear, stuck fast in his shield, dragging
    behind him,
When Lausus, his son, leaped forward and intervened in the
    combat:
Just as Aeneas was rising on tiptoe to slash Mezentius,
Lausus thrust out his own sword, parried the blow, and held
    him
In check. His comrades hailed the action with a loud shout,
And while the father drew back under cover of Lausus' shield
They tried to beat off Aeneas with volleys of missiles fired
From a distance. Aeneas, baffled and angry, kept his guard up.
It was like when the storm-clouds burst, scattering down their
    shrapnel
Of hailstones; all the ploughmen and labourers have dis-
    persed

Hurriedly from the fields, and the traveller is sheltering
    somewhere
In safety—beneath a river-bank, maybe, or a cornice of
    rock—
While the downpour drenches the earth; and they wait for
    the sun to come back
And let them get on with their work. Aeneas, snowed under
    with missiles
From every angle, endured the blizzard of war and waited
For it to be spent, taunting and threatening Lausus the
    while:—
  Why rush upon death like this? You're too rash, fighting
    out of your class;
And your loyalty's tempting you to your ruin.
                             But Lausus continued
His crazy defiance. And now the Trojan commander's rage
Boiled up more deeply, now the Fate-spinners passed
    through their fingers
The last threads of Lausus' life; yes, Aeneas drove his strong
    sword
Right through the young man's body, and buried it there to
    the hilt.
It penetrated his light shield, frail armour for so aggressive
A lad, and the tunic his mother had woven of pliant gold,
And soaked it with blood from his breast. Then the soul left
    the body,
Passing sadly away through the air to the land of shadows.
But when Aeneas beheld the dying boy's look, his face—
A face that by now was strangely grey—he felt pity for him,
And a deep sigh escaped him; he stretched out his hand to
    Lausus,
Who had conjured up for his mind's eye a picture of filial
    devotion:—
  Poor lad, what now can I give you, to show how I honour
    your brave deed,
Or worthy of such a fine character? What can Aeneas do?

These arms you were so proud of, keep them; also, for what
It is worth, I give you back to the ashes and shades of your
    fathers.
At least it shall soften the edge of your piteous death for you,
That the great Aeneas caused it.

                     What's more, he rebuked the hesitant
Comrades of Lausus, and lifted the body, its neatly ordered
Hair befouled with blood, and gave it into their hands.*
   Meantime, beside the stream of Tiber, the father of Lausus
Was cleansing his wound with water, as he reclined with his
    back
Propped up against a tree-trunk. His bronze helmet is hung
On a branch nearby, and his heavy accoutrements rest on the
    grass.
Round him the bodyguard stands: Mezentius, sick and gasp-
    ing,
Eases his neck, and the beard flows down to cover his chest.
He keeps on asking about his son, keeps sending messengers
Bearing commands from an anxious sire to recall him from
    battle.
But Lausus' friends were bearing his lifeless body, in tears,
On his shield—a heroic lad laid low by a wound from a hero.
Mezentius, who had a premonition of evil, sensed
Their grief from afar. He sullied his grey hair with dust,
    extended
To heaven his clasped hands, and clung to his son's body:—
   My son, was I so eager to go on living that I
Allowed you to take my place, to take the enemy's sword—
You, my own son? Oh, that I should have been saved by these
    wounds!
Alive because you are dead! Ah, god, the bitterness
Of death comes home to me now at last! the wound goes deep!
For I have tarnished your name with my own disrepute, as
    well,
Since I was driven from the throne of my fathers in execra-
    tion.

Long had I owed my country, my people who loathed me,
    atonement.
I was the guilty one. Would I had died a thousand deaths!
Instead, I live on, mankind and the light of day still un-
    relinquished.
But leave them I will.

              So saying, he struggles up onto his wounded
Thigh; and although the deep wound drains his strength and
    hampers him,
Will not give in, but orders his horse to be brought. His
    treasure
And comfort this animal was: he had ridden it out of every
Battle, victorious. Now he addressed the sorrowing beast:—
    Rhaebus, we have lived long, if anything can be called
        long
In human affairs. Today you shall bear back triumphantly
Aeneas' head and his bloodstained armour, sharing with me
Revenge for the pangs of Lausus; or else, if that end is be-
    yond
Our strength, we shall fall together. Brave steed, you would
    never consent,
I know it, to have a new master—a Trojan, least of all.
    He spoke; then, mounting the beast and settling himself on
        its back
As so often he'd done, bronze helmet glinting and horse-hair
    plume
Flaunting, he took sharp-pointed lances in either hand.
Thus armed, he went into the fray at full gallop. His heart
    was seething
With deep shame and the very ecstasy of grief,
With love driven wild by loss, and awareness of his own
    valour.
Now he called out 'Aeneas', in a loud voice, three times.
Aeneas recognized that voice, and prayed with a glad heart:—
    So may the Father of heaven and glorious Apollo grant it!
To it, then! Start the fight!

Without more words, spear levelled, he went to meet
      Mezentius,
Who cried:—

  Do you think to frighten me, now you have taken my son,
You murderer? That was the only way you could really
      destroy me.
I'm not afraid of death, nor yet will I spare your gods.
Enough! I have come to die; but first, here are some presents
I've brought you.

            So saying, Mezentius hurled a spear at his foe,
Another then, and another, sending them in as he wheeled
      round
Aeneas in a wide circle; but the gold-bossed shield with-
      stood them.
Three times he galloped, anti-clockwise, around his vigilant
Enemy, shooting: three times the Trojan hero pivoted,
His bronze shield bearing an ever-increasing harvest of
      javelins.
Then, tired of these long-drawn defensive tactics and pulling
      out spearpoints,
Finding himself hard-pressed in such an unequal combat,
Aeneas, after much thought, at last rushed forward and
      hurled
His spear, to strike Mezentius' charger right in the fore-
      head.
The beast reared up and hung there; its forefeet pawed at
      the air,
Its rider was unseated: then the horse came down on top of
      him,
Pinned him, and lay there, its shoulder put out and its head
      drooping.
The shouts of Trojans and Latins roared like flames in the
      sky.
Aeneas ran up, unsheathed his sword, stood over Mezentius,
And said:—

            Where is that hot-head Mezentius now, and all his

Brutal ferocity?
                    The Tuscan, recovering consciousness,
Gazing up at the sky, gulping the air, answered:—
   Harsh foe, you need not rail, or waste words on your
      deadly purpose.
No crime in killing: I never supposed there was, when I
      made war.
Mercy is not in the bond my Lausus made between us.
I ask but one thing—if the conquered has any right to a
      favour—
Allow my body interment. I know I'm beset by my people's
Bitter hatred. I ask you, protect my remains from their fury,
And let me rest in the same sepulchre as my son.
   He spoke, and deliberately offered his throat to the sword,
      and received it.
His life went out in waves of blood all over his armour.

BOOK XI

Night came and went. Aurora rose up, leaving the ocean.
Aeneas, although he felt a pressing duty to make time
For burying his friends, and was greatly distressed by the
    death of Pallas,
First, at daybreak, fulfilled the vows he had made for victory.
Lopping the branches all round*from a giant oak, he erects it
Upon a mound, and dresses the trunk with gleaming armour
He'd stripped from the enemy general, Mezentius, as a
    trophy
To the great War-god. He fastens up the blood-dabbled
    plumes,
The broken-off spears of his foe, the breastplate which had
    been struck
And pierced in twelve places; upon the left side he secures
The shield of bronze, and hangs from the neck the ivory
    scabbard.
Then, for his field commanders were all mustered around
    him
Closely, he made his triumphant comrades a rousing
    speech:—
    Gentlemen, we've performed our hardest task; for the rest
We need have no apprehension. Here are the spoils, our first-
    fruits,
From an insolent king, Mezentius: he's here in these arms
    my sword won.
Now we must march on Latium's capital and king.
With courage make ready to fight, work out the war in your
    minds,
So that there'll be no hitch, no unpreparedness, the moment
The gods say Lift your standards and lead the troops out of
    camp—

No delays through the over-caution that comes from a
  faltering purpose.
But first, let us commit to earth our unburied comrades,
For that is the only honour the world of the dead acknow-
  ledges.
Go now, and pay your last respects to those gallant hearts
Who shed their blood to win us this Italy for our homeland:
Before anything else, convey to Evander's mourning city*
The body of Pallas, our brave, good comrade, whom a dark
  day
Stole from us and plunged in the bitter waters of death.
  Thus spoke Aeneas, weeping; then he retired to his tent
  door
Where old Acoetes watched over the lifeless body of Pallas
Which had been laid there: Acoetes had served as squire to
  Evander
In the old days in Arcadia; but then, beneath a less fortunate
Star, he went as an aide to his dear foster-son, Pallas.
All the servants were gathered round, and a crowd of
  Trojans,
With Trojan women whose hair streamed loose in the manner
  of mourning.
But when Aeneas entered the lofty door, they raised
To heaven a loud, long sound of keening, and beat their
  breasts;
The royal tent was one great moan of grief and wailing.
Aeneas, looking at Pallas' head on the pillow there,
The snow-white face, the open wound in his young breast
Made by the spear of Mezentius, spoke amid rising tears:—
  Poor lad, alas that Fortune, in the hour she smiled on me,
Grudged me one thing—your life—and would not let you
  behold
My kingdom or ride back to your father's home in triumph!
How different from all I promised Evander to do for you,
That day I left him, when he embraced me and sent me forth
To my imperial destiny! He felt some fear, and warned me

How dangerous was the foe, how tough the people I'd fight
  with.
This very moment—who knows?—quite beguiled by a
  groundless hope,
He may be paying his vows and loading the altars with offer-
  ings;
While we, with mourning tributes useless to him, attend
Dead Pallas, who now owes nothing to any of the gods in
  heaven.
Evander, poor man, shall see his son buried, and break his
  heart.
So much for our triumphal return that he is awaiting!
So much for my solemn promise! But at least Evander will
  not
Look on a son wounded in cowardly flight, or pray for
A death made accursed by the son's living on in dishonour.
  Alas,
What a tower of strength is lost to Italy, lost to Ascanius!
  When he had made lamentation, Aeneas bade them lift up
The piteous corpse, and choosing a thousand men from his
  whole
Army, detailed them to form the solemn cortege and to
  share in
The tears of the bereaved Evander—small consolation
In such great grief, but one that was due to a sorrowing father.
Others quickly construct a resilient wickerwork bier,
Wattling switches of oak and shoots from the arbutus tree,
Then shade the built-up bier with a canopy of foliage.
Now they are laying young Pallas aloft on that country bed;
And he resembles a flower plucked by a girl's fingers—
A gentle violet, perhaps, or a fainting hyacinth—
Whose sheen and shape are not yet lost, not yet departed,
Though mother earth no longer can give it sap or strength.
Aeneas now brought out two purple robes that were richly
Brocaded in golden thread: Sidonian Dido had made them
With her own hands, in the old days, interweaving the fabric

With threads of gold, and giving all her heart to the work.*
In one of these robes he sadly wrapped Pallas—a farewell
    gesture,
Hooding with it the hair that would soon be burned to
    ashes:
He made a great heap, as well, of spoil they had won in the
    battle
Against the Laurentines, and had it borne in a long pro-
    cession—
Horses and weapons, too, they had taken from the enemy.
Manacled captives there were, consigned to be gifts to the
    dead—*
Victims whose blood would be sprinkled upon the altar
    flames.
He bade the leaders themselves to carry tree-trunks adorned
    with
Enemy armour, the names of the fallen foes attached to them.
Forlorn Acoetes, feeble and old, was supported along,
Beating his breast with his fists, tearing his cheeks with his
    nails,
And often prostrating himself full length upon the ground.
There were chariots in the cortege, splashed with Italian
    blood.
Behind them paced Pallas' war-horse, Aethon, without its
    trappings:
It wept as it walked—yes, big tears were rolling down its
    muzzle.
Others bore the helmet and spear of Pallas; the rest of
His armour, victorious Turnus had taken. Now followed a
    phalanx
Of mourners—Trojans, all the Etruscans, Arcadians bearing
Their arms reversed. When the files of his comrades had gone
    some distance
Forward, Aeneas stopped, sighed heavily, then spoke:—
    The same dread fate of war summons me hence to weep
For other dead. Brave Pallas, salute for evermore!

For evermore, farewell!

                    Aeneas said nothing further,

But turned towards the ramparts and made his way into
    camp.

    Envoys had just arrived from the capital of Latium,

Decked in olive branches*and bringing a plea that Aeneas

Hand over to them their fallen, whose bodies lay everywhere

On the field, and let them bury the dead in a common grave:

One could have no quarrel, they said, with men defeated and
    lifeless;

They'd once been his hosts, had promised his men their
    daughters, and therefore

He should show mercy. Aeneas courteously granted the
    plea—

He could not well reject it—and said these words besides:—

    It was indeed a malignant fate that involved you Latins

In such a terrible war, and caused you to flout our friendship.

You ask me to make peace with the dead, whom the fortunes
    of battle

Have killed: believe me, I'd like to make peace with the living
    equally.

I would not be here, but that destiny said it should be my
    home.

It is not your people that I'm at war with, only your king,

Who broke off relations with me, put faith in the weapons of
    Turnus.

Fairer if Turnus had stayed to face the death which your
    friends met.

If he's so keen to force an issue and drive out us Trojans

By fighting, he ought to have met me here in single combat:

The better man, or the one heaven favoured, would have
    survived.

Go now, and burn your unfortunate comrades upon the pyre.

    Aeneas had spoken. The envoys were taken aback, could
    find nothing

To say for a while, but silently searched one another's faces.

Then Drances, an old man, no friend to the young prince,
    Turnus,
Who always indulged his dislike by speaking against him,
    began
To answer Aeneas thus:—
                  Sir Trojan, great your fame
And greater your deeds. What words can I find to extol your
    glory?
Your fairness, your feats in battle—which is the more
    remarkable?
Most gladly we shall report in our city what you have just
    said:
Moreover, if circumstance makes it possible, we shall unite
    you
With king Latinus. Let Turnus look for his own alliances.
Nay, we'll delight to help you build the great walls of your
    destined
City, and bear on our shoulders the stones for the second
    Troy.
  So Drances spoke, and his colleagues all voiced their entire
    agreement.
A twelve-day truce was arranged; under its mediation
Trojans and Latins wandered amicably together
Over the wooded heights. Ash trees rang with the blows
Of axes, and the soaring spires of pine trees were felled;
There was no end to the splitting of oakwood and fragrant
    cedar
With wedges, the carting away of rowans in creaking wagons.
  And now winged Rumour*came, first herald of great grief,
To Evander's ears, to his palace and all his city—Rumour
Which only just now was reporting that Pallas had beaten
    the Latins.
Hurriedly seizing funeral torches—an antique custom—
The Arcadians ran to their gates: the long, torchlight pro-
    cession
They formed shone like a broad parting across the fields.

The Trojan cortege moved on to meet them: the mourning
     columns
Merged into one. When the mothers saw it enter the city,
Their shrieking ran like wildfire through the afflicted streets.
No force on earth could restrain Evander now. He rushed out
Into the crowds, and as soon as the bier was set down,
     prostrated
Himself upon Pallas, clung to the body, weeping and moan-
     ing.
For a while grief choked him: at last he just managed to find
     his voice:—
    Oh, Pallas, this was not the promise you gave your father—
That you'd be careful how you ventured into the grim fight!
But I knew too well how great is the lure of glory in battle
For a young man, how sweet to win fame in his first engage-
     ment.
Bitter your youth's first-fruits, harsh your initiation
Into this war so near home! Alas that not one of the gods
Gave ear to my vows and prayers! My blessed wife, how lucky
You were to die before such anguish could come upon you!
But I have lived on, exceeding my natural term—lived on
For what?—to survive my own son. Why didn't I march with
     our Trojan
Allies, and fall to the enemy's fire? Would *I* had perished,
And this cortege was carrying me, not Pallas, home!
Yet, Trojans, don't think I am blaming you, or our pact, or
     the joining
Of our right hands in friendship. What has happened—fate
     surely had it
In store for my old age. But though an untimely death
Was awaiting my son, I'll be proud that he died leading the
     Teucrians*
Into Latium, with thousands of enemy dead to his credit.
Besides, I could not grace you with a worthier funeral, Pallas,
Than this which Aeneas the true, the mighty Trojans, the
     generals

Of the Etruscans and their whole army are giving you.
They bear great trophies, symbols of those who fell by your
    hand.
You too, Turnus, would be here—a trophy,*a giant tree-trunk
Adorned with arms—had your age and the strength of your
    years been no more than
My son's. But why do I let my own tragedy keep you Trojans
From war? Go forth, and forget not to take back these words
    to your king;
Tell him I linger on,* though I care not for life now Pallas
Is gone, to receive the debt which he knows is owing to father
And son—vengeance on Turnus:- it's the sole task that
    remains for
His courage and luck to accomplish. I ask it, not to gladden
My life—that were wrong—but to bring the good news to my
    son in the Underworld.
    Meanwhile Aurora had lifted her cordial light above
Suffering humanity, and the daily round began again.
Pyres were built up on the shore of the bay by lord Aeneas
And Tarchon*now. Each, after his own traditional usage,
Brought hither his dead. They applied to the pyres the
    funereal torches,
And smoke rolled up, spreading out and palling the sky
    above.
Clad in their gleaming accoutrements, they marched three
    times around
The blazing pyres: three times they circled the melancholy
Flames of the dead, on horseback, and uttered the cries of
    mourning.
With tears the earth was sprinkled, their armour was wet
    with tears.
A lamentation of men arose, and a bray of trumpets.
Now some of them threw on the flames equipment which had
    been taken
From the enemy dead—helmets, fine swords, bridles, and
    chariot

Wheels that had scorched into battle; while others were
    throwing the shields
And unlucky weapons of their own fallen—familiar objects.
They were sacrificing oxen all round to the god of death,
Slaughtering bristle-haired swine and sheep, for which they
    had scoured
The countryside, to lay on the burning pyres. The whole
    length of
The shore, they look at their comrades burning, keep watch
    beside
Those charred pyres: nothing can drag them away, till dewy
    night
Unrolls a heaven thickly jewelled with sparkling stars.
  Some distance off, the dejected Italians too had built
Countless funeral pyres: such numbers of dead there were,
They buried some on the spot, lifted up others and bore them
Into adjacent fields or sent them back to their city;
While for the rest, a huge indiscriminate pile of corpses—
They burnt them, uncounted, anonymous. All round about,
    the desolate
Countryside was dotted with pyre after blazing pyre.
When a third dawn had peeled the chill darkness off the sky,
Sadly they swept the ashes and bones into a heap from
The smouldering pyres, and built up a barrow of still-warm
    earth
Above them. But in the houses of wealthy Latinus' city
The noise of mourning was loudest, greatest the long-drawn
    agony.
Mothers, sick-hearted brides, loved sisters bewailing their
    brothers,
Children whose fathers had fallen, here in the city were
    cursing
The war that had brought them ruin, the betrothal of Turnus
    that caused it.
Let him who claims for himself this realm and sovereign
    power here—

Let him, they cry, decide the issue* in single combat.
Drances aggravates this vindictively, making it known
That Turnus, and Turnus alone, is called on, is challenged to
    fight.
All the same, there was much support for Turnus, expressed
    in
Various arguments: the queen's great name protected him;
Also, his fame and the trophies he'd won told in his favour.
    In the middle of these cross-currents, when partisan feel-
    ing had reached
High pressure, to crown it all, the envoys returned with their
    answer
From Diomed's city,* in deep depression. For all the pains
They had taken, they'd got nowhere: Diomed was impervious
To presents, to gold, to urgent entreaties; he said the Latins
Must look for allies elsewhere, or come to terms with Aeneas.
Latinus himself collapsed under his load of anguish:
The wrath of the gods, the new graves in front of his eyes,
    told him
Heaven's will was beyond dispute and Aeneas had fate
    behind him.
Therefore Latinus convened a privy council, commanding
The foremost of his people to appear in his lofty palace.
They came together, their numbers crowding the streets as
    they flocked
To the royal home. Latinus, the eldest and wielding supreme
Authority, sat in their midst, a gloomy look on his face.
And now he bade the envoys returned from the Aetolian
City to make their report, and to set out in full detail
What Diomed had replied. Absolute silence followed
As Venulus, obeying the king, began to speak:—
    Citizens, we accomplished our journey, surmounting all its
Hazards: we saw Diomed in his Argive settlement,
And pressed the hand which wiped out the country of Ilium.
He was building a city, Arpi,* named after his father's people,
On land he had won in war round about Apulian Garganus.*

Entering his palace, we sought and were given a personal
  interview:
So we presented our gifts to him, told him our names and
  nation,
What had brought us to Arpi and who had invaded our
  country.
Diomed heard us out, then replied, with an equable mien:—
  You people of ancient Italy, from the kingdom of old
    Saturn,*
So blessed by fortune, what ill wind is troubling your calm
    régime
And driving you to provoke war, who have no experience in
  warfare?
All we who profaned with the sword the land of Ilium—I leave
Aside what we went through during the battles beneath
  Troy's walls,
And our heroic dead engulfed in the Simois—all of us
Suffered condign and terrible retribution, wherever
We went, so that even Priam must pity us: look at the storm
  that
Wrathful Athene*raised, wrecking Ajax on Cape Caphereus
In Euboea. After that war, driven to wide-apart coasts,
Menelaus, the son of Atreus, was exiled far away
At the pillars of Proteus, Ulysses beheld the Cyclops of Aetna*.
Neoptolemus' kingdom partitioned,* Idomeneus'* home
  broken up—
Why talk of them?—or the Locrians*compelled to settle in
  Africa?
Agamemnon*himself, the leader of our Greek expedition,
Fell at the hands of his damnable wife in the first hour of
His homecoming, for an adulterer lurked behind conquered
  Asia.
Look how the gods have grudged me a sight of the wife I
  long for
And beautiful Calydon*—stopped me returning to my home
  altars!

Even now I'm pursued by things of ill omen, dreadful

To look at: my own lost comrades,* changed into birds, made off

To the sky—an uncanny retribution they suffer, haunting

The streams, and the cliffs are loud with their melancholy cries.

What else could I expect but horrors such as these

From the moment I raised my sword* to the person of a divinity,

Wounding the hand of Venus, committing a sacrilege on her?

No, no, don't push me into another war like that!

No quarrel have I with the Teucrians since Troy's annihilation,

Nor does it give me pleasure to recall those bad old days.

As for the presents you've brought me out of your native land—

Give them instead to Aeneas. We've faced his tigerish weapons,

Have met him hand to hand. Believe me, I know from experience

How he springs at you, with his shield up, how his spear comes at you like

A hurricane. If two other champions of equal calibre

Had risen in Troyland, the Dardans would have stormed up to the cities

Of Greece—aye, fate had changed sides and it's Greece would be mourning today.

That we stayed so long investing the walls of stubborn Troy,

That victory kept on eluding the Greeks and came not until

The tenth year, was due to the efforts of Hector and Aeneas.

Both were outstanding in courage* and feats of arms; but the latter

Stood first in devotion of heart. I advise you, make terms with him

As best you may: don't risk fighting it out on the battlefield.

Good king, you have heard the reply king Diomed sent, and
    with it
The views he expressed about this great war that we are
    engaged in.
  The envoys had barely finished, when a mutter of conflict-
    ing
Comment arose among the uneasy Italians: so, when
A torrent is checked by boulders, it frets against them and
    babbles,
And the banks on either side resound with chattering water.
As soon as they had calmed down and their anxious murmurs
    were silenced,
The king, first invoking heaven, spoke from his lofty
    throne:—
  I could wish, and it would have been better, gentlemen,
    that we had reached
Some decision ere now on so crucial a matter—not had to
    call
A meeting at a time like this, when the enemy's at our gates.
We are waging an ill-advised war, fellow-citizens, with a
    people
Of heavenly descent, unconquerable*: no amount of fighting
Wears them down; though beaten, they never relinquish the
    sword.
If you had any hopes of an armed alliance with the Aetolians,
Resign them. Our only hope is in ourselves, and you see
How slim it is. That, apart from Diomed's refusal,
Our fortunes are a total wreck, is plain and palpable.
I am not blaming anyone: whatever a people's valour
Could do, was done: our realm put all it had into the struggle.
Give me your close attention while I explain briefly
What seems to me, though I'm not sure, best to do in our
    present dilemma.
I possess land along the Tiber—it's been Crown property
From ancient times—stretching westwards far, right up to
    and over

The Sicilians' frontier*: Auruncans and Rutuli farm it, work-
  ing
The stony hills with the plough and grazing their roughest
  slopes.
Let us cede the whole of this area, with its pine-covered
  mountain ridge,
To gain the goodwill of the Trojans. Let us draw up a treaty,
  fair to
Both sides, and invite them to partner us in the kingdom.
If they want it so much, let them found a city and settle down
  here.
But if they intend to possess themselves of the land of some
  other
Nation, and are at liberty to leave this soil of ours,
Let us build them twenty ships of Italian oak—or more,
If they can man them: all the raw material lies
At the water's edge; they can say what class of ships and how
  many
They want: we will supply the bronze, the labour, the ship-
  yards.
Further, to take our proposals and ratify the agreement,
I would send a hundred envoys, men of our most dis-
  tinguished
Families: they should offer the olive branch to Aeneas,
Bearing as presents gold and ivory, a talent of each,
With the chair and purple robe—the insignia of my king-
  ship.*
Now express your own views. Our affairs are desperate. You
  must mend them.
    Then Drances, hostile as ever to Turnus, whose high
  renown
Pin-pricked him with sour envy to intrigue against him—
  a man
Influential through his wealth,* an able speaker, but no
Lion at fighting; one whose advice in debate was accounted
Weighty; a force in political faction—(his well-born mother

Gave him great pride of race; there was nothing to say of his
    father)—

Drances got up, and stoked the high feeling there with a
    speech:—

  Your gracious Majesty, the issue you ask our advice on

Is crystal-clear and does not require our comments. Every-
    one

Admittedly knows what this crisis demands, but they shrink
    from expressing it.

Let *him* but allow us to speak and refrain from his usual
    blustering,

Him whose unlucky star and perverseness of mind have
    caused—

No, I *will* speak, though he mortally menaces me with his
    violence—

Have caused the death of so many of our brightest captains,
    and drowned

The whole city in mourning, while he, confident of his own
    get-away,

Attacked the Trojan encampment and scared with his
    weapons the blue sky.*

You should add one more to those many presents you bid us
    take

And promise to the Dardan people—just one thing more,
    most gracious

Of kings; and let not anyone's intransigeance have the power
    to

Prevent you giving your daughter in honourable marriage

To an excellent man, thus cementing a peace between us for
    ever.

But if our hearts and minds are obsessed by terror of Turnus,

Let us implore and beseech him in his infinite grace to stand
    down,

And restore to his king and country the marriage-rights he
    lays claim to.

O head and source of these disasters to Latium, why

Are you always thrusting her luckless folk into obvious peril?

Fighting will not save us: it's peace that we all demand of you,

Turnus, and with it the one pledge of peace that cannot be broken.

I, whom you claim to be hostile to you—well, what if I am?—

I take the lead in imploring you—look at me! Pity your people!

Strip off your pride! Admit yourself beaten, and go! We have seen

Enough deaths, in this rout, have unpopulated our countryside.

But, if you lust for glory, if you're so hardy of heart,

And if you're so set upon a royal bride, a king's palace,

Be bold, trust in your own strength, and face Aeneas in combat.

Good god! are we, we no-account souls, to litter the plains,

A multitude unburied and unmourned, so that Turnus

May marry the heir to the throne? Yes, you, if you've anything in you,

Any of the fighting spirit of your fathers, look at me, answer

My challenge!

   The impulsive, intransigeant Turnus blazed up in rage at this speech:

He gave a groan of anger, then passionately broke out:—

   Words, words, words! You've always plenty of them, Drances,

When war is asking for deeds. Let a council be summoned, and you

Are the first to appear. But we don't want big talk from an armchair critic

Like you just now in this House, while our battlements still keep

The foe at arm's length, and the moat is not yet swimming in blood.

Go pounding on with your usual rhetoric, and accuse me

Of cowardice, Drances—you whose strong right hand has
    inflicted

Such wonderful slaughter upon the Trojans, and set up
    notable

Trophies all over the battlefield. There's nothing to stop you
    trying

What real courage can do: you needn't go far, I assure you,

To find the enemy; they are massed all round our walls.

Are we going to meet them? What, no move from you? Is
    your bellicose

Spirit permanently confined to a windy tongue and a

Clean pair of heels?

So I'm to 'admit myself beaten'? You clot, could anyone
    really

Argue I'm beaten, after he'd seen the Tiber in spate with

Trojan blood, and the whole house of Evander*prostrate,

Root and branch, and his Arcadians stripped of their arms?

Bitias and huge Pandarus*did not find me a weakling,

Nor the countless men my conquering arm despatched to
    Hades

When I was shut up in the enemy's walls, with their ramparts
    around me.

'Fighting will not save us': you're raving! Keep those mor-
    bid

Forecasts for yourself and Aeneas! Ah, go on creating

Alarm and despondency everywhere, cracking up the im-
    mense strength

Of a twice-conquered nation and slandering our own army!

You'll be telling us next the Myrmidon*generals are all
    quaking

At the Phrygian forces—Diomed and Larissaean*Achilles—

And Aufidus*river is scampering back from the Adriatic.

Yes, and look how this artist in scheming gives out he's in
    terror of threats

From me, thus using fear to sharpen the edge of his calumny!

Don't be alarmed, I would never degrade myself by taking

A life like yours: you can keep it, tucked up in your cowardly
  breast.
Now, sire, I revert to you and the problems you've laid
  before us.
If you have no more faith in the armed forces, if we
Are really abandoned by all, if to suffer a single reverse
Means our whole cause is lost and there's no chance of
  recovery,
Then let us lay down our arms and helplessly sue for peace.
Yet I would that some gleam of our traditional valour would
  show itself!
I would esteem that man most fortunate in his exertions
And noblest in soul of us all, who, rather than witness so
  shameful
An end, has fallen and died, has bit the dust once for all.
But suppose we have resources and manpower still un-
  tapped,
Potential allies left among the peoples of Italy;
Suppose, too, that the Trojans have paid for success with
  heavy
Losses—they had their dead all right, the same storm blasted
Both sides:—then why are we fainting in the first lap of the
  war
And disgracing ourselves? Why tremble before the trumpet
  has blown?
Time, and man's versatile efforts over the shifting years,
Have often changed things for the better: fortune's vicissi-
  tudes
Make fools of us often, and then set our feet again upon firm
  ground.
Diomed and his Aetolians will give us no help, you say:
Yes, but we have Messapus and heaven's favourite, Tolum-
  nius,*
And captains sent by many peoples; great glory, too,
Will attend the flower of Latium and the Laurentine fields.
Then there's Camilla,* from the illustrious Volscian nation,

Leading her regiment of horse, her squadrons blooming in
    bronze.
But if the Trojans demand to fight with none but me—
If such is your will, and otherwise I'm ruinous to our cause—
Victory has not been such a total stranger to me that
I'd refuse any venture which held out such great possi-
    bilities.
Though he's Achilles' equal and carries weapons, as he did,
Made by Vulcan* himself, I'll go out and face Aeneas
With all my heart. I, Turnus, second in courage to none of
Our ancestors, solemnly vow my life to you and Latinus
Whose son I would be. Aeneas challenges me alone—
I welcome it. Whether it's heaven's wrath or honour and
    glory that's in it,
I would not let Drances be martyr to one or crowned with the
    other.
  So the Italians were hotly debating these controversial
Issues. Meanwhile Aeneas moved out of camp and advanced.
Through the palace a messenger hurried, spreading great
    consternation
Around him, so that the whole town was seized with panic:
    he said
The Trojans and the Etruscan forces were sweeping down
    from
The Tiber in battle formation, deploying across the plain.
At once the populace rose up, their minds in confusion, their
    feelings
Shocked, but their temper aroused by strenuous excitement.
Wildly they clamour for action. To arms! the young men
    shout;
While the senators gloomily weep and mutter. A monstrous
    din
Went up now all over the town as men argued and wrangled
    together:
So it is when a flock of birds have alighted upon
The tree-tops in some wood, or the fish-haunted river Padusa*

Resounds with the harsh screaming of swans till its pools are
    a bedlam.
Turnus, seizing the opportunity, cried:—
                       Fellow-citizens,
Talk on—that's right—and tamely sing the praises of peace,
Though the enemy's launched an offensive against us!
                    Without a word more
He whirled away and ran out from the high-vaulted cham-
    ber:—
  Volusus, order the Volscian squadrons to stand to arms,
And lead forth the Rutuli! Messapus, Coras and your brother,
Get your cavalry moving, deploy them out in the open!
Let every approach to the city be blocked, and the turrets
    manned!
The rest will be under my orders, to counter-attack where I
    tell them.
  At once from all over the city they raced up to line the
    battlements.
Meanwhile Latinus adjourned the meeting and left, post-
    poning
His grand design, depressed and upset by what had just
    happened:
He censured himself severely for not accepting Aeneas
Of his own free will, or attaching him to the Crown through
    marriage.
Now they are digging trenches in front of the gates and
    bringing up
Stones and stakes. The hoarse trumpet blares the alarum for
    bloody
Battle. Around the walls there is stretched a motley chain
Of women and boys; the supreme ordeal calls upon everyone.
Now, a great throng of mothers about her, the queen* is
    driving
Uphill to the temple and heights of Pallas Athene: she bears
Offerings, and has beside her the girl, Lavinia, the cause of
These terrible evils, sitting with eyes prettily downcast.

The mothers pass into the temple, fill it with smoke of
    incense,
And mournfully utter a prayer as they stand at the door of the
    sanctuary:—
    O puissant in arms, O regent of war, Tritonian maiden,
Break with your hand the spear of the Trojan marauder, and
    lay him
Prostrate upon our soil, yea, let him fall in the gateway!
    Turnus, enraged, is eagerly girding himself for battle.
Now he has donned the breastplate whose scales of rugged
    bronze
Glow like embers, and fastened the gold greaves on his legs:
Head still unhelmeted, he has strapped the sword to his side
And is running down from the citadel heights, a flash of gold,
And exults in anticipation of coming to grips with the enemy.
So, when a horse has broken its tether and galloped away
    from
The paddock, free at last, out on the open plains,
Look how he makes for the meadow where herds of mares are
    grazing,
Or else he plunges into some well-known stream, as he
    loves to,
Then leaps out, and throwing his muzzle high, so the mane is
    tossed
Over neck and shoulders, he whinnies in wild exhilaration!
Camilla hastened to meet him, leading the Volscian
    squadrons:
Right at the gate the princess jumped down from her horse,
    and the whole
Contingent, taking their cue from her, dismounted smartly
And stood beside their horses: then did Camilla say:—
    Turnus, the brave are surely entitled to feel self-con-
    fidence;
Therefore I dare and I promise to engage the mounted
    brigade of
Aeneas, and meet the Etruscan cavalry single-handed.

Let me be the first to encounter the hazards of war, while you
Remain with the infantry here and guard the walls of the
    town.
   Eyes fixed on the redoubtable Camilla, Turnus answered:—
Princess, Italy's proud of you. How can I ever express
Or prove my gratitude? But I know your spirit's above
All thoughts of recompense, so share this task with me.—
I had got wind, and now my reconnaissance has confirmed it,
That Aeneas has actually thrown forward a wave of light-
    armed
Horsemen to sweep the plain, while he moves on the town
    himself
Over the deserted mountain heights, through a pass.
I am planning an ambush,* to block both ends of the glen with
    troops
Where his route is a sunken road through heavily-wooded
    terrain.
You are to meet the Etruscan cavalry and engage them:
You will have the gallant Messapus with you, the Latin
    squadrons
And the troops of Tiburtus. Take over command, and thus
    share the task with me.
   So saying, he briefed Messapus and the other allied com-
    manders
In similar terms for the fight, then moved against the enemy.
There is a winding glen, a place cut out for ambush
And bloody stratagems: hill-slopes enclose it on either flank,
Darkening it with dense leafage: to reach it, you pass down
    a narrow
Track, through a bottleneck—a nasty, confined approach.
Overlooking this from above, at the summit on either side,
Are plateaux, invisible from beneath—a sound position
Whether you wanted to charge down the slopes at the
    enemy's flanks
Or to sit tight on the ridge and roll down boulders upon
    him.

Turnus arrived at this spot by a route he knew well, occupied
    it,
Disposed his men in the woods there—a dangerous threat to
    Aeneas.
    Meanwhile, in the abodes of heaven above, Diana*
Was speaking to swift-footed Opis, one of the sacred band
Of nymphs who attended her, and in a despondent tone
Was saying:—
                    Camilla goes forth to war and its savagery.
She's dear to me, girl, beyond all others; and yet our weapons
She's girding on cannot save her. Ah yes, this is no new
    love,
Shaking the heart with sweet surprise, that I am feeling.
Listen. When Metabus left the ancient town of Privernum,*
Expelled by the people, who hated his tyrannous use of
    power,
He smuggled out with him, as he fled through the street-
    fighting,
His baby daughter, to be a companion in exile; he named
    her
After her mother, Casmilla, just changing the name to
    Camilla.
Carrying her against his breast, he made for the mountains—
A long ridge, wooded and lonely: pursuers were close
    behind him,
And Volscian soldiers were skimming round to cut off his
    retreat.
All at once, as he fled, there was the Amasenus
In front of him, running bank-high, in full spate after a recent
Cloudburst. He is eager to swim for it, but is held back
By love and fear for the infant he tenderly carries. Casting
About in his mind, of a sudden this desperate remedy dawns
    on him:
Taking the mighty spear he had with him for self-defence—
A solid, gnarled, well-seasoned piece of wood—he fastened
The baby to its shaft, cocooning her first in bark

From a cork tree, and fixed her right at its point of balance
    for throwing;
Then poised the spear in his huge hand, praying aloud to
    heaven:—
  O kindly Diana the Virgin, patron of woodlands, I,
Her father, vow this child to your service. Yours the first
    weapon
She holds to, a suppliant, fleeing the foe. I invoke you, O
    goddess—
Accept her for yours, whom now I commit to the chancy
    breezes.
  So saying, he drew back his arm and sent the spearshaft
    spinning.
The waters roared beneath: over the racing river
The spear went whirring; upon it, hurtled poor little Camilla.
But Metabus, since a great pack of pursuers was now draw-
    ing closer,
Dived into the stream, and triumphantly plucked from the
    turf on the far side
The spear, with his babe still attached—his present to Diana.
No city offered him home or shelter: he'd not have accepted it
Anyway, being averse to civilization: instead
He lived out his life among shepherds in desolate mountain
    country.
Here, in the thickets, the tangled coverts where wild beasts
    prowled,
He nursed the baby girl on milk drawn from the breast of
A brood-mare, milking the teats into her delicate mouth.
But as soon as the child had found her feet and learnt to walk,
Metabus put a pointed javelin in her hand
And slung a bow and a quiver across her little shoulder.
Instead of a golden clasp for her locks, and a trailing robe,
A tiger-skin hooded her hair and cloaked her from head to
    foot.
Even then, her soft, child's hand could hurl miniature
    weapons;

And, whirling the sling around her head by its twisted thong,
She could bring down a white swan or a crane from the river
     Strymon.*
There were many mothers in the Etruscan cities who vainly
Sighed for her as a daughter. She was well pleased to serve
Diana alone, to remain a virgin for ever, worshipping
Chastity and the chase. Would she had not succumbed to
Desire for such service as this, or attempted to challenge the
     Trojans!
Then she'd be one of my train still, and I could love and pro-
     tect her.
But come, since a bitter, untimely doom is surely upon her,
Glide down from the sky, Opis, and visit the land of Latium
Where, under no lucky star for her, grim battle is toward.
Take my bow and quiver: draw out an avenging arrow:
With it, exact retribution in blood for me from the man who
Wounds and profanes her hallowed flesh—Italian or Trojan.
Then I shall bear away in the womb of a cloud her piteous
Body, her weapons intact, to a grave in her own country.
     Diana had spoken. Opis swooped rustling down from
     above
Through the light airs of heaven, wrapped in a dark storm-
     cloud.
     Meantime the enemy force approaches the walls of
     Latium—
The whole brigade of cavalry, with its Etruscan officers,
Moving in squadron formation. Over the plain's expanse
The chargers prance and neigh, swerving this way and that
As they fight the restraining curb. The field is all iron, one
     endless
Bristle of lances; the plains flash with uplifted weapons.
Against them move Messapus, the swift-riding Latins, Coras
With his brother, and the wing led by the maiden Camilla:
These now emerge on the plain and range themselves op-
     posite; hands drawn
Well back, they hold the lance in rest or brandish the javelin.

Warriors advancing, horses neighing—the moment kindles.
And now each side had moved forward into spear-range, and
    there
Halted. Then with a sudden yell they all charged, spurring
Their maddened horses, and hurled as they charged volleys
    of weapons
Which stormed as thick as a blizzard, darkening the very sky.
Tyrrhenus and gallant Aconteus rode each at the other in-
    continent,
Lances in rest; were the first to meet, to crash with a noise
    like
Thunder, and fall: their horses collided, head on, so that
    breast
Was broken and shattered on breast: the impact unseated
    Aconteus
And hurled him afar, like a meteorite or a great stone fired
From a catapult; he died before he hit the ground.
At once the formations were thrown into disorder: the Latins
Wheeled round and galloped towards the walls, with their
    shields behind them.
The Trojans pursued hotly, Asilas leading their squadrons.
Then, as they neared the gates, the Latins raised the war-cry
Again, and pulled at the sinuous necks of their horses, to
    turn them.
So now the Trojans went back a long way in flight, with loose
    reins.
It was like the to-fro rhythm of the sea, when a wave runs
    forward,
Comes charging against the shore, rides over the rocks in a
    smother
Of spray, and drenches the sand far up on the beach where the
    swell breaks;
Then rapidly draws away, the force of its undertow sucking
The pebbles back, swirls out, grows shallow, is gone from the
    shore.
Twice the Etruscans drove to the walls the fleeing Rutuli,

Twice galloped back, looking over their shoulders, with
    shields held behind
For protection. But when the opposing forces clashed for a
    third time,
The lines were locked together, and each man marked his
    man:
Then the groans of the dying were heard—it was all a welter
    of blood,
A tangle of weapons and bodies, with mortally-wounded
    horses
Plunging amid dead riders: bitterly swelled the struggle.
Orsilochus dared not meet Remulus hand to hand,
But threw a spear at his charger, which lodged under its
    ear:
Driven mad by the blow, the unendurable pain of this wound,
The horse reared up its great chest, its forelegs thrashing the
    air,
And Remulus was hurled to the ground. Catillus struck down
Iollas and Herminius—a man of great courage, a giant
In shoulder and trunk, whose auburn hair was unhelmeted*
And his shoulders bare; he had no terror of wounds, so much
Of himself he exposed to the enemy. Driven through his
    broad shoulders,
The spear stuck, quivering, and doubled him up with agony.
Everywhere streams the dark blood. They struggle; they
    deal out doom
With the sword, and offer themselves to a glorious death in
    the combat.
    Right in the thick of the slaughter, with one breast bared*
    for the fray
Like an Amazon, was exulting the archeress, Camilla.
Now she delivers a quick fire of whippy javelins, now
Unwearied she whirls a powerful battle-axe with her right
    hand.
Tapping her shoulder, hung the gold bow, Diana's weapon.
Even when she was driven back and in flight, she loosed

Her shafts at the foe as she fled, turning the bow round to
    shoot them.
Her bodyguard kept close about her—the maiden Larina,
Tulla, Tarpeia who brandished a battle-axe of bronze—
Italian girls, whom the godlike Camilla had chosen to grace
    her
Retinue: good supporters they were in peace and in war.
They resembled the Amazon women of Thrace when they
    go to battle
In blazoned armour, their horse-hooves stamping the frozen
    river
Thermodon,* escorting queen Hippolyta, or the martial
Penthesilea when she returns from a war in her chariot,
A woman-host with crescent-shaped bucklers screaming
    around her
In triumph. Ferocious Camilla, whom first did your hand
    lay low,
Whom last? How many men did you strike to the earth,
    dying?
Euneus was the first, Clytius' son: her long
Pinewood spear crashed through his unguarded chest as he
    faced her:
Coughing up streams of blood, Euneus fell; he bit
The ensanguined earth, and dying, he spun round on his
    wound.
Next she killed Liris, and Pagasus over him: one had been
    thrown
When his horse was stabbed in the belly, and was gathering
    up the reins;
The other was stretching his free hand to help the dazed man
    to his feet:
Side by side they fell headlong. Camilla killed, too, Amastrus,
Hippotas' son, and flung spears with a long follow-through
    from a distance
At Tereus and Harpalycus, Demophoon and Chromis:
For every single missile the princess aimed and threw,

A Phrygian warrior fell. Far off, queerly accoutred,
Was riding the hunter, Ornytus, upon his Apulian steed:
He wore for battle the hide of a bullock swathed about his
Broad shoulders, while his head was helmeted in a wolf's
    mask
Whose gaping mouth with its white-fanged jaws served for a
    visor:
A rustic hunting spear was his weapon. Ornytus turned,
With horsemen everywhere round him, overtopping all by a
    head.
She caught him—no difficult task in the jam of a routed
    formation,
Pierced him, and over his body spoke these unmerciful
    words:—
  Did you think you were hunting game in your own forest,
    Etruscan?
The day has come when a woman's weapons shall hurl your
    people's
Boasting back in their teeth. Never mind, you will go to the
    shades of
Your fathers with one piece of glory—you fell by the hand
    of Camilla.
  Next she killed Orsilochus and Butes, two great champions
Of Troy. Butes she hit with a spear, while he was turned
Away, just where the rider's neck showed between helmet
And breastplate, where the shield hangs down from the left
    shoulder.
Orsilochus she fled from, riding in a wide circle,
Then tightening her circle, tricked him, herself became the
    pursuer.
Now, standing up in the stirrups, she hacked her strong axe
    through his armour
And bones, though he begged and prayed for mercy, sending
    in blow
Upon blow: warm brains from his cloven skull spattered his
    face.

A warrior, the son of Aunus, an Apennine farmer, now
    happened
Her way, stood rooted to earth by shock and panic at seeing
    her:
Not least of Ligurian tricksters he, while fate allowed him
To cheat. When he saw it was too late now to avoid an
    encounter
Or to divert Camilla's onset by running away,
He tried to take her in with guileful provocative words,
Beginning thus:—
        You're a woman, but must you rely on a strong steed
To win you distinction? Get rid of that chance to escape, and
    meet me
Fair and square on the ground—if you dare—yes, fight me on
    foot:
You'll soon find out who is bluffing and boasting, and who'll
    be undone by it.
  Stung by these words to bitter resentment, Camilla, in high
    rage,
Gave up her horse to a comrade, and fearlessly faced him on
    foot
With no advantage in weapons—drawn sword and un-
    blazoned shield.
The Ligurian, however, believing he'd gained his ends by
    this ruse,
Promptly wheeled round his horse and started away—the
    coward—
In flight, plying the fleet-footed steed with his iron spurs:—
  Deluded fool, you have over-reached yourself with your
    own
Conceit! You think you're a smart boy, but all the smooth
    tricks you have learnt
From your folk won't get you back to your crooked father or
    save you!
  So saying, Camilla ran, swift as a bush-fire, after him,
Headed him off, stood full in his horse's path; then seizing

Its reins, she took her revenge deep in the blood of her enemy.
With the same ease will a falcon, prophetic bird, take off from
A crag to pursue the dove which is flying high overhead,
Will catch it, seize it, slash out its bowels with hooked talons,
So blood and a scatter of feathers come floating down from the sky.
  But the Father of gods and men, aloft on the heights of Olympus,
Did not observe these events with an indifferent eye.
He inspired the Etruscan, Tarchon, to fight with greater ferocity,
Spurred him roughly on, whetted the edge of his anger;
So Tarchon rode amongst the wavering formations,
The slaughter, goading his squadrons with shouts of abuse and encouragement,
Calling each man by name, and rallied his broken forces:—
  Can nothing shame you, Etruscans? Will you never snap out of your lethargy?
What are you scared of? Why this shocking display of cowardice?
So now a woman can send you flying and rout our proud ranks!
What are your swords meant for? Why carry arms and not use them?
You're vigorous enough where girls are concerned and tussles in bed,
Or when a dance is on and the curved flute of Bacchus invites you;
Well, keep your strength for the banquet, the groaning table, the wine cups—
If guzzling is all you care for—and wait till the priest has announced
Good omens, and you can picnic off the rich meat of the sacrifice!
  So saying, he spurred his charger into the fray, as ready

To risk his own life as his men's lives, and swept like a
  cyclone on Venulus.
Tearing him off his horse, Tarchon furiously galloped
Away, with his right arm clamping the man to the saddle in
  front of him.
All the Latins turned their eyes on the spectacle. Shouts
Went up to the sky. Now Tarchon streaks over the plain like
  wildfire,
Carrying the man and his weapons: he breaks off the business
  end of
His enemy's spear, and with it probes for a joint in his
  armour
Through which he can give him the death-blow: but Venulus
  fights back
To hold off Tarchon's hand from his throat, pitting strength
  against violence.
It was like when a golden eagle soars aloft with a snake
In its grip, twined round its feet, held fast by the claws that
  impale it:
But the snake, though wounded, writhes about with its whip-
  like coils,
And its scales stand up on end, and it hisses in fury, rearing
Its head to strike; while, fiercely as ever, the bird's hooked
  beak
Darts at the lashing snake, and its pinions thrash the air.
Just so did Tarchon triumphantly bear off his prey from the
  ranks
Of Tiburtines. Fired by their general's success, the Etruscans
  followed
His lead, and charged. Now Arruns, that fateful and fated
  man,
Circled round the fast-riding Camilla, javelin in hand,
  cleverly
Anticipating her movements, seeking the best way to strike.
Wherever the berserk princess rode in the thick of the mêlée,
There Arruns would appear, shadowing her unobtrusively:

When she withdrew from some successful foray at the foe,
This warrior stealthily wheeled his swift horse and kept con-
    tact with her.
Hefting his sure-as-doom spear—nothing would foil him—
    he tried for
One opening after another, circling and circling about her.
It befell that Chloreus, a one-time priest in the service of
    Cybele,
Showed at a distance, the shining Phrygian armour*con-
    spicuous,
Spurring his foam-flecked mount, which wore a horse-
    cloth—a hide
Armoured with scales of bronze, like plumage, and buckled
    with gold.
Chloreus himself, resplendent in dusky, exotic purple,
Was shooting Cretan arrows from a bow of Lycian*make:
Golden the bow this warrior carried, and gold the helmet
He wore; his mantle was made of linen, a saffron colour,
And a red-gold brooch held fastened its rustling folds; his
    tunic
And oriental trews were embroidered with golden thread.
Whether she wished to hang up his Trojan arms in a temple
Or to strip off his gold and wear it herself, Camilla
Picked out this man from the mass of combatants there, and
    trailed him,
Blind to all else, in full cry, recklessly ranging amid
The battle, on fire with a woman's desire for another's finery.
Now had come Arruns' chance, at last. From where he was
    lurking
He lifted his spear, poised it, prayed to the heavens above:—
    Most worshipful god, Apollo, guardian of blest Soracte,*
Where we, your chief devotees, heap up in your honour the
    blazing
Pine logs and walk through the midst of the flames, sure in
    our faith,
Treading the high-piled embers as we perform your rites—

Apollo, puissant in battle, grant that I may rub out
This stain on our escutcheon! I ask no spoils, no trophy
Of her defeat; it is not loot that I want: I'll be famous
For other deeds: let me but strike down this pestilent fury,
And I will gladly return home, taking no credit for it.

  Apollo silently gave his assent to one part of Arruns'
Prayer, but the rest he tore up and threw to the four winds.
He granted his wish to take Camilla off guard and deal her
A mortal wound; but that ever he should return to his own
    land,
He granted not—those words were snatched away on the
    breezes.
So, when the spear of Arruns went whistling from his hand,
The Volscians turned their fiercely expectant minds and eyes,
All, upon the queen Camilla. She was oblivious—
No wind, no sound of the hurtling weapon she got: next
    moment
The spear went into her body, just under the naked breast,
And stuck there, deeply drinking the maiden blood where it
    lodged;
In consternation her friends rushed up and caught their
    queen
As she collapsed. Most frightened of all was Arruns: in fear
Mingled with exultation, he fled; he would not trust his
Weapon, or dare to face Camilla's, a moment longer.
Just as, before the armed pursuers can get on his trail,
Some cowardly wolf, which has killed a shepherd or a big
    steer,
Makes rapidly off, avoiding the beaten paths, to hide in
The mountains; and knowing quite well he has done wrong,
    he runs to
The wooded heights, with his quivering tail between his
    legs—
Even so did Arruns remove himself from their view, all
    wrought up,
And vanished into the ruck of the fighters, glad just to escape.

Camilla, dying, tugged at the spear; but its iron blade,
Deep in her body, was firmly fastened between the ribs there.
She is sinking, faint from loss of blood: her fainting eyes
Are glazed with the frost of death: the colour ebbs from her
    face.
Now, with her last breath, she spoke to Acca, a girl of
Her own age, one who had been her confidante and of all
Her companions was the truest. These were the words she
    spoke:—
    Acca, dear, I can do no more. This bitter wound
Is the end of me. Shadows are falling, it's growing dark all
    round me.
Make your best speed and bring this last message of mine to
    Turnus—
He must take my place here and fight the Trojans off from the
    city.
Now, good-bye.
                So saying, she loosed her grip on the reins
And helplessly slid to the ground. Then, little by little, her
    body
Grew numb and released its hold upon life; her neck was
    drooping,
Her head bowed down to victorious death: she let go of her
    weapons,
And with a moan her protesting spirit fled to the shades.
Then, oh, then a terrific outcry arose, the welkin
Rang, and the fight grew fiercer because of Camilla's death.
All the Teucrian force, the Etruscan captains, Evander's
Arcadian squadrons—all of them launched a concerted attack.
    But Opis, Diana's observer, had long been watching the
    fight,
Unflinching, from where she sat on a high mountain-top.
Now when she beheld from afar Camilla, right there in the
    yelling
Mêlée of warriors, struck down and dying a piteous death,
Opis heavily sighed and spoke with deepest emotion:—

Ah, cruel, too bitterly cruel, poor lass, the forfeit you've
    paid
For having dared to challenge the Teucrian host in battle!
You lived alone in the wildwood, you served Diana and
    carried
Our quiver upon your shoulder; but none of this saved you
    now.
Still, your mistress has seen that you shall not be left dis-
    honoured
In death's last hour; your dying shall be a famous thing
Among the nations—they shall not say you were unavenged.
Whoever it was that wounded and desecrated your body
Shall get the death he deserves.

                   Under that mountain height
There was a huge barrow, the tomb of an old Laurentine
King, Dercennus,* lying beneath the shade of holm-oaks.
First, then, the beautiful nymph, with a movement swift as
    light,
Came and stood here, from the top of the mound looking out
    for Arruns.
When she saw him, shining in armour and swelling with idle
    vanity,
She said:—

               Why are you moving away? Come over here,
Come deathwards, come and receive the reward you deserve
    for killing
Camilla! Yes, you're a wretch, but you'll die by Diana's
    weapons.
  So saying, the Thracian nymph took from her quiver of
    gold
A flighted arrow, and stretched her bow, aiming at Arruns:
She drew the string right back, till the ends of the curving
    bow
Had almost met, her hands level, the left supporting
The arrow's point, the right hand drawing the string to her
    nipple.

Next moment, Arruns heard the whizz of a shaft, the whirring
It made through the air, and the arrow pierced him that very
    same instant.
His comrades, unconcerned, left him gasping and moaning
With his last breath on the dust of the plain—an inglorious
    end,
While Opis winged her way back to the heights of Olympus.
  Their mistress fallen, Camilla's light brigade were the first
To fly; then the Rutulians and gallant Atinas broke
In panic; detachments left leaderless, officers who had lost
    touch with
Their troops, now wheeled away and raced back to the cover
    of the walls.
There was no holding the Trojans' deadly, remorseless pres-
    sure,
However hard you fought, no standing against them. The
    Latins,
Slinging their unstrung bows on weary shoulders, retired,
And as they galloped away the hammering hooves shook the
    dry flats.
A dust cloud, dark and whirling, rolls up to the city walls,
Where mothers stand in the watch-towers and, as they gaze
    forth, beat
Their breasts; the shrieks of women go up to the heavens
    above.
Those who first poured in through the open gates at a gallop
Had a crowd of the enemy hard on their heels, even riding
    amongst them,
And did not escape a cruel death: at the actual gateways,
Within the walls, and worse—in the houses where they took
    refuge—
They were speared, and breathed their last. Some of them
    shut the gates,
Barring their comrades out, and for all their appeals, dared
    not
Admit them to the city. A tragic slaughter ensued

Between those defending the gates and their own friends
   fighting to enter.
Of those shut out, in full view of their weeping parents, one
   lot
Were tumbled into the moat by the pressure of those in panic
Behind them, while others with loose rein were blindly riding
   full tilt
Into, the solid doors that stood in their way, and ramming
   them.
The mothers themselves, on the battlements—they had seen
   Camilla's example,
And genuine love of their country showed them the way—
   with the utmost
Energy hastened to hurl down missiles, impulsively making
Tough poles of oak and fire-hardened stakes do the work of
   cold steel:
Eager they were to be first to die in defence of the city.
   Meantime desperate tidings came to the ears of Turnus
While he lay in the woods, for Acca brought word of the
   grave disaster—
How the Volscian forces had been wiped out, and Camilla
   had fallen;
How the foe were attacking fiercely, the battle had gone their
   way
And they'd swept all before them; panic now lapped at the
   town walls.
Turnus in anger—for so the stern will of Jove required—
Moved off from his menacing ambush among the trees on the
   hill-side.
He had scarcely marched out of sight of that place and
   reached the plain
Below, when Aeneas entered the pass, now unobstructed,
Surmounted the ridge and debouched from the dark woods
   with his army.
So both of them, leading their columns, were rapidly march-
   ing towards

The city, with no great interval between them. At one and
the same
Moment Aeneas descried at a distance ahead the plain
Smoking with dust, the Laurentine forces moving across it,
And Turnus became aware of the armed array of relentless
Aeneas, heard the tramp of feet and the snorting of chargers.
They would have joined battle and fought it out immedi-
ately,
But that the roseate sun now dipped his weary steeds in
The Iberian*sea, and day was darkening to night. So both of
them,
Camping outside the city, consolidate their positions.

BOOK XII

When Turnus saw that the Latins were crushed by defeat
    and in lowest
Spirits—saw, too, that all eyes were upon him as if demand-
    ing
That now he should make good his promise,* he burned with
    a mood all the more
Uncompromising; his temper sharpened. Just as an African
Lion, when he's received a bad wound in the breast from the
    hunters,
Then at last becomes really dangerous, gleefully tosses
The shaggy mane from his neck, and uncowed snaps at the
    assailant's
Arrow stuck in him, breaks it, roars with his mouth all
    bloody:
So Turnus looks; his violent intransigeance kindles and
    mounts up.
Now, with an outburst of passion, he speaks to Latinus,
    saying:—
  I am not holding back. Those yellow Trojans have no
    cause
To swallow their words or renounce their agreement, as far
    as I am
Concerned. I shall fight him. Make ready the rites and frame
    the terms.
Either this hand of mine will send that Dardan, that run-
    away
Asiatic, to hell—the Latins may sit and look on at us—
And with my sword I'll wipe out the slur on our people's
    good name,
Or he'll have Lavinia in marriage and the rest of you in sub-
    jection.

Latinus would not be rushed off his feet: he replied
    equably:—
Prince, I admire your spirit; but the higher your passionate
    courage
Rises, the deeper and more attentively I must ponder
What's best; I have to be cautious and weigh all sides of the
    question.
You own the realm of your father, Daunus, and many cities
You've captured in war; while I have gold, and am not close-
    fisted.
Are there not other unmarried girls of good birth in Latium
And the Laurentine land? To speak with brutal frankness
And lay all my cards on the table—please take to heart what
    I'm saying—
I never had the right to promise my daughter to any
Of her old suitors: both oracles*and popular feeling forbade it.
But, overborne by my affection for you, by our kinship
And the tears of my grieving wife, I disregarded all vetoes:
I cheated Aeneas of his bride, and took up arms in a bad
    cause.
What a disastrous war has resulted from this, you can
    see,
And how great are the evils, Turnus, which you are the first
    to suffer.
Twice beaten in full-scale battles, we can hardly hold this
    town now—
Italy's last hope. The Tiber is still running warm with
Our blood, and our people's bones are blanching the plain
    all over.
My mind yaws like a madman's, for ever washed back to the
    same point.
If I'm prepared to make friends with the Trojans, on Turnus'
    death,
Why don't I end the conflict while he is still alive?
Think what your Rutulian kinsmen, what all Italy
Would say, if I were responsible for Turnus getting killed

(God save the mark!) through his desire to marry my
    daughter.
Reflect how war can change men's fortunes. Be sympathetic
Towards your old father who grieves for you, cut off as he is
    in his native
Ardea.
        These words made no impression at all upon Turnus'
Intransigence—nay, it increased, the cure only inflamed it.
As soon as he was able to speak, he began like this:—
    The anxiety you show for me, most gracious king, I
        implore you
For my sake to discard: let me purchase fame with death.
I am no weakling, sire, I too can rain blows and deliver
Fusillades; men bleed when I wound them—same as Aeneas:
His goddess mother*will not be on hand, concealed in mere
        shadow,
To cover his flight with a cloud delusive as woman herself.
    But the queen, greatly alarmed by this new turn of the
        struggle,
Clung to the hot-headed Turnus, weeping, knowing her
        death near:—
    By these tears of mine, by whatever love and respect you
        feel
For me, I implore you, Turnus—since you are my one hope
        now,
Sole stay of my sad old age; since Latinus' honour, authority
Rest in your charge; but for you we should collapse al-
        together—
One thing I beg, give up this idea of fighting the Trojan.
Whatever hazards await you in such a duel, the same
Await me too: if you die, then will I quit a life
I hate; Aeneas shall not be my son, nor I his captive.
    Lavinia listened while her mother was speaking: tears
Flowed down her burning cheeks, suffused with a deep
        crimson
Blush that spread all over the glowing face. Imagine

A piece of Indian ivory stained with a blood-red dye
By a craftsman, or a bouquet of white lilies blended with
  many
Red roses: that was how the hues in the girl's face looked.
Turnus, deeply moved by love, gazed hard at Lavinia.
More eager than ever to fight, he spoke to the queen briefly:—
  Please do not send me forth to the tough encounter before
    me
With tears and with such defeatist, ominous words, Amata.
If I'm to die, it's not in my power to postpone the hour of it.
Idmon, act as my herald and take this word to the Phrygian*
Despot—it won't amuse him: as soon as tomorrow's dawn
Rides up the sky in its rosy car and flushes it, let him
Not lead the Teucrians against us, let there be armistice
For Trojans and Rutuli, while he and I settle the war
Between us: that fight shall decide who is to have Lavinia.
  When he had finished speaking, he quickly withdrew to
    his own place
And called for his horses, happy to see them neighing before
    him—
Those steeds, more dazzling white than snow, swifter than
    winds,
Which Orithyia* herself had graciously given to Pilumnus.
The charioteers stand busily round them, slapping their
    resonant
Barrels with open hand, and comb the luxurious manes.
Turnus then put over his shoulders a corselet stiff with
Gold and pale orichalc,* at the same time fitting on ready
His sword, his shield, and the helmet with sockets to hold its
    red crest.
The sword had been made for Daunus, his father, by the
    Fire-lord's*
Own hands, who had tempered the white-hot blade in the
    waters of Styx.
Now he snatched quickly up his powerful spear, which was
    leaning

Against a mighty column in the central courtyard (he'd
      won it
As spoil from Auruncan Actor), and shouted aloud as he
      shook
The vibrating shaft:—
            Ha! now is your chance, my spear! You have never
Failed me when I have called on you. Actor, a great champion,
Carried you once. Now Turnus hefts you. Together we'll
      bring
That Phrygian pansy*down, tear open and rend off
His corselet by main force; we'll dabble in the dust those love
      locks
He crisps and dolls up with curling-tongs and smarms with
      perfumed grease!
   He was wildly wrought up, so burning for battle that all
      his countenance
Seemed to shoot sparks, and darts of fire to come from his
      fierce eyes.
So it is when a bull bellows out its first terrible challenge to
      combat,
And practises throwing all its fury into its horns
By goring trunks of trees, butts at the air in anger,
Paws and tosses the sand as a prelude of coming battle.
   Aeneas the while, a grim figure in the arms his mother had
      brought him,
Was whetting no less his desire for the fight, and keying him-
      self up
With anger, glad of the chance to settle the war on these
      terms.
Now he comforts his friends and the dreadfully anxious
      Ascanius
With things the fates have told him, bids officers take to
      Latinus
A definite answer and to dictate the conditions of peace.
   The morrow's dawn was just beginning to shower its
      light on

The mountain-tops, and out of the deepsea the sun's horses
Were starting to climb and breathing the day from uplifted
        nostrils,
When Trojans and Rutuli paced out on the plain, beneath
The great town walls, the lists for the combat and made them
        ready,
Setting up braziers and altars of turf to the gods they both
        worshipped
In the middle of the arena. Some, wearing the priestly aprons
And garlanded with field herbs, were bringing fire and spring
        water.
Now the Italian army moved off, surged out through the
        gates
Marching in close column. From the other side the Etruscan
And Trojan forces streamed on, with their diverse equip-
        ment,
Heavily armed and in formation, as if for the stern
Arbitrament of battle. Amongst the assembled thousands
The captains move about, haughty in gold and purple—
Mnestheus of the Assaracan line, valiant Asilas,
Messapus too, the tamer of horses, the scion of Neptune.
When the signal is given, each side retires to the area allotted
        it;
Planting their spears in the ground, they lean their shields
        up against them.
Then the women came running out excitedly, with the un-
        armed
Civilians and frail old men, to throng the towers and the
        roofs of
The houses, while other spectators stood by the tall gateways.
    But Juno, looking forth from the eminence which today
We call the Alban hill*(then, it had neither name
Nor fame), was attentively gazing at the Laurentine ranks,
And the Trojan, arrayed upon the plain, and Latinus' city.
At once she addressed Juturna,* the sister of Turnus, deity
Speaking to deity, she being goddess of lakes and sounding

Rivers; for Jove himself, king of high heaven, had conferred
This office on her in return for the maidenhead he had
ravished:—
    Water-spirit, most dear to my heart, pride of the rivers,
You know that, of all the Italian maids who have mounted
into
The unrewarding bed of large-hearted Jove,* I have singled
You out and gladly promoted you to a place in heaven:
I must tell you what pain is in store for you, lest you blame me
for causing it.
As far as fortune seemed to allow and the Fate-spinners
granted
That Latium's affairs should go well, I have shielded your
walls and your brother.
But now I see he is facing a destiny loaded against him:
The day of doom is here, the enemy's hand is upon him.
I cannot endure to look on at this duel or its preliminaries.
If you dare do anything more effective to aid your brother,
Do it: *you* may. You and he may yet have a chance, poor souls.
    She had hardly finished speaking when Juturna burst into
tears
And violently struck her beautiful breast, three times and
again.
Saturnian Juno cried:—
                This is no time for weeping.
Hurry, and if there's a way, rescue your brother from death!
Or start them all fighting, arrange that this embryo peace be
stillborn!
I am behind you, whatever you venture.
                      With such encouragement
Juno left her, bemused, unsettled, in agony of mind.
    Meantime the kings came forth, Latinus, heroic of stature,
Riding a four-horse chariot, his temples crowned and
brilliant
With coronet of twelve gold rays, an emblem of
His ancestor the Sun,* while Turnus rode behind a

White pair, swinging a couple of broad-bladed javelins.
Over there, lord Aeneas, father of the Roman nation,
Bright in the armour from heaven, his shield like a star
    flashing,
Moves out of camp, with Ascanius beside him, the other hope
For Rome's great future: a priest, clothed in immaculate
    vestments,
Has led up the young of a bristly boar and with it an unshorn
Two-year-old sheep, and brought the beasts to the flaming
    altars.
The heroes, turning their eyes towards the rising sun,
Sprinkle the salted meal from their hands, cut off with a
    knife
The victims' forelocks, and pour libations from bowls on the
    altars.
Then did Aeneas the true, drawing his sword, pray:—
    Let the Sun witness my invocation now, and this Earth
For whose sake I have endured to go through such terrible
    travails,
And you, Father almighty, and you, Saturnian Juno,
Kindlier-disposed to me now, I hope and pray; and you,
Famed Mars, whose providence governs and shapes all wars:
And I call upon Springs and Rivers, on all the dread powers
    of the sky
Above us, and every deity haunting the cobalt sea—
If so it be that the victory goes to Italian Turnus,
It's agreed that the vanquished side shall withdraw to
    Evander's city;
Ascanius shall quit this soil, and my people shall never renew
The war thereafter, or challenge Latium with the sword.
But if victory falls to me in this fight—as I deem more likely,
And may the assent of the gods confirm me in so believing!—
I shall not make the Italians a subject race to the Trojans,*
Nor do I seek this realm for my own: let both our peoples,
Unconquered, as equal partners be joined in a league for
    ever.

The gods and the hallows I'll give*: Latinus shall keep, as my
    father,
His arms and his rightful authority. The Trojans shall build
    for me
My city walls, and Lavinia shall give her name to the city.
  Aeneas spoke first, like that. Then did Latinus follow,
Gazing up at the heavens, stretching his right hand towards
    them:—
  I too, Aeneas, swear by Earth, by Sea, by Sky,
By Apollo and Diana, by Janus-facing-both-ways,
By the power of the Underworld gods and the shrine of Dis,
    the merciless:
May the Father, whose lightning sanctions our treaties, hear
    me!
I touch the altar, I call on the fire and the godhead between us:
Never, for us Italians, shall this peace treaty be broken,
However things betide, no force of circumstance make me
Swerve from it of my own free will, not even though a flood
Should melt all earth into sea and heaven be dissolved in
    hell;
As sure as this sceptre of mine, which I hold in my right hand,
    never
Could put out new shoots and be dressed in light leaves to
    give men shade,
Once it was cut away from low down on its parent tree
In the forest, shedding its twigs and foliage to the knife:
It was a growing thing, but the hand of a craftsman encased it
In elegant bronze and made it the sceptre of the kings of
    Latium.
  So, in full view of the princes assembled, they ratify
The treaty between them in these terms. Then are the cere-
    monial
Victims solemnly sacrificed, hard by the fires, their living
Entrails torn out, and the altars loaded with high-piled dishes.
  But for some time the Italians had been in a vacillating,
Uneasy state of mind, thinking the fight an unfair one;

All the more now, when they saw from close up that the
    principals were not
Equally matched for it. Turnus heightened the feeling, as
    mutely
He went to the altar, and humbly worshipped with downcast
    eyes—
They noticed how pale he was too, how wasted his cheeks had
    become.
As soon as his sister, Juturna, perceived that the mutters of
    unrest
Were growing, that public opinion was wavering and
    irresolute,
Into the crowd she moved, assuming the likeness of Camers,
A man of distinguished family, whose father was widely
    renowned for
His valour, and who was himself a most active soldier; she
    went
Into the ranks of the Rutuli, a definite plan in her head,
And started a whispering campaign with remarks like this:—
    Aren't you ashamed, you Italians, at risking one hero's
        life
To save an army like ours? Are we not equal in numbers
And strength to the foe? Arcadians and Trojans—look, they
    are all there,
With the doom-ridden Etruscans intent upon Turnus' death.
Why, if half of us fought them, they'd hardly have men to
    equal us.
Turnus shall mount on wings of fame to the gods whose
    altars
He vows his life to, and live on the lips of men for ever;
But we shall lose our country and have to obey those arrogant
Masters, because we choose to sit here now and do nothing.
    More and more did these words inflame the mood of
        resentment
Among the Rutulian soldiers; muttering crept through the
    ranks:

Even the Laurentines and Latins began to change their atti-
tude.
Men who'd been dreaming of rest from the struggle, of going
about
Their affairs in peace, now wanted to fight, prayed that the
treaty
Be void, and felt pity for Turnus in his unfair predicament.
Here Juturna threw in a heavier weight, a delusive
Portent, giving a sign from the skies above,* which worked on
The minds of the Italians more strongly than anything else.
A golden eagle, Juppiter's bird, aloft in the red sky,
Was chasing a pack of water-fowl, which uttered clamorous
sounds
As they flew before it: suddenly swooping down to the water,
It greedily seized a magnificent swan in its hook-like claws.
The Italians grew tense as they watched. Now the whole
flock of water-fowl
Wheeled from their flight, screaming—a regular marvel to
see—
And darkening the sky with their wings, closed up, a cloud
of them, mobbed
The eagle, and drove it before them, until, overborne by their
fury
And the sheer weight of its burden, it weakened, dropping
the victim
Into the river below, and fled to the cover of a cloud.
This, of course, the Rutulians hailed with shouts as an
augury;
Their hands flew to their sword hilts. Tolumnius,* the augur,
at once cried:—
    This, aye this was what I have often prayed for! I mark
And acknowledge this sign from above. Out with your swords
and follow me,
You downtrodden folk, whom, like a flock of birds at his
mercy,
A greedy adventurer terrorizes, and violently plunders

Your coasts! Now *he*'ll have to fly, sail far away and take
　　cover
Out on the deep. Close up your ranks, then, with one accord,
And fight to defend the prince whom that bird of prey has
　　seized.
　　So saying, he ran forward and launched a weapon right at
The foe: his spear of cornel-wood cut through the air,
　　whining,
Accurate in aim. At once a great roar went up; all the rows of
Spectators broke out in a frenzy of uncontrollable passion.
That spear flew on. Now it happened nine brothers stood in
　　its path—
Young men of splendid physique, all were the sons of
　　Arcadian
Gylippus by one faithful wife, an Etruscan woman:
One of these, a handsome fellow in shining armour,
Was hit by the spear, at his waist, where his stomach was
　　chafed by the belt
Heavily sewn at the buckle which clasped it tightly together.
It skewered him through the ribs, and laid him dead on the
　　brown sand.
His brothers, crazy with grief, brave as they come, in a body
Charged at the foe head down, unsheathing their swords or
　　snatching up
Iron-tipped javelins. The army of the Laurentines
Ran forward to meet them; and then, once again, streamed
　　forth a great flood
Of Trojans, of Caeretans, and Arcadians with blazoned arms.
All are devoured by one passion, to fight it out with the sword.
The altars stood dismantled: a whirling barrage of missiles
Darkened the sky like a storm-cloud, the blizzard of iron
　　grew thicker.
The bowls and the fires were removed from the altars.
　　Latinus himself,
Now the treaty was void, picked up the images of his defeated
Gods,* and fled. Men harnessed their chariot horses or leapt

Astride their chargers, and raced with drawn swords to the
    fray.
Messapus, eager to tear up the treaty, rode at Aulestes,
A Tuscan king, who bore the insignia of his kingship,
And frightened him into recoiling: Aulestes, reeling back-
    wards,
Unluckily tumbled over an altar behind him and fell
On his head and shoulders. Messapus was up to him in a
    flash
With his lance, and towering above him on horseback,
    fiercely stabbed down
At him, for all his entreaties, with the massive weapon, and
    cried:—
    He's had it! This best of victims I've sacrificed*to the gods.
    The Italians ran to the spot and despoiled the still-warm
    corpse.
As Ebysus came at him, ready to strike, Corynaeus, full in
His path, snatched up a red-hot brand from an altar*and
    thrust
The blaze of it into his face: the man's great beard caught
    fire
And gave off a smell of singeing: Corynaeus followed it up
By gripping the hair of his dazed antagonist in his left hand,
Bringing a knee up against him and thrusting him hard to the
    ground,
Then slashed him in the side with his tempered blade.
    Podalirius
Bore down with uplifted sword on Alsus the shepherd, just
    as he
Charged through the missiles there in the front rank: Alsus,
    however,
Swung back his axe and bisected his enemy's head from brow
To chin, so that his armour was spattered with blood all
    over.
Unkind repose, the iron sleep weighed down Podalirius'
Eyes: his eyelids closed for everlasting night.

But Aeneas the true,* his head unhelmeted, put out his right
    hand
Which held no weapon, and shouted appeals to his own
    comrades:—
  Where are you off to? Why this sudden outbreak of
    violence?
Pull yourselves together! The truce has been made and its
    terms
Are all fixed now: I am the only man who's allowed to fight.
Leave it to me, and no more of this panicking! I will con-
    firm
The pact with my arms; the rites we've performed make
    Turnus my business.
  Even as he spoke, before he'd finished appealing, an
    arrow—
Imagine it!—winged its way towards him, whizzing: nobody
Knows who drew the bowstring, who sent that arrow flying,
Who won, whether by accident or heavenly aid, such glory
For the Italians: no one claimed the renown for so splendid
A feat, or ever boasted of having wounded Aeneas.
When Turnus saw Aeneas retire from the field, and his
    officers
Gravely disturbed, with a sudden access of glowing con-
    fidence
He called for his weapons and horses, proudly leapt up at one
    bound
Into his chariot, and fought to control the plunging team:
Then, careering about the field, he killed many brave
    warriors,
Bowled many over, mortally wounded, knocked down whole
    ranks with
His chariot wheels, sent a quick fire of spears at the fleeing
    enemy.
As, by the banks of icy Hebrus,* ensanguined Mars,
Driving his horses at full pelt, clangs out on his shield the
    alarum

Of war: the horses are furiously galloping over the broad
    plains,
Faster than South wind or West; their drumming hooves
    make the furthest
Regions of Thrace reverberate: Fear, with its louring visage,
Angers and Stratagems*speed on in the train of the War-
    god—
Exultant as this now, Turnus is lashing on through the battle
His horses, streaming with sweat: he tramples over the
    horribly
Slaughtered foe, while showers of blood fly out from be-
    neath
The galloping hooves as they stamp the sand into bloody
    paste.
Sthenelus now he killed, Thamyrus, Pholus—the first
From a distance, the other two at close quarters: he killed
    with spear-casts
The sons of Imbrasus, Glaucus and Lades, brought up by
    their father
In Lycia; he had equipped them with arms equally suitable
For close fighting on foot or charging on wind-swift horses.
On another sector Eumedes hurled himself into the fighting,
The war-famed son of that Dolon*widely renowned of old,
Having his grandsire's name, the courage and strength of his
    father
Who once, for venturing into the Danaan camp as a spy,
Demanded that his reward should be nothing less than
    Achilles'
Horses: but Diomed gave him a very different reward for
His daring—a dead man cannot aspire to the team of Achilles.
Well, Turnus noticed Eumedes far off on the open plain,
And hitting him first with a long-range javelin shot, drove
    over,
Pulled up his pair of horses, leapt down from the chariot,
    straddled
The fallen, dying man, and putting his foot hard down

On his neck, twisted the sword out of his hand, to plunge
    its
Glittering blade deep into his throat; then spoke these
    words:—
  Lie there, measure out with your length, you Trojan, the
    land of Hesperia
You wanted to grab by aggression. This is the pay-off they
    get
Who dare to take arms against me: thus do they found their
    city.
  Then, hurling his spear, he sent Asbutes to keep him
    company,
Chloreus and Sybaris, Thersilochus and Dares,
Thymoetes too, who had fallen, pitched over his horse's
    head.
As when a northerly gale from Thrace is roaring over
The Aegean, and driving shorewards rank upon rank of
    waves,
And clouds go flying in the sky where squalls of wind have
    flailed them,
So the formations give way, the ranks turn round and run
Wherever Turnus cleaves a path, carried on by his own
Momentum, his plumes fluttering in the wind of the chariot's
    passage.
Phegeus, enraged at this onset and Turnus' arrogant shout-
    ing,
Now threw himself in the chariot's path; and seizing the
    foam-flecked
Bridles of the frenzied horses, he wrenched them off their
    course.
As gripping the yoke, he was dragged along, the broad-
    bladed lance
Of Turnus found his unshielded side, broke through the
    joint of
His corselet where it was thrust, and gave him a slight flesh-
    wound.

But Phegeus turned on his foe, shield up, and was trying to
get at him,
To draw his sword and make a fight of it, when the wheel,
With the impetus of the hurtling chariot behind it, sent him
Spinning and crashed him to earth; Turnus at once followed
up with
A sword slash between the helmet's lower rim and the top of
The corselet, which took off his head and left his trunk on the
sand.
  Now while the victorious Turnus littered the battlefield
With dead, Aeneas, bleeding, was helped into camp by his
best friend,
Achates, and by Mnestheus, Ascanius beside them: he leant
Heavily on his tall spear at every other step.
Bitterly chagrined he was; he strove to pluck out the head of
The broken arrow, told them to give him a rough and ready
Treatment—to cut out the barb with a sword, open up the
flesh
Where it was lodged so deep, and get him back into the
fighting.
At this point Iapis, the son of Iasus, came up: this man
Was specially dear to Apollo, who, seized by intense passion*
For him, had delightedly offered him once his own arts, his
own powers—
Of divination, of music, of shooting the swift-flying arrow.
Iapis, to lengthen the life of a father desperately ill,
Elected the knowledge of healing herbs, the science of medi-
cine,
Choosing to practise an art which has little status, in obscurity.
Aeneas, chafing and fuming, stood there propped on his giant
Spear, a great crowd of soldiers about him, with young
Ascanius
Grieving, himself unmoved by their tears. Now the aged
Iapis,
With sleeves rolled up and gown close-girdled, as doctors
have them,

Rapidly tried many methods, applying the curative herbs
Of Apollo; but all were useless, and vainly too did he work
To coax the arrowhead out of the wound in the grip of his
    forceps.
Fortune gave him no clue, nor did his patron, Apollo,
Assist him; and all the time the terrible roar of battle
Was mounting, disaster nearing. The fighters saw no sky
But a canopy of dust; the enemy horsemen charged closer;
    and missiles
Fell thickly right in the camp. The din of warriors fighting
And falling as they struggled went hideously up to the
    heavens.
Now Venus, greatly distressed by her son's unmerited suffer-
    ing,
With a mother's solicitude plucked, from Ida in Crete,* a
    root of
Dittany, full-grown, with down on its leaves and a crimson
Flower: the plant is one not unfamiliar to wild goats,
Which get relief from it when they've been stuck by an
    arrow.
Putting a veil of mist around her, the goddess brought
This herb and made an infusion of it, in a cauldron, with
    sparkling
Water—none saw her doing it—adding drops of the juice
Of health-giving ambrosia*and fragrant panacea.*
The aged Iapis bathed the wound with that infusion,
Quite unaware of its provenance: at once, as might be
    expected,
The pain all went and the flow of blood from the deep wound
    stopped.
So then the barb came away in his hand—no force was
    needed—
And fell out: Aeneas' strength was renewed, he was strong
    as ever.
Iapis immediately roused up their fighting spirit by shout-
    ing:—

Jump to it! Fetch our commander his weapons! Don't
    stand about there!
This cure has been brought to pass by no human means, no
    medical
Mastery of mine. It is not my skill that has saved you,
    Aeneas.
One greater, a god, is behind it, restores you for deeds yet
    greater.
    Aeneas, thirsting for battle, irked by delay, had put on
His golden greaves—left leg, right leg; now he brandished
    his spear.
As soon as the corselet was on and the shield at his side in
    position,
He folded his son, Ascanius, in a mailed embrace; and lightly
Kissing his lips through the helmet's open visor, he said:—
    From me you may learn courage and what real effort is;
From others, the meaning of fortune. Today this hand will
    see
You're protected in war, and take you to where war's prizes
    are found.
Be sure that, when you have grown to your full manhood,
    you do not
Forget; but rather, dwelling upon your kinsmen's example,
Be inspired by your father Aeneas, your uncle Hector.
    When he had spoken, Aeneas sallied forth in his might,
Shaking his massive spear, Antheus and Mnestheus with
    him—
A close-packed column of warriors rapidly moving forwards
And leaving the camp deserted. Then was the plain a flurry
Of blinding dust, and the ground thrilled with the tramp of
    feet.
Turnus, upon a rampart opposite, saw them advancing;
The Italians saw it, and tremors of icy fear pervaded
Their inmost hearts. Before any of the Latins, Juturna heard
That marching sound and knew what it meant, and fled in
    terror.

Aeneas raced on, his column sweeping and darkening the
      plain.
As when a storm has burst and a cyclone strides across
The sea towards the land, and forewarned from afar the
      hearts of
Poor countrymen are appalled—that storm is going to fell
Their trees and flatten their growing crops, create havoc
      everywhere;
Gusts, blowing in from the sea, trumpet the gale's ap-
      proach—
So did the Trojan commander launch a frontal attack
On the enemy, with his men all rallying to him, compact in
Arrowhead formations. Thymbraeus struck down big Osiris,
Mnestheus killed Arcetius, Achates killed Epulo,
Gyas killed Ufens; even the augur, Tolumnius,* fell—
He who had been the first to fire at the Trojan ranks.
A din rose up to the sky, as the Rutuli, routed in their turn,
Took to their heels and fled over the field in a cloud of dust.
Aeneas was not concerned to slaughter these fugitives, nor
      did he
Follow up such as opposed him, foot to foot, or were threaten-
      ing
To shoot at him: Turnus alone was his quarry; for Turnus he
      peered
Through the fog of battle, tracking him, calling on him to
      fight.
Shaken by fear of this, the warrior maid Juturna
Pushed out of Turnus' chariot his driver, Metiscus, who
      stood
With the reins about him: striking the pole, he fell to the
      ground
And lay far in their wake. Juturna, taking his place and
      transformed to
His likeness—in voice, physique, armour—now handled the
      rippling reins.
Just as a blue-black swallow flits through the villa of some

Rich lord; weaving a skein of flight in the fine big halls, she
Gathers up crumbs of food, tit-bits for her chirruping
nestlings—
You can hear her twittering, now through the empty colon-
nades,
Now by the tanks in the garden: so Juturna went darting
Amid the foe, her chariot flying all over the battlefield.
Now here, now there she gave them a glimpse of her conquer-
ing brother,
But allowed no encounter—next moment she's off and safely
away.
Aeneas, for all that, followed their mazy trail, determined
To meet him; he dogged Turnus through all the confusion
of battle,
Shouting his challenge. Whenever he set eyes on his enemy
And tried to outmatch the speed of those galloping horses by
running,
So often Juturna steered the chariot away at a tangent.
What was Aeneas to do? He was at a loss, undecided,
With different ideas ebbing and flowing across his mind.
Just then Messapus, who carried two whippy javelins,
pointed
With steel, in his left hand—a fighter quick off the mark—
poised one
And with unerring aim hurled it straight at Aeneas.
He stood his ground, and covering up behind his shield,
Sank down upon one knee; but the flying javelin took off
The peak of his helmet, shearing away the crest from its top.
Aeneas then got really angry: his hand had been forced by
Their treachery. Seeing that Turnus had driven off, well out
of reach,
He repeatedly called to witness* Jove and the altar of the
broken
Treaty, and then at last went in at the foe, with the flood-tide
Of battle behind him, gave rein to the pent-up fury within
him,

And terribly unleashed a fierce, indiscriminate slaughter.

Have I the inspiration now to do justice to so many

Horrors, to such a gamut of carnage—the deaths of captains

Driven all over the field by Turnus now, and now by

The Trojan prince? Juppiter, was it your will*that nations,

Destined to live at peace for ever, should clash so bitterly?

Well, the first combat to hold up the Trojans' assault, though not

For long, was when Aeneas met the Rutulian, Sucro:

He got him soon in the side, where death comes quickest, driving

His merciless sword through the ribs, the palisade of the chest.

Turnus, unhorsing Amycus and also his brother Diores,

Went for them on foot, nailed one with his long spear as he advanced,

Struck down with his sword the other; then cut off both their heads*

And drove away with those blood-dripping heads attached to his chariot.

Aeneas despatched Talos, Tanais and the brave

Cethegus, all three at one killing, and slew the dejected Onites,

A man of Theban stock, his mother's name Peridia.

Turnus killed the brothers who'd come from Apollo's land

Of Lycia; also Menoetes, a man who loathed war, but that didn't

Help him—he was Arcadian, a fisherman living in humble

Circumstances near the waters of Lerna, a stranger

To the mansions of the great, the son of a tenant-farmer.

You know how it is when fires have been kindled on either side

Of a wood that is dry as tinder, dense-grown with crackling laurel;

Or when from the mountain heights two torrents, foaming in spate,

Come rapidly roaring down and race towards the sea,
Leaving behind them a trail of devastation: Aeneas
And Turnus tore through the battle with the same violence.
   Now
Does an eagre of wrath sweep them, their hearts cannot
   contain it
Or imagine defeat; they charge on the enemy's weapons at
   full power.
Murranus, who was sounding off about his ancestors,
The whole of his ancient pedigree traced through the kings
   of Latium,
Was struck by a rock which Aeneas whirled at him, and sent
   flying
Out of his chariot full length on the ground: the wheels
   rolled him forward
Under the traces and yoke of his horses, which trampled
   him down
With a flurry of galloping hooves, and no thought for their
   master's life.
Turnus encountered Hyllus charging and yelling out savage
War-cries; he flung a spear at the man's gold-helmeted head:
The weapon pierced the helmet of Hyllus and lodged in his
   brain.
His strong arm did not preserve the bravest of the Arcadians,
Cretheus, from Turnus: nor did his gods protect Cupencus
When Aeneas came his way, but he took the cold steel full in
The breast, poor fellow—his bronze shield could not arrest
   the blow.
Now the Laurentine plain saw Aeolus perish too,
His body sprawling upon the ground—that Aeolus
Whom all the armies of Greece had never been able to bring
   down,
Nor even Achilles who overthrew the kingdom of Priam:
Here he came to the finish; he had a fine home at Lyrnesus
Under Mount Ida—a fine home, but he sleeps in Laurentine
   soil.*

The whole of each army had now been thrown into the
    battle—
All the Latins and Trojans, Mnestheus and gallant Serestus,
Messapus, the tamer of horses, brave Asilas, the whole
Etruscan division, Evander's Arcadian cavalry squadrons.
They struggled, with every man putting all he had into the
    struggle;
No hanging back, no respite: they fought to the death every-
    where.
    Then did his lovely mother put into the head of Aeneas
That he should move on the city, divert his men to a sud-
    den
Assault on its walls, and surprising the Latins, disorganize
And defeat them. Scouring the various battle sectors for
    Turnus,
And looking all round him, this way and that, he viewed the
    city
Untouched by all this fighting, peaceful and undisturbed.
At once his imagination was lit by the thought of a greater
Battle. He called up Mnestheus, Sergestus and brave
    Serestus,
His staff, and took his stand on a hillock: the rest of the
    Trojan
Force gathered to him, tight-packed, but did not ground
    their shields
Or spears. Then, standing above the ring of warriors, he
    said:—
    I want my orders obeyed instantly. Juppiter's with us.
My plan may surprise you, but that must be no excuse for
    half-heartedness.
Look at the city, the cause of this war, the seat of Latinus'
Power!—unless they admit they are beaten and owe us
    obedience,
This day I'll destroy it and raze its smoking roofs to the
    ground.
Do I have to wait until Turnus feels like facing the ordeal

Of combat? is willing to meet me again, after once being
    beaten?*
Here is the heart, the centre of this cursed war, my men.
Get torches! Hurry! Fire shall exact the terms of the treaty.
  Upon these words, they all are seized by an equal enthu-
    siasm,
Get into wedge formation, drive solidly at the walls.
In a moment ladders appear, incendiaries the same instant.
Some of them run to the several gates, cut down the guards
    there;
While others darken the sky with a covering fire of arrows.
Aeneas, in the forward party, stretches his right hand
Up at the battlements, loudly rebukes Latinus, and calls
The gods to witness that once again a fight is forced on him,
Twice the Italians have broken a treaty*and been the aggressors.
The citizens' nervous excitement bursts out into violent dis-
    sension,
One party demanding the gates be unbarred, the town thrown
    open
To the Trojans, and Latinus himself haled onto the walls:
The others took arms and ran to the defence of their city.
So, when a shepherd has traced a swarm of bees to their
    chamber
Deep in some porous rock, and filled it with acrid smoke,
The bees within, alarmed for their community, scurry
About the wax castle, and raise their temper with high-
    pitched buzzing:
Black, pungent smoke rolls through their cells; the hollow
    rock
Is all one inward humming; smoke trickles out from its
    crannies.
  A further calamity now befell the war-weary Latins,
Shaking the town to its very foundations, and causing great
    grief.
The queen, looking forth from her roof-top, saw the advance
    of the foe,

Their assault on the walls, the flaming material flung at the houses,
But nowhere the Rutuli, no opposition from Turnus.
She believed, alas, that her warrior had lost his life in the desperate
Fighting. The shock and anguish of this unsettled her mind:
Crying out that she was the cause, she only to blame for disaster,
Talking wildly, distracted by paroxysms of grief,
Death in her heart, she tore the crimson gown she was wearing
And hung from a beam the noose that would horribly make an end of her.
When the poor Latin women got word of this calamity,
Led by the queen's daughter, who tore at her flower-bright tresses
And rose-petal cheeks, they soon were all of them in a frenzy
Of grief around her: the palace resounded with lamentations.
From there the appalling story spread through the city everywhere.
All were dismayed: Latinus, rending his clothes, went about
In a daze at the tragic end of his wife and his city's downfall,
Sprinkling upon his grey head handfuls of unclean dust,
And censured himself severely for not accepting Aeneas
Of his own free will, or attaching him to the Crown through marriage.

   Meanwhile, at the far side of the plain, Turnus is fighting,
Pursuing a few stragglers, but not with such spirit now,
With less and less enjoyment in the action of his horses.
Borne on the wind, there came to him now an outcry, vague
But frightening: he strained his ears; he had to listen; he heard
The sound of a city in tumult, a murmur of no good cheer:—
   O god! What is all that noise coming from the distant city?
What has happened to shake the walls with such sounds of grief?

So Turnus spoke, and wild with anxiety reined up his
    horses.
Whereat his sister who, still in the likeness of Metiscus,
His charioteer, was controlling the horses and driving the
    chariot
Countered his thoughts by saying:—

                           Let us pursue those Trojans:
That way lies the path to immediate victory, Turnus.
Others there are to defend the town, and quite competent
    for it.
Aeneas is battling and fully committed against the Italians,
Let us deal merciless havoc upon the Trojans here.
You'll win as much glory as he, and have no fewer dead to
    your credit.
  Turnus replied:—
  Sister, I recognized you long ago, the first moment you
    cleverly
Caused the pact to be broken, embroiled yourself in this
    war;
And I'm not deceived now by this mortal disguise of yours.
    But who was it
Sent you down from Olympus to go through so great an
    ordeal?
To witness the hard death your unfortunate brother must
    die?
For what can I do? What chance or warrant have I of sur-
    vival?
I have seen Murranus*—and no one is left whom I love so
    well—
A champion slain by a wound from a champion fighter, fall
Before my very eyes, calling on me for aid.
The ill-starred Ufens*died, rather than look upon
Our dishonour: the Trojans now possess his corpse and his
    armour.
Am I to let our homes be destroyed—the one disaster
I have been spared—and not give the lie to Drances' slanders*

By fighting? What? Turn my back? My country to see me a
     runaway?
Death is not all that dreadful. You Shades, be kind to me,
Since now the Powers above have taken their goodwill from
     me.
I shall come down to you, a soul unstained, with no cowardice
Upon my conscience to make me unworthy of my great
     ancestors.
  He'd barely finished when Saces came racing up on his
     lathered
Horse, having ridden right through the enemy, though he
     was wounded
By an arrow full in the face: he cried out to Turnus for aid:—
  Turnus, you are our last hope, pity your people and save
     them!
Aeneas attacks like a thunderbolt, threatens to batter down
The citadel of the Italians and blast us with total destruction.
Already they're shooting up fire at our roofs. The Latins
     look to you,
Pray to you. King Latinus debates with himself, uncertain
Which alliance to favour and whom to have for Lavinia.
And listen—the queen, your most trustworthy supporter,
     has died
By her own hand: she was frightened out of her wits, and
     killed herself.
Messapus and gallant Atinas alone, in defence of the gates,
Are holding our men together. Around them, on flank and
     front,
The hostile formations are pressing, a thick-set bristling
     crop of
Cold steel, while you're joy-riding over these empty fields.
  The picture of their changed fortunes struck Turnus
     dumb, bewildered him.
Speechless and staring, he stood there, his heart in a violent
     conflict,
Torn by humiliation, by grief shot through with madness,

By love's tormenting jealousy and a sense of his own true
    courage.
As soon as the mists parted and he could think again clearly,
He turned his blazing eyes upon the walls, in great
Distress of mind, looked back at the city there from his
    chariot.
He saw a whirling spire of flame which was leaping upwards,
Wave after wave, through the floors of a turret, had got a
    firm grip on it:
Turnus had built this turret*himself, a solid construction
Of planking, with wheels to move on, and gangways rigged
    aloft:—
    The fates are too strong for me, sister—I see it now. Don't
    hold me back;
Let me go where God and my own unmerciful fortune call me.
I am resolved to fight Aeneas, to bear whatever
Bitterness death holds for me. You shall not see me disgraced
Any longer. Just let me indulge this madness of mine ere I
    die.
    So saying, Turnus at once leapt down to the ground from
    his chariot,
And leaving his sister sorrowing, dashed through the enemy,
    ran
The gauntlet of fire, his impetus breaking a way through
    their midst.
Even as a boulder that rolls straight down from a mountain
    summit,
Dislodged by a gust of wind—a cloudburst has washed away
The soil it was fast in, perhaps, or the passage of time has
    loosened it;
Down, with terrific momentum, the huge thing insensately
    bounces
Over the ground, steep down, carrying trees, flocks, men
Before it: just like this did Turnus speed to the city,
Scattering the foe from his path, and run to the walls where
    the earth was

Most deeply drenched with blood and the air screeched with
    missiles.

He held up his hand as a signal, shouted for all to hear:—
    Rutuli, put up your weapons! Cease fire, you Latins!
    Whatever

The issue is, I shoulder it. Better that I redeem

For you the breaking of the treaty, and decide all, in a duel.
    So then they drew apart, leaving a space in the midst for
    the combat.

But lord Aeneas, as soon as he heard the name of Turnus,

Hurried away from the walls, from the towers he was then
    attacking,

Broke off the whole engagement, impatient of any delay,

Overjoyed at the prospect of meeting Turnus; and terribly
    clashed his

Sword on his shield. Gigantic as Athos* he looked, as
    Eryx,*

As our own Appennine range when a storm roars in its oak
    trees

Dancing their leaves, and its snowy peaks soar joyfully sky-
    wards.

Now did the Rutuli, the Trojans and all the Italians

Excitedly gaze at their two champions—those who were
    up on

The battlements, and those who were thumping the walls
    below

With a ram. All laid down their shields. Latinus himself
    marvelled

To see those giants, born in different parts of the world,

Now met together to fight it out in single combat.

They, as soon as the lists were cleared on the open plain,

Exchanged spear-shots from a distance and then advanced
    at a run

Into the fight and met with a clang of their bronzen shields.

Earth groaned beneath the encounter: the sword strokes
    rained so fast

You could not see which hits were lucky and which were
    skilful.
As on the ranges of Sila*or a plateau of Taburnus*
Two bulls charge at each other, head on, determined to fight
To the death; the herdsmen have backed away from the
    combat in terror,
And the whole herd stands mute with fear, the heifers
    wondering
Which will be lord of the forest and sultan of all the herd:
The two bulls furiously tussle, wounding each other
    repeatedly,
Horns straining together and butting, blood running down
Their necks and shoulders in streams; the woodland rings
    with their bellowing:
Equal to this was the fray between Trojan Aeneas and Turnus
Of Italy: shield against shield, they collide with the sound
    of a thunderclap.
Juppiter holds the scales in his own hand: empty, they
    balance:
And then he puts in the scales the different fates of the two
    men,
To see which weight sinks down, meaning defeat and death.
Turnus sprang forward that moment, thinking he saw a safe
    opening,
Rose on tiptoe, whirled up his sword, and with all his
    strength
Behind it, struck. The Trojans and the excited Latins
Cried out. Both sides were tense, keyed-up. But the
    treacherous blade
Snapped—yes, right in midstroke it failed the fiery Turnus,
Left him no choice but to flee. When he realised he was dis-
    armed
And the sword-hilt he held was not even his own, he ran like
    the wind.
The story goes*that, when he was mounting in haste for
    battle

Behind his chariot team, he snatched up the sword of
  Metiscus,
His driver, instead of his father's blade, being blind with
  excitement.
That sword was good enough to deal with the routed
  Trojans:
But it was only a mortal blade; so, when it struck
On armour made by the Fire-god, it shivered to bits at the
  blow,
Like brittle ice, and its fragments lay glittering on the brown
  sand.
So Turnus in desperation tried this way and that to escape
Out onto the open plain, running in circles erratically,
Since all about him the Trojans had formed a ring, and
  besides
A wide-spreading marsh cut off one escape-route, the steep
  walls another.
  Aeneas pursued the while, though hampered and slowed
  down
At times by the arrow-wound he had received in his leg:
Still, he pressed hard and hotly upon his panting foe.
It was like the scene when a hound has got a stag cut off by
A river, or headed off by the nets with their crimson feathers
Which scare it: the hound, baying, follows up close on its
  heels;
The quarry, frightened both by the snares and the river-
  bank's steepness,
Turns on its tracks again and again; but the spirited stag-
  hound
Sticks to it, jaws agape—has he got it?—you'd think he had
  got it,
The way his teeth snap like a trap, but he's bitten the air and
  is baffled.
Then what a din arose! The river-banks and the marsh pools
Echoed and echoed all round, the sky roared with the shout-
  ing.

Even as he fled, Turnus cursed the Rutulians who stood
    there,

Calling on men by their names, demanding they give him his
    own sword.

Aeneas stopped that by threatening immediate death for
    any

Who went near Turnus, terrorized the already unnerved
    Rutulians

By swearing he'd wreck their whole city; kept on in spite of
    his wound.

Five times the pair ran in a circle, then changing direction,
    returned

On their own tracks: no light-hearted sporting event it was,
    though—

The prize they ran for being the very life-blood of Turnus.

Now it happened a bitter-leafed wild olive, sacred to Faunus,*

Had stood here—a tree from of old held in great reverence
    by sailors

Who, when they'd escaped from drowning, would hang on
    its boughs their offerings

To the Laurentine god, hang up the clothing they'd vowed
    him.

But the Trojans,* to clear the arena for the two combatants,

Had removed the trunk of this tree with no regard for its
    sanctity.

Here, in the stump, was sticking Aeneas' spear: the momen-
    tum

Of flight had carried it here and wedged it firm in the tough
    wood.

Aeneas now strained every muscle in an attempt to extract

The weapon, wanting to catch with a missile the foe he could
    not

Catch up by running. Turnus cried out in extremity of
    fear:—

  Faunus, I beg you, take pity! Dear native earth, hold
    fast to

That spear! Remember how I have always paid you reverence,
And how the Trojans profaned you to clear the field for our
    combat!
  This prayer to the god for help did not fall upon deaf ears.
Aeneas, though long he struggled, bent over the tough-
    grained stump,
Could not by any effort manage to free his spear
From the bite of the wood. While he fought and strained with
    violent exertions,
The nymph Juturna, changing again into Metiscus
The charioteer, ran forward and gave her brother his own
    sword.
Venus, annoyed that the nymph was granted such freedom
    of action,
Approached and tore out the spear from the deep grip of the
    tree stump.
Now in high heart the two champions, their arms and their
    spirits restored,
One with his trusted sword, one erect and aggressive holding
His spear, stand facing each other, breathing hard, in the lists.
  Meantime the king of all-powerful Olympus addresses
    Juno
As she looks down at the combat out of a golden cloud:—
  My wife, how shall it end now? What more is there you
    can do?
For you know, and admit the knowledge, that Aeneas is
    called of heaven
As a national hero, and fate is exalting him to the stars.*
What are you planning? Why do you linger here in the chill
    clouds?
Was it right that Aeneas, the heaven-born, should be hurt by
    the hand of a mortal?
Or that Juturna should give back the missing sword to her
    brother—
Ah yes, without you she was powerless—and strengthen the
    loser's hand?

Then yield to my persuasions, give up the long feud now at
    last!

No more of the hidden rancour that so consumes you, the
    sullen

Recriminations your sweet lips have troubled me with so
    often!

This is the end, I say. You had power to harry the Trojans

All over lands and seas, to kindle accursed war,

Bring tragic disgrace on a king's home and drape a betrothal
    in mourning.

I forbid you to carry the feud any further.

                               So Juppiter spoke.

Juno, the daughter of Saturn, with lowered eyes, replied:—

    It is because your wishes, great consort, were known to
    me,

That I have reluctantly given up Turnus and quit the earth.

Otherwise I'd not be sitting apart here and putting up with

Every humiliation: no, armed with flame, I'd be there

In action, dragging the Trojans into a fatal fight.

I admit I encouraged Juturna to go and help her unfortunate

Brother, approved of her acting more boldly still to preserve
    him;

But not that she should use her bow and shoot at the Trojans:

This I swear by the source of the inexorable river,

Styx—the one dreadful and binding oath for us heaven-
    dwellers.

And now I do truly yield; I give up the fight—I am sick of it.

One thing, and no ruling of fate forbids you to grant it, I do

Entreat, for Latium's sake and the dignity of your own kin:

When they make peace through a prosperous—aye, let it be
    so—a prosperous

Marriage, and when they are making agreements and laws
    to unite them,

Do not command the indigenous Latins* to change their
    ancient

Name, to become Trojans and to be called the Teucrians:

Allow them to keep the old language and their traditional
    dress:
Let it be Latium for ever, and the kings be Alban kings;*
Let the line be Roman, the qualities making it great be Italian.
Troy's gone; may it be gone in name as well as reality.

    The creator of man and of all things replied to her with a
        smile:—
Jove's sister you are indeed and the second child of Saturn,
So powerful the tides of wrath sweeping within your breast!
But come, there was no need for this violent emotion; calm
    yourself.
Willingly I grant what you ask: you have won me over.
The Italians shall keep their native tongue and their old
    traditions;
Their name shall not be altered. The Trojans will but sink
    down in
The mass and be made one with them. I'll add the rites and
    usage
Of Trojan worship*to theirs. All will be Latins, speaking
One tongue. From this blend of Italian and Trojan blood
    shall arise
A people surpassing all men, nay even the gods, in godliness.*
No other nation on earth will pay such reverence to Juno.

    The goddess bowed and agreed, glad now to change her
        whole policy,
Passed forthwith from the sky, leaving her place in the
    clouds.

    This being accomplished, the Father brooded awhile on
        another
Question—how to detach from her brother's side Juturna.
Two demon fiends there are, called by the name of Furies,*
Whom darkest Night brought forth at one and the same birth
    with
Hellish Megaera, breeding all three alike*with the twining
Coils of serpents and giving them wings like the wind. These
    creatures

Attend on Juppiter's throne, at the house of heaven's stern
    Ruler,
Ready to stab fear into the hearts of anguished mortals
Whenever the king of the gods is dealing out pestilences
And hideous death, or affrighting guilty cities with war.
Juppiter now sent one of these demons hurrying down from
Heaven, to confront Juturna with a forbidding omen.
Off she flew, and swiftly was borne to earth in a whirlwind.
Just as an arrow flies through the clouds from a bowstring—
    a shaft
Whose tip some Parthian or Cretan*archer has doped with a
    deadly
Poison, and then shot it; fatal the wound it will give—
Whirring and unsuspected it flies through the mirk of the
    clouds:
So sped the spawn of Night upon her way to the earth.
When she could see the Trojan lines and Turnus' army,
She suddenly dwindled and changed into the shape of that
    small owl
Which often at night, when no one's about, perches on
    tombs
Or gables, and hoots for hours disquietingly through the
    darkness.
Thus transformed, the Fury flittered about the face of
Turnus, screeching, and kept on bumping his shield with
    her wings.
The thing was so uncanny that he went numb with fear
And his hair stood on end, and the voice died in his throat.
But Juturna recognized from afar the creaking wings of
The demon. It broke her spirit: she rent her dishevelled hair,
Scratched at her cheeks and beat her breast in grief for her
    brother:—
    Oh, Turnus, what can your sister do for you now? What
      worse
Remains for this much-tried heart? I have used all my powers
To save you. But how can I face a manifestation so dreadful?

No, no, I give up the fight now. I tremble—oh, spare me your
     terrors,
You sinister bird: I know the beat of your wings, I know that
They sound the tocsin of death, and Jove's high purpose has
     given
These high-handed orders. So thus he requites me who took
     my virginity!
Why did he make me immortal? disfranchise me from the
     common
Law of death? But for that, I could end my terrible anguish
This very moment, and go through the shades with my poor
     brother.
I immortal! What joy can I have from immortal life,
Bereft of my brother? Alas, that nowhere may earth yawn
     deep
And let me go down to the ghosts below, for I am a deity!
     So saying, the goddess veiled her face in her grey-green
     mantle,
And heavily sighing, vanished into the depths of the river.*
     Aeneas moved up on his enemy, hefting and flashing his
     spear
Which was huge as a tree, and shouted out with extreme
     ferocity:—
     Turnus, you'll get no more reprieves. Are you still recoil-
     ing?
It's cold steel now, hand to hand, not fleetness of foot, that
     will tell.
Try all the transformations of Proteus! Summon up
Your powers, whether of courage or magic! Take wings, if
     you like,
And shoot straight up to the stars, or go to ground in the deep
     earth!
     Turnus, shaking his head, replied:—
                                   It's the gods and Juppiter's
Enmity frighten me, not your sneers or your bloodthirsty
     speeches.

Without a word more he looked round and his eyes lit
on a huge stone—
A huge old stone which for years had been lying there on the
plain
As a boundary mark between fields, to prevent disputes
about ownership.
Hardly could twelve strong men, of such physique as the
earth
Produces nowadays, pick up and carry it on their shoulders.
Well, Turnus pounced on it, lifted it, and taking a run to
give it
More impetus, hurled this stone from his full height at
Aeneas.
But as he moved, as he ran, as he raised his hands, as he
threw
That boulder, for him it was just as if somebody else were
doing it.
Ice-bound were his veins, and his legs felt like water.
So too the stone he hurled, flying through empty air,
Failed to make the distance, fell short of its objective.
But, as it is in a nightmare, when sleep's narcotic hand
Is leaden upon our eyes, we seem to be desperately trying
To run and run, but we cannot—for all our efforts, we sink
down
Nerveless; our usual strength is just not there, and our
tongue
Won't work at all—we can't utter a word or produce one
sound:
So with Turnus, each move he bravely attempted to make,
The unearthly demon brought it to nothing. Now did his
feelings
Veer this way and that in distraction: he gazed at the city,
the Rutuli;
Faltered with fear; trembled at the weapon menacing him.
He could see no way to escape and no way to get at Aeneas;
His chariot, his sister who drove it, were nowhere to be seen.

So Turnus faltered: the other brandished his fateful spear,
And watching out for an opening, hurled it with all his might
From a distance. The noise it made was louder than that of
    any
Great stone projected by siege artillery, louder than
A meteorite's explosion. The spear flew on its sinister
Mission of death like a black tornado, and piercing the
    edge of
The seven-fold shield, laid open the corselet of Turnus, low
    down.
Right through his thigh it ripped, with a hideous sound. The
    impact
Brought giant Turnus down on bent knee to the earth.
The Italians sprang to their feet, crying out: the hills all
    round
Bayed back their howl of dismay, far and wide the deep
    woods echoed it.
Turnus, brought low, stretched out a pleading hand, looked
    up at
His foe in appeal:—
                    I know, I've deserved it. I'll not beg life.
Yours was the luck. Make the most of it. But if the thought of
    a father's
Unhappiness can move you—a father such as you had
In Anchises—I ask you, show compassion for aged Daunus,
And give me back to him; or if that is the way it must be,
Give back my dead body. You have won. The Italians have
    seen me
Beaten, these hands outstretched. Lavinia is yours to wed.
Don't carry hatred further.
                    Aeneas stood over him, poised
On the edge of the stroke; but his eyes were restless, he did
    not strike.
And now what Turnus had said was taking effect, was
    making him
More and more indecisive, when on his enemy's shoulder

He noticed the fatal baldric,* the belt with its glittering
    studs—
How well he knew it!—which Turnus had stripped from
    young Pallas after
He'd killed him, and put on himself—a symbol of triumph
    and doom.
Aeneas fastened his eyes on this relic, this sad reminder
Of all the pain Pallas' death had caused. Rage shook him.*
    He looked
Frightening. He said:—
            Do you hope to get off now, wearing the spoils
You took from my Pallas? It's he, it's Pallas who strikes this
    blow—
The victim shedding his murderer's blood in retribution!
  So saying, Aeneas angrily plunged his sword full into
Turnus' breast. The body went limp and cold. With a deep
    sigh
The unconsenting spirit fled to the shades below.

EXPLANATORY NOTES

BOOK I

2   *Lavinian shores*: Lavinium, an ancient town on the coast twenty miles south of the site of Rome. This is the town which Aeneas will actually found.

7   *royal line of Alba*: Alba Longa, between Lavinium and Rome, will be founded by Aeneas' son Ascanius/Iulus. From here the family of the Iulii came to Rome. Cf. Book I, 267 ff.

27   *judgement of Paris*: the Trojan prince Paris gave the prize for beauty to Venus, who promised him Helen, over Juno and Athene.

28   *Ganymede*: a boy of the Trojan royal family, carried off and beloved by Jupiter.

41   *Ajax*: the lesser Ajax, son of Oileus, ravished Cassandra at the sack of Troy, tearing her away from Athene's altar. The goddess punished him, and the failure of the Greeks to stone him for sacrilege, by sending a storm to wreck their ships.

67   *Tyrrhene sea*: the sea to the west of Italy.

108 ff.   *Three times did the South wind . . .* : more accurately, 'Three ships did the South wind spin towards an ambush . . . three did the East wind Drive in to the Syrtes shoal.'

111   *Syrtes shoal*: off the north coast of Africa.

144   *Nereid and Triton*: sea-goddess and sea-god.

174   *Achates*: chief named subordinate of Aeneas. Regularly called 'loyal Achates'.

177   *Ceres*: goddess of corn.

195   *shared out the wine . . . Acestes*: in Sicily, cf. Book V, 746ff.

200   *Scylla*: cf. Book III, 420 ff.

201   *Cyclops*: cf. Book III, 641 ff.

241   *Antenor*: Trojan chief who made his way to North Italy and founded Patavium (Padua).

272 *third summer ... three hundred years*: observe the artful crescendo: three years—thirty years—three hundred years—no limit in time or space.

273 *priestess ... Trojan blood*: Ilia, mother by the god Mars of the twins Romulus and Remus.

286 *a Caesar*: ambiguously expressed between Julius Caesar and Augustus, but the reference to the East shows it is really the latter who is meant. After his death he will be deified.

293 *gates of War*: the temple of Janus at Rome was open in time of war, closed in peace: cf. Book VII, 607 ff.

317 *Thracian Harpalyce*: Harpalyce was an Amazon. Spartan girls were famous for their outdoor sports.

329 *sister of Phoebus*: the goddess Diana.

338 *Agenor*: mythical king of Tyre, the mother city of Carthage.

367 *'Bull's Hide'*: the citadel of Carthage was called Bosra: Greeks heard this as Byrsa (in Greek, 'bull's hide') and made up the story that the settlers were sold 'as much land as a hide would hold': they cut the hide into threads and circled a large area with it.

380 *my own land, Italy*: Dardanus, ancestor of the Trojans, came originally from Italy; cf. Book III, 167 ff., Book VII, 205 ff., Book VIII, 37.

415 *Paphos*: cult-centre of Venus on Cyprus.

416 *Sabaean*: i.e. Arabian.

444 *skull of a spirited horse*: a horse appears on many Carthaginian coins. Compare the omen of the sow given to Aeneas, Book III, 388 ff., and Book VIII, 81 ff.

450 *Dido's fear*: more accurately, 'This grove first soothed Aeneas' fear'.

458 *the sons of Atreus*: Agamemnon and Menelaus. This passage lists many scenes from Homer's *Iliad*.

469 *tents of Rhesus*: this night attack is related in the Tenth Book of the *Iliad*.

474 *Troilus*: son of Priam.

484 *thrice round the walls . . . lifeless body*: the events of *Iliad*, Books XXII and XXIV.

489 *black Memnon*: Memnon the Aethiop, son of the Dawn, and Penthesilea the Amazon came to help Troy after the death of Hector. Achilles slew both.

498 *banks of Eurotas . . . Cynthian slopes*: Eurotas is the river of Sparta, Cynthus the hill on the island of Delos.

499 *Oreads*: mountain nymphs.

530 *Hesperia*: 'the western land', a Greek name for Italy.

550 *Acestes*: cf. Book V, 35 ff.

569 *Saturn*: father of Jupiter, who once ruled in Italy (the 'Age of Saturn' was the Golden Age).

619 *Teucer*: Greek hero, half-brother of the greater Ajax: in exile from Greek Salamis after the Trojan War, he founded Salamis on Cyprus.

649 *Argive Helen*: this foreshadows the forbidden love of Dido for Aeneas and its disastrous outcome.

667 *Your own brother, Aeneas*: strictly, half-brother. A rather frivolous point, much relished by Ovid.

681 *Cythera . . . Idalium*: Cythera, an island off the Spartan coast; Idalium, on Cyprus.

741 *long-haired Iopas . . . zither*: a song from a bard at a feast is regular in the *Odyssey*; the unexpectedly philosophical subject of this one has led to many speculations about Virgil's purpose.

751 *son of Aurora*: Memnon; cf. Book I, 489.

BOOK II

7 *what Myrmidon*: the Myrmidons were Achilles' troops at Troy.

14 *Broken in war . . . slipping away*: the Greeks had been besieging Troy for ten years. This account of their defeat is of course very different from the picture in the *Iliad*.

82 *Palamedes*: a Greek leader, rival in cleverness of Ulysses, who out of envy devised his death; not in Homer, the story is popular with later poets.

100 *Calchas*: soothsayer of the Greek army.

117 *a young girl's blood . . . Troy*: Iphigeneia, daughter of Agamemnon, had to be sacrificed to Diana to get a favourable wind for sailing to Troy.

166 *Athene's image . . . holy place*: the two Greek chieftains entered Troy and carried off the Palladium, an image of Athene which by its presence in Troy guaranteed the city from capture. Sinon's strange version of the story is untrue—Athene is not angry with the Greeks.

189 *Minerva*: Latin name of Athene.

197 *Larrissaean*: i.e. Thessalian.

246 *Cassandra*: a Trojan princess, gifted with prophetic power but fated never to be believed.

263 *Neoptolemus*: (also called Pyrrhus) the son of Achilles and grandson of Peleus.

270 *Hector*: the great champion of Troy, slain by Achilles (*Iliad*, Book XXII) and dragged behind his chariot.

275 *arrayed in the armour of Achilles*: Hector killed Achilles' friend Patroclus who was dressed in Achilles' armour, stripped him, and wore it (*Iliad*, Book XVII).

293 *Her holy things . . . keeping*: These gods, the Penates of Troy, are handed over to Aeneas by the priest Panthus, line 320.

296 *Vesta*: goddess of the hearth, and akin to the household Penates. An important state cult in Rome tended an undying fire of the goddess, in the care of the Vestal Virgins; that too, Virgil suggests, goes back to Troy.

310 *Deiophobus*: Trojan prince, husband of Helen after the death of Paris: cf. Book VI, 495 ff.

320 *his conquered divinities*: cf. line 293. Rome claimed to have inherited the Penates of Troy; this guaranteed the unbroken survival of Troy in Rome.

325 *Ilium*: another name for Troy. This Teucer (not the one named at Book I, 619) is a Trojan king of an earlier generation: cf. Book III, 108.

392 *all our warriors*: Observe that Aeneas himself is not said to have

resorted to this trick—not a very heroic one, and ultimately disastrous.

456 *Andromache*: the wife of Hector. Cf. *Iliad*, VI, 390 ff., the scene where Hector meets his wife on the wall, with the baby Astyanax.

469 *Pyrrhus*: cf. note on Book II, 263.

500 *The brothers Atrides*: Agamemnon and Menelaus.

501 *Hecuba with her hundred princesses*: Priam traditionally had fifty sons; Virgil adds fifty daughters to his fifty daughters-in-law.

526 *Polites*: this son of Priam is mentioned by Homer as a fast runner, *Iliad*, II, 791.

543 *gave up the bloodless remains*: refers to *Iliad*, XXIV.

557 *A great trunk . . . body without a name*: it was not usually said that Priam's body was beheaded, or that it lay 'on the shore'. Virgil seems to be glancing at the fate of Pompey; having been the conqueror of the East and the greatest man in Rome, he fled from Caesar to Egypt and was beheaded on the sea-shore (48 BC). His fate horrified Romans, and this covert glance at it added, for a Roman, to the pathos of Priam's death.

562 *Creusa*: Aeneas' wife.

567–87 *Yes, I was now . . . appeasing my people's ashes*: this passage is not present in the best manuscripts of Virgil, and its authenticity is hotly disputed. Some scholars regard it as unfinished, others as a post-Virgilian insertion. The case against it is certainly not proven.

602 ff. *The gods, the gods, I tell you*: this scene reinforces the vital point that Aeneas did not abandon Troy when heroic fighting could have saved it. The gods had finally doomed Troy, and here we see them actually demolishing the city.

624 *and Neptune's Troy quite overthrown*: the normal story was that the Greeks took Troy and then burned it at their leisure, before their departure. Virgil insists that it was destroyed at once, both for the sinister grandeur of the scene, and to show Aeneas not leaving the city while it still stood. 'Neptune's Troy', because Neptune and Apollo built its walls.

643 *Enough . . . survived her capture*: these lines allude to the earlier sack of Troy by Hercules, in the time of King Laomedon.

649 *Bid me farewell . . . levin-flash*: Anchises was a cripple. This was often the fate of men who slept with goddesses, something which Jupiter tended to resent. It explains why Aeneas had to carry him out of Troy; and it is emphasized here, whereas often it is lost sight of, to underline his querulous helplessness at this crucial moment.

664 *Was it for this . . . another's blood?*: Aeneas finds the divine promises hard to rely on, as often in the first half of the *Aeneid*.

680 *a wonderful miracle*: this is a manifestation of the divine will: in terms of Roman religion, an 'offered augury' (as opposed to one which has been asked for). The flame links Ascanius with Aeneas (X. 261), Romulus (VI. 779), and Augustus (VIII. 680).

691 *grant your aid*: Anchises asks for a second sign, of the other category recognized in Roman religion.

693 *from our left hand . . . a shooting star*: the left side is the favourable one in Roman augury. The star hints at the comet which appeared at the funeral of Julius Caesar and was held to show that his soul had ascended to heaven; cf. note on Book V, 522.

703 *This sign is yours . . . keeping*: Troy has fallen, but its continuity is unbroken and assured.

711 *Creusa . . . a distance*: Virgil needs to disembarrass Aeneas of his wife, who obviously cannot come to Carthage.

772 *The very ghost of Creusa . . . life*: the disappearance of Creusa, a Virgilian invention, remains mysterious. As with other events in the poem—the death of Dido (Book IV), the killing of Lausus (Book X)—it is not exactly Aeneas' fault, and yet he feels a certain guilt. Creusa is larger than life because of her association with the goddess, a kind of partial apotheosis. Gods are bigger than men.

781 *Lydian*: the Etruscans, who now live by the Tiber, came originally from Lydia (in Asia Minor). Creusa predicts the goal of the Trojan wanderings clearly: in Book III it is unknown. Virgil has altered his conception and not lived to remove the traces. The royal bride is Lavinia, daughter of King Latinus.

788 *Mother of the gods*: Cybele, who was worshipped on Mount Ida near Troy.

797 *I was astonished to find*: Virgil solves the problem of giving Aeneas enough men for his venture, without raising the possibility of his leading them in the defence of Troy.

BOOK III

7 *Not knowing where*: the Trojans do not know where they are to go: cf. note on Book II, 781.

9 *Father Anchises*: it is stressed in Book III that Anchises was in command. This is part of the *pietas* of Aeneas: submission to his father.

18 *Aenea*: connection with Aeneas explains the origin of the place name. There was a town called Aenus in Thrace, and one called Aeneia in Chalcidice. Virgil avoids settling for one rather than the other.

35 *Gradivus*: a title of Mars.

45 *Polydorus*: the story of his sending out of Troy and of his murder comes from the *Hecuba* of Euripides; the bleeding myrtle shoots seem to be Virgil's own addition.

67 *we lay the ghost*: the hope is that the dead man will now find rest.

76 *A floating island*: Delos, the sacred island of Apollo, which used to be a floating wanderer, according to the myth. It is loved by the sea-gods for its beauty. Myconos and Gyarus are two (very small) neighbouring islands.

90 *a sudden tremor*: these signs mark the presence of the oracular god.

94 *the land which first produced*: Apollo means Italy, the original home of Dardanus; Anchises thinks the god means Crete.

105 *a Mount Ida*: there is a Mount Ida in Crete, as well as the one near Troy: that suggested a connection. The cymbals and the lions which drew her chariot were characteristic of Cybele.

122 *Idomeneus*: commander of a Cretan contingent at Troy. He shares in the general disaster of Troy's conquerors. Cf. Book III, 401.

133 *Pergamea*: another place name explained, this time from the Trojan citadel of Pergamum.

163 *Hesperia*: Italy is reintroduced (cf. Book II, 781) as if for the first time.

167 *Dardanus*: on the Italian origin of Dardanus, cf. note on Book I, 380.

170 *Corythus*: a city south of Rome, traditionally identified as Cortona.

202 *Palinurus*: his story is told in Book V, 827 ff., and Book VI, 337 ff.

209 *Strophades*: small islands to the west of the Peloponnese.

213 *Phineus*: punished by the gods with incursions of the Harpies, who stole and befouled his food. Eventually the two sons of the North Wind, coming to his country among the Argonauts, drove them away. The Harpies, originally spirits of the storm-wind, are represented as women-faced birds.

239 *Misenus*: his death is recounted in Book VI, 162 f.

248 *Laomedon*: as king of Troy he broke his promise to pay Apollo and Neptune for building the walls of the city. Calling the Trojans by this name often has overtones of guilt; cf. Book IV, 542; Book V, 811.

256 *chew your tables*: the prediction is fulfilled in Book VII, 109 ff. —where by an uncorrected change of plan it is attributed not to the curse of the Harpy but to a prophecy by Anchises. Cf. Book III, 394.

270 *Zacynthus*: the Trojans sail up the west of Greece, past Ithaca.

280 *Actium*: Virgil emphasizes the visit to Actium, site of Octavian's defeat of Antony in 31 BC: a connection with the Games established there by Augustus is deliberate.

288 *DANAI*: a title of the Greeks who fought at Troy.

291 *Corcyra*: the modern Corfu. Buthrotum is in Epirus.

297 *Andromache*: Hector's widow, taken by Achilles' son Pyrrhus at the fall of Troy. After his death she married another Trojan survivor and set up a little Troy (349 ff.): there they live in endless nostalgia. This road Aeneas must avoid: cf. Book V, 632 ff.

302 *Simois*: a local stream has been named after the Trojan river Simois.

322 *that maiden daughter of Priam*: Polyxena, sacrificed on the grave of Achilles.

328 *Hermione*: daughter of Menelaus, king of Sparta, by Helen, daughter of Leda. Orestes, son of Agamemnon, slew Pyrrhus for Hermione.

332 *at his father's altar*: this recalls (and avenges) Pyrrhus' killing of Priam at the altar: Book II, 550.

335 *Chaon*: unknown and perhaps invented.

343 *his uncle, Hector*: Creusa, Aeneas' wife, was Hector's sister.

381 *First, then, the Italy*: they must go right round the south of Italy.

386 *the infernal lakes*: the Lucrine and Avernian lakes, which Aeneas must pass at the beginning of Book VI; the Avernian has an entrance to the Underworld, where he must go.

Circe: she is passed in Book VII, 10 ff.

390 *a sow*: this portent appears in the story at an early date. It is predicted again at Book VIII, 42, and it occurs in Book VIII, 81 ff.

399 *the Locri*: the leaderless followers of the lesser Ajax (cf. note on Book I, 41); Idomeneus the Cretan (cf. note on Book III, 122) and Philoctetes the Thessalian were Greek leaders at Troy. For them, at least as much as for the Trojans, the Trojan War has meant suffering and loss of home.

405 *Remember to veil your head*: this explains the Roman custom of covering the head while offering sacrifice: Greeks, by contrast, did it with heads bare.

411 *Pelorus*: the north-east tip of Sicily.

420 *Scylla . . . Charybdis*: monsters from the *Odyssey* (Book XII). Cf. Book III, 555 ff.

429 *Pachynum*: the south-east tip of Sicily. Helenus is advising Aeneas to sail right round the island, avoiding the Straits of Messina.

437 *It's paramount . . . homage*: Jupiter repeats that the Romans will outdo all peoples in devotion to Juno (Book XII, 840). They do not, in the poem, succeed in mollifying her.

441 *Cumae*: near Naples; the oldest Greek colony in Italy, home of the Sibyl. Aeneas comes to her in Book VI.

466 *Dodona*: sacred place of Zeus/Jupiter in Northern Greece. The booming of brazen cauldrons played a part in divination there.

476 *twice saved*: i.e. from the sack of Troy by Hercules (II. 643) as well as that by Agamemnon.

492 *Long may you live and lucky*: Aeneas shows some natural envy of those who, unlike him, have at least achieved peace.

505 *Let that be a charge*: this difficult passage seems to allude to the fact that Augustus, when he founded Nicopolis ('City of Victory') nearby, close to the site of Actium, said that its people were to be treated as akin to the Romans.

506 *Forth we went*: they sail north to the point where the crossing to the heel of Italy is the shortest.

531 *Minerva's Height*: Castrum Minervae in Calabria.

537 *Here, an initial omen*: the Trojans will find both war and peace in Italy.

547 *Argive Juno*: Juno (or, in Greek, Hera) was the chief goddess of Argos, as Athene was of Athens.

551 *Next we raised*: they cross the Gulf of Taranto, from the heel of Italy to the toe, and come in sight of Sicily (Mount Etna).

564 *We were tossed up high*: Odysseus, in the *Odyssey*, avoided Charybdis and was plagued by Scylla; Aeneas, as a literary variation on Virgil's part, experiences Charybdis but not Scylla.

578 *Enceladus*: the giant Enceladus, or the monster Typhoeus, was buried under Etna: his writhings producing the local earthquakes and volcanic eruptions.

590 *When suddenly there stepped ... individual*: again, a variant on Homer's Cyclops episode in *Odyssey* Book IX. Achaemenides is an invention, it seems, of Virgil. The heartless Greek Ulysses abandoned his own man; the Trojans, still nobly trustful even after their deception by Sinon in Book II, take him to their hearts. The Cyclops is a one-eyed, man-eating giant. Aeneas can hardly be imagined in the grip of such a monster; as with Circe (Book VII, 10 ff.) he is kept in the distance.

682 *Our panic prompted us ... run for it*: i.e. (apparently) the Trojans in panic made off to the north, then remembered Helenus' advice

and turned south into the wind—which changed in their favour. They now sail south down the eastern side of Sicily.

696 *Arethusa's fount*: at Syracuse, the spring Arethusa was said to be the re-emergence of a spring which flowed under the sea from the Peloponnese; myth said that the nymph of the spring was in flight from the amorous River Alpheus, who pursued her and was united with her beyond the sea, in Sicily.

701 *Camarina*: 'Do not move Camarina' was a Greek proverb. The people of Camarina drained a marsh and were conquered by an army which came by the way the marsh had been.

703 *Acragas*: Agrigento. They are now sailing along the southern shore of Sicily.

706 *Lilybaeum*: the western promontory of Sicily. It was as they turned this corner that Anchises died—leaving Aeneas bereaved and vulnerable—and the storm blew them back to Africa.

BOOK IV

11 *how powerful in chest and shoulders!*: *armis* here is more likely to mean 'weapons' than 'shoulders'. Probably Dido's utterance should be translated 'how powerful in chest, how formidable in armour!'

20 *poor Sychaeus*: the story of Sychaeus' murder is told in Book I, 340 ff.; Dido's brother is still a threat, cf. below, lines 43 f., 325.

27 *pure widowhood's claim*: in Rome, as in early Christianity, special esteem was given to widows who did not remarry.

36 *Iarbas*: cf. below, lines 196 ff., 326.

40 *Gaetuli, Numidians*, and *Barcaei*: African tribes; the *Syrtes* are the great sandbanks north of Cyrenaica.

64 *poring over the victims' Opened bodies*: the only mention in the *Aeneid* of the practice, borrowed by Rome from the Etruscans, of enquiring the will of the gods by examining the entrails of sacrificed animals ('extispicy'). Dido in her frantic eagerness pores over the entrails herself.

73 *Dictaean*: Cretan. Cretans were famous archers.

81 *lies down on her bed*: this refers not to a bed but to the couch on

which she had reclined at dinner. She returns to the scene of her enchantment.

113 *You are his wife*: heavy irony: Venus knows that Juno is perfectly aware of Jupiter's determination. There is a certain feminine malice in the exchanges between the two goddesses, and Juno in her reply reasserts her dignity.

127 *Hymen*: god of the marriage ceremony.

129 *Aurora*: goddess of dawn.

143 *Lycia*: in Asia Minor. Apollo is a god who travels, spending different seasons at different shrines. On his island of Delos he delights in the dances of his worshippers. The Agathyrsi are not even Greeks: they come from Thrace.

147 *Cynthian range*: Cynthus is the hill on Delos.

168 *wedding*: this episode, a skilful invention, both is and is not a real wedding. Juno (see line 59) is the goddess of marriage.

179 *Enceladus*: a giant.
Coeus: a Titan. Rumour is personified as a tremendous monster.

199 *Ammon*: an African god, identified with Jupiter; whose son Iarbas thus is.

215 *that philanderer*: Aeneas is seen by his enemies as another Paris (cf. Book VII, 321 and 363)—a glamorous Trojan seducer. Dido is bewitched like Helen. This hostile view of Trojans, usually called 'Phrygians' in this context, recurs at Book IX, 598 ff., and Book XII, 99.

222 *Mercury*: the winged messenger of the gods.

228 *twice*: once in the *Iliad*, Book V, 311 ff.; again at the fall of Troy.

242 *Orcus*: the Underworld.
Tartarus: the place of punishment within it.

247 *Atlas*: the mountain, turned to stone by the head of Medusa, had been a giant, father of Cyllene, Mercury's mother (below, line 258).

260 *superintending the work*: Aeneas is actually helping to found Rome's enemy, Carthage.

301 *Bacchante*: possessed worshipper of Bacchus. Cithaeron is the

Boeotian mountain where the Bacchantes kill Pentheus in Euripides' *Bacchae*.

335 *Elissa*: Dido's other name, like Iulus/Ascanius.

346 *Lycia*: in Asia Minor, a place which belongs to Apollo. This oracle is not narrated in the poem.

365 *Dardanus*: Trojan king of an earlier generation.

366 *Hyrcania*: near the Caspian Sea: therefore utterly remote and barbarous.

379 *the calm of The gods*: Dido glances (anachronistically) at the doctrine of Epicurus: the gods live in undisturbed serenity.

382 *just spirits*: the word she uses is *pius*—Aeneas' own epithet and quality. He has got into a position where, with a certain amount of justice, she can turn it against him.

393 *god-fearing*: again, *pius* is the word. Aeneas regains his title, but in painful circumstances.

421 *You were the only confidante*: a version of the myth, not followed by Virgil, said it was Anna whom Aeneas loved. Virgil takes a hint from that for a good piece of psychology.

426 *Aulis*: where the Greek fleet assembled to sail against Troy.

449 *her tears*: the Latin more naturally means 'his tears': a point not without importance.

469 *Just so does the raving Pentheus*: the comparison of Dido to figures in tragic drama—Pentheus in Euripides' *Bacchae*, 918 ff., Orestes in the *Oresteia* of Aeschylus—is a bold and surprising one. Such a 'literary' comparison is without parallel in Homer or elsewhere in the *Aeneid*.

483 *Massylian*: i.e. Numidian. The Garden of the Hesperides ('Daughters of Evening') was imagined by Greeks in the far West, somewhere in North Africa. The nymphs looked after a tree, on which grew golden apples, guarded by a serpent: a symbol, originally, of immortality.

510 *Erebus, Chaos, Hacate*: powers of the Underworld. Hecate, sometimes identified with Diana, was an alarming goddess, worshipped at cross-roads and represented as a triple figure facing in three directions. Cf. below, line 609.

512 *Avernus*: in South Italy: an entrance to the Underworld. Cf. Book VI, 201 ff.

515 *a gland*: a growth believed to occur on the forehead of newborn foals. The mother tried to eat it; if secured, it had magic powers.

542 *Laomedon*: cf. note on Book III, 248.

585 *Tithonus*: mortal paramour of Aurora, the goddess of the dawn; carried off by her for his beauty.

602 *served him up for his father*: Dido thinks of some horrific revenges in mythology, as when Procne killed and served up her son to his father Tereus, who had raped her sister Philomela.

614 *May he be harried*: this curse is fulfilled in the second half of the poem.

619 *But fall before his time*: Aeneas reigned for only three years in Lavinium (Book I, 265). There was a tradition, here glanced at, that his body was never found.

625 *Rise up from my dead bones*: Roman readers would think of Hannibal, the Carthaginian general who ravaged Italy and won great victories over Rome from 218 to 204 BC.

653 *I have lived*: Dido speaks her own epitaph, in the high Roman manner.

681 *I, the cause of your troubles*: probably Anna means to reproach Dido rather than herself: 'So that you might lie on it, and I, through your cruelty, should not be there'.

684 *if any last breath is fluttering*: a last gesture towards the dying in Roman practice, to prevent the passing spirit from being lost.

694 *Iris*: goddess of the rainbow, often an emissary of Juno.

698 *Proserpine*: the first gesture at an animal sacrifice was the cutting off of a lock of its hair: this marked the victim for death. Virgil here imagines Proserpine (another name of Persephone) doing the same for dying men and women. Until it is done, Dido cannot die. This is a poetic invention, not a real belief.

BOOK V

2 *North wind*: Aeneas heads north, for Italy; he is forced to make for Sicily again.

24 *Eryx*: the town and mountain of Eryx in Sicily are named after Eryx, son of Venus by Butes and so half-brother to Aeneas.

30 *Acestes*: we hear about Acestes, a Trojan chief already in Italy, a good deal in Book V: cf. the portent given him at lines 519 ff., and his foundation of Acesta, 718 ff.

31 *Anchises*: he died when the Trojans were in Italy before, cf. Book III, 709.

45 *Dardans*: Trojans, from Dardanus.

51 *Syrtes*: The African sandbanks, cf. note on Book IV, 40.

66 *Trojan Games*: the episode recalls the funeral games of Patroclus in *Iliad*, 23, combined with the Troy Game patronized in Rome by Augustus. Cf. below, note on line 556.

78 *he poured on the earth*: drink-offerings to the dead.

84 *a giant snake*: snakes, mysterious creatures which emerge from the earth, were often identified or connected with the souls of the dead.

117 *the Memmian clan*: a number of aristocratic Roman families claimed to descend from Trojan ancestors. The best known of the Memmii was C. Memmius, patron of the poet Lucretius who dedicated his great poem to him; hated and attacked by Catullus.

121 *the Sergian family*: the only prominent Sergius in recent history was Catiline, the revolutionary enemy of Cicero. Sergestus runs his ship aground: that foreshadows the recklessness of his violent descendant.

123 *Cluentius*: the Cluentii were not a very prominent family.

192 *Gaetulian*: i.e. off the coast of Africa.

193 *Malea*: the southern tip of the Peloponnese.

203 *too narrow*: cf. note on line 121 above.

233 *Cloanthus*: Virgil intends the moral to be felt: recklessness and folly lead to disaster, human effort alone wins second place, but victory needs (as with Aeneas in the story as a whole) both human effort and also piety.

241 *Portunus*: an old Italian god of ports. The other sea-deities named are Greek.

251 *Meliboean*: i.e. Thessalian, from the source of the purple dye.

252 *Ganymede*: beautiful Trojan boy, abducted by Jupiter, who sent his eagle to carry him off.

284 *Minerva's tasks*: that is, skilled at weaving.

294 *Nisus and Euryalus*: these two are introduced afresh at the beginning of their night-expedition in Book IX, 176 ff. Homosexual love, even of this high-minded sort, is altogether absent from Homer. Cf. note on Book X. 325.

298 *Salius and Patron*: both, surprisingly, Greeks. We are free to suppose that they joined Aeneas when he was staying with Helenus at Buthrotum: Book III, 292 ff.

306 *Gnossian*: i.e. Cretan. Crete was famous for archers.

343 *Euryalus*: he is to be imagined as about fourteen. There can of course be no doubt that what Nisus did was, by ancient as well as by modern standards, cheating.

360 *Neptune's temple*: at least it is clear that this very special shield was taken from the temple by Greeks, not by pious Trojans, but the story is hard to reconstruct.

373 *Butes*: Amycus, king of the Bebrycians, forced all comers to box with him for their lives. In the end Pollux, coming with the Argonauts, beat him. So Butes came from a race of pugilistic monsters. He is not the same man as the one mentioned in the note on line 24 above.

387 *Entellus*: a name connected with the Sicilian town Entella.

392 *Eryx*: see note on Book V, 24.

401 *Boxing gloves*: among the Greeks, boxing had been a sport for gentlemen; at Rome it was a brutal business, the *caestus* (we are not to think of modern, padded boxing gloves) being savagely hard and heavy. Virgil prefers not to let any ancestor of a Roman family indulge in it—neither Dares nor Entellus appears again in the *Aeneid*.

411 *Eryx . . . great Hercules*: Eryx was killed by Hercules, having challenged him to fight.

448 *Ida or Erymanthus*: Mount Ida is in the Troad, Mount Erymanthus in Arcadia.

495 *Pandarus*: induced by Athene to break this truce, *Iliad* IV. 72 ff.

He was killed by Diomede (*Iliad* V. 290 ff.); as a dead archer he is imagined as able to assist (see line 514 below).

522 *A startling phenomenon*: the archery is modelled on the contest in *Iliad* XXIII. 850 ff., which ends with the shooting of the dove. The episode of Acestes' flaming arrow foretells the success of Acestes in founding Acesta (cf. note below on line 718), but also doubtless reminds the Roman reader of the 'Julian star' (cf. note on Book I, 693) which marked the deification of Julius Caesar. That, too, is foreshadowed in the *Aeneid*.

537 *Cisseus*: father of Hecuba, cf. Book VII, 320.

553 *fathers*: the games are an all-male affair. We shall soon see what the women get up to, left to themselves (lines 613 ff.).

556 *They wear on their hair*: this equestrian display by the boys is made the heroic model of the Troy Game, an event for well-born boys greatly favoured by Augustus. That links past and present, and Augustus with Aeneas; cf. below, lines 596 ff.

568 *The Latin Atii*: not an eminent family, but Augustus' mother was an Atia, his grandparents being an Atius and a Julia: hence the insistence here that the ancestors of the two families (Ascanius being the other name of Iulus) were already devoted friends.

588 *The fabled Labyrinth*: the deadly maze in which King Minos kept the Minotaur.

595 *Carpathian*: the island of Carpathus lies between Crete and Rhodes.

596 *This kind of cavalry tournament*: cf. above, note on line 556.

606 *Iris*: cf. note on Book IV, 694.

620 *Tmarian*: an unexpected epithet for a Trojan; Mount Tmaros is in Epirus. Cf. note above, on line 298: a similar background can be constructed for this matron, if one chooses: married to an Epirote, she joined Aeneas at Buthrotum. Beroe is away ill: line 650.

626 *the seventh summer*: it is a chronological difficulty that this identical line is used in Book I, 755—a year earlier. Probably an unfinished change of plan by Virgil is at the root of this problem.

633 *If Troy-town's walls*: she demands not Rome but a second Troy, like that founded by Helenus and Andromache, cf. note on Book

III, 297: again the temptation of nostalgia. Cf. the names 'Ilium' and 'Troy', line 756.

637 *Cassandra*: cf. note on Book II, 246. The story here of course is a lie.

661 *Some strip the altars*: wild behaviour is characteristic of Virgil's women. To take fire from the altars added sacrilege to sabotage and treason.

704 *Nautes*: the name means, in Greek, 'sailor', This man is the ancestor of the family of the Nautii at Rome.

710 *Whatever may happen*: this is a sentiment of Stoic philosophy rather than archaic heroism—a deliberately anachronistic touch. Aeneas is not simply an archaic hero.

718 *Acesta*: the town was called Egesta by Greeks, Segesta by Romans. It was to be conspicuously loyal to Rome in the wars with Carthage, in the third century BC.

730 *tough and primitive are the people*: the Italians find the Trojans soft (cf. Book XI, 598 ff.); the civilization of Troy and the toughness of Italy must combine to produce Rome.

733 *Avernus*: cf. note on Book IV, 512.

735 *Here, when you've sacrificed*: the events of Book VI are predicted.

756 *named one quarter of the town 'Ilium'*: cf. note above on line 633.

759 *Eryx*: the cult of Venus on Mount Eryx was one of great celebrity.

760 *Idalian*: cf. note on Book I, 681.

789 *Libyan sea*: cf. Book I, 84 ff.

799 *Saturn's son*: Neptune, like Jupiter, is a son of Saturn.

801 *Where you were born*: Venus arose from the sea.

803 *Xanthus and Simois*: rivers of Troy. The rescue of Aeneas took place in the *Iliad*, Book XX, 318 ff.

811 *perjured Troy*: cf. note on Book III, 248.

817 *Her father put the gold yoke*: Venus is the daughter of Jupiter (*Aeneid*, I. 254), not of Neptune, who here receives the title of 'father' as a general term of honour.

822 *retainers, diverse in appearance*: a verbal representation of the cortège of sea-deities so popular in art.

838 *Sleep*: the personifying god of Sleep.

854 *Lethe*: the Underworld ('Stygian') river of Oblivion.

864 *the Sirens*: they vainly tried to lure Ulysses (*Odyssey* XII. 105 ff.) and killed themselves in despair at their failure.

870 *O Palinurus*: Palinurus' ghost encounters Aeneas: Book VI, 337 ff.

BOOK VI

2 *Euboean Cumae*: Cumae was originally founded *c.*750 BC by Greek colonists from Chalcis in Euboea.

9 *Apollo*: the temple of Apollo and the cave of his inspired prophetess, the Sibyl.

14 *Daedalus*: the great craftsman who built the Cretan labyrinth. He escaped from the island by making wings for himself and his son Icarus (line 31), but Icarus flew too near the sun, the wax of his wings melted, and he fell into the sea. Daedalus reached Italy and built a temple to Apollo, on the doors of which he depicted these stories.

20 *Androgeos*: son of Minos, murdered at Athens. Minos forced the Athenians to send an annual tribute of seven young men, who were killed in the labyrinth by the Minotaur, offspring of Minos' queen Pasiphae by a bull.

28 *Ariadne*: Minos' daughter, who fell in love with Theseus, one of the Athenian victims. Daedalus showed her how to guide Theseus through the labyrinth and kill the Minotaur. Consequently Daedalus had to flee.

35 *Trivia*: Diana, Apollo's sister.

42 *There's a huge cave*: excavation reveals a great subterranean complex, based on natural caves, used for religious purposes, from about 500 BC.

57 *Paris against Achilles*: the killing of Achilles 'by Paris and Apollo' is predicted in the *Iliad*, XXII. 359 f., and was narrated in later poetry.

60 *Massylian*: in North Africa.

69 *Then will I found a temple*: this glances at the temple of Apollo

which Augustus built on the Palatine: Augustus and Aeneas are again connected.

71 *You too shall have your holy place*: an official collector of Sibylline oracles was housed under the Palatine temple and consulted in times of crisis.

73 *priesthood*: the Board of Fifteen in charge of the Sibylline Books.

88 *a Simois, a Xanthus*: the rivers of Troy.

89 *a new Achilles*: Turnus, son of the nymph Venilia, as Achilles was son of the goddess Thetis.

93 *Once more it's an alien bride*: first it was the wedding of Helen, now that of Lavinia: two foreign princesses.

97 *a Greek city*: Pallanteum, the city of Evander (Book VIII).

107 *Acheron*: a river of the Underworld.

118 *Hecate*: cf. note on Book IV, 510.

119 *Orpheus, Pollux, Theseus, Hercules*: heroes who have succeeded in going down to the Underworld: Orpheus, to fetch his wife Eurydice; Pollux, who is alive and dead on alternate days with his brother Castor; Theseus, who helped his friend Pirithous in his doomed attempt to carry off Persephone (cf. line 397); Hercules, who brought back the hell-hound Cerberus (cf. line 395 f.).

132 *Cocytus*: 'Lamentation', another Underworld river.

137 *a golden bough*: this is a Virgilian invention.

149 *a friend*: Misenus: below, 162 ff. A headland is named after him, below, 234 f.

173 *Triton*: a sea-god, often represented blowing a conch shell.

193 *His mother's birds*: doves are often associated with Venus.

201 *Avernus*: a lake, in an area marked by earthquakes and volcanoes: traditionally an entrance to the Underworld.

237 *a deep, deep cave*: this cave, archaeologists report, is a fiction.

240 *miasma*: these mephitic exhalations also are a fantasy, aided by the fanciful derivation of 'Avernus' from the Greek for 'birdless', *aornos*.

250 *Furies*: (cf. 555) Tisiphone, the eldest of the three.

257 *Hecate*: see note on Book IV, 510. She often hunts by night with

hounds. Only those who have been initiated into her secret cult are allowed to see what happens next.

265 *Phlegethon*: fiery river of the Underworld.

269 *Dis*: a name of Hades.

273 *Orcus*: the Underworld.

283 *Dreams*: this is Virgil's own idea, as far as is known.

284 *many varieties of monsters*: the complex monsters—man–horse Centaurs and the rest—are put with the Dreams; perhaps with a hint of their impossibility.

299 *Charon*: Like the monsters, he is not in the Underworld of *Odyssey*, Book XI. He was a favourite demon with the Etruscans.

323 *the Stygian marsh*: gods took their most solemn oaths by the infernal River Styx.

333 *Leucaspis and Orontes*: men lost on the ship of Orontes, sunk in the storm: cf. Book I, 113 ff.

337 *Palinurus*: for his loss, cf. Book V, 838 ff.

343 *this one answer*: this oracle is not narrated in the poem.

348 *nor was I drowned by a god*: naturally Palinurus does not know of the action of the god of Sleep.

366 *Velia*: near Cape Palinurus. Aeneas would have to sail back quite a long way to do this.

381 *Palinurus*: like Misenus, Palinurus explains the name of a place in Italy; cf. also Caieta, Book VII, 1–4.

392 *Hercules*: for these stories see note on line 119 above.

400 *the huge watch-dog*: Cerberus; cf. below, 417 ff.

413 *The ramshackle craft creaked under his weight*: Aeneas, not being a shade, is much heavier than Charon's other passengers.

417 *Cerberus*: three-headed hound who guards the entrance to Hell.

426 *Ghosts of infants*: various categories of the dead who are neither punished in Tartarus nor blessed in Elysium: infants, those unjustly condemned, suicides, those who died for love, warriors. They all died an untimely death.

432 *Minos*: a just king in life, now a judge of the dead.

445 *Here Aeneas descried Phaedra and Procris*: those who died for love

seem to be all women. Phaedra killed herself after failing to seduce her stepson Hippolytus; Procris was killed accidentally by her husband, as she jealously spied on him while he was hunting; Eriphyle caused the death of her husband and was killed by her son; Evadne threw herself on to her husband's funeral pyre; Pasiphae loved a bull and gave birth to the Minotaur; Laodamia's young husband was killed at Troy, and she mourned for him so inconsolably that he was allowed to come back to her for one night, in which she died in his arms; Caeneus was originally a girl named Caenis: Neptune ravished her and then granted her wish —to become a man, and to be invulnerable. The absence of moral criterion in the selection of these women is remarkable.

474 *Sychaeus*: cf. Book I, 343 ff.

479 *Tydeus*: the father of Diomede, one of the Seven against Thebes, as were Parthenopaeus and Adrastus. Their expedition was a disaster.

485 *Idaeus*: the charioteer and armour-bearer of Priam, King of Troy.

492 *In the old days*: refers to the time when Hector beat them back to their ships, in *Iliad* XV and XVI.

495 *Deiphobus*: cf. note on Book II, 310. That the wounded are still mangled in the Underworld is a grisly conception, alien to Homer.

505 *Rhoetean*: the shore north of Troy.

511 *Lacaenian*: i.e. Spartan: Helen. She betrays her new husband to the old.

542 *Elysium*: the place of the blessed.

555 *Tisiphone*: chief of the Furies.

566 *Rhadamanthus*: brother of Minos; another judge of the dead.

576 *Hydra*: a monster with many snaky heads which infested Lerna, in Arcadia.

580 *Titans*: the older generation of gods, defeated and cast down by Jupiter.

582 *the twin sons of Aloeus*: giants, blitzed by Jupiter before they attained their full stature.

586 *Salmoneus*: king of Elis in the Peloponnese (and so of Olympia): tried to rival Jupiter.

595 *Tityos*: a giant: tried to ravish Leto, the mother of Apollo.

601 *Ixion*: tried to ravish Hera and was bound on a whirling wheel (616);
Pirithous tried to carry off Persephone.

603 *a black crag hangs*: confusingly, the traditional punishment of Tantalus is put here.

616 *Some have to roll huge rocks*: the stone is the traditional punishment of Sisyphus (not named here), the wheel of Ixion (601).

617 *Theseus*: he assisted the reckless attempt of Pirithous and was condemned to sit on a rock in Hell for ever. Other versions of the myth said that Hercules brought him up.

618 *Phlegyas*: set fire to a temple of Apollo.

630 *The Cyclops' furnaces*: they sometimes appear as supernatural smiths. Cf. Book VIII, 424 ff.

645 *Orpheus*: the greatest musician of mythology, famous also as a religious teacher.

650 *Ilus, Assaracus, and Dardanus*: Trojan kings of earlier generations.

659 *Eridanus*: semi-mythical river of the north-west: by Virgil identified with the River Po.

667 *Musaeus*: another mythical musician and teacher, often associated with Orpheus.

694 *How I dreaded . . . Carthage!*: a delicate reproach to Aeneas.

705 *Lethe*: river of Oblivion. Souls which are to be reincarnated must forget their former lives.

726 *immanent Mind*: a sort of pantheism is preached here. It is not easy to reconcile it with the supreme importance of nationalism elsewhere in the *Aeneid*. Virgil draws on several strands of Greek philosophical speculation.

762 *Silvius*: usually the emphasis in the *Aeneid* is not on Aeneas' late-born son by Lavinia but on Ascanius/Iulus, his son by his first wife, who is the founder of Alba Longa (Book I, 267 ff.). What is said here is not irreconcilable with that.

767 *Procas, Capys, Numitor, Silvius Aeneas*: these are mythical kings of Alba Longa—a shadowy collection.

773 *Nomentum, Gabii and Fidenae*: historic places in Latium. Virgil values these touches of specifically Italian tradition.

778 *Romulus*: he is of Trojan descent (Assaracus), and son of the god Mars. Cf. Book I, 277.

786 *Cybele*: cf. note on Book II, 788. Cybele's chariot was traditionally drawn by lions.

793 *Saturn*: cf. note on Book I, 569. The new Golden Age, like the first, shall have overtones of Italian moral simplicity.

795 *Garamants*: Africans.

801 *Hercules*: in the course of his Twelve Labours, three of which are mentioned here, Hercules had to traverse the world. On Mount Erymanthus he captured a boar, at Lerna he disposed of the hydra (cf. note above on line 576).

805 *Bacchus*: he conquered India, converting the Indians to drinking wine. Mount Nysa is the legendary mountain where the god (Dionysus in Greek) was brought up.

807 *Ausonia*: Italy.

809 *That Roman king*: kings of Rome in succession to Romulus. Numa was a priestly and pacific character, Tullus Hostilius a conqueror, Ancus Marcius a demagogue; of the two Tarquins the second, Tarquinius the Proud (Superbus) was ejected.

818 *Brutus*: Lucius Iunius Brutus, who expelled the king and established the Republic. His sons conspired with the Tarquin, and as consul he condemned them to death.

824 *the Decii, the Drusi, Torquatus . . . Camillus*: these are all great figures and generals from early Republican history.

826 *those twin souls*: Caesar and Pompey. Pompey married Caesar's daughter Julia: that made their civil war all the more shocking.

834 *my son of heavenly lineage*: Caesar.

836 *That one shall ride*: Lucius Mummius, who in 146 BC destroyed Corinth. His conquest of Greece avenges the Greek conquest of Troy.

839 *Aeacus*: an ancestor of Achilles.

840 *sacrilege*: cf. note on Book I, 41.

841 *Cato . . . Serranus*: more Republican conquerors.

845 *Fabius*: Quintus Fabius Maximus ('Greatest') succeeded in wearing down Hannibal by avoiding pitched battles. The next line quotes a celebrated verse in his praise by Ennius, 150 years before Virgil.

847 *others*: these 'others' must be the Greeks: they have the arts and the sciences.

853 *To practise men in the habit of peace*: should be translated 'impose peace and then civilization'.

855 *Marcellus*: Marcus Claudius Marcellus, consul in 222 BC, was a great general: he was one of only three Roman commanders (one of the others being Romulus) to win the *spolia opima*, the reward of killing an opposing commander in battle with his own hand. The captured armour was dedicated to Quirinus (859), another name for Romulus.

861 *A youth of fine appearance*: the reason for the special emphasis on the elder Marcellus is Virgil's interest in the younger Marcellus, nephew and son-in-law of Augustus and intended to be his successor, who died in 23 BC at the age of 19. The lament for him must have pleased Augustus, as well as ending the parade of heroes on a note of pathos.

873 *Campus Martius*: the site of Marcellus' funeral.

891 *Laurentines*: the people of King Latinus in Latium. 'Laurentines' is an archaic and mysterious name for them; cf. Book VII, 63.

893 *two gates of Sleep*: these gates derive from Homer, *Odyssey*, XIX. 562 ff. It is not clear what Virgil means by introducing them here: perhaps that Aeneas' descent to the Underworld was in a way analogous to a dream.

BOOK VII

1 *Caieta*: Cape Caieta is two-thirds of the way from Cumae to Circeii.

10 *Circe*: an important figure in the *Odyssey*, an enchantress, daughter of the Sun, who turns Ulysses' men into pigs. Like the

Cyclopes (cf. note on Book III, 590) she appears in the *Aeneid* only in the distance: almost explicitly a literary allusion.

30 *Tiber*: the River Tiber, in Virgil's day busy and prosaic, is imagined as it was in its innocence.

37 *Muse of Love*: Erato by name. Why this Muse? Presumably because of the love-story of Lavinia, Turnus, and Aeneas.

45 *Latinus*: some earlier versions of the myth made Latinus fight the Trojans and be killed by them. Virgil avoids this by making him old and no longer firmly in control of events: cf. below, line 599.

47 *Faunus*: a rustic god of Italy. On Saturn, cf. note on Book I, 569; on Picus see below, 189 ff.

56 *Turnus*: he is to be the great antagonist of Aeneas.

62 *Laurentes*: cf. note on Book VI, 891.

82 *Albunea*: a sulphurous lake, fountain, and forest.

84 *Oenotrians*: Italians: a poetry-name.

116 *We're eating our tables*: this fulfils the prophecy uttered, as a curse, by the Harpy, Book III, 256; see the note on that passage.

123 *My father Anchises*: cf. note on Book III, 256.

139 *Juppiter, patron of Ida*: that is, the gods of Troy.

150 *Numicius*: river near Lavinium.

154 *Garlanded all with olive branches*: in token of coming on an embassy.

178 *Italus*: the eponymous ancestor of the Italians, as Sabinus is of the Sabines, an important Italian people. The Sabines grew good wine. The ancestry here ascribed to Latinus looks different from that given at lines 47 ff. above: a mark of the poem's lack of final revision?

180 *Saturn*: cf. note on Book I, 569.
Janus: the god of doorways and of beginnings (so his month January begins the year), represented with two heads: one facing forwards, to the future; the other back, to the past.

187 *the augur's staff*: the special staff held by the augurs, priestly specialists in foretelling the future.

189 *Picus*: the name means 'woodpecker'; perhaps originally a

totem-figure. The story of Circe, rebuffed, turning him into that bird, is told in Ovid's *Metamorphoses*, Book XIV.

198 *Ausonian*: Italian.

206 *Auruncan*: a primeval Italian people. On the Italian origin of the Trojan Dardanus, cf. Book III, 167.

208 *Samothrace*: island in the north-east Aegean, near Troy.

209 *Truscan home of Corythus*: cf. note on Book III, 179. Tuscan: in, or near, Etruria.

222 *a storm, unleashed from cruel Mycenae*: the war unleashed on Troy by Agamemnon, king of Mycenae.

282 *Circe*: cf. note above, on line 10.

286 *Inachus*: mythical Argive king, father of Io. Juno was patroness of Argos.

289 *Pachynus*: the south-east tip of Sicily.

301 *Against the Trojans I spent . . . sea and sky*: this and the next line refer to the storm in Book I and the perils of Book III.

304 *Mars had the power . . . Calydon*: the city of Calydon earned the anger of Diana by omitting her from divine honours. The story of Mars and the Lapiths (mythical people who fought the centaurs) is unknown.

319 *Hecuba*: before giving birth to Paris, Hecuba dreamed that she gave birth to a firebrand: this predicted that he would be the ruin of his country. Aeneas compared to Paris: cf. note on Book IV, 215. Torches were a feature of ancient weddings.

323 *Allecto*: a Fury. Juno's speech and this scene are meant to recall her monologue and bribery of Aeolus in Book I.

342 *the Laurentine monarch*: Latinus. Amata is Latinus' wife.

363 *Paris*: cf. note on Book IV, 215. Helen was the daughter of Leda.

372 *Mycenaean*: this detail (see note below, on line 410) adds the opposition of Greek and Trojan to his rivalry with Aeneas; it goes with his connection with the Argive goddess Juno. Mycenae is near Argos; Acrisius and Inachus are ancient Argive kings.

392 *a mass hysteria*: Amata resembles Dido in her Bacchic wildness: Book IV, 68 ff. and 300 ff. The women of Latium are as prone to madness as the Trojan matrons: Book V, 659 ff.

410 *Danae*: an Argive princess, daughter of Acrisius; so her foundation of the city of Ardea would explain Turnus' Argive connection. Ardea is near the coast, five miles from Lavinium.

426 *Tuscans*: Etruscans.

472 *The Rutuli*: Turnus' people. Ardea is their capital.

500 *Wounded, the animal ran*: compare the simile of Dido, Book IV, 68 ff.

516 *The lake of Diana*: The lake of Aricia, not far from Ardea; but also the Veline lake and the River Nar, which are in the Sabine country, at least fifty miles away. 'Nar' is said to be the Sabine word for sulphur.

557 *The Father, supreme lord of Olympus, would not be pleased*: a strikingly hypocritical speech in Juno's mouth. She is ashamed of the hellish instrument which she has had to use.

565 *Amsanctus*: a small lake which bubbles noisily with sulphuretted hydrogen; hence thought to be an entrance to the Underworld.

599 *Latinus*: cf. note above, on line 45.

604 *Getae*: peoples on the Danube. These three lines refer to campaigns, actual or mooted, of Augustus.

605 *Hyrcanians*: peoples near the Caspian Sea.

606 *the Parthians*: lived in what had been Persia. They had defeated a Roman army in 53 BC and captured its standards; Augustus made great play with his success in retrieving them—by diplomatic, not military, means.

607 *twin gates of War*: cf. note on Book I, 293. Here the hate-filled goddess performs the ritual act herself.

612 *grand in Quirinal robe*: this line refers to the special way of girding the toga for religious acts—of which declaring war was one.

630 *powerful Atina . . . Antemnae*: five historic places in Latium. In Virgil's time Tibur was opulent and flourishing, but Antemnae had disappeared.

641 *Helicon*: sacred mountain of the Muses. In traditional epic style Virgil makes a fresh invocation of the Muse before his Catalogue of the Italian contingents.

648 *Mezentius*: Etruscan king, exiled for his cruelties: cf. Book VIII,

481 ff. for horrid details. The 'scorner of the gods' (cf. Book X, 773 f. for a startling blasphemy) appropriately heads the list of the antagonists of the pious Aeneas.

649 *Lausus*: the pathetic fate of Lausus is narrated at Book X, 789 ff.

655 *Aventinus*: presumably the eponym of the Aventine hill in Rome.

658 *Hydra*: killed by Hercules: cf. note on Book VI, 801. Hercules was born in the Argive city of Tiryns.

662 *Geryon*: three-bodied monster. Hercules killed him in Spain and drove his cattle to Italy: cf. Book VIII, 201 ff.

670 *Tibur*: cf. note above, on line 630.

675 *Homole or snow-capped Othrys*: mountains in Thessaly.

681 *Caeculus*: Praeneste is the modern Palestrina. The places named in lines 682 ff. are all in the neighbourhood and indicate a substantial kingdom for Caeculus, who was in some way engendered (as son of Vulcan) by fire: the usual story is that a spark from the hearth leapt out into the lap of a virgin sitting by the fire.

691 *Messapus*: he must have begun as the eponym of the Messapians, in the heel of Italy; Virgil transposes him to the border of northern Latium with Etruria. That is where the places named in lines 695–7 are.

701 *Caÿster*: an Asian river, because Virgil is thinking of a simile in the *Iliad*, Book II. 459 ff., which locates the birds there.

707 *the Claudian clan*: the Claudii were one of the most eminent of Roman patrician families: the Emperors Tiberius and Claudius belonged to it. Of ultimately Sabine origin. The place-names are Sabine.

717 *Allia*: site of a disastrous Roman defeat by an invading horde of Gauls in 390 BC.

721 *Hermus . . . Lycia*: the river of Lydia. Lydia and Lycia are fertile areas in Asia Minor.

723 *Halaesus*: perhaps 'countryman of Agamemnon' rather than his son. Another Greek exile in the West. Virgil puts him in northern Campania, the area of the place names in lines 726–30.

734 *Oebalus . . . Abella*: this contingent is from southern Campania.

Oebalus is otherwise unknown. The place names, some of which are never mentioned elsewhere, lie in that district.

744 *Nursae*: a region of hardy mountaineers, who in Virgil's time still did not live in towns.

750 *Marruvian*: the Marsi, in the very centre of Italy. Archippus' name is derived from the town Archippe, Umbro's from the river Umbro: perhaps both invented by Virgil. The Marsians were proverbial for their skill as snake-charmers. The Lacus Fucinus, in a basin in the hills, is their centre; there was a wood there sacred to the local goddess Angitia.

762 *Virbius*: a local god associated in cult with Diana at Aricia, which is in Latium (by the lake of Nemora, in the Alban hills). Horses were taboo in the precinct, and that seems to have suggested that Virbius was identical with Hippolytus, or with a son of his. Hippolytus, son of Theseus, was loved by his stepmother Phaedra; he rebuffed her, she denounced him, and in consequence of his father's curse he was killed when his horses bolted and wrecked his chariot. His chastity was connected with his devotion to the virgin goddess Artemis (cf. Euripides' *Hippolytus*).

769 *Aesculapius*: son of Apollo, a great healer. Jupiter intervened when he went too far by raising the dead.

776 *Egeria*: a local nymph of a spring in the precinct of Diana at Aricia.

785 *Chimaera*: fire-breathing complex monster (lion plus goat plus serpent). Turnus is leader of the Rutulians: the place-names, some of which are puzzling, relate to his kingdom in southern Latium (794 ff.).

788 *Io*: daughter of the Argive king Inachus; beloved by Jupiter and changed into a cow by the jealous Juno, who then set Argus to watch her. Inachus is also the god of the Argive river of the same name.

803 *Camilla*: an invention of Virgil's, an Italian counterpart to the Amazons of Greek myth. Here she leads the Volscians, but the story told at Book XI, 535 ff., presents her as an exile, living in the woods. Her death: Book XI, 815 ff.

BOOK VIII

1 *Laurentine*: cf. note on Book VI, 891.

9 *Diomedes*: a Greek chieftain at Troy, who had migrated to the west after its fall and founded the city of Arpi in Apulia. Cf. Book XI, 226 ff., for the failure of the Latin appeal to him.

31 *Tiberinus*: the god of the River Tiber appears, appropriately enough, to the founder of Rome.

37 *back to us*: cf. note on Book I, 380.

42 *A great white sow*: this portent, traditional in the legend, was predicted at Book III, 390 ff., by Helenus: that is ignored here. Doubtless another loose end which Virgil would have tidied up.

48 *Alba*: Alba Longa, cf. Book I, 271. *Alba* means 'white'.

51 *Pallas*: the Arcadian connection was suggested, it seems, by finding an etymology for the Palatine hill in Rome in the name of the Arcadian hero Pallas, grandfather of Evander, whose son is also called Pallas.

77 *horned River*: river-gods are regularly depicted with the heads and horns of bulls.

99 *Rome's dominion*: Virgil conveys both pride at Rome's greatness and also a sense of the loss of rustic innocence.

103 *Amphitryon*: the mortal 'father' of Hercules; his real father was Jupiter.

130 *Atridae*: Agamemnon and Menelaus.

134 *Dardanus*: fanciful mythologizing establishes hereditary connection between Aeneas and Evander, both descended from Atlas.

146 *Daunian people*: Daunus is the father of Turnus.

157 *Hesione's kingdom*: Hesione, a Trojan princess, married Telamon, King of Salamis, in the generation before the Trojan War. Evander equals Aeneas in mythological reminiscence.

165 *Pheneus*: town in Arcadia.

166 *Lycian arrows*: the Lycians, great archers, were allies of the Trojans.

194 *Cacus*: the defeat of Cacus, here related at full length, was

celebrated yearly at Rome at the Ara Maxima ('greatest altar') in the Oxen Forum. Virgil gives the origin of the cult. Probably he was influenced by the fact that this festival was held on 12 August, while on 13 August in 29 BC Augustus entered Rome in a spectacular triple triumph over Antony and Cleopatra and other enemies: cf. below, on line 714. Like Hercules, Augustus is a deliverer from monsters. The myth of Cacus is old, but it was Virgil who made him into a fire-breathing demon. His cave was under the Aventine hill.

202 *Geryon*: cf. note on Book VII, 662.

219 *Alcides*: a title ('mighty one') of Hercules himself, rather than his father.

269 *Potitius*: the families of the Potitii and Pinarii had the hereditary care of the cult (see note above on line 194). In 29, the year of Augustus' triple triumph, one of the Potitii was consul: another connection which will have pleased Virgil.

285 *The Salii*: ancient college of dancing priests at Rome.

288 *Hercules*: Jupiter's son by Alcmena. Juno, Jupiter's wife, attempted to dispose of him as a baby by sending two serpents: the baby throttled them.

291 *Troy and Oechalia*: Hercules sacked Troy because he was cheated by King Laomedon, Oechalia to get the princess Iole.

293 *Eurystheus*: Hercules was forced to carry out the Twelve Labours at the bidding of Eurystheus, king of Argos, including the destruction of the Centaurs, the wild bull of Crete, the Nemean lion and the Hydra. He brought up Cerberus from the Underworld and fought the horrific monster Typhoeus (or Typhon).

300 *the Lernaean dragon*: the Hydra: cf. note on Book VI, 576.

315 *spring from hard-wood oaks*: that the first men sprang from trees or stones was an ancient fantasy. Here it goes with the characteristic toughness of the ancient peoples of Italy.

319 *Saturn*: Jupiter's father, deposed by him. His rule in Latium was a golden age: subsequent ages decline through bronze to iron.

323 *Latium*: Virgil etymologizes 'Latium' from *latēre*, to lie hidden (whence English 'latent').

328 *Ausonian hordes*: Virgil conveys—no doubt possesses—only a vague idea of these invasions and changes of name.

330 *Thybris*: Virgil usually calls the Tiber not by its ordinary name of *Tiberis* but by the grander-sounding *Thybris*. Here he produces a man after whom the river was named.

336 *Carmentis*: also called Carmenta, an Italian goddess. Virgil connects her name with *carmen*, which often means 'prophetic utterance'. We should not miss the point that, like Aeneas, Evander, Dardanus, and Saturn are all exiles and immigrants; Evander was guided by the gods, as Aeneas is.

342 *a Retreat*: Romulus, to encourage settlers and increase the young city, set up 'asylum' for any man on the run from his home. Aeneas is shown the most venerable and emotional sites in Rome.

343 *the Lupercal*: a cave under the Palatine. The Luperci conducted a ritual, of primeval antiquity, once a year. Their name suggested a derivation from *lupus*, 'wolf'; and so another Arcadian link, with the cult of Pan Lycaeus (*lycus*, 'wolf', in Greek).

345 *Argiletum*: site of a temple of Janus. *Argi letum*, as two words, would mean in Latin 'Argos' doom'.

347 *the Capitol*: site of the great temple of Jupiter and epitome of Rome, had a place on its southern side where traitors were thrown down to death: the Tarpeian Rock.

357 *Janiculum*: another of the hills of Rome. Saturn reigned on the Capitol before Jupiter.

361 *the Forum of Rome and the elegant Ship-Place*: the Forum was the centre of Rome, where business was conducted and the Senate met. The Ship-Place (Carinae) was, in Virgil's day, a fashionable residential area; on the Esquiline Hill.

372 *Vulcan*: the lame blacksmith god.

383 *Thetis*: mother of Achilles. She persuaded Vulcan to make armour for her son (*Iliad*, Book XVIII); the goddess of the Dawn —lover of Tithonus—induced him to do the same for her son Memnon.

417 *Lipare*: the largest of seven volcanic islands off the coast of Sicily. The island in Virgil's mind is doubtless the one still named, as Vulcan's workshop, Vulcano (cf. line 422).

418 *the Cyclops' fires*: cf. note on Book VI, 630.

425 *Brontes and Steropes, Pyracmon*: the names of the Cyclopes mean Thunderer, Lightning, Fire-Anvil.

435 *the aegis*: the goat-skin mantle, with gold tassels and the head of the Gorgon, worn by Athene.

440 *Aetna*: being a volcano, it was also suitable for this sort of thing. Virgil is indifferent to consistent topography.

455 *Aeolian shores*: these islands (cf. above, note on line 417) were the place where Aeolus imprisoned the winds. Lemnos is an island, in the Aegean, which belonged especially to Hephaestus (= Vulcan).

458 *Tyrrhene clogs . . . sword of Tegea*: Etruscan shoes, because he is in Italy; Arcadian sword (Tegea is an Arcadian town) because he is an Arcadian by origin.

470 *Teucrians*: Trojans.

473 *Rutuli*: the people of Turnus.

479 *Caere*: Etruscan hill-town north of Rome. The Etruscans were often said to have come to Italy from Lydia in Asia Minor.

482 *Mezentius*: cf. note on Book VII, 648.

506 *Tarchon*: a great name, recurring several times among the Etruscans.

513 *most valiant leader of Trojans and of Italians*: a resounding line, beyond its immediate context. Rome needs the combination of Trojan and Italian elements.

526 *Etruscan trumpets*: trumpets were said to be an Etruscan invention.

560 *If Juppiter would only restore those bygone years*: this reminiscence of Evander is modelled on those of Homer's Nestor. Virgil thinks particularly of Nestor's tale of his youthful exploit in killing the Siamese twins of Greek myth, the Molione; and of the three-bodied Geryon (above, line 202).
Erulus: not mentioned elsewhere; his mother Feronia is an Italian, probably Sabine, goddess. Erulus seems to have three complete bodies, and so to have to be killed three times.

600 *Pelasgians*: vaguely used for any pre-Greek, or (as here)

pre-Roman population; but usually in Virgil it means Greeks.

602 *Silvanus*: god of the wild woodland; later also of agriculture.

615 *Cythera*: an island sacred to Venus.

626 *Italian history*: Virgil's model, the shield of Achilles (*Iliad*, Book XVIII) represented the whole world; Virgil's conception, by contrast, is nationalistic.

631 *the twin boy babies*: Romulus and Remus, suckled by a she-wolf.

635 *the Sabine women*: to remedy a shortage of women in his new city, Romulus invited the Sabines to come with their womenfolk to an athletic spectacle; the Romans then forcibly carried off the Sabine women. This led to war with Titus Tatius and the Sabine army, but the women intervened and reconciled the two sides.

642 *Mettus*: as dictator of Alba Longa he broke a treaty with Rome. He was torn apart between two chariots.

646 *Porsenna*: Lars Porsenna, ruler of the Etruscan city of Clusium, attempted to restore Tarquinius, the ejected king of Rome, by force.

650 *Cocles*: Horatius Cocles defended the wooden bridge against Porsenna while the Romans destroyed it behind him; Cloelia, in Porsenna's grasp, escaped and swam the Tiber.

652 *Manlius*: in 390 BC, when the Gauls captured Rome, the Capitol was saved when Juno's geese gave the alarm; Manlius led the defence.

663 *Salii*: cf. above, note on line 285; on the Luperci, cf. above, note on line 343.

664 *the shields that fell from Heaven*: the *ancilia*. One of these shields fell from heaven; eleven more were made to match, to baffle thieves.

665 *ladies*: the *matronae* of Rome rode in carriages, and had a prominent role, at public thanksgivings.

668 *Catiline*: even the next world is Roman. Catiline was the revolutionary leader suppressed in 63 BC, Cato the embodiment of unbending Republican virtue in the generation before that of Virgil.

675 *Actium*: the sea serves as a setting for Augustus' victory over Antony and Cleopatra at Actium (31 BC).

681 *The Italians*: the civil war battle is presented as one between virtuous West (Italians, Senate) and monstrous East. Like Aeneas, Augustus has the *Penates*, the household gods of Rome.

682 *Agrippa*: Augustus' great admiral. The naval crown, adorned with the beaks of ships, was awarded for victories at sea.

688 *his Egyptian wife*: Cleopatra.

696 *timbrel*: a rattling instrument used in Eastern cults. Virgil imagines her using this exotic and disreputable instrument instead of trumpet or drum.

698 *Anubis*: jackal-headed Egyptian deity.

703 *Bellona*: goddess who embodies war.

704 *Apollo of Actium*: Apollo, Augustus' divine patron, had a temple on the promontory of Actium.

713 *triumphal procession*: Augustus' triumph, 13 August 29, over Illyricum, Actium, and Egypt.

716 *three hundred great shrines*: Augustus actually claimed to have established 12 new shrines and restored 82 old ones.

720 *the marble-white temple*: Augustus' temple to Apollo on the Palatine.

724 *Nomads*: Berbers, Africans, hellenized peoples of Asia Minor (the Leleges and Carians), Scythians.

727 *Morini*: near Boulogne.

728 *Araxes*: the great river of Armenia.

BOOK IX

4 *Pilumnus*: minor Italian deity.

5 *Iris*: cf. note on Book IV, 694.

11 *Lydian*: i.e. Etruscan: cf. note on Book VIII, 479.

80 *Ida*: mountain near Troy, the haunt of Cybele, mother of the gods.

82 *Cybele*: here identified with Rhea, the obscure goddess traditionally named as the mother of Zeus. The identification is found as early as the fifth century BC.

88 *Dardan*: i.e. Trojan. Aeneas needed a fleet to sail from Troy.

102 *Goddesses of the great deep*: Nereids, the mermaids of antiquity.

104 *by the stream of his Stygian brother*: cf. note on Book VI, 323: gods swore their oaths by the Underworld river Styx.

112 *Cybele's cymbals*: the worship of Cybele was accompanied by ecstatic music: percussion and wind instruments, not strings.

123 *Rutuli*: Turnus' men.

145 *Built by the hand of Neptune*: cf. note on Book II, 624.

150 *Athene's image*: the Palladium: cf. note on Book II, 166.

151 *a horse's dark paunch*: the Trojan Horse.

153 *Danaans*: a title of the Greek warriors at Troy. 'Pelasgian' here also means Greek.

176 *Nisus*: on Nisus and Euryalus cf. note on Book V, 294.

196 *Pallanteum*: the city of Evander.

218 *Acestes' city*: the other matrons preferred to stay in Sicily, where Acestes founded a city: Book V, 746 ff.

259 *Assaracus*: ancestral king of Troy.

264 *Arisba*: a place near Troy. The myth, if not an invention of Virgil's, is unknown.

297 *Creusa*: Ascanius' mother, left behind in Troy: cf. Book II, 768 ff.

360 *Remulus of Tibur*: it is in the Homeric manner to give a precious sword or other treasure a provenance through the hands of distinguished and heroic owners. The details of this story are obscure.

370 ff.:   *Volscens* should be 'Volcens'.

387 *Alba*: apparently a district between Alba Longa and Rome, known as 'the Alban area'. Albanus is unknown.

446 *Ah, fortunate pair!*: a remarkable departure from the dispassionate manner of the Homeric epic. 'The house of Aeneas' doubtless includes both the Julian family and the Roman people as a whole. 'The head of the Roman family' is a deliberately unclear expression: its reference is at least in part to Augustus and his successors.

460 *Aurora*: the goddess of dawn. Tithonus is her lover.

476 *the shuttle*: she was weaving at the loom—the typical occupation of women in the heroic age.

525 *Calliope*: cf. note on Book VII, 525. Calliope is sometimes said to be the chief of the Muses.

546 *Lydian*: this time not Etruscan but a king of Lydia in Asia Minor.

564 *the war-bird of Jove*: the eagle is specially the bird of Jupiter.

584 *Symaethus*: river in Sicily. The Palici are twin gods of the native (non-Greek) Sicilian population.

599 *twice-captured Troy*: cf. note on Book II, line 643. Troy has been captured twice: once by Hercules, once by Agamemnon.

617 *You Phrygian women*: cf. note on Book IV, 215.

618 *Dindymus*: Trojan mountain where the ecstatic cult of Cybele was carried on; see note on line 112, above. Italian toughness despises such oriental goings-on. See the final reconciliation of Jupiter and Juno, Book XII, 827.

659 *The Trojan commanders recognized him for a god*: it is in the Homeric manner for a god to reveal his true identity only at departure: cf. the more poignant example in Book I, 403 ff. Apollo is an archer, hence the quiver.

668 *Goat-stars*: the Haedi, two stars in the constellation Auriga; they rise in October, a stormy month.

673 *dryad*: tree-nymph.

710 *Baiae*: a contemporary simile, of a sort not traditional in epic. Baiae was a popular seaside resort.

715 *Inarime*: the shock is felt by the nearby islands. Inarime, or Arime, is the traditional name for the place where the monster Typhoeus was buried under a mountain: his movements cause earthquakes. Virgil transfers the myth from the far East, where the Greeks had set it, to a seismic area of Italy.

737 *Amata*: Latinus' queen and mother of the heiress Lavinia.

757 *And if only the conquering Turnus . . .*: this is the Turnus who abandons an ambush too soon (Book XI, 901) and takes the wrong sword for his duel with Aeneas (Book XII, 735): violent, a loser.

BOOK X

2 *a council was called*: Homer's epic contains a number of scenes of discussions on Olympus (which means 'heaven' as well as the mountain in northern Greece). Virgil compresses this feature of Homeric epic into this one scene.

12 *One day when barbarous Carthage . . .*: Juppiter predicts the Second Punic War (218–2 BC), in which Hannibal crossed the Alps and for years dominated Italy, at one time seeming likely to take Rome itself.

29 *Diomed*: Greek hero at Troy, now in Italy, where he has founded a city. Cf. note on Book VIII, 9. In the fifth book of the *Iliad* he wounded Aphrodite/Venus: rhetorically she says that no doubt it will happen again.

36 *the burning of their fleet*: this refers to Book V, 604 ff.

37 *the suborning of the Storm-king*: in Book I, 65 ff.

38 *Iris*: in Book IX, 2 ff.

39 *Allecto*: in Book VII, 323 ff.

51 *Amathus, Mount Paphus, Cythera, And a shrine in Idalia*: these places are all on Cyprus except for the island of Cythera. They are cult-centres of Venus.

60 *Xanthus and Simois*: the rivers of Troy.

68 *Cassandra*: cf. note on Book II, 246.

76 *grandson of Pilumnus*: Turnus is descended from minor deities. Venilia, like Achilles' mother Thetis, is a sea-nymph.

81 *You may filch your Aeneas*: refers to a scene where Aphrodite rescued Aeneas in battle in the *Iliad*, Book V, 311 ff.

83 *You may transform his vessels*: refers to Book IX, 77 ff.

89 *What started Europe and Asia . . . each other?*: Juno refers to her standing grievance (Book I, 26) of the Judgement of Paris, the 'Dardan philanderer', which led to the abduction of Helen and so to the Trojan War. It was all Venus' fault!

105 *Teucrians*: i.e. Trojans.

113 *By the stream of his Stygian brother*: cf. note on Book VI, 323.

142 *Pactolus*: river in Lydia, from which gold was panned.

145 *the town in Campania*: the great Campanian city of Capua.

156 *Phrygian lions*: the chariot of Cybele, mother of the gods, was drawn by lions: she was at home on the Phrygian Mount Ida.

163 *Helicon*: cf. note on Book VII, 641. This is another little Catalogue.

167 *Clusium … fighters all*: Clusium, Cosae, and Populonia are Etruscan towns. Ilva is the island of Elba, where the Etruscans mined iron.

175 *A master at divining*: these arts of divination were an Etruscan speciality.

179 *Etruscan Pisa*: Pisa had the same name as a town at Olympia in Greece. Hence it was supposed that it was founded by people from there. The Alpheus is the river at Olympia.

183 *Caere, Pyrgi, Gravisca*: more Etruscan places.

185 *the Ligurians*: north-west of Etruria, in what is still called Liguria.

189 *Cycnus*: his name means 'swan' in Greek.

190 *Phaethon*: son of the Sun-god; he drove his father's chariot, went out of control, and crashed; the site of his fall was often put on the coast of northern Italy. His sisters, inconsolable, were metamorphosed into poplar trees.

200 *Mantua*: Virgil's birthplace, so he goes into detail. The 'three clans' are mysterious: perhaps Etruscans, Gauls, and Umbrians. Manto was the daughter of Tiresias. The Mincius (206) is the local river.

220 *the nymphs, the ships that kindly Cybele had turned into nymphs*: cf. Book IX, 77 ff.

252 *lady of Ida*: Cybele, mother of the gods. Cf. note on Book IX, 618.

265 *Strymon*: river in Thrace.

316 *consecrated to Phoebus*: we are told that all those born by Caesarian section had a special link with Apollo as god of medicine.

319 *Hercules*: he typically used a club, not a spear. That is one of the things which mark him as a hero of a particularly primitive sort. This Melampus is unknown.

325 *oblivious of all his youthful loves*: another homosexual touch, cf.

Cycnus above, line 187 ff., and Nisus and Euryalus, and Book XII, 392. The theme is alien to Homeric epic.

350 *Boreas*: the North Wind. From the point of view of the Greeks it blew from Thrace.

389 *a man of Rhoetus' ancient line*: it is in the Homeric manner to give short accounts of minor heroes as they are killed; what is said of this man, however, is unthinkable in such an 'epitaph' in Homer.

426 *Lausus*: son of the blasphemous Etruscan tyrant Mezentius.

433 *Here Pallas strains*: both Pallas and Lausus are marked for death. Like Nisus and Euryalus, they move Virgil powerfully.

461 *Hercules, I implore you*: refers to the story told by Evander in Book VIII, 200 ff.

471 *Sarpedon*: the death of Sarpedon is narrated in the sixteenth book of the *Iliad*.

497 *a legendary crime*: the daughters of Danaus, obliged to marry their cousins, all (with one exception) killed their husbands on the wedding night. Perhaps a connection is intended with the fate of Pallas, killed on his first day of battle.

503 *For Turnus a time is coming*: see Book XII, 940 ff.

518 *designing to sacrifice them*: Aeneas, in his rage at the death of Pallas, emulates the action of Achilles in his rage at the death of Patroclus (*Iliad*, Book XXIII, 175 ff.). It is meant to come as a shock: such are the consequences of anger. Cf. Book XI, 81 ff.

542 *as a trophy for Mars*: this pious action perhaps suggests what Turnus should have done with the sword-belt of Pallas. Cf. Book XI, 5 ff.

551 *Faunus*: cf. note on Book VII, 47.

564 *Amyclae*: in south Italy. Legend said that after many false alarms it was forbidden to sound the alarm at Amyclae at all; hence the town was captured by enemies.

565 *Aegaeon*: primeval giant. Usually he is on Jupiter's side.

581 *the horses of Diomed*: refers to passages in the *Iliad*. Aeneas narrowly escape with his life from Diomede (Book V, 311) and from Achilles (Book XX, 290).

607 *it's Venus*: Jupiter teases Juno: Aeneas is not so dependent, after all.

619 *Pilumnus*: a minor Italian deity. Cf. note above, on line 76.

637 *a strengthless and insubstantial Wraith*: this episode was perhaps suggested to Virgil by *Iliad*, Book V, 449 ff., where Apollo substitutes a bogus Aeneas for the real one.

689 *Mezentius*: cf. note on Book VII, 648.

704 *Pregnant with fire*: cf. note on Book VII, 319.

708 *Vesulus*: mountain where the River Po rises.

719 *Corythus*: cf. note on Book III, 170.

758 *In the halls of Jove*: this expresses the feeling of the blessed gods, that mortals are miserable enough already, without this kind of suffering.

761 *Tisiphone*: cf. note on Book VI, 555.

763 *Orion*: a giant, blinded for attempted rape, striding over land and sea.

773 *which is god to me*: a traditional blasphemy, ascribed to several excessively violent and arrogant figures of myth.

792 *because long tradition allows us to do so*: a very ambiguous remark. The episode is probably invented by Virgil himself.

831 *What's more, he rebuked . . . into their hands*: this tableau—the hero lamenting as he holds in his arms the body of the charming boy he has been forced to kill—stands with the ruin of Dido as symbolic of Virgil's picture of the hard doom of the imperialist. Cf. note on Book XII, 946.

BOOK XI

5 ff. *lopping the branches all round*: with this pious gesture compare the note on Book X, 542. The trophy is a kind of reconstitution of the slain enemy, the trunk of the tree representing his body. Cf. below, 173.

26 *Evander's mourning city*: Evander, in his city of Pallanteum, does not yet know of the death of his son.

75 *giving all her heart to the work*: a closer translation would be 'happy in her work'. That is a detail of telling pathos.

81 *consigned to the gifts to the dead*: cf. note on Book X, 518.

101 *Decked in olive branches*: cf. note on Book VII, 154.

139 *Rumour*: cf. note on Book IV, 173 ff.

168 *Teucrians*: i.e. Trojans.

173 *a trophy*: cf. note above, on line 5.

177 *Tell him I linger on*: this claim for vengeance on Turnus is important in the end of the poem, Book XII, 947.

184 *Tarchon*: leader of the Etruscans.

219 *Let him, they cry, decide the issue*: refers back to 115 ff., above.

225 *from Diomed's city*: cf. note on Book VIII, 9. Virgil takes the opportunity to make this great Greek hero glorify Aeneas (252 ff.).

246 *Arpi*: roughly etymologized as coming from the Greek *Argos Hippion*.

247 *Garganus*: mountain in Apulia.

252 *Saturn*: cf. note on Book VIII, 319.

259 *Wrathful Athene*: cf. note on Book I, 41.

262 *At the pillars of Proteus . . . Aetna*: i.e. Egypt. Menelaus tells this story in the fourth book of the *Odyssey*. Ulysses faced the Cyclops in the ninth book of the *Odyssey*.

264 *Neoptolemus' kingdom partitioned*: after the killing by Orestes of Neoptolemus/Pyrrhus, son of Achilles, his kingdom seems to have been fragmented. Helenus and Andromache have carved their little Troy out of it, Book III, 333.
Idomeneus: cf. note on Book III, 122. His wife, when he came home, was unfaithful.

265 *the Locrians*: obscure. It seems that there was a story that some of the followers of the lesser Ajax, after his death (cf. note on Book I, 41), settled in Africa.

266 *Agamemnon*: he was murdered by his wife Clytemnestra and her paramour Aegisthus.

270 *beautiful Calydon*: Diomede's own fate: unable to return to Calydon, the Aetolian city of his origin, and punished for his attack on Venus at Troy, cf. note on Book X, 29.

272 *my own lost comrades*: on the 'Diomede islands' off the coast of Apulia there were sea-birds, perhaps a kind of puffin, who were thought to be the metamorphosed men of Diomede.

275 *From the moment I raised my sword*: cf. note above, on line 270.

291 *Both were outstanding in courage*: Virgil here makes Aeneas the greatest of the Trojan warriors—not the impression left by the *Iliad*. The supremacy claimed for Aeneas in *pietas*, devotion, is noteworthy.

306 *unconquerable*: Roman pride here insists that the Trojans were not defeated at all.

318 *The Sicilians' frontier*: this would place this land on the bank of the Tiber, stretching north of Laurentum: the site of Aeneas' eventual city. These 'Sicilians'—*Sicani* is Virgil's word—are not in Sicily; cf. Book VII, 795.

334 *the insignia of my kingship*: this amounts to recognizing Aeneas as a king like himself.

338 *influential through his wealth*: Drances represents a type familiar in the historic perod but alien to the heroic world as imagined by Homer.

350 *Attacked the Trojan encampment and scared with his weapons the blue sky*: this very rhetorical expression seems to refer to Turnus' exploits in the Trojan camp (Book IX, 727 ff.) and his deluded pursuit of the phantom Aeneas (Book X, 636 ff.).

394 *the whole house of Evander*: refers to the killing of Evander's son Pallas.

396 *Bitias and huge Pandarus*: cf. Book IX, 672 ff.

403 *Myrmidon*: the people of Achilles.

404 *Larissaean*: i.e. Thessalian.

405 *Aufidus*: great river of southern Italy.

429 *Tolumnius*: he is an augur, an interpreter of the will of heaven. At Book XII, 258, he breaks the truce; at Book XII, 460, he is killed.

432 *Camilla*: cf. note on Book VII, 803.

439 *Made by Vulcan*: cf. note on Book VIII, 383.

457 *Padusa*: one of the mouths of the Po.

478 *the queen*: Latinus' queen, Amata.

483 *Tritonian maiden*: a title of Athena.

515 *I am planning an ambush*: cf. note on Book IX, 757.

534 *Diana*: the virgin hunter goddess is naturally a patron of the outdoor girl and virgin Camilla.

540 *Privernum*: city in Latium. The Amasenus (547) is a local river.

580 *Strymon*: river in Thrace.

643 *whose auburn hair was unhelmeted*: looks like a reminiscence of the Berserker warriors of the Germanic north.

649 *with one breast bared*: the usual dress of Amazons.

659 f. *Thermodon ... Hippolyta ... Penthesilea*: Thermodon was a Thracian river. Hippolyta was queen of the Amazons, subdued by Theseus. Penthesilea was an Amazon who came to the rescue of Troy after Hector's death and was killed by Achilles.

769 *the shining Phrygian armour*: there is a hint that his golden armour marks him as a dandy, not a warrior. He is a Phrygian: cf. note on Book IV, 215.

773 *Cretan ... Lycian*: the epithets are decorative. Both Crete and Lycia were famous for archery.

784 *Soracte*: Monte Soratte, twenty miles north of Rome. People known as the Hirpini possessed the power of walking on hot coals in cult there.

850 *Dercennus*: a shadowy name from the mythology of early Latium.

914 *Iberian*: i.e. Western.

BOOK XII

3 *his promise*: cf. Book XI, 434 ff.

28 *oracles*: cf. Book VII, 96 ff.

52 *His goddess mother*: a reference to her rescuing him in the *Iliad*, Book V, 311 ff.

75 *Phrygian*: cf. note on Book IV, 215.

83 *Orithyia*: the wife of Boreas, who lived with him in Thrace.

87 *orichalc*: a blend of silver and gold; the word has fabulous overtones.

90 *the Fire-lord's*: i.e. Vulcan's. Dipping in the Underworld river of course made the weapon more deadly.

99 *that Phrygian pansy*: cf. note on Book IV, 215.

134 *the Alban hill*: an ancient cult centre of Latium.

137 *Juturna*: a local nymph or goddess of springs; she had a sacred fountain in the Roman Forum. Virgil makes her Turnus' sister, etymologizing her name as 'Help Turnus'.

144 *bed of large-hearted Jove*: Juturna's immortality is explained by her affair with Jupiter; that in turn makes her intimacy with Juno need an explanation.

164 *His ancestor the Sun*: apparently a different genealogy from that set out in Book VII, 47 ff.

189 *I shall not make the Italians . . . Trojans*: cf. below, 820 ff. Virgil attached importance to this point.

192 *The gods and the hallows I'll give*: the vital contribution of Troy to Rome is her gods. Cf. below, line 836.

245 *a sign from the skies above*: this is trespassing on Jupiter's sphere in a particularly shocking way.

258 *Tolumnius*: cf. note on Book XI, 429. The trick of the goddess deceives the credulous augur.

287 *picked up the images . . . Gods*: a symbolic act.

296 *This best of victims I sacrifice*: a blasphemous utterance.

298 *from an altar*: these killings at the altar underline the sacrilege of the breach of the truce.

311 *Aeneas the true*: the epithet *pius* has much more than simple formulaic force here.

331 *Hebrus*: Thracian river. The war god was particularly worshipped in Thrace.

335 *Fear . . . Angers . . . Stratagems*: these are personifications, necessarily attending on war.

347 *Dolon*: his disastrous night-expedition is described in the *Iliad*, Book X. Diomede killed him.

392 *intense passion*: cf. note on Book X, 325. Apollo was patron-god of medicine.

412 *Ida in Crete*: cf. note on Book III, 105.

419 *ambrosia*: 'deathlessness'; the gods drink it.
panacea: 'cure-all'.

434 *Kissing his lips through the helmet's open visor*: the kiss through the helmet is another symbol of the subjection of the emotions to war and duty. Aeneas' speech represses, yet conveys, bitterness.

460 *Tolumnius*: cf. note on Book XI, 429.

496 *He repeatedly called to witness*: the inseparable union of justified duty with violent passion in the act of conquest is here underlined.

503 *Juppiter, was it your will*: the poet leaves his epic objectivity to remonstrate with the gods of his own story.

511 *cut off both their heads*: a characterizing gesture for Turnus.

547 *in Laurentine soil*: the pathos is his death so far from home.

571 *after once being beaten?*: that is: by avoiding me, Turnus admits defeat.

582 *Twice the Italians have broken a treaty*: once in Book VII, the second time in Book XII.

639 *Murranus*: see above, line 529.

641 *Ufens*: above, at line 460.

644 *Drances' slanders*: cf. Book XI, 336 ff.

674 *Turnus had built this turret*: symbolic: Turnus' power is on the point of collapse.

701 *Athos*: a mountain in Chalcidice, in northern Greece.
Eryx: a mountain in Sicily.

715 *Sila*: a forest in the Abruzzi.
Taburnus: a mountain in Campania.

735 *The story goes*: cf. note on Book IX, 757. Turnus, like Aeneas, has a sword of divine manufacture.

766 *Faunus*: cf. note on Book VII, 47.

770 *the Trojans*: an uncharacteristically impious act for the Trojans—who are punished for it (778 ff.).

795 *to the stars*: i.e. as a god, after his death.

823 *Do not command the indigenous Latins*: the great goddess must save face as she yields; and Virgil is anxious to make it clear that the peoples of Italy were not simply conquered by an external power. Rome needs both the Italian and the Trojan contribution. Cf. above, note on line 189; and below, line 826, on the qualities of the Italians.

826 *Alban kings*: the kings of Alba Longa, the city which is to precede Rome: cf. Book I, 271 ff.

836 *Trojan worship*: cf. above, note on 192.

839 *A people surpassing all men, nay even the gods, in godliness*: a line of inexhaustible resonance.

845 *Furies*; cf. Book VI, 505, 665; Book VII, 323 ff.

847 *all three alike*: i.e. there are three Furies in all.

857 *Parthian or Cretan*: typical archers.

886 *vanished into the depths of the river*: Juturna is a goddess of springs, cf. above, note on line 137.

942 *the fatal baldric*: stripped in Book X, 496 ff.

946 *Rage shook him*: the killing of Turnus, deliberately made rather disquieting, is a last image of the nature of imperialism: the conqueror finds himself forced to destroy—with justification, but but also with guilt. Cf. note on Book X, 831.

American Literature

British and Irish Literature

Children's Literature

Classics and Ancient Literature

Colonial Literature

Eastern Literature

European Literature

History

Medieval Literature

Oxford English Drama

Poetry

Philosophy

Politics

Religion

The Oxford Shakespeare

A complete list of Oxford Paperbacks, including Oxford World's Classics, Oxford Shakespeare, Oxford Drama, and Oxford Paperback Reference, is available in the UK from the Academic Division Publicity Department, Oxford University Press, Great Clarendon Street, Oxford OX2 6DP.

In the USA, complete lists are available from the Paperbacks Marketing Manager, Oxford University Press, 198 Madison Avenue, New York, NY 10016.

Oxford Paperbacks are available from all good bookshops. In case of difficulty, customers in the UK can order direct from Oxford University Press Bookshop, Freepost, 116 High Street, Oxford OX1 4BR, enclosing full payment. Please add 10 per cent of published price for postage and packing.